TAKING SIDES

Clashing Views in

Public Policy, Justice, and the Law

D0217048

TAKING SIDES

Clashing Views in

Public Policy, Justice, and the Law

Selected, Edited, and with Introductions by

Marie D. Natoli
Emmanuel College

Mc Graw Hill **Contemporary Learning Series**

A Division of The McGraw-Hill Companies

To my two best friends—Kathy and Jonathan—and to all of my students—past, present, and future—in hopes that they will work at ridding this society and the world of injustice.

Photo Acknowledgment
Cover image: Photos.com

Cover Acknowledgment
Maggie Lytle

Printed on Recycled Paper

Preface

$\mathbf{T}$he nineteenth-century philosopher John Stuart Mill, in his work entitled *On Liberty,* provided a poignant definition of "the free and open market place of ideas." Wrote Mill,

> If all mankind minus one were of one opinion, and only one man were of the contrary opinion, mankind would be no more justified in silencing that one man, than he, if he had the power, would be justified in silencing mankind.

Conflicting ideas and the respect for differences of opinion are critical to the political, economic, and social health of a democracy. Perhaps it *is* only one person who has seen the "truth." Perhaps s/he is wrong, or what s/he sees is only part of the truth. Perhaps, however, even misperceptions may *lead* to the discernment of the truth. The point is that not only the preservation of, but also the *encouragement* of, conflicting views is paramount to a society's health and well-being. In a democracy, there can never be too many points of view.

This is important for all to see. It is especially important for students to see this. Oftentimes, students will assume the veracity of a statement "because it is written down," or "because it is in a book or an article," or because a learned professor had proclaimed it so.

The Taking Sides volumes are devoted to exposing students not only to substantive information contained in any one volume, but more pervasively, the Taking Sides volumes aim to have students become habituated to seeking and evaluating both sides of an issue. Indeed, the Taking Sides volumes are devoted to "the free and open market place of ideas." So, in the Taking Sides volumes, substance and process blend.

The purpose of this new Taking Sides volume on public policy, justice, and the law is to explore areas and issues in the public policy arena in which the law may have created, ignored, or perpetuated injustices in society. Only when injustices are discerned can public policy efforts be made to write a wrong. And only when wrongs are eliminated can we say that justice truly exists.

Plan of the Book   Each issue has an issue *introduction* so that the "yes" and "no" selections will have a context. Following each issue is a "Postscript" that will highlight salient points stemming from the "yes" and "no" selections. All of this material is intended for you to *think about the issue* and form your own conclusions based upon what you have read here and through other readings. *Suggested further readings* will be included with each "Postscript." Appropriate Internet site addresses (URLs) are included on the *On the Internet* page at the beginning of each part opening. At the back of the book will be a list of contributors, their credentials, and their affiliations. It is always important to know *who* wrote something before drawing your own conclusions about the validity of that person's views.

A Word to the Instructor   An *Instructor's Manual With Test Questions* (multiple choice and essay) is available through the publisher for the instructors using *Taking Sides* in the classroom. A general guidebook, *Using Taking Sides in the Classroom,* that discusses methods and techniques for integrating the pro-con approach into any classroom setting, is also available. An online version of Using *Taking Sides in the Classroom* and a correspondence service for *Taking Sides* adopters can be found at http://www.mhcls.com/usingts/.

   Taking Sides: Clashing Views in Public Policy, Justice, and the Law is only one title in the Taking Sides series. If you are interested in seeing the table of contents for any of the other titles, please visit the Taking Sides Web site at http://www.mhcls.com/takingsides/.

Acknowledgments   I am grateful to all of my family, friends, and colleagues who have supported me in this endeavor. I have been "pontificating" for quite some time about injustices in society (indeed, I even went to law school to try to better understand this problem!) and appreciate the urging of students to write a work on the subject. I am also grateful to Larry Loepke of McGrawHill Contemporary Learning Series for having seen the worth of such a volume. And a very special thank you goes to Nichole Altman for her patience with an absent-minded professor and for her editing efforts in this work. Without Nichole, this volume would not be here.

Marie D. Natoli
Emmanuel College

Contents In Brief

Contents

Author Ron Stewart's work is a case study of the black male population in Buffalo, New York. Stewart explores not only the pattern of black male incarceration, but focuses on the experiences and perceptions of black males in relation to the U.S. criminal justice system and the local police department. D'Alessio and Stolzenberg challenge the typically held view that racial discrimination by police is the reason for the very high rate of male African-American incarceration. The authors also criticize the use of social factors—especially poverty, economic inequality, social disruption, segregation and family structure—to explain the differences in crime patterns between the races.

Author Heather Mac Donald reviews and disputes the allegations of police profiling and explores the daily demands on police officers. Mac Donald also discusses the justification for using race in investigating crime. Richard G. Scott draws the distinctions between legitimate "stops" versus those based upon racial characteristics. Scott includes an overview of Constitutional protections aimed at preventing police profiling and points to the need for proper police training.

Nagel and Johnson argue that recent social and historical events have resulted in race, gender, and class discrimination. They argue that the current emphasis is on the crime committed, rather than who committed the crime. Gaskins argues that women suffer disproportionately by virtue of being caught in the circumstance of serving as conspirators to males in drug conspiracy. She further argues that such "trapped" women should be given preferential treatment because of their role as mothers.

The National Organization for Women (NOW) argues that the privatization of Social Security will be detrimental to women. Women rely upon current Social Security benefits and would fare poorly under privatization. Authors Shirley and Spiegler argue that women will do very well under the privatization of Social Security because the current Social Security system is detrimental to women.

Cathy Young cites judicial leniency toward women, arguing that women do indeed receive lesser sentences for the same crime. Through the issue of capital punishment, Barbara Cruikshank explores the dilemmas posed by feminist thinking that would argue for equality vs. special consideration for women. If there is to be equality of the sexes, gender cannot be considered in sentencing.

PART 3   SEXUAL ORIENTATION   179

Elena Grigera argues that since the state has a legitimate interest in implementing harsh penalties for hate crimes, hate crime legislation is constitutional. Andrew Sullivan agrees that hate crimes are despicable and that government should work toward eliminating violence. But, he argues, a crime is a crime and should not be treated differently depending upon the victim. Sullivan further argues that waging war on beliefs is unconstitutional.

Lara Schwartz, Human Rights Campaign senior staff counsel, argues that any other form of same-sex uniform denies equality, financial benefits and security, and social recognition. Settling for anything less than "marriage" would be to abandon the quest for equality. Edith M. Humphrey argues that same-sex marriages are contrary to biblical teaching. Marriage, she argues, is not a human creation but one enacted by god himself.

Citing cases of well-adjusted children of gay/lesbian parents, Ellen C. Perrin argues in favor of adoption rights for homosexual individuals and couples. Timothy J. Dailey argues that children of gay/lesbian parents are endangered as a result of many factors, including lack of role models, homosexual behavior, and the need for a "traditional" (i.e., mother/father) family structure.

PART 4   SOCIO-ECONOMICS   239

Sloan, Clarke, and Engelberg argue that while the 1963 Supreme Court decision in *Gideon v. Wainwright* held that everyone is entitled to a

Introduction

The Relationship of Public Policy, Justice, and the Law

There is an inextricable link among public policy, justice, and law. It would be impossible to include in this volume all the areas that warrant discussion. This volume will focus upon several of the most controversial public policy areas that raise the question of whether or not the law/law enforcement have created, ignored, or perpetuated injustice. A word regarding terminology is necessary. "Law" as it is being used in this volume includes not only "rules" that have been made by legislatures, or that have been delineated by court decisions and actions of the executive and regulatory agencies. "Law" for the purposes of this volume also includes the judicial and law enforcement processes.

If we were to envision "public policy," "law," and "justice" as three circles we can then determine what the relationship among these circles is in a particular society and what they should be in a *just* society (figure 1). The sets of relationships might not be the same. The purpose of this volume is to explore the dynamics among these circles and to determine if a more equitable alignment might be not only in the interests of society, but especially in the interests of its people.

To view the circles as separate entities with no overlap is erroneous. While it is true that in a particular society "justice" may stand alone, it is impossible for "public policy" and "law" to do so. Not all public policy is created by laws enacted by legislative bodies, but a great deal of it is. So, in the hypothetical, we might visualize that overlap as in which some portion of

Figure 1

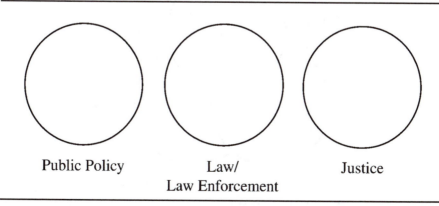

Public Policy   Law/   Justice
                 Law Enforcement

public policy (arbitrarily depicted in figure 2) is created by legislatively enacted law, while other portions of public policy have been created by other forces and factors, such as court rulings, executive actions, and regulatory agency actions. The thrust of this volume is to determine how the "justice" circle fits in. Figure 3 shows one hypothetical.

In this hypothetical depiction, some parts of public policy and law/law enforcement would be "just," but not all. This illustration is meant to portray just one variation on many possible relationships among the three.

Figure 2

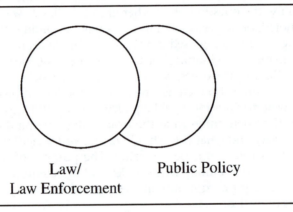

Figure 3

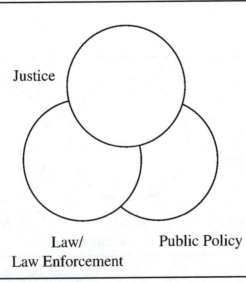

Public Policy

In the above configuration, it is clear that only parts of the law and public policy are just, while many parts are not. The ideal goal of a society that espouses equality and justice under the law would have the justice circle completely aligned with the law circle as well as the public policy circle, because no law or public policy should be unjust. For illustrative purposes, imagine figures 4 and 5, in which the "law/law enforcement" circle and the "justice" circles align so completely that it is impossible to distinguish between the two, as do the "public policy" and "justice" circles.

Thus, the "law/law enforcement" circle fully aligns with justice, as does the "public policy" circle.

In no society is public policy created in a vacuum. Rather, it is the product of a society's values, culture, norms, and demands. The U.S. political culture has long roots in the protestant work ethic that demands hard work to achieve success and presumes that those who are successful must have worked

Figure 4

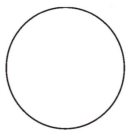

Law/Law Enforcement and Justice

Figure 5

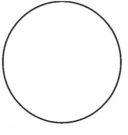

Public Policy and Justice

hard. There are long roots, too, in social darwinism, which applies "survival of the fittest" to a society and is a "logical" corollary to the protestant work ethic. Those who have not done well are those who didn't work hard, and they deserve nothing from those who have. Much of U.S. policy stems from this combination of beliefs, for those who promulgate the law are elected by constituents who embody these views.

Many years ago, Marc Ryan wrote a seminal work entitled *Blaming the Victim,* in which he talks about the poor in society upon whom is placed the blame—and typically the shame—for their plight. Ryan argues, however, that the poor are victims of society and its policies. Much of this Taking Sides volume will be viewing the issue of just how much justice is meted out to those on the bottom of the socioeconomic ladder.

We must be wary of labels. Because "public policy" is thus labeled does not mean it is necessarily in the best interests of the public. Before appropriate policy should be enacted, certain steps are necessary. First, there should be the proper identification of the problem, and this should occur before the problem becomes a crisis.

Misidentification of a problem leads to the adoption of inadequate or totally inappropriate public policy. Then, various "solutions" to the problem should be carefully scrutinized to make sure that not only is the adopted solution the appropriate one, but to insure that the adoption of a "solution" does not lead to other, or worse, problems. One example of this, as will be seen in this volume, may have been the adoption of the Federal Sentencing Guidelines.

The Law

Much as public policy, laws are not created in a vacuum. The same can be said of law enforcement. Public policy, law, and law enforcement reflect a society's values, culture, norms, and demands. What is appropriate at one point in time may not be so at another. People's views and demands change, and these changes impact the way in which the legislature behaves and which law enforcement agencies treat society and societal issues. Thus, there is a *dynamic* among law and public policy. This dynamic has an impact upon whether the practices of a society are just or unjust.

People's demands affect how law enforcement officials work. Simply stated, when people are frightened, they are not only happy to have law enforcement agents working on their behalf, they often demand it. If this results in the denial of individual (or group) rights, if a society comes down on the side of "crime control" rather than individual (or group) rights, is justice being served?

Justice

It is in the nature of most individuals' political socialization to assume that laws, by virtue of being laws, must be just. This fallacy typically results in a lack of questioning of "the way things are." "Why can't I do *x*?" or "Why must I do *y*?" someone might ask. And the reflexive response will most likely be "Because it's the law." Relatedly, we might assume that because a public policy exists, it must be the correct policy.

Periodically, some are brave enough to question the relationship among public policy, laws, and justice. One of the most eloquent statements questioning this relationship came to us from the Rev. Martin Luther King, Jr.'s "Letter from a Birmingham Jail." King's advocacy of civil disobedience is not new. But his message is powerful, and the distinctions he makes between just and unjust laws can help us as we explore the topics in this volume.

King wrote, "Some may well ask 'How can you advocate obeying some laws while disobeying others?'" This is certainly a dilemma for any thinking person. King's answer hinges on the distinction between just and unjust laws. Indeed, King suggests that "an unjust law is no law at all."

As did King, we must keep in mind that laws are created by humans, and humans can make mistakes. It is also possible that humans may intentionally create unjust laws. There is no doubt that southern legislatures intentionally codified rampant segregation statutes that took decades to be declared unconstitutional. And even the Supreme Court rendered decisions that had the effect of upholding segregation statutes, such as in *Plessey v. Ferguson* (1896), in which the Court held that "separate but equal facilities" were constitutional. Fifty-eight years elapsed before the Court was willing to see the folly and injustice of that holding, as *Brown v. Board of Education* proclaimed that "separate but equal is inherently unequal."

Moreover, it is possible that well-intentioned laws may have unjust results. By way of example, the federal food stamp program enacted under President Lyndon Johnson's administration initially allowed the poor to purchase $100 worth of food stamps for a "mere" $12, not realizing that in some parts of the country, the poor often didn't have $12 all at once, if at all. So it is important to be open to questioning the validity of laws in any society. As King noted, "Injustice anywhere is a threat to justice everywhere."

King presents very clear distinctions between "just" and "unjust" laws. Just laws uphold human dignity; unjust laws degrade it. Just laws are enacted by a majority, but both the majority and the minority obey these laws. Individuals must have a role in enacting the laws that affect them. Laws must not only be just on their face but just in their application. And here is where our cases enter, both in terms of illustrating the Rev. King's perspectives and in demonstrating that public policy is a reflection of the moment in society.

Application of These Concepts

Part I of this volume deals with how minorities fare under various aspects of the law/law enforcement system and public policy. By virtue of being a "process," it would appear that the judicial process would be uniform.

The authors of articles in Issue 1, "Does the Judicial Process Result in Racial Discrimination?" have divergent perspectives. Does the process result in discrimination, or is it simply the case that minorities engage in more criminal behavior? If it is the former, then the Rev. King's perspective on facially neutral policies would be applicable.

Issue 2 presents us with the scenario of whether circumstances set the scene for law enforcement. Although the articles in Issue 2 were written pre–9/11 and are principally dealing with African-Americans, the topic is all the more poignant following the events of September 11, 2001 and the government's and public response to the profiling of individuals. Again the issue is one of crime control versus individual rights.

Issue 3 presents an example of Rev. King's statement of a law (in this case, a procedure) that is just on its face, but unjust in its application. Plea bargaining is available to everyone, but if the reality is that minorities and the indigent are more likely to plea bargain for lack of adequate defense, then the process is unjust in its application.

The same is true of Issue 4. Federal sentencing guidelines apply to *everyone*, but if minorities tend to commit particular *types* of crimes that have been correlated with a definitive sentence, minorities will suffer disproportionately. The "guidelines," designed to result in equality, may have had the opposite effect.

Relatedly, Issue 5, dealing with mandatory minimum sentences, reflects a policy designed to remove judicial discretion from the equation. But if this "equality" cannot take extenuating circumstances into consideration, has "justice" been served?

Part II, which deals with gender issues, is not confined to women, since, as we will see, Issue 6 deals with whether "affirmative action" programs, designed to address minority grievances coming out of the past, are in the present hurting others, especially white males.

Issues 7 and 9 return us to the issue of equalizing punishment, but raises compelling questions about whether women, who are often the victims, should be treated comparably by the judicial system. If women want equality, why not across the board?

This is also true of Issue 8, an economic issue. Women have fought a political battle for equality with men. Yet if this is the goal, why should women expect to be taken in special consideration when it comes to facially neutral policies (in this case, the privatization of social security)?

Part III brings us to the contemporary and very controversial issue of sexual orientation and its so many related issues.

Issue 10 can and should be applied to other minorities. Are hate crimes a "special" kind of crime that should be met differently by society? Or is "a crime a crime," regardless of whom the victim is?

Issue 11 brings us to the cultural values that contribute to public policy and justice. If a society espouses true equality, how can it deny basic rights to everyone in that society? By way of background, it is wise to be reminded of a 1967 Supreme Court case, *Loving v. Virginia*, in which the Supreme Court invalidated a state law that prohibited interracial marriages. A compelling argument in the case was that it is a basic human right to be able to go to sleep at night next to the person one loves. This case continued the "right to privacy" many believe to be implicit in the U.S. Constitution and elucidated in case law in *Griswold v. Connecticut* (1965), in which the Supreme Court invalidated a state law that prohibited the dissemination of information regarding birth control. The phrase that emerged from that case was, "What is more private than the marital bedroom?"

Issue 12 is a logical extension of Issue 11. If society were to grant gays and lesbians the right to marry—and even if not—should individuals of a sexual orientation that is a minority be denied the rights that the majority have—in this case, adoption? The arguments flare on both sides, based upon what might be the effects on an adopted child by an individual or couple who is/are homosexual.

Part IV deals with socio-economics public policies, law, and justice. We return to some of the former issues. Can those who are indigent receive the same treatment in the courts as those who are more affluent? Can they afford the "expert witnesses" who might aid their case? Reflect back on Part I, Issue 3, that of plea bargaining.

Part V brings us to educational issues. Education is the key to a person's future. That said, are all children in the United States afforded the same opportunities, or are we in a vicious circle in which the poor, who live in neighborhoods with typically lower-quality schools, will have their children receive an inferior education? What, then, shall we do? Do we require schools to "measure up," as the No Child Left Behind Act would warrant?

The last sentence ended with a question mark. This is what the Taking Sides volumes are all about. We *must* leave you with questions about which to think.

On the Internet . . .

Policy Library

Policy Library provides numerous documents concerning social and policy issues from a diversity of sources, including international research organization.

http://www.policylibrary.com/US/index.html

New American Studies

New American Studies Web provides Internet links for a range of issues in American studies and is particularly useful for studies in race and minority issues.

http://www.georgetown.edu/crossroads/asw

Office of the High Commissioner for Human Rights

This site provides up-to-date information on the activities of the Working Group on Minorities, along with information on legal standards and procedures available for the protection and promotion of minority rights, especially at the international level.

http://www.unhchr.ch/minorities/

Supreme Court Collection

Supreme Court Collection is crucial for researching key decisions of the Supreme Court.

http://supct.law.cornell.edu/supct/inex.html

PART 1

Race

*T*he United States likes to see itself as the great "melting pot." The practice of slavery and immigration in our history have made us a heterogeneous society. In a society that prides itself on political, social, and economic equality, we must ask ourselves whether all of these forms of equality truly exist. We may even have to ask ourselves if any of these exist. Indeed, we have to ask ourselves what "equality" is and whether it can possibly be achieved in any society.

While many might be tempted to see the word "minority" in a very narrow numerical sense, it is important to view "minorities" as those groups in society who have been disadvantaged in the past and may continue to be disadvantaged. We must also see "minorities" as those who, despite their numbers, are expected to submit to the dominant culture that has been established by white Anglo-Saxon Protestant men who have dominated the political and economic sectors of society for over 200 years. Has this dominant culture made efforts to translate the myth into reality? Or do minorities still suffer from the policies and laws delineated by the dominant culture? In this section, we address public policy, justice, and legal issues related to some of the problems faced by ethnic and racial minorities as they face the established judicial system.

- Does the Judicial Process Result in Racial Discrimination?

- Is Racial Profiling Necessary to Law Enforcement?

- Is Plea Bargaining Fair?

- Do Minorities Receive Tougher Sentencing?

- Are Mandatory Minimum Sentences Fair and Effective?

ISSUE 1

Does the Judicial Process Result in Racial Discrimination?

YES: Ron Stewart, from "African American Males' Reported Involvement in the Criminal Justice System: A Descriptive Analysis," *Journal of African American Men* (Fall 2000)

NO: Stewart J. D'Alessio and Lisa Stolzenberg, from "Race and the Probability of Arrest," *Social Forces* (June 2003)

ISSUE SUMMARY

YES: Author Ron Stewart's work is a case study of the black male population in Buffalo, New York. Stewart explores not only the pattern of black male incarceration, but focuses on the experiences and perceptions of black males in relation to the U.S. criminal justice system and the local police department.

NO: D'Alessio and Stolzenberg challenge the typically held view that racial discrimination by police is the reason for the very high rate of male African-American incarceration. The authors also criticize the use of social factors—especially poverty, economic inequality, social disruption, segregation and family structure—to explain the differences in crime patterns between the races.

The essence of a judicial system in an open, fair, and just society should be its impartiality. Justice in the United States is said to be "blind." But if it discriminates in any way, it is not blind but crippled.

The figures regarding the disproportionate number of racial and ethnic minorities living lives of incarceration are staggering. Is the judicial system to blame, or is the judicial system merely the end of the road for people whose lives lead them on a steady, almost direct, path to the courthouse door? Are the courts responding to a public opinion that stereotypes minorities as prone to crime?

As we begin to examine the relationship of public policy, justice, and the law, it behooves us to keep in mind the proverbial chicken-egg dilemma. Once caught up in the vicious cycle of poverty as so many minorities are, can the courthouse door be avoided? Can the children with either one or both parents incarcerated break the cycle? Can children who are surrounded day in and day out by crime and violence on their streets and in their neighborhoods—and who have thousands of "miles" on them well beyond their years—avoid the cycle as teens and adults? As the protagonist in the film *The Year of Living Dangerously* asked of the poverty he witnessed in Sukarno's Indonesia, "What then must we do?"

Arguing that the judicial system discriminates, Ron Stewart provides us with the staggering figures of the prison population. How is it that prison inmates are comprised of 49 percent of African Americans, when their percentage of the entire country's population is just 13 percent? Should society merely accept these numbers, or should we be proactive in working on the roots and real causes of this path to first the courthouse—and then the jailhouse—door?

Stewart raises another interesting question by citing Angela Davis' observation of a potentially unconscionable phenomenon. Davis notes:

> Seemingly, there is a correlation between the high rates of involvement [of African American males] and the proliferation of new penal institutions, i.e., the penal industrial complex. Moreover, what is so interesting about the alarming incarceration rates is the fact that not only are Black males supplying the penal industrial complex with the human capital, i.e., free labor, needed to sustain itself, but Black women as well as other minorities also.

If this were true, there is more wrong with our system than we suspect. But this is a subject for further research. Suffice it to say that society may not realize the loss it is sustaining by having so many people incarcerated, and not just in the simplistic terms of the annual cost of incarceration. Much more important is the human cost to those incarcerated, to their families, and to the institutionalized cycle of intergenerational incarceration.

The opposing side of the argument is presented by Stewart J. D'Alessio and Lisa Stolzenberg, who argue that it is not necessarily clear why blacks constitute such a proportion of the incarcerated. Do the police perform in a discriminatory manner? That blacks are arrested in disproportionate numbers does not make this case, they argue. Rather, D'Alessio and Stolzenberg suggest, "the elevated arrest rate for blacks may simply reflect their greater involvement in criminal activities." The authors report that their research "find[s] no evidence of racial discrimination, [but] such discrimination may manifest itself at later states in the legal process."

Ron Stewart  **YES**

African American Males' Reported Involvement in the Criminal Justice System: A Descriptive Analysis

Introduction

Upon examination of the conditions of Black males in urban environments, it becomes apparent that they face a plethora of obstacles. A sampling of such difficulties include decreasing life expectancy, unemployment, high homicide rates and inadequate education. In addition, there are other problems such as drug abuse, AIDS, and violence that adversely impact African American males (Marable 1994; Majors and Gordon 1994; Austin 1996). These problems suggest the need for innovative initiatives. Nowhere is the need more pronounced than the problem of African American males' involvement in the criminal justice system. Consider the following statistics from Mauer (1999):

- 49 percent of prison inmates nationally are African American, compared to their 13 percent share of the overall population.
- Nearly one in three (32%) black males in the age group 20–29 is under some form of correctional control, e.g., incarceration, probation, or parole (with the recent spate of unarmed Black men being killed by police officers, it is conceivable that we may have to add a new dimension to their involvement, i.e., incarceration, probation, parole and murdered), as is 1 in 15 young white males and 1 in 8 young Hispanic males.
- As of 1995, one in fourteen (7%) adult black males was incarcerated in prison or jail on any given day, representing a doubling of this rate from 1985. The 1995 figure for white males was 1 percent.
- A black male born in 1991 has a 29 percent chance of spending time in prison at some point in his life. The figure for white males is 4 percent, and for Hispanics, 16 percent (Mauer 1999, p. 2).

Illustrative of the high involvement of African American males in the criminal justice system is the number of arrests for the year 1997. Data reveal that of the 8,070,225 total arrests, 2,675,786 were Black Americans that translates

From *Journal of African American Men,* vol. 5, issue 2, Fall 2000, pp. 55–70. Copyright © 2000 by as conveyed via the Copyright Clearance Center. Reprinted by permission.

into 33 percent of the total arrests for the year (U.S. Department of Justice, 1997). Adding to these statistics is Miller's startling calculation that "the chance of a black male city resident being arrested at some time in his life for a nontraffic offense is as high as 90 percent with 51 percent being charged with a felony (1996, p. 5)." According to Miller, the twelve-year span between ages eighteen and thirty appear to be the most vulnerable period for arrest among Black males. Not to suggest that they are a focus of this research, but black women are also experiencing dramatic growth in their involvement in the criminal justice system. According to Mauer (1999), African American women are now incarcerated at a rate seven times that of white women. According to Davis (1999), the prolific speaker and renowned activist, fueling what she refers to as the "feminization of the imprisoned population" is, in part, the disestablishment of the welfare system. Welfare "reform" has prompted a large number of women to participate in alternative economies such as the drug and sex trades which has as a consequence their participation in the criminal justice system, i.e., prison (Davis 1999, p. 207). It appears as if the United States' criminal justice system has no shame in sending people of color to prison and jail. Indeed, the system is an equal opportunity incarcerator, for it does not discriminate among Black men and women and other nonwhites (see Mauer 1997; Monteiro 1994). Confirming this contention, again Angela Davis' words are telling. Quoting her, Gordon (1998/99) writes that: "Almost two million people are currently locked up in the immense network of US prisons and jails. More than 70 percent of the imprisoned population are people of color."

As these statistics indicate, the United States' current "mass incarceration policy" has and continues to have its greatest impact on minorities in general and African Americans in particular. From Boston to Seattle, Miami to Detroit or any large urban area the statistics are the same, an exorbitant number of African Americans are involved in the criminal justice system. In terms of the statistics for the city examined in this research, Reasons (1999) writes:

> In Erie County (the county in which Buffalo, NY is located), Blacks represent about 11 percent of the population, but they accounted for 62 percent of the inmates passing through Erie County jails in 1998. In the City of Buffalo, approximately 31 percent of the population is African American while 63 percent of arrests are of African Americans. . .

Such ominous statistics do not bode well in terms of the likelihood of young Black males not being involved in the criminal justice system prior to their thirtieth birthday. Indeed, Miller (1996) contends involvement in the criminal justice system is so pervasive among young Black males that it is a "rite of passage." The criminal justice involvement [as] rites of passage are evidenced by the fact that ". . . Black males are now routinely socialized to the routines of arrest, booking, jailing, detention, and imprisonment. . . ." Moreover, most citizens in America can attest to having seen the image of young Blacks prone on the ground, handcuffed against walls, or over the hoods of police cars.

Statement of the Problem

Given the high likelihood of involvement in the criminal justice system by so many young Black males and given the city's racial composition, there is [in] particular a need to assess the involvement of young African American males in the city of Buffalo, NY. More specifically, the purpose of this investigation is to examine the perceptions and experiences of Black males between the ages of eighteen and thirty-five as it relates to their involvement in the criminal justice system. In addition to examining their reported involvement, an assessment of African American males' perceived satisfaction with the Buffalo Police Department is also examined. Lastly, how well Black males perceive themselves as getting along with the Buffalo Police Department is investigated.

Methods

Respondents

Respondents for this research were residents of the city of Buffalo, NY, where African Americans at the time the research was conducted constituted 31 percent of the population. The data were collected in the summer of 1995. A non-probability sampling procedure was used. As a result, this research is limited in terms of its ability to generalize to all Black males in the city of Buffalo. However, it is thought that some valuable information about the involvement of Black males in the criminal justice system can be learned from this analysis. Further, the use of the sampling design is justified because young African American males are persons likely to be missed by traditional survey research methods. A self-administered questionnaire was distributed to 216 males found at five sites within the city. The target age group was eighteen to thirty-five years of age. This particular age-cohort was selected because it represents a critical period in the life course of individuals. Early adulthood, the period involving movement beyond adolescence, is encompassed within these years. Normatively, at this stage in the life course, it is believed young males should choose an initial occupation and establish a family through marriage. Moreover, this period is characterized by an interest in forward progress in terms of property, power, and prestige (Shepard, 1999). Of course, as noted earlier, it also turns out to be a period with high risk for arrest. The sample sites were: (1) Buffalo State College; (2) a mall in the central business district; (3) a barber shop catering to African Americans located in a predominantly Black part of the city; (4) The Juneteenth Festival in Martin Luther King Park; and (5) the basketball courts located in the city's largest park.

Given the lack of representation, the generalization about the results is limited to sample respondents. Non-response was also a significant problem in collecting the data. Many potential respondents were reluctant to participate in the investigation, i.e., there was an inordinate number of refusals. Reasons for refusals included but were not limited to the following:

1. Afraid of having their illiteracy exposed.

2. Parental obligations (Many potential respondents were "father sitting." The idea of father sitting is important because it relates to the unrepresentative number of respondents in the sample with children. The fact that the sample sites were public places required those Black males with children to be cognizant of what their children were doing and where they were at all times. Thus, many could not participate because they were watching their children).
3. Vending (Many potential respondents were selling products).
4. Heat irritation.
5. Peer pressure for potential respondents not to participate.
6. Some were intoxicated.
7. Questionnaire was thought to be too long, i.e., about 14 pages with about 170 variables.
8. Some of the potential respondents felt threatened, i.e., as if they were taking a test.

An overarching reason for refusal among the target population related to privacy concerns. There were a number of sensitive items on the questionnaire. For example, aside from the usual demographic questions, respondents were asked questions related to nutrition, health and health services utilization, victimization, political participation, religiosity, racial solidarity, substance abuse, and of course involvement in the criminal justice system.

. . . Most respondents (57.8%) were under the age of twenty-five years old, the sample's average age. The same fraction of respondents had completed more than a high school education in terms of educational attainment. Fifty-four percent had income less than $15,000. Eighty-six percent of the respondents were employed while approximately a fifth were married.

Limitations with the sampling procedures include the fact that a representative sample of African American males in the city of Buffalo may not have been drawn. Nonprobability sampling techniques lend themselves to criticisms for not resulting in a representative sample of respondents.

Measures

Involvement in the criminal justice system. Respondents' perception of involvement in the criminal justice system, the primary focus variable, was measured by asking the respondents if, other than a traffic violation, they had ever been involved in the criminal justice system (had to go to court or had been arrested). If respondents answered yes to this question, they were then asked to indicate the way(s) they had been involved in the criminal justice system.

Police satisfaction Respondents' satisfaction with the Buffalo Police Department was operationalized by an item on the questionnaire that asked subjects how satisfied they were with the overall performance of the Buffalo Police Department.

Gang activity Operationalized by an item that asked "Have you ever been involved in gang activity?"

Getting along with police   Measured by an item asking respondents how well they and the people in their neighborhood get along with the police.

Demographic characteristics   The demographic variables included in the analysis were age (age at last birthday), marital status (married, divorced or separated, widowed, or never married), education (highest grade completed), household income (all sources of income for all members of the household), and employment status (employed or unemployed).

Analysis

Analysis examined the univariate distribution of responses to the two key variables in the data set. Frequency distributions were employed to determine respondents' perception of their involvement in the criminal justice system and their satisfaction with the Buffalo Police Department.

Results

Involvement in Criminal Justice System. The reported involvement of respondents in the criminal justice system was assessed by an item on the questionnaire asking if respondents have ever been involved in the criminal justice system. Results suggest a little over a fourth (28.1%) have been involved in the criminal justice system. When respondents were asked to indicate how they were involved in the criminal justice system, a variety of ways were mentioned. However, substance abuse was the modal response (N = 18 or 31% of sample respondents) in terms of their reported involvement. Their experiences with victimization is also assessed in these data. . . . The results revealed 20 percent of the respondents were very or somewhat satisfied with the Buffalo Police Department.

More were undecided (27.5%) about their satisfaction with the Buffalo Police Department than were those satisfied. The percentage (52%) of respondents who said they were either somewhat or very dissatisfied with the Buffalo Police Department was close to double that of those undecided. (Given that 69% or 124 cases of the sample indicated experiencing racial discrimination in contacts with the police, it is not surprising that greater than 50 percent would say they were dissatisfied with the Buffalo Police Department.) These results were consistent with results obtained by Backman and Stewart (1995) in their study of the community's satisfaction with policing in the city of Buffalo. They found that approximately 50 percent of the non-white, non-Hispanic population reported general dissatisfaction with the police (N = 136 minority in a sample of 497 households). The actual number of Black males in the Backman and Stewart study eighteen to thirty-five years old was only thirteen. The percentage (46.2) of their dissatisfaction with the Buffalo Police Department almost approximates the percentage for the current analysis. Relatedly, the 1995 investigation indicated African American males found the overall Buffalo Police Department level and quality of service to be fair (53% and 46%, respectively).

In the present investigation, respondents were also asked how well they and their neighbors got along with the Buffalo Police Department. Results indicate there is low satisfaction in terms of how well Black males get along with city police. Almost as many do not get along well or not well at all with the Buffalo Police Department as do—43.1 versus 48.8 percent, respectively. Eight percent of the sample were undecided about how well they get along with the Buffalo Police Department.

Closely related to respondents' involvement in the criminal justice system is their participation in gang activity. The theory is that those involved in such activity are more likely to find themselves involved in the criminal justice system (Cohen 1955; Yablonsky 2000). To that end, respondents were asked if they had been involved in gang activity. If they answered yes to this question they were then asked to indicate the ways involved. In response to the first question related to gang involvement, 17.2 percent of the respondents said they had been involved in a gang. Burglary, armed robbery, assault, gang membership, and other forms of gang activity represented the specific kinds of gang behavior.

Discussion

Consistent with literature on the involvement of Black males in the criminal justice system, this investigation revealed that at least one out of four respondents (25%) have been involved in the criminal justice system. That is a lot; however, the percentage is lower than official estimates of criminal justice involvement. The Reasons (1999) statistics on Black male involvement cited earlier indicated that 63 percent of arrests were African Americans. Yet, these data reveal a smaller percentage as self-reported involvement. With the numbers being as different as they are the question of why must be addressed. The 63 percent includes both males and females of all age ranges, but this fact still does not adequately explain why the numbers in this sample do not match official statistics. It could be argued that this analysis did not examine the reported involvement of those African American males under arrest and this would be a valid argument. But seemingly some other factor may account for the differences in numbers.

Should the veracity of the respondents be questioned? Were the measures so ambiguous that respondents did not clearly understand what information was being solicited?

Possible explanations might include: (1) many arrests are re-arrests of the same persons; (2) if one does not adjust for re-arrests, a significant percentage of the African American population was in jail in 1998; and (3) lifetime estimates of involvement overstate involvement for the men in the current analysis because most of the respondents were less than twenty-five years in age.

Also important is the fact that a significant number of urban Black males are or have been involved with gang activity. In terms of the reasons for such involvement, the literature is replete with explanations. The sociocultural theories offered by sociology provide some explanation by suggesting "that gangs are a status-generating medium for boys whose aspirations cannot be realized by legitimate means" (Siegal and Senna 1991, 299). Still, the idea of status legitimation does not adequately explain why African American males find themselves participating in gangs. Were it not for the pervasiveness of violence in gangs, there may be some redeeming quality to gang membership. Perhaps we will never know why gangs appeal to males in general and Black males in particular.

Regarding the quarter of the sample analyzed here being involved in the criminal justice system, the circumstances are clearer. According to Mauer (1994):

> Except for the relative handful who have been unjustly convicted, clearly all the Black men in the system have committed a crime (or have been charged with a crime, as is the case for pretrial detainees in jail).

Reinforcing this point, Maurer (1999) answers the question of why has the situation of black males within the criminal justice worsened considerably to the point where it threatens the viability of an entire generation by positing that, although unfortunate, the criminal justice involvement outcome is inevitable given high black rates of crime. Thus, we cannot overlook the culpability of Black males themselves in terms of why so many are involved in the criminal justice system.

However, one of the more telling reasons why Black male[s] are involved in the criminal justice system is, in two words: "it pays!!!" [though] not for African American males). Angela Davis addresses the profit making ability of large numbers of minority group members being involved in the criminal justice system when she contends that:

> Seemingly, there is a correlation between the high rates of involvement and the proliferation of new penal institutions, i.e., the penal industrial complex. Moreover, what is so interesting about the alarming incarceration rates is the fact that not only are Black males supplying the penal industrial complex with the human capital, i.e., free labor, needed to sustain itself, but Black women as well as other minorities also.
>
> Vast numbers of handcuffed and shackled people are moved across state borders as they are transferred from one state or federal prison to another. All this work, which used to be the primary province of government, is now also performed by private corporations, whose links to government in the field of what is euphemistically called 'corrections' reveal dangerous resonances with the military industrial complex. The corporations that accrue from investment in the punishment industry, like those that accrue from investment in weapons production, only amount to social destruction. Taking into account the structural similarities and profitability of business-government linkages in the realm of military production and public punishment, the expanding penal system can now be characterized as a 'prison industrial complex' (see Gordon 1998/99 p. 146).

Another factor contributing to Black males' involvement in the criminal justice system is the unprecedented expansion of the criminal justice system.

Over the past two decades we have witnessed a vast expansion in the criminal justice system. Jerome Miller (1996) wrote:

> With the passage of federal crime legislation and the rush to enact similar measures across the nation, the U.S. was spending in excess of $200 billion annually on the crime control industry by the mid-1990s (Miller, 1996 p. 12).

The electronic news media and Americans' insatiable appetite for titillating news stories is another reason fueling Black males' involvement in the criminal justice system. That is, the media bombarding us with crime stories, daily. As a result, we have become cognizant of the so-called pervasiveness of crime and we want something done about it. If this "something" entails locking up literally hundreds of thousands of young Black males, admittedly in most cases for the commission of a crime, so be it (Miller 1996). Mathiesen (1995) in an insightful report on the media as a driving force behind prison growth asserts that the media's propensity to sensationalize minor forms of criminality also contributes to involvement in the criminal justice system.

Lastly, according to Mauer (1994), other factors leading to a disproportionate number of African American males being involved in the criminal justice system include but are not limited to: (1) limited occupational opportunities; (2) U.S. law enforcement being disproportionately concerned with crimes of the poor; (3) the so-called "war" on drugs (some derisively refer to this "war" as a war on minority rights); and (4) racism, e.g., though Blacks are only 13 percent of the population, they represent 50 percent of the prison population and 40 percent of those persons on death row. The next section of the analysis addresses what can be done to curtail the involvement of so many Black men in the criminal justice system.

Conclusion

It is painfully obvious that the reported involvement of Black males in the city of Buffalo with the criminal justice system mirrors the involvement of Black males in cities throughout the United States. Thus, there is a critical need for innovative policies for reducing such a waste of human productivity. To that end, several scholars have proposed a number of efforts to curtail the involvement of African American males in the criminal justice system. [Maurer's] (1994) innovative strategies could prove pivotal. A summary of his strategies follows.

First, an increase in the diversion of many first-time offenders from the criminal justice system would reduce the exorbitant numbers. Second, a focus of the "war on drugs" upon prevention rather than law enforcement would be helpful as well. One of the factors fueling the increased number of African American males in the system is the fact that many of those involved are actually low-level drug offenders. This writer would go so far as to propose decriminalization of certain substances. Massing (1999) stated:

> Virtually all liberals, for instance, would like to see the police stop making so many drug arrests, which currently number more than 1.5 million a

year. Everyone, too, would like to see an overhaul of the nation's harsh and discriminatory drug-sentencing laws-a step that would, among other things, reverse the relentless flow of black and Latino men into prison (Massing, 1999 p. 11).

The reduction of lengthy and inefficient prison terms is the third strategy proposed. Many readers are aware of the ongoing saga of Kemba Smith, a young Black woman facing twenty-four years in federal prison; she is a victim of "get-tough" mandatory sentencing laws (see Stuart 1996). Sentencing to ameliorate racial disparities is the fourth strategy while an increase in the use of alternatives to incarceration is the final proposal for reducing Black males' involvement in the criminal justice system. Recently, Mauer (1999) augmented his earlier proposals by suggesting (1) legislative actions that involve: (a) a reconsideration of mandatory sentencing policies; (b) equalization of penalties for crack and powder cocaine; (c) development of racial/ethnic impact statements of sentencing policy; (d) establishment of a goal of reducing the non-violent offender population by 50 percent over ten years; and (e) increased funding for indigent defense and sentencing advocacy; (2) criminal justice officials' initiatives that involve: (a) expanded drug policy options; (b) expanded use of alternative sentencing (mentioned earlier as diversionary programs); (c) the monitoring of alternative sentencing programs to assess racial balance; and (3) criminal justice/community partnerships that involve: (a) increase community-based diversion from the criminal justice system, and (b) strengthening the link between communities and the justice system.

This writer wholeheartedly agrees with Mauer and would go a step further by seriously reviewing the sentences of the current first-time offenders who committed nonviolent victimless crimes, i.e., the sale and use of illicit substances. Having already served some time in the harshest aspect of the criminal justice system, these young men could have their sentences commuted and re-sentenced to do public service work for a specified number of months or years. There is always a need to improve the infrastructure, e.g., public highways and buildings of this country. Additionally, it is possible that public work might improve their overall self-esteem, a factor, perhaps, in their initial involvement in the criminal justice system.

In sum, to reduce the number of Black males involved in the criminal justice system, there must be a concerted effort involving government, law enforcement, community organizations, parents, educators, clergy, and employers. Collaboration by these entities holds the key to unlocking a system of incarceration that has literally taken an entire generation of potentially productive young Black males from society in general and the Black community in particular. Additionally, by harnessing the unchecked power of police officers, a reduction in the number of Black males in penal institutions may decrease. It is widely recognized that police officers wield tremendous powers (read discretion) in determining who goes to jail and who does not. If they use their discretion correctly, instead of wantonly, many young lives will not be destroyed due to unnecessary involvement in the criminal justice system. Indeed, if many police officers used a stern admonition, i.e., scared straight, when Black males engage in victimless crimes such as the sale of crack cocaine, instead of arrest and criminal adjudication, perhaps we would see a substantial reduction in the number of Black males involved in the criminal justice system and, concomitantly, African American males might be more satisfied with police officers and their efforts to fight crime. In sum, at a minimum, an effort must be started immediately to reduce the numbers of young Black males involved in the criminal justice system because America and the African American community can ill afford to lose another generation of its future to the criminal justice system.

Implications for Future Research

Given that this research analyzed African American males' reported involvement in the criminal system using a nonprobability sampling design and descriptive statistics with a relatively small sample, future research in this area should expand the analysis by using a much larger probability sample and statistical procedures that are both descriptive and inferential. In addition, measures that get at why Black males think they are involved in the criminal justice systems could prove to be enlightening. Further, with the number of women incarcerated increasing to unparalleled highs, an examination of the reasons why, other than those alluded to in this research, should occur as well. Lastly, the long-term impact on the Black community's ability to remain viable with so many of its young men behind bars warrants investigating. It is a fact that high rates of incarceration disenfranchises large numbers of potential voters (Mauer 1999), but what other consequences result from the wholesale imprisonment of tens of thousands of young African American males? These and many more are research question[s] deserving of immediate attention. Indeed, the field of African American males' involvement in the criminal justice system is ripe for empirical harvesting. The information presented here are the seeds needed in the long and arduous process of understanding how and why Black males are involved in the criminal justice system and, more importantly, what can be done to reduce such involvement.

References

Austin, B.W. (1996). *Repairing the breach: Key ways to support family life, reclaim our streets and rebuild civil society in America's communities.* Chicago: Noble Press, Inc.

Backman, C. B. & Ron Stewart (1995). "Policing in Buffalo: The community's attitudes, opinions, and preferences." Unpublished Manuscript. SUNY-Buffalo State College.

Cohen, A. (1955). *Delinquent boys: The culture of the gang.* Glencoe: Free Press.

Davis, A. (1999). Prison Abolition. In W. Mosley, M. Diawara, C. Taylor, and R. Austin (ed.) *Black Genius: African American Solutions to African American Problems* (196–214). New York: W. W. Norton.

Gordon, A.V. (1998/99). Globalism and the prison industrial complex: An interview with Angela Davis. *Race & Class,* 40(2/3):145–157.

Marable, M. (1994) The black male: Searching beyond stereotypes. In R. Staples (ed.) *The black family: Essays and studies* (pp. 91–96). Belmont, CA: Wadsworth Publishing Company.

Majors, R., Gordon, J. (1994). *The American black male: His present status and his future.* Chicago: Nelson-Hall.

Massing, M. (1999). Beyond legalization: New ideas for ending the war on drugs. *The Nation* V269(8), 11–15.

Mathiesen, T. (1995). *Driving forces behind prison growth: The mass media.* Washington, DC: The Sentencing Project.

Mauer, M. (1994). A generation behind bars: Black males and the criminal justice system. In R. Majors and J.U. Gordon's (ed.) *The American Black Male: His Present Status and His Future* (81–93). Chicago: Nelson Hall.

Mauer, M. (1997). *M. Mauer before the Congressional Symposium on the federal sentencing guidelines.* Washington, DC: The Sentencing Project.

Mauer, M. (1999). *The crisis of the young African American male and the criminal justice system.* Washington, DC: The Sentencing Project.

Miller, J. G. (1996). *Search and destroy: African American males in the criminal justice system.* New York: Cambridge University Press.

Monteiro, T. (1994). The new face of racism. *Peace-Review,* 6(2):139–147.

Reasons, C. E. (1999). The color of justice," *Art Voice,* V10 (8):8–14.

Shepard, J. M. (1999). *Sociology,* 7th ed. CA: Wadsworth.

Siegel, L. J. and Senna, J.J. (1991). *Juvenile delinquency: Theory, practice, and law,* (4th ed.). New York: West Publishing Company.

Stuart, R. (1996). Kemba's nightmare. *Emerge,* 7(7):28–48.

U.S. Department of Justice, Federal Bureau of Investigation (1997). *Crime in the United States.* Washington, DC: Government Printing Office.

Yablonsky, L. (2000). *Juvenile delinquency into the 21st century.* Belmont, CA: Wadsworth.

Stewart J. D'Alessio
and Lisa Stolzenberg

Race and the Probability of Arrest

The relationship between race and arrest remains a topic of contentious debate. While blacks constitute about 12.8% of the population, they accounted for 38% of the arrests for violent crimes and 31% of the arrests for property crimes in 2000 (Federal Bureau of Investigation 2001; U.S. Census Bureau 2001). Although it is readily acknowledged that blacks are arrested in numbers far out of proportion to their numbers in the population, considerable disagreement exists as to what this finding exactly means. Social scientists have proferred two major explanations. The first and most broadly solicited explanation employs normative theories to explain the overrepresentation of black citizens in official arrest statistics. Normative theories view the enforcing of criminal laws as unbiased, with little or no consideration being given to the offender's race or other demographic characteristics. These type of theories purport to explain most of the disparity in arrest statistics between blacks and whites to differences in criminal involvement. It is argued that racial differences in arrest patterns occur primarily because blacks violate the law more frequently and commit more serious crimes than do whites.

Normative theories typically emphasize the nexus between social factors and crime to explicate differences in crime patterns between the races. The social factors most highlighted in the literature include poverty, economic inequality, deprivation, social disorganization, segregation, and family structure (Wilson & Petersilia 2002). Constitutional factors such as intelligence have also been adduced as engendering race differences in criminal behavior, but research on this topic is highly controversial (Fischer et al. 1996; Herrnstein & Murry 1994).

An alternative explanation for the differential arrest patterns of whites and blacks focuses on racially biased law enforcement practices. This perspective draws from conflict theory, which posits that the elevated arrest rate for black citizens is the consequence of discrimination by police. Conflict theorists view society as consisting of groups with differing and conflicting values and maintain that the state is organized to represent the interests of citizens who are wealthy and powerful. Criminal law is conceived as an instrument to protect the interests of the elite, and the severity of criminal sanction is based

From *Social Sources*, vol. 81, issue 4, June 2003, pp. 1381–1397. Copyright © 2003 by Social Forces. Reprinted by permission.

to a large degree on extralegal factors such as race and social class (Turk 1969; Quinney 1977). Consequently, groups that challenge the status quo are more apt to be subjected to criminalization, arrest, and increased incarceration compared to groups that are perceived as less menacing. The conflict perspective thus suggests that blacks and other racial minorities will be more susceptible to biased law enforcement practices in order to ensure they are brought under state control (Greenberg, Kessler & Loftin 1985). As Chambliss (1969:86) points out, blacks are more likely to be scrutinized and therefore to be observed in any violation of the law and more likely to be arrested and discovered under suspicious circumstances.

It is also asserted that blacks, especially young black males, face a higher probability of arrest because the police have a negative perception of them. Disparaging labels such as "delinquents," 'dope addicts,' and "welfare pimps" are used frequently to depict black males (Gibbs 1988:2). Black males also epitomize an aggressive behavior style that is perceived by many whites to be threatening (Tittle & Curran 1988). The media often acts to render these stereotypes more negative. In his study of local news broadcasts, Entman (1992) reports that violent crimes committed by blacks comprise a substantial portion of the coverage of news stories that centrally feature blacks. He reports that blacks are not only more likely than whites to be characterized as criminal offenders in news stories about violent crime, but that they are also more likely to be depicted as physically intimidating, a pattern also noted by Jamieson (1992) in national network portrayals. This general stereotype of blacks, especially young black males, as being dangerous and criminally inclined is thought to compel police to monitor and arrest black citizens more frequently than warranted based on their actual criminal behavior. . . .

Using data from the NIBRS [National Incident-Based Reporting System], we attempt to determine the extent that black overrepresentation in official arrest statistics is explained by differential offending or by differential selection into the criminal justice system via arrests by police. NIBRS represents the next generation of crime data and it is designed to replace the nearly 70-year-old UCR. The intent of NIBRS is "to enhance the quantity, quality, and timeliness of crime statistical data collected by the law enforcement community and to improve the methodology used for compiling, analyzing, auditing, and publishing the collected crime data" (Federal Bureau of Investigation 2000:1). NIBRS is unique because rather than being restricted to a group of eight Index crimes that the summary-based program uses, it gathers information from individual crime reports recorded by police officers at the time of the crime incident for 57 different criminal offenses. The information collected by police typically includes victim and offender demographics, victim/offender relationship, time and place of occurrence, weapon use, and victim injuries. Because NIBRS is capable of producing more detailed and meaningful data than that generated by the traditional UCR, it is a valuable tool in the study of crime.[1]

NIBRS data are well suited for our intentions because it is possible to link a reported crime incident to a subsequent arrest that was heretofore not feasible with the UCR. The ability to merge crime incident data with arrest data enables researchers to calculate the actual probability of arrest by race for crimes communicated to the police where the victim is able to identify the race of the offender. This is the most appropriate strategy for evaluating the discriminatory use of the arrest sanction because the police can only act upon illegal behaviors that come to their attention. These data also afford us the opportunity to examine how the arrest sanction is influenced by a number of salient factors about which Hindelang lacked data, such as whether the victim was injured, the race of the victim, the victim/offender relationship, and weapon use. . . .

Given that prior research reports that a victim's race is often important in determining severity of criminal sanction, we felt it prudent to assess whether a victim's race interacts with a criminal offender's race in predicting the probability of arrest. It is often argued that when blacks victimize whites, the high value attached to a white victim and the racial fears of authorities engender severe treatment (Black 1976). The race of the victim is reported to play an important role in the punishment of rapists (LaFree 1980), robbers (Thomson & Zingraff 1981), murderers (Kleck 1981) and other types of criminal offenders (Myers 1979). . . .

✦✦✦

Debate persists as to whether the police perform their duties in a racially dis-criminatory fashion. The most frequently cited evidence for this assertion is the observation that blacks are arrested in numbers far out of proportion to their numbers in the general population. This observation, however, cannot in itself be taken as evidence of racial discrimination, since the elevated arrest rate for blacks may simply reflect their greater involvement in criminal activ-ities. Because our legal system's claim to legitimacy is especially dependent on the public's perception of fairness and equity in the decision to arrest, we took a closer look at the evidence bearing on this issue.

Using data from the new NIBRS, we analyzed the effect of an offender's race, as perceived by the crime victim, on the probability of arrest for 335,619 incidents of forcible rape, robbery, aggravated assault, and simple assault in 17 states during 1999. Contrary to the theoretical arguments of the differential arrest hypothesis, and consistent with the tenants of the differential offending perspective, our analyses show that whites are considerably more likely than blacks to be arrested for robbery, aggravated assault, and simple assault. There are also no glaring differences in the data between white and black offenders regard-ing their chances of being arrested for forcible rape. This null finding also tends to refute the argument that racial bias in policing is affecting the arrest rate for blacks. Such findings beg the question: How can it be that whites and not blacks are more likely to be arrested for robbery and for assault, when many individuals who write about the criminal justice system assume precisely the opposite?

One likely explanation for our findings relates to black citizens' distrust of the police. In police work there are two basic ways that an individual is initially linked with the commission of a crime: (1) the police officer can observe the criminal offense and (2) a citizen can give testimony against the individual. In most cases, however, the police officer usually arrives too late to witness the criminal offense. Accordingly, the police are often forced to rely on the testimony of witnesses to gather the necessary evidence to effectuate an arrest. Our finding that whites are more likely to be arrested than blacks should be understood in this context. It is well known that blacks distrust the police more than whites (Sherman 2002; Weitzer 2000). For example, a recent national Gallup Poll showed that 36% of black citizens, as compared to 13% of white citizens, have an unfavorable opinion of the local police (Gallup & Gallup 1999). Although speculative, this interpretation most likely explains our findings. Only future research designed to test this hypothesis can ascertain whether it is more than merely plausible and whether it actually produces the patterns we observe in this study.

Although our analyses present empirical evidence that whites generally have a higher expectation of arrest, our findings should be qualified by the fact that we analyze only certain types of crimes and cannot definitely say what the effects of an offender's race might be for other offenses. Our analyses are limited to rape, robbery, and assault because it is in these types of crimes that the victim is confronted by the offender and hence is able to infer his or her physical characteristics. Further insight into the nature and strength of the underlying structural relationship between race and the probability of arrest for other crimes such drug or property offenses must await the development of richer data sets.

Contextual analyses are also needed because it is plausible that the impact of an offender's race on the likelihood of arrest varies across social contexts. It is often argued that the amount of social control experienced by blacks in society is greatest in areas where the size of the black population presents a serious challenge to the political and economic power of whites (Blalock 1967; Jacobs & Wood 1999). On the basis of this research, we believe that future investigations should concentrate on multilevel studies in which police actions are nested within differing social contexts.

Finally, our findings do not negate the possibility that some individual police officers discriminate against black citizens. What the present analysis does show is that regardless of whatever discrimination is present at the arrest stage, the outcome is generally a lower chance of arrest for blacks than for whites. If there is discrimination against blacks by some police officers, then, given the observed net result, it appears that there must also be some compensating effect. It is also important to consider that although we find no evidence of racial discrimination, such discrimination may manifest itself at later stages in the legal process.

A paramount concern about racial discrimination in the administration of the justice relates to the unequal treatment of similarly situated individuals by law enforcement officials. Our findings have profound implications since they bear directly on the current debate as to whether the police perform their duties in a racially discriminatory fashion. The results of this study suggest that the disproportionately high arrest rate for black citizens is most likely ascribable to differential criminal participation in reported crime rather than to racially biased law enforcement practices. The new data presented here also suggest some caution in the pervasive practice of employing race-specific arrest rates as a surrogate measure of race-specific criminal offending, at least for the crimes of robbery, aggravated assault and simple assault.

Note

1. For an overview of NIBRS and how the system differs from summary reporting, see the National Incident-Based Reporting System, Volume 1: Data Collection Guidelines (Federal Bureau of Investigation 2000). The NIBRS data are archived at the National Archive of Criminal Justice Data, University of Michigan (www.icpsr.umich.edu/NACJD).

References

Black, Donald J. 1976. *The Behavior of Law*. Academic Press.

Blalock, Herbert M., Jr. 1967. *Toward a Theory of Minority-Group Relations*. Capricorn Books.

Chambliss, William. 1969. *Crime and the Legal Process*. McGraw-Hill.

Entman, Robert. 1992. "Blacks in the News." *Journalism Quarterly* 69:341–61.

Federal Bureau of Investigation. 2000. National Incident-Based Reporting System, Volume 1: Data Collection Guidelines. Government Printing Office.

———. 2001. Crime in the United States, 2000. Government Printing Office.

Fischer, Claude S., Michael Rout, Martin Sanchez Jankowski, Samuel Lucas, Ann Swidler, and Kim Voss. 1996. *Inequality by Design*. Princeton University Press.

Gallup, George, Jr., and Alec Gallup. 1999. *The Gallup Poll Monthly*, No 411. Gallup Poll.

Gibbs, Jewelle. 1988. *Young, Black, and Male in America*. Auburn House.

Greenberg, David F., Ronald C. Kessler, and Colin Loftin. 1985. "Social Inequality and Crime Control." *Journal of Criminal Law and Criminology* 76:684–704.

Herrnstein, Richard J., and Charles Murry. 1994. *The Bell Curve: Intelligence and Class Structure in American Life*. Free Press.

Jacobs, David, and Katherine Wood. 1999. "Interracial Conflict and Interracial Homicide: Do Political and Economic Rivalries Explain White Killings of Blacks or Black Killings of Whites?" *American Journal of Sociology* 105:157–90.

Jamieson, Kathleen H. 1992. *Dirty Politics: Deception, Distraction, and Democracy*. Oxford University Press.

Kleck, Gary. 1981. "Racial Discrimination in Criminal Sentencing: A Critical Evaluation with Additional Evidence on the Death Penalty." *American Sociological Review* 46:783–805.

LaFree, Gary. 1980. :"The Effect of Sexual Stratification by Race on Official Reactions to Rape." *American Sociological Review* 45:842–54.

Myers, Martha A. 1979. "Offended Parties and Official Reactions: Victims and the Sentencing of Criminal Defendants." *Sociological Quarterly* 20:529–40.

Quinney, Richard. 1977. *Class, State and Crime*. McKay.

———. 2002. "Trust and Confidence in Criminal Justice." *NIJ Journal* 248:23–31.

Thomson, Randall J., and Matthew T. Zingraff. 1981. "Detecting Sentencing Disparity: Some Problems and Evidence." *American Journal of Sociology* 86:869–80.

Tittle, Charles R., and Debra A. Curran. 1988. "Contingencies for Dispositional Disparities in Juvenile Justice." *Social Forces* 67:23–58.

Turk, Austin T. 1969. *Criminality and Legal Order*. Chicago: Rand-McNally.

U.S. Census Bureau. 2001. Resident Population Estimates of the United States by Sex, Race, and Hispanic Origin: April 1, 1990 to July 1, 999, with Short-term Projection to November 1, 2000. Government Printing Office.

Weitzer, Ronald. 2000. "Racialized Policing: Resident's Perceptions in Three Neighborhoods." *Law and Society Review* 34:129–55.

Wilson, James Q., and Joan Petersilia, eds. 2002. *Crime: Public Policies for Crime Control*. ICS Press.

POSTSCRIPT

Does the Judicial Process Result in Racial Discrimination?

The race-arrest relationship is a complex one. Clearly the data tell us that there is a disproportionately African-American male prison population. But to what can we attribute this phenomenon? Are more arrests made when African Americans (especially males) are involved in a criminal activity? Are the police biased and less likely to mete out the same punishment to whites who commit the same crime? Or are there other factors in play?

Ron Stewart presents the demographics that may help to explain the overrepresentation of young African-American males in the criminal justice system. Under what social and economic conditions does the typical African-American male live? Data tell us that most of the incarcerated African-American males are poorly educated, which contributes to a high unemployment rate. The low level of self-esteem that results may help us to understand why this population is more likely to engage in activities that lead to arrest—drug abuse and drug dealing, or violent and often homicidal behavior. Stewart also discusses the results of a self-administered questionnaire given to a sample of African-American males in sectors of Buffalo, New York, and how understanding the perceptions of these individuals may lead to policy changes.

Stewart J. D'Alessio and Lisa Stolzenberg present a summary of normative theories, which view enforcement of criminal laws as unbiased versus conflict theory, which looks to biased law enforcement practices. While D'Alessio and Stolzenberg concede that some police officers may be biased, they argue that on the whole the police are simply arresting those who commit crimes.

Public policy questions emerge regarding what can be done to ameliorate the plight of this "subculture" of society. One might say, "If the answer were a simple one, then the problem would have been solved." This is extremely simplistic; indeed, it is naïve. The answer *is* a simple one: Give those in this subculture something for which to live. This would mean enhancing educational opportunities and encouraging students with a meaningful curriculum and positive reinforcement. Psychological studies tell us that individuals live up to the expectations held of them. Society, as a whole, has very low expectations for the young African-American male. The prophecy is self-fulfilling, and the cycle is a vicious one. Among the developing literature on this subject, two works are particularly worthwhile for future reading: Heather MacDonald, *Are Cops Racist,* and David Cole, *No Equal Justice.* Thomas Ross, Just Stories: *How the Law Embodies Racism and Bias* presents an interesting commentary about the views and stereotypes the "powerful" (judges, bureaucrats, jurors) have of the poor, blacks, and women. Linda Gayle Mills' *A Penchant for Prejudice* presents an argument that disputes the possibility of judicial impartiality.

ISSUE 2

Is Racial Profiling Necessary to Law Enforcement?

YES: Heather Mac Donald, from "The Myth of Racial Profiling," *City Journal* (Spring 2001)

NO: Richard G. Schott, from "The Role of Race in Law Enforcement: Racial Profiling or Legitimate Use?" (Federal Bureau of Investigation, 2001)

ISSUE SUMMARY

YES: Author Heather Mac Donald reviews and disputes the allegations of police profiling and explores the daily demands on police officers. Mac Donald also discusses the justification for using race in investigating crime.

NO: Richard G. Scott draws the distinctions between legitimate "stops" versus those based upon racial characteristics. Scott includes an overview of Constitutional protections aimed at preventing police profiling and points to the need for proper police training.

It is ironic that at the same time the public and politicians alike rail against the injustice of racial profiling, the practice continues. It is almost as if rhetoric alone will ameliorate the continuation of the practicing. Do we even know what we are talking about when we use the term "racial profiling"?

Post–9/11, "racial profiling" has come to have an added dimension to it—and somewhat of a rhetorical justification. But the process has always been controversial. It goes to the heart of properly conducted police activities. If, just if, racial profiling leads to curtailing crime, the argument might go, or catching just one more criminal, is it worth trading off individual rights and individual human dignity in an allegedly just society? Recall Martin Luther King, Jr.'s view that any law (and we will include procedure here) that degrades human dignity is unjust. Is it dignified to be pulled out of a car if one is black in a white neighborhood? Is it dignified to be removed from an airplane because another passenger complains of one's skin tone and garb? If these practices degrade human dignity, then these are unjust practices. If a society claims these to be critical to its well-being, that society must acknowledge that it is behaving unjustly. That society cannot have it both ways. What every thinking person has to question is if the trade-off of security—be it from criminals or terrorists—is worth our civil liberties. Once any person's civil liberties are infringed upon, then everyone's civil liberties are infringed upon. We must be mindful of Benjamin Franklin's remark that "Those who trade liberty for security deserve neither."

Richard G. Schott traces the historical use of race in the law and the distinctions between the legitimate use of profiling by the police versus the abuse of the process. Any first-year law school student knows that laws that are focused on any "protected class" (race, sex, religion) are subject to "strict scrutiny" by the courts. It is incumbent upon the government to prove that such laws serve a compelling governmental interest. But what about the process of what might be racially motivated police activities? If these do occur, they occur long before any case comes to a court's attention. Schott argues that proper police training will avoid the necessity of racial profiling, and that "it is critically important for law enforcement officers to understand the difference between legitimate and illegitimate uses of race in their law enforcement activities to maintain credibility within their communities."

Heather Mac Donald comes down firmly on the side that racial profiling by police is a "myth." Mac Donald argues that it is certainly within the realm of police conduct to use race as a criterion for assessing criminal activity. Police, she maintains, do not use race exclusively, but as one of many criteria. She refers to this as "soft" racial profiling. How do we determine if this is what has occurred in a particular instance?

Schott's citing of a particular incident reminds us of the difficulty.

On May 14, 2001, three young African-American males were pulled over by the Indianapolis, Indiana, Police [sic] Department. According to one of the passenger's stepfather, the stop was a blatant example of racial profiling. According to the officers on the scene, it was a legitimate traffic stop for failure to signal a turn. Which one of these characterizations was correct? Were both viewpoints arguable?

As you read the articles in this section, think about this scenario and the dilemma such occurrences present to a society that would strive for justice.

Heather Mac Donald

The Myth of Racial Profiling

The anti-"racial profiling" juggernaut must be stopped, before it obliterates the crime-fighting gains of the last decade, especially in inner cities. The anti-profiling crusade thrives on an ignorance of policing and a willful blindness to the demographics of crime. . . .

The ultimate question in the profiling controversy is whether the disproportionate involvement of blacks and Hispanics with law enforcement reflects police racism or the consequences of disproportionate minority crime. Anti-profiling activists hope to make police racism an all but irrebuttable presumption whenever enforcement statistics show high rates of minority stops and arrests. But not so fast.

Two meanings of "racial profiling" intermingle in the activists' rhetoric. What we may call "hard" profiling uses race as the *only* factor in assessing criminal suspiciousness: an officer sees a black person and, without more to go on, pulls him over for a pat-down on the chance that he may be carrying drugs or weapons. "Soft" racial profiling is using race as one factor among others in gauging criminal suspiciousness: the highway police, for example, have intelligence that Jamaican drug posses with a fondness for Nissan Pathfinders are transporting marijuana along the northeast corridor. A New Jersey trooper sees a black motorist speeding in a Pathfinder and pulls him over in the hope of finding drugs.

The racial profiling debate focuses primarily on highway stops. The police are pulling over a disproportionate number of minority drivers for traffic offenses, goes the argument, in order to look for drugs. Sure, the driver committed an infraction, but the reason the trooper chose to stop *him*, rather than the speeder next to him, was his race.

But the profiling critics also fault both the searches that sometimes follow a highway stop and the tactics of urban policing. Any evaluation of the evidence for, and the appropriateness of, the use of race in policing must keep these contexts distinct. Highway stops should almost always be color-blind, I'll argue, but in other policing environments (including highway searches), where an officer has many clues to go on, race may be among them. Ironi-cally, effective urban policing shows that the more additional factors an officer has in his criminal profile, the more valid race becomes—and the less signifi-cant, almost to the point of irrelevance.

⚫⟨◉⟩⚫

Before reviewing the evidence that profiling critics offer, recall the demands that the police face every day, far from anti-police agitators and their journalist acolytes.

February 22, 2001, a town-hall meeting at P.S. 153 in Harlem between New York mayor Rudolph Giuliani and Harlem residents: a woman sarcasti-cally asks Giuliani if police officers downtown are paid more than uptown officers, "because we don't have any quality of life in Harlem, none whatso-ever. Drug dealers are allowed to stand out in front of our houses every day, to practically invade us, and nothing's done about it." Another woman com-plains that dealers are back on the street the day after being arrested, and notes that "addicts are so bold that we have to get off the sidewalk and go around *them*!" She calls for the declaration of a state of emergency. A man wonders if cop-basher congressman Charles Rangel, present at the meeting, could "endow the police with more power," and suggests that the NYPD coor-dinate with the federal Drug Enforcement Administration, the INS, and the IRS to bring order to the streets.

The audience meets Giuliani's assertions that the police have brought crime down sharply in Harlem with hoots of derision. No one mentions "police brutality." . . .

February 12, 2001, the fifth floor of a hulking yellow apartment building on Lenox Road in Flatbush, Brooklyn: two officers from the 67th Precinct investigate an anonymous call reporting a group of youths smoking mari-juana in the hallway. The boys have disappeared. As officers check the stair-well, a gaunt middle-aged man sporting a wildly patterned black-and-white tie courteously introduces himself as Mr. Johnson, the building superintendent. After slowly bending down to pick up a discarded cigarette butt, he asks politely if anything more can be done about the kids who come from the next building to smoke pot in his hallway.

⚫⟨◉⟩⚫

This is the demand—often angry, sometimes wistful—that urban police forces constantly hear: *get rid of the drugs!* These recent appeals come *after* the most successful war on crime that New York City has ever conducted. A decade and a half ago, when drug-related drive-by shootings became epidemic, inner-city residents nationwide were calling even more frantically for protection from drug violence. When New Jersey, a key state on the drug corridor from Central America to New England, sent its state highway troopers to do foot patrols in Camden and Trenton, residents met them with cheers.

In New York, the mayhem eventually led to the development of the Giuliani administration's assertive policing that strives, quite successfully, to prevent crime from happening. Outside of New York, the widespread pleas to stop drug violence led the Drug Enforcement Administration to enlist state highway police in their anti-drug efforts. The DEA and the Customs Service had been using intelligence about drug routes and the typical itineraries of couriers to interdict drugs at airports; now the interdiction war would expand to the nation's highways, the major artery of the cocaine trade.

The DEA taught state troopers some common identifying signs of drug couriers: nervousness; conflicting information about origin and destination cities among vehicle occupants; no luggage for a long trip; lots of cash; lack of a driver's license or insurance; the spare tire in the back seat; rental license plates or plates from key source states like Arizona and New Mexico; loose screws or scratches near a vehicle's hollow spaces, which can be converted to hiding places for drugs and guns. The agency also shared intelligence about the types of cars that couriers favored on certain routes, as well as about the ethnic makeup of drug-trafficking organizations. A typical DEA report from the early 1990s noted that "large-scale interstate trafficking networks controlled by Jamaicans, Haitians, and black street gangs dominate the manufacture and distribution of crack." The 1999 "Heroin Trends" report out of Newark declared that "predominant wholesale traffickers are Colombian, followed by Dominicans, Chinese, West African/Nigerian, Pakistani, Hispanic and Indian. Mid-levels are dominated by Dominicans, Colombians, Puerto Ricans, African-Americans and Nigerians."

꿏

According to the racial profiling crowd, the war on drugs immediately became a war on minorities, on the highways and off. Their alleged evidence for racial profiling comes in two varieties: anecdotal, which is of limited value, and statistical, which on examination proves entirely worthless.

The most notorious racial profiling anecdote may have nothing to do with racial profiling at all. On April 23, 1998, two New Jersey state troopers pulled over a van that they say was traveling at 74 miles an hour in a 55-mile-an-hour zone on the New Jersey Turnpike. As they approached on foot, the van backed toward them, knocking one trooper down, hitting the patrol car, and then getting sideswiped as it entered the traffic lane still in reverse. The troopers fired 11 rounds at the van, wounding three of the four passengers, two critically.

Attorneys for the van passengers deny that the van was speeding. The only reason the cops pulled it over, critics say, was that its occupants were black and Hispanic.

If the troopers' version of the incident proves true, it is hard to see how racial profiling enters the picture. The van's alleged speed would have legitimately drawn the attention of the police. As for the shooting: whether justified or not, it surely was prompted by the possibly deadly trajectory of the van, not the race of the occupants. Nevertheless, on talk show after talk show, in every newspaper story denouncing racial profiling, the turnpike shooting has come to symbolize the lethal dangers of "driving while black."

Less notoriously, black motorists today almost routinely claim that the only reason they are pulled over for highway stops is their race. Once they are pulled over, they say, they are subject to harassment, including traumatic searches. Some of these tales are undoubtedly true. Without question, there are obnoxious officers out there, and some officers may ignore their training and target minorities. But since the advent of video cameras in patrol cars, installed in the wake of the racial profiling controversy, most charges of police racism, testified to under oath, have been disproved as lies.

∾◈∾

The allegation that police systematically single out minorities for unjustified law enforcement ultimately stands or falls on numbers. In suits against police departments across the country, the ACLU and the Justice Department have waved studies aplenty allegedly demonstrating selective enforcement. None of them holds up to scrutiny.

The typical study purports to show that minority motorists are subject to disproportionate traffic stops. Trouble is, no one yet has devised an adequate benchmark against which to measure if police are pulling over, searching, or arresting "too many" blacks and Hispanics. The question must always be: *too many compared with what?* Even anti-profiling activists generally concede that police pull drivers over for an actual traffic violation, not for no reason whatsoever, so a valid benchmark for stops would be the number of serious traffic violators, not just drivers. If it turns out that minorities tend to drive more recklessly, say, or have more equipment violations, you'd expect them to be subject to more stops. But to benchmark accurately, you'd also need to know the number of miles driven by different racial groups, so that you'd compare stops per man-mile, not just per person. Throw in age demographics as well: if a minority group has more young people—read: immature drivers—than whites do, expect more traffic stops of that group. The final analysis must then compare police deployment patterns with racial driving patterns: if more police are on the road when a higher proportion of blacks are driving—on weekend nights, say—stops of blacks will rise.

No traffic-stop study to date comes near the requisite sophistication. Most simply compare the number of minority stops with some crude population measure, and all contain huge and fatal data gaps. An ACLU analysis of Philadelphia traffic stops, for example, merely used the percentage of blacks in the 1990 census as a benchmark for stops made seven years later. In about half the stops that the ACLU studied, the officer did not record the race of the motorist. The study ignored the rate of traffic violations by race, so its grand conclusion of selective enforcement is meaningless. . . .

Do minorities commit more of the kinds of traffic violations that police target? This is a taboo question among the racial profiling crowd; to ask it is to reveal one's racism. No one has studied it. But some evidence suggests that it may be the case. The National Highway Traffic Safety Administration found that blacks were 10 percent of drivers nationally, 13 percent of drivers in fatal accidents, and 16 percent of drivers in injury accidents. (Lower rates of seat-belt use may contribute to these numbers.) Random national surveys of drivers on weekend nights in 1973, 1986, and 1996 found that blacks were more likely to fail breathalyzer tests than whites. In Illinois, blacks have a higher motorist fatality rate than whites. Blacks in one New Jersey study were 23 percent of all drivers arrested at the scene of an accident for driving drunk, though only 13.5 percent of highway users. In San Diego, blacks have more accidents than their population figures would predict. Hispanics get in a disproportionate number of accidents nationally. . . .

Despite the hue and cry, there is nothing illegal about using race as one factor among others in assessing criminal suspiciousness. Nevertheless, the initial decision to pull a car over should be based almost always on seriousness of traffic violation alone—unless, of course, evidence of other law-breaking, such as drug use, is visible. If the result is that drug couriers assiduously observe the speed limit, fine. But compared with most other policing environments, highways are relatively cueless places. In assessing the potential criminality of a driver speeding along with the pack on an eight-lane highway, an officer normally has much less to work with than on a city street or sidewalk. His locational cues—traveling on an interstate pointed toward a drug market, say—are crude, compared with those in a city, where an officer can ask if this particular block is a drug bazaar. His ability to observe the behavior of a suspect over time is limited by the speed of travel. In such an environment, blacks traveling 78 mph should not face a greater chance of getting pulled over than white speeders just because they are black and happen to be driving a car said to be favored by drug mules. . . .

The most important victory of the anti-racial profiling agitators occurred not on the traffic-stop battlefield, but on the very different terrain of the searches that sometimes follow a stop. And here is where people who care about law enforcement should really start to worry. On April 20, 1999, New Jersey's then-attorney general Peter Verniero issued his "Interim Report of the State Police Review Team Regarding Allegations of Racial Profiling." It was a bombshell, whose repercussions haven't stopped yet.

"The problem of disparate treatment [of blacks] is real, not imagined," the report famously declared. Governor Christine Todd Whitman chimed in: "There is no question that racial profiling exists at some level." The media triumphantly broadcast the findings as conclusive proof of racial profiling not just in the Garden State but nationally. The *New York Times* started regularly referring to New Jersey's "racial bias" on the highways as incontrovertible fact. Defense attorneys and their clients celebrated as well. "Whenever I have a state police case, I file a suppression motion . . . alleging that the stop was based on color of skin and therefore illegal," a Trenton criminal defense attorney told the *New York Times*. "And now guess what? The state agrees with me!"

Yet the report's influential analysis is shoddy beyond belief. Contrary to popular perception, Verniero did not reach any conclusions about racial profiling in stops. His finding of "disparate treatment" is based on the percentage of "consent searches" performed on minorities *after* a stop has occurred. (In a consent search, the motorist agrees to allow the trooper to search his car and person, without a warrant or probable cause.) Between 1994 and 1998, claims the report, 53 percent of consent searches on the southern end of the New Jersey Turnpike involved a black person, 21 percent involved whites, and overall, 77 percent involved minorities. But these figures are meaningless, because Verniero does not include racial information about search requests that were denied, and his report mixes stops, searches, and arrests from different time periods.

But most important: Verniero finds culpable racial imbalance in the search figures without suggesting a proper benchmark. He simply assumes that 53 percent black consent searches is too high. Compared with what? If blacks in fact carry drugs at a higher rate than do whites, then this search rate merely reflects good law enforcement. If the police are now to be accused of racism every time that they go where the crime is, that's the end of public safety.

◆

The hue and cry over the alleged New Jersey search rate makes sense only if we assume that drug trafficking is spread evenly across the entire population and that officers are unable to detect the signs of a courier once they have pulled over a car. There are powerful reasons to reject both these assumptions.

Judging by arrest rates, minorities are vastly overrepresented among drug traffickers. Blacks make up over 60 percent of arrests in New Jersey for drugs and weapons, though they are 13.5 percent of the population. Against such a benchmark, the state police search rates look proportionate.

The attorney general's report dismissed this comparison with an argument that has become *de rigueur* among the anti-racial profiling crowd, even in Congress: the "circularity" argument. Arrest and conviction data for drugs and weapons are virtually meaningless, said Verniero. They tell you nothing about the world and everything about the false stereotypes that guide the police. If the police find more contraband on blacks and Hispanics, that is merely because they are looking harder for it, driven by prejudiced assumptions. If the police were to target whites with as much enforcement zeal, goes this reasoning, they would find comparable levels of criminality. David Harris, a University of Toledo law school professor and the leading expert for the anti-profiling forces, makes this preposterous argument. An enforcement effort directed at 40-year-old white law professors, he assures a Senate subcommittee, would yield noticeable busts. The disproportionate minority arrests then reinforce the initial, racist stereotypes, and the vicious cycle begins all over again—too many minorities arrested, too many whites going free.

The circularity argument is an insult to law enforcement and a prime example of the anti-police advocates' willingness to rewrite reality. Though it is hard to prove a negative—in this case, that there is *not* a large cadre of white drug lords operating in the inner cities—circumstantial evidence rebuts the activists' insinuation. Between 1976 and 1994, 64 percent of the homicide victims in drug turf wars were black, according to a Heritage Foundation analysis of FBI data. Sixty-seven percent of known perpetrators were also black. Likewise, some 60 percent of victims and perpetrators in drug-induced fatal brawls are black. These figures match the roughly 60 percent of drug offenders in state prison who are black. Unless you believe that white traffickers are less violent than black traffickers, the arrest, conviction, and imprisonment rate for blacks on drug charges appears consistent with the level of drug activity in the black population. (And were it true that white dealers *are* less violent, wouldn't we expect police to concentrate their enforcement efforts on the most dangerous parts of the drug trade?)

The notion that there are lots of heavy-duty white dealers sneaking by undetected contradicts the street experience of just about every narcotics cop you will ever talk to—though such anecdotal evidence, of course, would fail to convince the ACLU, convinced as it is of the blinding racism that afflicts most officers. "The hard-core sellers are where the hard-core users are—places like 129th Street in Harlem," observes Patrick Harnett, retired chief of the narcotics division for the NYPD. "It's not white kids from Rockland County who are keeping black sellers in business."

The cops go where the deals are. When white club owners, along with Israelis and Russians, still dominated the Ecstasy trade, that's whom the cops were arresting. Recently, however, big shipments have been going to minority neighborhoods; subsequent arrests will reflect crime intelligence, not racism.

There's not a single narcotics officer who won't freely admit that there are cocaine buys going down in the men's bathrooms of Wall Street investment firms—though at a small fraction of the amount found on 129th Street. But that is not where community outrage, such as that Mayor Giuliani heard in Harlem, is directing the police, because they don't produce violence and street intimidation.

Ultimately, the circularity argument rests on a massive denial of reality, one that is remarkably vigorous and widespread. In March, 2000, for example, New Jersey senator Robert Torricelli asserted before then-senator John Ashcroft's Judiciary Subcommittee: "Statistically it cannot bear evidence [*sic*] to those who suggest, as our former superintendent of the state police suggested, that certain ethnic or racial groups disproportionately commit crimes. They do not." Needless to say, Torricelli did not provide any statistics.

The second condition necessary to explain the higher minority search rates on the highway is patrol officers' ability to detect drug trafficking. Unlike the initial decision to pull over a car, the decision to request permission to search rests on a wealth of cues. One of the most frequent is conflicting narratives among passengers and driver. "If a group in a car is carrying drugs, there will always be inconsistencies in their stories," reports Ed Lennon, head of the New Jersey Troopers Union. "It's unbelievable. A lot of times the driver won't know the passengers' first or last names—'I only know him as Bill'—or they'll get the names completely wrong. Sometimes they'll have a preplanned answer regarding their destination, but their purpose in being on the road will vary."

A driver's demeanor may also be a tip-off. "I've stopped white guys in pick-up trucks with a camper compartment on top," recalls Lennon. "Their chest is pounding; they're sweating, though it's the dead of winter. They won't look at you." And they're also hiding drugs.

Once a trooper stops a car, he can see the amount of luggage and its fit with the alleged itinerary, the accumulation of trash that suggests long stretches without stopping, the signs of drug use, the lack of a license and registration, the single key in the ignition and no trunk key, or the signs that the vehicle may have been fitted out with drug and weapon compartments. Some New York narcotics officers recently pulled over an Azusa SUV and noticed welding marks along the rain gutter on top. The occupants had raised the entire roof four inches to create a drug vault. If a car's windows don't roll all the way down, drugs may be concealed in the doors.

The fact that hit rates for contraband tend to be equal across racial groups, even though blacks and Hispanics are searched at higher rates, suggests that the police are successfully targeting dealers, not minorities. Race may play a role in that targeting, or it may not. Most cues of trafficking are race-neutral; it may be that race often correlates with the decision to search rather than causing it. But if race does play a role in the request to search, it is a much diminished one compared with a car stop based on a courier profile. When an officer has many independent indices of suspicion, adding his knowledge of the race of major trafficking groups to the mix is both legitimate and not overly burdensome on law-abiding minorities.

Amazingly, Attorney General Verniero acknowledges that the police merely try to maximize their hit rates in deciding whom to search, but he *blames* them for doing so. "The state police reward system gave practical impetus to the use of these inappropriate stereotypes about drug dealers" by rewarding big busts, he frets. But if the police were seeking to maximize their contraband yields, and the alleged "inappropriate stereotypes" were not helping them do so, presumably they would abandon those "stereotypes" and find some other set of cues—unless, of course, they were merely out to harass minorities for the thrill of it. But in that case, their hit rates would be lower for minorities than for whites, which they were not.

The bottom line is this: the New Jersey attorney general has branded the state police as racist without a scintilla of analysis for his finding. Yet New Jersey is the wave of the future, for racial profiling data-collection initiatives are sweeping the country. At least 30 states could soon require their state police to collect racial data on all traffic stops and searches, with the stated end of eliminating "racial profiling." Urban forces are under identical pressure. Virtually every major law-enforcement organization opposes these bills, because of their failure to deal with the benchmarking problem. Until someone devises an adequately sophisticated benchmark that takes into account population patterns on the roads, degrees of law-breaking, police deployment patterns, and the nuances of police decision making, stop data are as meaningless as they are politically explosive. Attorney General John Ashcroft has encouraged these data-gathering initiatives; he should instead withhold his support, unless local proponents can prove that they will capture the complex realities of law enforcement.

⋅≪◉≫⋅

Unfortunately, the flurry of racial profiling analysis is not confined to the highways. It will wreak the most havoc on urban policing. Despite the racket by protesters, it is in city policing that race probably plays its least significant role, because officers have so many other cues from the environment. In assessing whether a pedestrian is behaving suspiciously, for example, they might already know that he is at a drug corner, about which they have received numerous complaints. They know if there has been a string of burglaries in the neighborhood. As they observe him, they can assess with whom he is interacting, and how.

A New York Street Crime Unit sergeant in Queens describes having stopped white pedestrians who had immediately changed directions as soon as they saw his unmarked car or ducked into an alley or a store for eight seconds and then looked for him once they came out. The night I spoke to him, he was patrolling the 102nd Precinct in Woodhaven, a largely white and Hispanic neighborhood. He had earlier questioned a white kid hanging out in front of a factory. "He was breaking his neck looking back at us; we thought he was a burglar." It turns out he was waiting for a friend. Another night in another precinct, the sergeant saw two black kids on bikes. "One guy's arm was hanging straight down, like he was carrying a gun. When they saw us, the other guy took off on his bike and threw a bag away. It was felony-weight drugs." Are you ignoring whites with guns? I asked him. "Of course not; I could see the same thing tonight," he said impatiently. "I don't use race at all. The only question is: are you raising my level of suspicion? Fifteen minutes after a stop, I may not even be able to tell you the color of the guy."

Even car stops on city streets usually have more context than on a highway. "If we pass four or five guys in a car going the opposite direction," explains the Queens sergeant, "and they're all craning their necks to see if we notice them, we may reverse and follow them for a while. We won't pull them over, but our suspicion is up. We'll run their plates. If the plates don't check out, they're done. If they commit a traffic violation, we won't pull everyone out of the car yet; we'll just interview the driver. If he doesn't have paperwork, it may be a stolen car. Now everyone's coming out to be frisked."

Hard as it is to believe, criminals actually do keep turning around to look at officers, though it would seem an obvious give-away. "Thank God they're stupid, or we'd be out of a job," the sergeant laughs.

But urban policing depends on another race-neutral strength: it is data-driven. The greatest recent innovation in policing was New York's Compstat, the computer-generated crime analysis that allows police commanders to pinpoint their enforcement efforts, then allows top brass to hold them accountable for results. If robberies are up in Bushwick, Brooklyn, the precinct commander will strategically deploy his officers to find the perpetrators. Will all the suspects be black? Quite likely, for so is the neighborhood. Does that mean that the officers are racist? Hardly; they are simply going where the crime is. In most high-crime neighborhoods, race is wholly irrelevant to policing, because nearly all the residents are minorities.

❧❦❧

Urban police chiefs worry about the data-collection mania as much as highway patrol commanders do. Ed Flynn, chief of police for Virginia's Arlington County, explains why. Last year, the black community in his jurisdiction was demanding heavier drug enforcement. "We had a series of community meetings. The residents said to us: 'Years ago, you had control over the problem. Now the kids are starting to act out again.' They even asked us: 'Where are your jump-out squads [who observe drug deals from their cars, then jump out and nab the participants]?'" So Flynn and his local commander put together an energetic strategy to break up the drug trade. They instituted aggressive motor-vehicle checks throughout the problem neighborhood. Cracked windshield, too-dark windows, expired tags, driving too fast? You're getting stopped and questioned. "We wanted to increase our presence in the area and make it quite unpleasant for the dealers to operate," Flynn says. The Arlington officers also cracked down on quality-of-life offenses like public urination, and used undercover surveillance to take out the dealers.

By the end of the summer, the department had cleaned up the crime hot spots. Community newsletters thanked the cops for breaking up the dealing. But guess what? Says Flynn: "We had also just generated a lot of data showing 'disproportionate' minority arrests." The irony, in Flynn's view, is acute. "We are responding to heartfelt demands for increased police presence," he says. "But this places police departments in the position of producing data at the community's behest that can be used against them."

The racial profiling analysis profoundly confuses cause and effect. "Police develop tactics in response to the disproportionate victimization of minorities by minorities, and you are calling the *tactics* the problem?" Flynn marvels.

However much the racial profilers try to divert attention away from the facts of crime, those facts remain obdurate. Arlington has a 10 percent black population, but robbery victims identify nearly 70 percent of their assailants as black. In 1998, blacks in New York City were 13 times more likely than whites to commit a violent assault, according to victim reports. As long as

those numbers remain unchanged, police statistics will also look disproportionate. This is the crime problem that black leaders should be shouting
about.

⋘◉⋙

But the politics of racial profiling has taken over everything else. Here again,
New Jersey is a model of profiling pandering, and it foreshadows the irratio-
nality that will beset the rest of the country. In February 1999, New Jersey governor Christine Todd Whitman peremptorily fired the head of the state police,
Colonel Carl Williams, whose reputation for honesty had earned him the
nickname "The Truth." It was the truth that got him fired. The day before his
dismissal, Williams had had the temerity to tell a newspaper reporter that
minority groups dominate the cocaine and marijuana trade.

Of course, this information had constituted the heart of DEA reports for
years. No matter. Stating it publicly violated some collective fairy tale that all
groups commit drug crimes at equal rates. Whitman's future political career
depended on getting Williams's head, and she got it. One scapegoat was not
enough, however. The New Jersey state troopers who shot at the van are now
on trial for attempted murder—a wildly trumped-up charge—and the attorney general has been prosecuting the case in a flagrantly political fashion.

One way to make sure that nasty confrontations with the facts about
crime don't happen again is to stop publishing those facts. And so the New
Jersey state police no longer distribute a typical felony-offender profile to their
officers, because such profiles may contribute, in the attorney general's words,
to "inappropriate stereotypes" about criminals. Never mind that in law
enforcement, with its deadly risk, more information is always better than less.
Expect calls for the barring of racial information from crime analysis to spread
nationally.

The New Jersey attorney general's office has also dropped its appeal of a
devastating 1996 trial court decision that had declared the state police guilty
of "institutional racism." Using Lamberth's New Jersey traffic study as proof of
racial profiling, the court dismissed drug indictments against 17 blacks without so much as glancing at the facts of their cases. The court was wrong on the
evidence and wrong on the law, but the case now stands permanently on the
books as the most important judicial decision to date on racial profiling.

Next, the New Jersey attorney general himself dismissed *en masse* drug
and weapons charges against 128 defendants. The defendants all alleged that
state troopers had pulled them over merely because of race. The attorney general was not willing to defend the state's officers and so let the defendants go
free. In one case, the defendants' car allegedly passed a marked cruiser at
75 miles an hour; the occupants were openly smoking pot and drinking; the
trooper found cocaine—hardly a case of racial profiling, hard or soft. Numerous requests to the attorney general's office for comment on the case have
gone unanswered.

New Jersey will soon monitor the length of traffic stops that individual
officers make and correlate it to the race of the motorist. It will also monitor

by race the computer checks that individual officers run on license plates, on the theory that racist officers will spend more time bothering innocent black motorists and will improperly target them for background checks. Of course an officer's stop and arrest data will be closely scrutinized for racial patterns as well. And if in fact such investigatory techniques correlate with race because more minorities are breaking the law? Too bad for the cop. He will be red-flagged as a potential racist.

These programs monitoring individual officers are present in all jurisdictions that, like New Jersey, operate under a federal monitor. Along with the new state requirements for racial data collection on a department-wide basis, they will destroy assertive policing, for they penalize investigatory work. The political classes are telling police officers that if they have "too many" enforcement interactions with minorities, it is because they are racists. Officers are responding by cutting back enforcement. Drug arrests dropped 55 percent on the Garden State Parkway in New Jersey in 2000, and 25 percent on the turnpike and parkway combined. When the mayor and the police chief of Minneapolis accused Minneapolis officers of racial profiling, traffic stops dropped 63 percent. Pittsburgh officers, under a federal consent decree monitoring their individual enforcement actions, now report that they are arresting by racial quota. Arrests in Los Angeles, whose police department has been under fire from the Justice Department, dropped 25 percent in the first nine months of 2000, while homicides jumped 25 percent.

The Harlem residents who so angrily demanded more drug busts from Mayor Giuliani last February didn't care about the race of the criminals who were destroying their neighborhood. They didn't see "black" or "white." They only saw dealers—and they wanted them out. That is precisely the perspective of most police officers as well; their world is divided into "good people" and "bad people," not into this race or that.

If the racial profiling crusade shatters this commonality between law-abiding inner-city residents and the police, it will be just those law-abiding minorities who will pay the heaviest price.

Richard G. Schott  # NO

The Role of Race in Law Enforcement: Racial Profiling or Legitimate Use?

On May 14, 2001, three young African-American males were pulled over by the Indianapolis, Indiana, Police Department. According to one of the passenger's stepfather, the stop was a blatant example of racial profiling.[1] According to the officers on the scene, it was a legitimate traffic stop for failure to signal a turn. Which one of these characterizations was correct? Were both viewpoints arguable?

Few issues in society today generate as much controversy as the issue of racial profiling. It was a recurrent topic of debate during the 2000 presidential campaign, and racial profiling remains a frequently debated and divisive issue in many local communities. The highway traffic practices of New Jersey and Maryland State Police troopers have been called into question as racially discriminatory. As a result, both departments have been required to compile exhaustive statistics on all future traffic stops. Other states have passed legislation requiring all law enforcement agencies within that state to maintain similar statistics.[2] But, what is racial profiling? Are there legitimate uses for racial characteristics during an investigation or other law enforcement activity? It is critically important for law enforcement officers to understand the difference between legitimate and illegitimate uses of race in their law enforcement activities to maintain credibility within their communities.

This article explores the historical perspective of the use of race in the law, examines the constitutional challenges available to victims of racial profiling, and offers suggestions to rebut allegations of improper racial profiling.

It is important to define what is meant by racial profiling in this article and also to distinguish between the legitimate use of profiling and unlawful racial profiling. Profiles based on officers' training and experience are legitimate tools in police work. For example, the "drug courier profile"[3] has long been recognized as an investigative technique used by narcotics investigators.[4] This "drug courier profile" has been described as "the collective or distilled experience of narcotics officers concerning characteristics repeatedly seen in

Reprinted courtesy of the FBI Law Enforcement Bulletin.

drug smugglers."[5] Courts have held that matching a profile alone is not the equivalent of reasonable suspicion or probable cause necessary to conduct an investigative detention or arrest;[6] but, police officers are entitled to assess the totality of the circumstances surrounding the subject of their attention in light of their experience and training, which may include "instruction on a drug courier profile."[7] Therefore, profiles, combined with other facts and circumstances, can establish reasonable suspicion or probable cause.

On the other hand, while race or color may be a factor to consider during certain police activity,[8] race or color alone is insufficient for making a stop or arrest.[9] Therefore, for purposes of this article, the term "racial profiling" refers to action taken by law enforcement officers solely because of an individual's race. As the following discussion makes clear, this type of profiling has no place in law enforcement.

Historical Perspective

Historically, there have been two broad legal attacks upon laws on the basis of race. First, citizens have attacked statutes that clearly treat people differently on the basis of their race. Second, citizens have challenged laws that, on their face, are racially neutral, but are enforced in a way that causes an adverse impact upon only one racial group.

Laws that are clearly aimed at particular racial (or other protected classifications, such as sex or religion) groups are subject to exacting, strict scrutiny by the courts. The Supreme Court has said that "[l]egal restrictions which curtail the civil rights of a single racial group are immediately suspect."[10] Unless the government can show that distinguishing among racial groups serves a compelling governmental interest, the distinction is unconstitutional. This is the general principle that courts apply when examining the validity of laws that impact individuals of one race differently than members of other races. The Supreme Court has recognized, however, that "not all such restrictions are unconstitutional. Pressing public necessity may sometimes justify the existence of such restrictions; racial antagonism never can."[11] . . .

By far, the majority of today's claims of racially motivated police actions are based on two constitutional provisions: the reasonableness requirement of the Fourth Amendment and the Equal Protection Clause of the Fourteenth Amendment. The essence of these claims is that while the laws being enforced by the police are facially race neutral, the way the police are enforcing them has an adverse impact on members of a particular race. Each of these claims will be examined in turn. . . .

Many police seizures are challenged as being racially motivated. Clearly, officers who detain or arrest someone solely on the basis of race have violated the Fourth Amendment to the Constitution.[12] Seizures of people should be based on what they do and not who they are. A more difficult case arises under the Fourth Amendment when the claim is made that an officer's objectively reasonable seizure (i.e., a seizure based upon probable cause or reasonable suspicion) was only a pretext for racial profiling. The Supreme Court addressed the issue of pretextual seizures in a case decided in 1996. . . .

Many police searches also are attacked as racially motivated. The Supreme Court has held that a reasonable Fourth Amendment search is one conducted with a search warrant based upon probable cause to believe evidence of a crime is present or is justified by a recognized exception to the search warrant requirement.[13] As with seizures, searches conducted without probable cause, but solely because of the race of the person searched or the race of the property owner, clearly violate the Fourth Amendment. However, like Fourth Amendment seizures, the courts will not inquire into the subjective motivation of the police as long as their searches are objectively reasonable.

Claims of racial profiling most often arise from two warrantless police searches justified by exceptions to the Fourth Amendment's search warrant requirement.[14] It is the abuse of, not the exceptions themselves, that are challenged. These two exceptions are the consent search[15] and the search incident to a lawful arrest.[16]

The only legal requirement for a valid consent search is the voluntary consent of a person authorized to give it.[17] There is no warrant requirement nor any requirement that officers have probable cause to believe the person has committed a crime or that there is evidence of a crime present.[18] Consequently, the officer's motivation for asking for consent is irrelevant. As Justice Scalia recognized in the Whren case, even if officers ask for consent to search only because of the person's race, there is no Fourth Amendment violation.[19]

Another warrantless search often cited as racially motivated police action is the search incident to arrest. The only legal justification for the search incident to arrest is a lawful, custodial arrest.[20] An arrest is lawful when based on probable cause to believe the person arrested has committed or is committing a crime. The seizure also must be custodial to justify the search; mere temporary detention is insufficient.[21] As with other Fourth Amendment searches, the underlying motivation of the officer is irrelevant to the issue of lawfulness of the search incident to arrest provided the arrest itself was constitutional. . . .

The threshold burden has made statistical data an important component in most racial profiling challenges. The absence of data to support or defend many of these challenges has created the need to compile detailed statistics of everyday police actions. A 1995 federal court case demonstrates the importance of statistical analysis in equal protection cases. . . .

An important question not addressed in cases discussed thus far is whether race ever can be a valid consideration when conducting law enforcement activity.

Race can be a legitimate consideration for police officers. In the Travis[22] opinion, the majority concluded that "race or ethnic background may become a legitimate consideration when investigators have information on this subject about a particular suspect."[23] Clearly, this consideration is not only constitutional but efficient and logical as well. . . .

☙❦❧

The issue of racial profiling is one of great concern for law enforcement agencies throughout the country. Expensive statistical compilations have been mandated for some departments; many others have begun compiling records voluntarily. The same statistics can sometimes be interpreted by those on either side of a debate to support conflicting arguments. When claims of equal protection violations are made, statistical evidence is almost always used to support or defend the case.

Fourth Amendment challenges are analyzed in traditional terms to determine the reasonableness of a search or seizure. Depending on the circumstances of a particular seizure, police are required to possess either reasonable suspicion or probable cause. To conduct a valid search under the Fourth Amendment, either a warrant or an exception to the warrant requirement is necessary. The Supreme Court has consistently held that the subjective motivations of individual police officers do not make objectively reasonable Fourth Amendment searches and seizures unconstitutional. For this reason, few claims of racial profiling, even if race is the motivating factor of the officers involved, violate the Fourth Amendment. Only if actions are taken without the requisite reasonable suspicion, probable cause, warrant, or exception to the warrant requirement, will a search or seizure not pass Fourth Amendment muster.

Racially motivated police actions can be challenged using a Fourteenth Amendment Equal Protection clause argument. Individuals alleging an equal protection violation will have to produce evidence that they were subjected to police actions that were not initiated against similarly situated members of other races. This evidence usually comes in the form of statistics. However, statistics should not be accepted as definitive proof until they have been analyzed and put into the context in which they are being used. Many departments have begun compiling their own statistics to defend claims based on a different batch of statistics.

Training individual officers on the legal and practical issues involved with claims of racial profiling is of paramount importance. Preventing the improper use of race in policing is critical. It will not only help maintain credibility within the community, but it also may prevent civil liability on the part of the department and individual officers.

Endnotes

1. M.T. Sprinkles letter to Editor, The Indianapolis Star, May 19, 2001.
2. See, e.g., Missouri R.S. 5 90.650: 2. Each time a peace officer stops a driver of a motor vehicle for a violation of any motor vehicle statute or ordinance, that officer shall report the following information to the law enforcement agency that employs the officer: 1) The age, gender, and race or minority group of the individual stopped.
3. See, e.g., Florida v. Royer, 460 U.S. 491 (1983). Royer defined the "drug courier profile" as an abstract of characteristics found to be typical of persons transporting illegal drugs, note 2.
4. Id.
5. Florida v. Royer, 460 U.S. at 525, note 6 (Rehnquist, J., dissenting).
6. See, e.g., Reid v. Georgia, 448 U.S. 438 (1980) and Royer at 525, note 6.
7. Florida v. Royer, 460 U.S. at 525, note 6. See, also, Terry v. Ohio, 392 U.S. 1 (1968).

8. United Slates v. Brignoni-Ponce, 422 U.S. 873, 887 (1975).

9. Brignoni-Ponce, 422 U.S. at 886-887 (1975) (appearance of Mexican ancestry alone is insufficient to justify a stop or arrest under the Fourth Amendment); United Slates v. Bautista, 684 F.2d 1286, 1289 (9th Cir. 1982) (race or color alone is not a sufficient basis for making an investigatory stop); Rodriguez v. California Highway Patrol, 89 F. Supp. 2d 1131 (N.D. Cal. 2000) (race or appearance alone is insufficient to justify a stop or arrest, FN5).

10. Korematsu v. United States, 323 U.S. 214, 216 (1944).

11. Id.

12. Supra note 9.

13. Katz v. United States, 398 U.S. 347 (1967). The five exceptions to the search warrant requirement recognized by the Supreme Court are the consent search (Schneckloth v. Bustamonte, 412 U.S. 218 [1973]); the search incident to arrest (US. v. Robinson, 414 U.S. 218 [1973]); the emergency or exigent circumstances search (Warden v. Hayden, 387 U.S. 294 [1967]); the motor vehicle search (Carroll v. US., 267 U.S. 132 [1925]); and the inventory search (South Dakota v. Opperman, 428 U.S. 364 [1976]).

14. U.S. Const. amend. IV, states in pertinent part, ". . . no Warrants shall issue but upon probable cause, supported by Oath or affirmation, and particularly describing the place to be searched, and the persons or things to be seized."

15. See, e.g., Schneckloth v. Bustamonte, supra note 25.

16. See, e.g., Chimel v. California, 395 U.S. 752 (1969).

17. Ohio v. Robinette, 519 U.S. 33 (1996).

18. Schneckloth v. Bustamonte, supra note 25.

19. Whren, supra note 22 at 812-813.

20. US. v. Robinson, supra note 25.

21. Knowles v. Iowa, 525 U.S. 113 (1998).

22. Travis, supra note 54.

23. Id. at 174.

POSTSCRIPT

Is Racial Profiling Necessary to Law Enforcement?

Racial profiling has been a very visible and controversial topic since the 9/11/2001 terrorist attacks in the United States. But racial profiling has been at least a subcurrent of controversy long before 9/11. While post–9/11 subjects of racial profiling have had an Arab background, pre–9/11 subjects of profiling were racial minorities. Regardless of which group is the subject of racial profiling, the question remains whether the use of racial profiling is necessary to police/investigative work. Indeed, there are some who would argue, as does Heather MacDonald, that racial profiling is a "myth." The advocates of the need for racial profiling argue that it is absolutely necessary for policing and that the demographics of crime mandate such profiling.

Importantly, those who would support racial profiling would argue that race, of and by itself, cannot be the basis for assessing criminal suspiciousness. However, they would argue, race as *one* factor in a profile is justified. MacDonald refers to this as "soft" racial profiling. She argues, further, that one must take into consideration the demands the police face in their attempts to protect the public—and not just from the criminals they pursue, but from the public and the press.

By contrast, there are those, such as Richard G. Schott, who would argue that racially profiling typically encompasses only race, and that therein lies the travesty of justice. Indeed, the Supreme Court noted as early as *Korematsu v. United States* (323 U.S. 214, 216 [1944]) that "legal restrictions which curtail the civil rights of a single racial group are immediately suspect." Thus, a compelling governmental interest must be served before distinguishing among racial groups.

The problem that remains is one of insidious racial profiling, and how to prove that race has not been the single criterion upon which an individual has been singled out. The burden rests upon those whom have been the victims.

Professor David A. Harris is one of the leading scholars on the subject of racial profiling. Among his many works, several are particularly appropriate for further reading. *Profiles in Injustice: Why Racial Profiling Cannot Work* and *Good Cops: The Case for Preventing Profiling* provide analyses of the many types of police profiling, its injustice and ineffectiveness, and how police work can be effective without discrimination.

ISSUE 3

Is Plea Bargaining Fair?

YES: Timothy Sandefur, from "In Defense of Plea Bargaining: The Practice Is Flawed, but not Unconstitutional," *Regulation* (Fall 2003)

NO: Mike McConville and Chester Mirsky, from "Guilty Plea Courts: A Social Disciplinary Model of Criminal Justice," *Social Problems* (May 1995)

ISSUE SUMMARY

YES: Timothy Sandefur argues that, while plea bargaining can be abused, it is not necessarily unconstitutional, and that to the extent that flaws exist, they can be remedies.

NO: McConville and Mirsky argue that plea bargains form a system of imposing control and discipline upon vulnerable groups in society.

Martin Luther King, Jr. wrote, "Justice too long delayed is justice denied." He meant this, of course, as it applied to the denial of civil liberties for his fellow African Americans. But if a judicial system delays justice, it is in essence denying justice. But what is a society to do if its courts are overly burdened?

The U.S. judicial system is overloaded with cases on both the criminal and civil sides of the law. On the civil side, alternative dispute resolution (negotiation, mediation, arbitration) has held considerable promise. Indeed, the courts have moved toward requiring arbitration in many cases. But the criminal side presents a dilemma stemming from the Constitutional right to a jury trial. One of the key "solutions" to this has been the practice of "plea bargaining." Although everyone is entitled to a jury trial, if you plead guilty, you are "voluntarily" giving up the right to a trial by jury.

But plea bargaining goes beyond simply pleading guilty. It involves striking a deal. The accused, faced with the possibility of conviction and a particular sentence, comes to an agreement with the prosecutor: a guilty plea in exchange for a reduced sentence. This process certainly results in the desired "judicial efficiency." But is it just?

Justice in this case may be viewed from several perspectives. What if the accused is indeed guilty of the crime with which s/he has been charged? Are society's interests being justly served by having that individual serve less time? Alternatively, what if the accused is actually innocent but is fearful of conviction and a lengthier sentence—or even the death penalty in those states that still have it? Would an innocent person plead guilty? Is this just? One further thing to keep in mind about "plea bargaining" is that once one has pleaded guilty, there is no opportunity for an appeal.

Clearly, this subject relates to one that will be discussed in Issue 13, where we examine whether the poor can receive adequate criminal defense. Faced with the possibility of a lengthy sentence and being defended by a court-appointed attorney with little time for a truly effective defense, isn't it likely that the indigent accused is more likely to plea bargain and to be encouraged to plea-bargain? So, is plea bargaining fair?

Timothy Sandefur holds that plea bargaining is certainly subject to abuse, but that this possibility does not make the process unconstitutional or unfair, and "does not necessarily violate a defendant's rights." As Sandefur notes, approximately "90% of criminal cases end in a plea bargain." He argues that the accused is merely entering into a contract with the state.

Mike McConville and Chester Mirsky see plea bargaining as a form of social control, a "social disciplinary model," with a differential impact upon the poor, especially in large urban areas. They argue that this model has no concern for the "proof of either factual or legal guilt," or indeed the truth. Once the accused enters a guilty plea, the state is relieved of the burden to prove guilt beyond a reasonable doubt. While technically constitutional and "fair"—after all, the accused "voluntarily" accepted the agreement—the question of justice remains.

 **YES**

In Defense of Plea Bargaining: The Practice Is Flawed, But Not Unconstitutional

Plea bargaining, like all government activities, is liable to abuse. Defendants, often too poor to afford their own attorney, unfamiliar with court proceedings, and threatened by the full force of the prosecutor's office, are likely to be very intimidated. They find themselves confronted by experienced and confident officers of the state, in suits and robes, speaking the jargon of the law and possessing wide discretion to engage in hardball tactics before trial. Prosecutors know how to exploit limits on habeas corpus rights, mandatory sentencing rules, and loopholes that allow evidence collected under questionable circumstances to be admitted. All of this would scare even the most hardened criminal, let alone an innocent defendant. And it could intimidate a defendant into accepting a plea bargain that may not be truly just.

Yet the mere fact that a process can be abused does not necessarily make that process unconstitutional or immoral. Plea bargaining is rife with unfair prosecutorial tactics, and it needs reform. But the process itself is not unconstitutional, nor does it necessarily violate a defendant's rights.

An Alienable Right to Trial?

A plea bargain is a contract with the state. The defendant agrees to plead guilty to a lesser crime and receive a lesser sentence, rather than go to trial on a more severe charge where he faces the possibility of a harsher sentence. Plea bargaining is enormously popular with prosecutors; according to researcher Douglas Guidorizzi, something like 90 percent of criminal cases end in a plea bargain.

In recent decades, courts have upheld extreme and unfair prosecutorial tactics in negotiating plea bargains. Last year, in *United States v. Ruiz*, the U.S. Supreme Court held that the Constitution does not require prosecutors to inform defendants during plea bargaining negotiations of evidence that would lead to the impeachment of the prosecution's witnesses. As Timothy Lynch noted in his 2002 article "An Eerie Efficiency," this rule would allow the prosecution to not disclose during plea negotiations that its only witness was too drunk at the time of the crime to provide any reliable evidence. Such tactics are unfair. If a plea bargain is a contract, it should be subject to the same rules that apply to other contracts, including the requirement that parties disclose relevant information. If a car dealer must tell you that the car he sells you is defective, prosecutors ought to he required to disclose when their cases are defective. But the sad fact that such inappropriate bargaining tactics exist does not obviate the freedom of contract itself.

One argument against plea bargaining is that the Sixth Amendment guarantees a right to a jury trial, not to a faster, more potentially error-prone procedure like plea bargaining. As Lynch has written, "The Framers of the Constitution were aware of less time-consuming trial procedures when they wrote the Bill of Rights, but chose not to adopt them." But that does not prove plea bargaining is unconstitutional. After all, at the time the Sixth Amendment was written, there were no Federal Rules of Evidence, no Miranda rights, no court-appointed attorneys, and no bench trials. The Framers' notion of a "fair trial" differs greatly from ours. The Constitution's limits on criminal procedure are certainly indispensable protections for individual liberty, a great advance over British rule, and a testament to the Founders' greatness—but they only go so far.

The fundamental question is, is the right to a jury trial inalienable? Although some natural rights are inalienable, most rights make sense only if they can be bought and sold. In which category does the right to a trial belong? In early American history, a defendant could waive his right to a jury in felony cases, but by the time of the American Revolution, that practice had died out. In the 1858 case Cancemi v. People, a New York court held that a defendant could not waive a jury trial because, while "the law does recognize the doctrine of waiver to a great extent . . . even to the deprivation of constitutional private rights," the public's interest in fair trials overrode the defendant's right to choose his own trial tactics.

But after the Civil War, the bench trial reappeared. In 1879, the Iowa Supreme Court held in *State v. Kaufman* that a defendant could waive a jury trial if he wished—after all, defendants can waive other procedural rights, including the right to a speedy trial. A guilty plea, the court noted, also "dispenses with a jury trial, and it is thereby waived." Yet the defendant still had the right to plead guilty. "This, it seems to us, effectually destroys the force of the thought" that public interest could prohibit defendants from waiving their right to a jury. According to the court,

> Reasons other than the fact that he is guilty may induce a defendant to so plead . . . yet the state never actively interferes in such case, and the right of the defendant to so plead has never been doubted. He must be permitted to judge for himself in this respect. . . . Why should he not be permitted to do so? Why hamper him in this respect? Why restrain his liberty or right to do as he believed to be for his interests? Whatever rule is adopted affects not only the defendant, but all others similarly situated, no matter

how much they desire to avail themselves of the right to do what the defendant desires to repudiate. We are unwilling to establish such a rule.

The debate over inalienability continued, however. The Iowa Supreme Court changed its mind a few years later in *State v. Carman,* then changed back in the 1980 case *State v. Henderson.* Connecticut prohibited jury waivers in the 1878 case *State v. Worden;* Louisiana allowed them in the 1881 case *State v. State.* At the California Constitutional Convention of 1878, a lengthy debate ensued over a provision allowing criminal defendants to waive their right to a jury; proponents argued that a defendant had the right to do as he pleased in his own defense, while opponents claimed the public interest was too great and defendants were often too intimidated to make reasonable decisions in their own defense. The proposal was defeated, although today California does allow defendants to waive a jury trial.

The U.S. Supreme Court held in the 1979 case *Gannett Co. Inc. v. DePasquale* that the public does not "have an enforceable right to a public trial that can be asserted independently of the parties in the litigation." That seems reasonable; while requiring jury trials may make sense as a matter of policy, it is not an inalienable right. Life, liberty, and the pursuit of happiness are inalienable by nature. But the right to a jury is a civil right, not a natural right. If defendants can waive personal-jurisdiction, and waive their right to an attorney, there seems little sense in saying that the jury right is inalienable. Today, it seems to be universally conceded that the right to a jury trial is alienable, and nothing in the Constitution says otherwise. It follows that a defendant can "sell" his right to trial if he so chooses. And at least some defendants— often guilty ones—benefit from doing so.

The Right to Leniency?

Another argument against plea bargaining is that it punishes defendants for invoking their right to a trial. Consider the landmark case *Bordenkircher v. Hayes* (1978). The defendant, Paul Lewis Hayes, was indicted for a relatively minor fraud charge, punishable by a two- to 10-year sentence. The prosecutor offered Hayes a bargain: If he pled guilty, the prosecutor would seek a five-year sentence. If not, the prosecutor would indict him under the state's Habitual Criminal Act. Because he was a repeat offender, conviction under the Act meant a lifetime sentence. Hayes refused the deal, and the prosecutor got the second indictment. Hayes was tried and convicted under the Act, and given a life sentence. On appeal to the U.S. Supreme Court, he argued that the sentence was an unconstitutional punishment for insisting on his right to a jury trial.

The Court ruled against him. In a confusing opinion, it held that so long as the procedure included no actual coercion, the plea bargain did not amount to punishment. But the Court frankly appealed to necessity: "The imposition of these difficult choices," the Court wrote, is an "inevitable attribute of any legitimate system which tolerates and encourages the negotiation of pleas." The Court thus upheld the practice of plea bargaining solely on pragmatic grounds: "A rigid constitutional rule that would prohibit a prosecutor from acting forthrightly in his dealings with the defense could only invite unhealthy subterfuge that would drive the practice of plea bargaining back into the shadows from which it has so recently emerged."

This begs the question. If a practice offends the Constitution, it ought to be driven into the shadows, just as segregation was. By basing its entire theory on pragmatism rather than the Constitution, the Hayes Court opened itself to the charge that it was editing the Constitution to suit current needs. If a practice is unconstitutional, efficiency cannot excuse it. "It is highly probable that inconveniences will result from following the Constitution as it is written," wrote dissenting New York Court of Appeals chief judge Greene Bronson in the 1850 case *Oakley v. Aspinwall.* "But that consideration can have no weight with me. . . . There is always some plausible reason for the latitudinarian constructions which are resorted to for the purpose of acquiring power some evil to be avoided, or some good to be attained by pushing the powers of the government beyond their legitimate boundary. It is by yielding to such influences that constitutions are gradually undermined, and finally overthrown."

There is a far better reason for the Hayes decision: The defendant was simply not being punished for his refusal to plea bargain; he was being punished for violating the Habitual Criminal Act. Had he been tried for that at the outset—which he legitimately could have been—he would have received the very same punishment: life in prison. Regardless of whether such habitual offender laws are wise, Hayes violated that law, and had, so to speak, incurred the liability of a lifetime prison term. He thus had no right, strictly speaking, to any lesser sentence, let alone to escape indictment completely. Instead, the prosecution had the right to indict him for all the crimes he committed, and Hayes had the right to a jury trial on all those charges. Once each side possessed those rights and liabilities, they had the right to exchange them; Hayes could trade his jury right for prosecutorial leniency. The prosecution's bargaining tactics may have been severe, and perhaps statutory reform of those tactics is called for. But the legitimacy of the procedure itself is not refuted by abuses. In short, because Hayes had no right to leniency, his failure to get leniency is not a deprivation, and he could not claim his rights were violated when he failed to receive it.

Other analogies This is the response to Lynch's analogy regarding tourists arrested in Washington, D.C. for possessing firearms. He argues that the government must not permit the tourist to waive his right to a jury trial on the charge of firearm possession, because that decision is "coerced" by the fact that, if the tourist refuses to plead, the prosecutor will also bring charges for ammunition possession. But the tourist who possesses a gun and ammunition has violated both the gun law and the ammunition law; assuming those laws to be otherwise constitutional, the tourist has therefore incurred the liability of sentence for both crimes. There is nothing unjust (or, more relevantly, unconstitutional) in the prosecutor offering to drop one of the charges in exchange for a guilty plea on the other. If the tourist refuses and goes to trial on both charges, the tourist has incurred no greater punishment than he deserved at the outset.

Or consider another analogy Lynch adopts from the 1935 false imprisonment case Griffin v. Clark. In Clark, the defendant was found liable for false imprisonment when he seized the plaintiff's purse and would not return it unless she rode with him in a car. Since the plaintiff's freedom of movement could not rightly be conditioned on her giving up her purse, the court found that the defendant could not escape liability by arguing that he had not physically restrained her. Lynch argues that government bargains requiring defendants to give up the right to a trial are, in the same way, illusory choices.

But the analogy dissolves on closer inspection: The woman had a natural right to freedom of movement with her purse at any time. A criminal defendant, by contrast, has no right not to be indicted for his crimes. As Lynch says, the criminal may not walk away from the state; he is rightfully subject to any indictment consistent with the facts and law. The government may offer leniency and give up its right to indict him in exchange for a plea, just as it may offer to forgive other debts or confer other benefits. But the defendant has no grounds for complaint if the government chooses not to. (On the other hand, if the state indicts him without a factual or legal basis, his due process rights have been violated regardless of the legitimacy of plea bargaining.)

In the 2001 case *Berthoff v. United States,* Judge William Young decried the disparity of plea bargaining and criminal sentences:

> Between two similarly situated defendants . . . if the one who pleads and cooperates gets a four-year sentence, then the guideline sentence [imposed under federal sentencing rules] for the one who exercises his right to trial by jury and is convicted will be 20 years. Not surprisingly, such a disparity imposes an extraordinary burden on the free exercise of the right to an adjudication of guilt by one's peers. Criminal trial rates in the United States and in this District are plummeting due to the simple fact that today we punish people—punish them severely—simply for going to trial.

But both of the criminals in Judge Young's example committed crimes for which they might be sent to jail for 20 years; neither has a right to demand a four-year sentence. A four-year sentence for one does not increase the punishment for the other; it simply fails to decrease the other's sentence—something to which neither defendant is entitled to begin with. The disparity of their sentences does not represent greater punishment being visited on the party that refuses the bargain; rather, it represents a benefit conferred on the party that did bargain.

Conviction of the Innocent?

Some commentators claim that plea bargaining creates an incentive system designed to discourage the exercise of constitutionally protected rights. If the defendant faces a far greater potential sentence at trial than through a plea bargain, this increases the incentive to bargain, which increases the potential that innocent parties will be sent to prison for crimes they did not commit.

Government policies that chill the exercise of constitutional rights ought to be regarded with great suspicion. But they are not per se unconstitutional or unjust. Government, like private businesses, often purchases the rights of citizens: members of the military are forbidden to criticize the president, for instance, and private contractors doing business with the government must often comply with "living wage" requirements. Unwise as those policies may be, they are not a violation of anybody's rights, because they are based on the parties' consent. If the tactics used to induce consent are so overbearing as to obviate that consent, then the procedure should be reviewed under due process standards and, in a case in which the prosecution's tactics are fraudulent, they should be struck down. But where that is not the case, a plea bargain does not itself violate the Constitution.

Disparate Punishments

In short, Lynch's claim that plea bargaining is unconstitutional comes down to his complaint that "disparate punishments for the same offense [are not] sensible." But similarly situated defendants who make different choices in legal strategy often end up with different sentences. One defendant might choose to waive his right to testify, while another might exercise that right. The result might be disparate sentences, or even sentences that are insensible to outside observers. But that choice is entirely constitutional. The courtroom may not seem like a place for haggling, but that is exactly what it is, in both civil and criminal contexts. A civil defendant can settle his case for a certain sum; a criminal defendant for a certain amount of time. If the calculations made by prosecutors, or plaintiffs, and defendants are influenced by fear or intimidation rather than calm deliberation, then statutory reform is certainly warranted. But nothing in the Constitution compels it.

Lynch makes many valid points in criticizing plea bargaining. Ruiz was wrongly decided; courts should not give free reign to prosecutors; the criminal justice system should not be manipulated, or constitutional guarantees watered down, in order to prosecute the war on drugs more efficiently. But those criticisms surround plea bargaining without quite hitting the target. For instance, Lynch wrote in his 2002 article, "It is easy for some people to breezily proclaim that they would never plead guilty to a crime if they were truly innocent, but when one is confronted with the choice of two years in jail or quite possibly 20 years' imprisonment, the decision is not so easy." That is true, but note that Lynch assumes that the innocent defendant will be convicted and sentenced to 20 years. Without that assumption, the hypothetical defendant's risk profile changes, and surely innocent defendants have reason to believe that they are less likely to be convicted. If not, then our target should be the trial system, not plea bargaining.

Innocent defendants are convicted all too often, but if defendants are so afraid of trials that they regularly plead guilty to crimes they did not commit in order to avoid a trial, then that is an indictment of the trial system, not plea bargaining. And while it is true that plea bargains are often the product of overbearing prosecutorial bargaining tactics, that is a criticism of the negotiating process, not of the right to make the contract. Finally, it is true that the

Framers included a right to trial by jury among our vital constitutional guarantees, but that does not mean defendants lack the freedom to waive that right or trade it to the state in exchange for a lighter sentence. Mere efficiency does not justify resorting to a constitutionally flawed procedure. But there are sufficient justifications for plea bargaining. Its flaws are procedural, not constitutional, and it needs reform, not abolition.

Readings

"The Discretionary Power of 'Public' Prosecutors in Historical Perspective," by Carolyn Ramsey. *American Criminal Law Review*, Vol. 39 (2002).

"An Eerie Efficiency," by Timothy Lynch. *Cato Supreme Court Review*, Vol. 1 (2002).

"The Historical Origins of Bench Trial for Serious Crime," by Susan Towne. *American Journal of Legal History*, Vol. 26 (1982).

Rethinking the Petty Offense Doctrine," by Timothy Lynch. *Kansas Journal of Law and Public Policy*, Vol. 4 (1994).

"Should We Really 'Ban' Plea Bargaining? The Core Concerns of Plea Bargaining Critics," by Douglas Guidorizzi. *Emory Law Journal*, Vol. 47 (1998).

A Treatise on Constitutional Limitations on the Police Power of the States, by Thomas Cooley. Boston, Mass.: Little, Brown, 1868.

"The Waiver Paradox," by Jason Mazzone. *Northwestern University Law Review*, Vol. 97 (2003).

NO  Mike McConville and Chester Mirsky

Guilty Plea Courts: A Social Disciplinary Model of Criminal Justice

Introduction

The majority of routine felony cases, the day-to-day workload of criminal courts, are settled by guilty pleas.[1] Traditional accounts assume that those actually guilty of criminal acts adopt a cost-efficient method of confronting their guilt, make deals, and plead guilty (Alschuler 1976). Implicit in these accounts is the notion that the decision to offer or accept a plea is based on the weight of the evidence against the accused and the presence or absence of a viable legal defense (Walker 1993). Nardulli, Eisenstein, and Flemming (1988:210) contend, for example, that the "absence of factual ambiguity in most cases looms large as an explanation for the defendant's decision to plead guilty." The guilty plea is usually both inevitable and just (Feeley 1979; Maynard 1984).

Analysts and ideologues (defenders and supporters of the system) recognize that, without a trial, there is a risk that rights guaranteed to a criminal defendant may not be protected and that the factually innocent may be convicted. The assignment of legal counsel to all criminal defendants, guaranteed by *Gideon vs. Wainwright* (1963), is supposed to ensure the protection of individual rights and adequate scrutiny of the police evidence against a criminal defendant. In spite of legal representation, most criminal defendants still plead guilty because "[c]ourt personnel simply recognize the factual culpability of many defendants and the fruitlessness, at least in terms of case outcome, of going to trial" (Heumann 1978:156).

Indeed, many courtroom observers who defend the current system point to colloquies such as the following (which ended one of the cases discussed below), in which judges question defendants before allowing them to plead guilty, to show that factually guilty defendants' legal rights are respected and protected, even as they forego a public trial. (All names in this paper are pseudonyms.)

From *Social Problems*, vol. 42, no. 2, May 1995, pp. 216–234. Copyright © 1995 as conveyed via the Copyright Clearance Center. Reprinted by permission.

Q: "Have you had an opportunity to consult with your lawyer, Mr. Gartenstein, and to discuss the matter with him before choosing to plead guilty?"

A: "Yes."

Q: "Do you understand that by pleading guilty you have given up your right to trial by jury?"

A: "Yes."

Q: "Do you understand that by pleading guilty you have given up your right to confront and cross-examine witnesses against you, to testify, and to call witnesses on your own behalf?"

A: "Yes."

Q: "Do you understand that you have given up your right to remain silent and your privilege against self-incrimination?"

A: "Yes."

Q: "Do you understand that at a trial you are presumed innocent and that the prosecution has to prove your guilt beyond a reasonable doubt?"

A: "Yes."

Q: "Has anybody threatened or coerced you?"

A: "No."

Q: "Is your plea voluntary and of your own free will?"

A: "Yes."

Q: "Do you understand that in pleading guilty you have given up all these rights and that the conviction entered is the same as a conviction after trial?"

A: "Yes."

Q: "Did you along with McBride and Hervey forcibly steal property from the person of the complaining witness and possess what appeared to be a gun."

A: "Yes."[2]

The research reported in this paper comes to a different conclusion. We conclude that in large urban areas guilty pleas are part of a vertically integrated system of imposing control and discipline on highly visible sections of society, those who are perceived as dangerous because of their lack of involvement in an acceptable labor market and the intensity of their involvement with the criminal justice system (Simon 1993). This system often begins with proactive "sweeps" by specialized police units (such as narcotics control units); it extends through the system of assigning counsel to indigent defendants, and it concludes with a highly coercive drama in which defendants are first shown (by being made to watch others) that they will suffer greatly increased penalties if they refuse to plead guilty, and in which they are then given their 15 seconds to accept or reject the pleas and sentences offered to them by calendar judges.

We call this a social disciplinary model, a form of substantive rationality committed to achieving order through surveillance and control of the urban underclass (Simon 1993; Smith and Visher 1981; Smith, Visher, and Davidson 1984). Substantive rationality is concerned with "impact, effect, and ends" served by the criminal justice system (Savelsberg 1992:1348; Weber 1968). It involves "an intrusion of the state into society" and the "opening of state decision making to social (extralegal) criteria" (Savelsberg 1992:1348; Teubner 1987:10–12). As a form of substantive rationality, social discipline has little commitment to traditional notions of crime control through proof of either factual or legal guilt. The latter, often equated with legal rationality, furthers individual autonomy (Nonet and Selznick 1978) and is achieved through an analysis of the state's burden of proof, either informally at settlement conferences (Blumberg 1967a; Mnookin and Kornhauser 1979), or formally at hearings, motions, and trials. By contrast, a social disciplinary model, concerned with containment rather than crime control (Simon 1993), imposes judgments of conviction without restraint on how police power may be exercised against the individual. . . .

❧

Here we focus on one defense lawyer, Emerson, one criminal defendant, Roberto Santiago, and the events, including other cases heard that Emerson represented or that Santiago observed, that preceded Santiago's decision to plead guilty. A closer look at these actors and their cases produces a deeper understanding of the social disciplinary processes at work than a more circumscribed sample of data from a slightly larger number of cases.

Roberto Santiago was arrested as he left his apartment at 1:30 a.m. by police officers engaged in a sweep of the neighborhood. Before the arrest, undercover officers toured Santiago's neighborhood and radioed descriptions of suspected drug dealers to backup units whose officers swept the street for people they believed fit the descriptions. The sweep occurred once the police had decided to complete an operation in which undercover officers, posing as gypsy cab drivers, purchased cocaine and other drugs from street-level dealers. When Santiago was held later in a precinct, an undercover officer, looking through a two-way mirror, identified him as a person from whom the officer had purchased cocaine six months earlier.

By 1989, with the advent of the crack epidemic, drug arrests, often initiated by non-individuated sweeps, produced more than 50 percent of all superior court indictments in New York City (Division of Criminal Justice Services 1989). Santiago, along with more than 56 percent of those arrested who were indicted, pleaded guilty after appearing only before a calendar judge (Office of Court Administration 1984–1985; Miller, McDonald, and Cramer 1978).[3] Santiago was a person of color, and, during our observations, more than

80 percent of all arrested defendants were people of color (New York City Department of Corrections 1984; McConville and Mirsky 1986–87; Division of Criminal Justice Services 1989). Santiago was 21, and more than half of all arrested defendants were below age 30 (New York City Department of Corrections 1984). Santiago, with more than three-quarters of arrested defendants, was represented by a court-assigned lawyer (McConville and Mirsky 1986–87). Santiago, along with more than half of the arrested defendants we observed, was represented by a number of different court-assigned attorneys during several months (McConville and Mirsky 1986–87; Gilboy and Schmidt 1979). . . .

The Assignment of Counsel

Once Roberto Santiago's court papers were assembled, he was transferred to a holding cell behind the arraignment court to await the assignment of an attorney. A copy of the papers was first placed in a basket designated for the Legal Aid Society, the City's public defender agency (McConville and Mirsky 1986–87). The uneven work patterns of the Legal Aid Society staff attorneys, the number of staff attorneys at arraignment, and the availability of "18-B attorneys,"[4] however, often provoked judges to assign Legal Aid cases to 18-B regulars. These lawyers represented almost as many indicted defendants (roughly 30 percent) as the Legal Aid Society (roughly 40 percent) (McConville and Mirsky 1986–87). The regulars were solo practitioners; some subsisted on court assignments, while others prospered on these cases, earning more than $100,000 from court assignments (McConville and Mirsky 1986–87; Assael 1989; Fritsch and Purdy 1994). They stationed themselves in the court building, expecting to obtain case assignments on a moment's notice.

While Roberto Santiago sat in the court pen, the sight of Legal Aid staff attorneys in court chatting among themselves provoked Judge Lorraine to order the court captain to "find an 18-B who can help clear the docket." Lorraine was a Criminal (inferior) Court calendar judge who routinely processed more than 100 cases in an eight-hour arraignment shift, disposing of 50 percent through guilty pleas.

At the court captain's instigation, Emerson, the 18-B attorney assigned for the day to conflict cases, began to thumb through cases the clerk had placed in the basket. Emerson was a solo practitioner who came to criminal law practice after attending a local law school at night and working as a court officer in guilty plea court (Abel 1989; Wice 1978; Wood 1976). His practice was almost entirely court-assigned.

Emerson picked out some case files, briefly looked at the names and said: "I'm not interested in this, it's a burglary, and this is a robbery, a chain snatch. I can't stand these robberies, it's a horrible crime. I like narcotics, let's see." Then he found a case file that attracted him, looked through it quickly, and said, "I'll take this one." Soon, he had gathered three cases and walked away from the Legal Aid basket. Emerson had chosen the cases of Danny James, Monroe Hickson, and Roberto Santiago.

Emerson proceeded first with the case of Danny James, whose file had been placed in the Legal Aid basket by Jim, a staff attorney, after having interviewed the defendant. When Emerson attempted to dispose of James's case through a guilty plea, Jim intervened shouting; "What's going on it's my case. What's happening?" Lorraine said: "I don't know anything about this." Each pressed the file on the other, but eventually Emerson handed the file over to Jim and said: "It's your case, you keep it. I was helping out. I didn't want it anyway." A second call was ordered so that Jim could resume representation of Danny James.

Emerson's selection of cases was typical of the process we observed. Assignments depended on case backlog and the take-up rate of Legal Aid staff attorneys and 18-B regulars. A successful lawyer, one who received many arraignment assignments, was a lawyer who enabled the calendar judge either to immediately enter a guilty plea or to adjourn the case to another date. This was evident in the initial client interviews Emerson conducted of Hickson and Santiago before the court proceedings.

Emerson briefly interviewed Monroe Hickson, another defendant awaiting arraignment on a street-level drug sale. Emerson flicked through the file; as he picked up the last sheet, a great deal of writing appeared on the jacket containing the notes of an earlier interview of Hickson conducted by a Legal Aid attorney, before Emerson had removed Hickson's file from the Legal Aid basket. Emerson glanced at the writing and let the papers drop back into the file.

When Hickson's case was called, an Assistant District Attorney (ADA) served Emerson with notice that the case was about to be presented to a grand jury. Emerson interjected immediately: "May we approach?"

Lorraine: "Yes."

Emerson: "Is there an offer [guilty plea] in this case?"

ADA: "There is a warrant on him and we need to check."

Emerson: "Where? It's not in my papers."

Lorraine: "It's right there on the first sheet."

Emerson: "No it's not. There's nothing about it."

A court officer showed Emerson the warrant among Hickson's papers. Because of the confusion caused by the appearance of the warrant, the judge ordered a short second call. Emerson spoke to one of the authors at side-bar and said: "Fuck it. It's not such a good case." In Emerson's view, the only alternative was to adjourn the case to another date. At a later call on the calendar, Hickson appeared only to learn that, in his absence, Emerson had adjourned the case, while Lorraine had remanded him to jail.

Emerson began to work on the case of Roberto Santiago. As Santiago pulled on a cigarette and nervously moved around the pen, he looked drawn and frightened.

Emerson: "Okay. They say you sold some cocaine but here's the good news."

A voice from inside the pen intervened and said:
"It's your first offense."

Emerson: "That's right it's your first offense, and second, it happened six months ago. No there is no way in which you are going to be convicted by any jury on this. What happened, did you just get picked up? Were they just flushing the area?"

Santiago: "I don't know what happened, man. Oh, man! I was just coming out of my building and I was just grabbed, told to stand up against the wall. I've been here three days . . ."

Emerson: "Okay. So you were just grabbed. They grabbed everyone right?"

The "voice" appeared again (a white male aged about 35, blond with a mustache) and said:

"Look, they picked up the whole neighborhood."

Emerson then left to telephone Santiago's aunt to verify the information Santiago had provided concerning his employment and ties to the community. But the line was always busy and Emerson returned to speak with Santiago again. As he was speaking he flicked through the papers; he suddenly stopped and yelled, "What the fuck is this? There's a warrant out for you."

Santiago: "A warrant? It's not for me. Oh, no!"

Emerson: "The Navy, the Navy wants you. You are wanted by the Navy on a warrant. Did you quit before you did your time with them?"

Santiago: "I've never been in the Navy."

Emerson: "It must be a mistake. There are lots of Santiagos, but it will have to be checked. I'll go and see."

Emerson's interviews with Hickson and Santiago were perfunctory and public. Emerson spoke through the cell bars in the presence of other defendants and uniformed officers. As he returned to court after speaking to Santiago, Emerson said to us: "This [the Navy warrant] could screw it up today but he'll get an acquittal. They will never convict on this evidence." Emerson did not review the physical description of Santiageles to determine whether the warrant referred to someone else.[5]

Nor did Emerson obtain information from Santiago regarding his community ties and whether his family or friends had the capacity to post bail. Similarly, when a cell mate emphasized the non-individuated nature of Santiago's arrest. Emerson responded by referring to the date of the alleged sale as the important factor in determining whether the case would result in a conviction. Emerson never questioned the outcome of a case; he was able to attempt a guilty plea within moments of meeting a defendant or to adjourn cases without further delay.

Arraignment—The Commencement of Judicial Review

At arraignment, his first appearance before a judge, Roberto Santiago saw the futility of any legal challenge to the police case. When Santiago was produced before Judge Lorraine, Emerson's first act was to respond affirmatively to the court officer's request: "Do you waive the reading of the rights and charges?" Lorraine then asked the Assistant District Attorney (ADA) to address Santiago's release status:

ADA: "This case involves a sale of cocaine. The sale was hand to hand. It is a B felony, quite serious, and the Pre-Trial Services sheet indicates that this defendant has insufficient community ties to warrant parole at this point without a substantial cash bail. Therefore the People ask $3,000 cash bail."

Lorraine: "Mr. Emerson, you may be heard."

Emerson: "This is like when you go into a store to buy olives and someone tells you that there might be more than one quality of olives. You can get big olives or you can get giant olives or you can get absolutely colossal huge olives. Here the District Attorney's office is telling you they have giant olives, but in reality the olives in this case are very small ones. In fact I don't see how they are going to prosecute at all in this case because the sale took place so long ago. The sale took place almost six months ago, and I simply don't see how the state will bring charges successfully in this case. The identification evidence will never stand up. How are they going to produce a lab test? He has no prior arrests. I called his home phone number and it was busy."

Lorraine: "You obviously don't know anything about the Special Narcotics Prosecutor's Office."

Emerson: "They'll never make 180.80."[6]

Lorraine: "I don't think you understand how an undercover investigation works, Mr. Emerson. This is not abnormal at all. In fact, most undercover investigations work like this when the arrest occurs some times after the original sale. But you can keep the case and fight it as much as you want. I'll set bail at $1,500 cash or bond."

Lorraine set bail in an amount that a defendant requiring the assignment of counsel would be unlikely to post (Nagel 1983) without inquiring into the factual-legal basis for the undercover officer's identification (*Manson vs. Brathwaite* 1977), i.e., the opportunity to observe the person selling drugs, the cause for delay in arrest, or its effect on the reliability of the undercover officer's later identification of Santiago. Neither Emerson nor the judge made any reference to Roberto Santiago's community ties, and Emerson failed to challenge the ADA's repetition of the Pre-Trial Services finding of "insufficient community ties," other than to state that Santiago's phone was busy.

Emerson never discussed with Hickson or Santiago the rights that attach to arraignment. Nor did Lorraine inform either defendant that he had a right to remain silent, the right to a prompt hearing on the charges, the right to counsel, or the right to proceed without a lawyer and to represent himself (Criminal Procedure Law Sec. 180.10 [1985]). Instead, Emerson's presence satisfied legal formalism; it signified that a lawyer had so advised the defendants, that each defendant had asserted his right to silence and had requested the assignment of counsel, and that Emerson had agreed to act as the attorney-of-record.

Unless the ADA reduced the charge to a misdemeanor, Lorraine lacked jurisdiction to accept a guilty plea in Santiago's case (Criminal Procedure Law Sec. 10.30(2) [1982]). However, she could have required the ADA to amend the complaint to provide some basis for the undercover officer's identification. She also could have inquired into Santiago's community ties and employment history to determine whether Santiago should be released or detained. In addition, she could have refused to continue Emerson as Santiago's attorney, had she concluded that the lawyer's understanding was so flawed as to disable him from providing competent representation. Instead, Lorraine made no effort to expand the record or to provide a legal basis for her actions. Lorraine adjourned the case to another date without delay.

While in jail following the arraignment, Santiago called a neighbor who made contact with his family. His mother responded and, within a day, posted $1,500 to obtain his release. Santiago thereafter made three court appearances with a family member. Each time he waited until mid-afternoon to discover that the judge had adjourned his case because the grand jury had not yet indicted him. When the grand jury did act, the indictment alleged that the drug sale occurred *eighteen months,* not sixth months, before Santiago's arrest. However, Emerson had not attempted to reconstruct the events in question through an in-depth interview with the defendant, nor had he undertaken any independent factual and legal inquiry.

Public Education in the Courtroom and Guilty Plea Scripts

When Roberto Santiago first appeared in Supreme Court, 20 months had expired between the alleged incident and the filling of the indictment. Under formal legal rationality, the delay in arrest and indictment was reason enough to dismiss the charges, upon a showing that the delay was intentional, attributable to the police, and prejudicial to the defendant (*United States vs. Lavasco* 1977; Criminal Procedure Law Sec. 210.20(h) [1980]). Should Santiago refuse to plead guilty and insist upon litigating the propriety of the delay, however, Judge Roger, a calendar judge in guilty plea court with an intolerance for "dilatory tactics" would rule on the challenge. Roger was the calendar judge with the highest rate of dispositions and the largest caseload; his daily calendar often contained more than 50 indicted defendants.

All judges are rated according to their ability to dispose of large caseloads without hearing or trial. The calendar judges we observed in guilty plea courts were those with the highest rate of disposition measured in terms of total caseload.[7] These judges were fixtures in guilty plea court, while judges who compared unfavorably were routinely assigned to hearing and trial courts (Luskin 1989; Heydebrand and Seron 1987). During a one-year period of our observations, six calendar judges disposed of approximately 11,600 indictments, of which 4,126 (35 percent) were disposed of within 60 days and 3,581 (31 percent) between 61 and 135 days (Office of Court Administration 1984–85). These judges educated defendants and others present in their courtroom that the opportunity to contest the police case was limited (Pollner 1979; Resnick 1982).

As Roberto Santiago waited for his case to be called, he, along with other defendants, lawyers, and families and friends assembled, listened to the bench conferences Judge Roger conducted with prosecutors and defense attorneys, most of which led to guilty pleas. To be sure Roger appeared to comply with formal legal rationality, the defendants "voluntarily" waived their rights on the record. However, Roger relied upon police interrogation practices to ensure that defendants would become compliant (Rossett and Cressey 1976; Leo 1994). He manipulated the bail status of released defendants (Inciardi 1984)[8] by jailing those defendants who refused to plead guilty, despite the fact that a defendant who had been released at arraignment had voluntarily appeared on several adjourned dates. By contrast, Roger rewarded defendants who pleaded guilty by allowing them to remain free on bail, although they were now convicted and awaiting sentence. Roger raised the stakes on defendants who refused to admit guilt by threatening them with a greater sentence on any subsequent adjourned date (Brereton and Casper 1981; Uhlman and Walker 1980; National Minority Advisory Council 1980). Initial offers of probation, if refused, would later become fixed jail time, whereas offers of jail time once refused, would be increased into indeterminate state prison sentences. In the event of a conviction after a trial, Roger would impose a sentence that greatly exceeded the last guilty plea offer made.

These encounters, which Roger described to the authors as "tests of strength," placed a premium on the defendant's resolve, pitted against the judge's power to control the outcome. At these conferences, Roger reduced cases to skeletal outlines—a "chain snatch," and "undercover drug sale," a "break-in" (Sudnow 1965). All conversations at the bench and all statements made by Roger to lawyers and defendants were "off-the-record." Only the formal setting of bail, the adjourn date, and the entry of the guilty plea and sentence were "on-the-record."[9]

Roger first read a write-up of the state's evidence supplied by the ADA stationed in the calendar part. The central feature of the summary sheet was the prosecution's charge and sentence offer. Should the offer be acceptable to Roger, he would immediately repeat it to the defense lawyer. If Roger believed that the prosecution's offer failed to serve as adequate inducement for a plea, or if he believed it to be too generous, Roger would alter either the charge or the sentence. Should the ADA object, Roger would threaten the prosecution with an immediate trial (for which police and civilian witnesses were never immediately available), or he would insist that the ADA who presented the case to the grand jury or a supervisor immediately appear in court to defend the original offer. When confronted with Roger's displeasure, the ADA usually agreed to Roger's demands, after which Roger would describe the offer to the defense lawyer. Roger then would tell the lawyer to speak to the defendant about pleading guilty.

In Judge Roger's court, the advice that lawyers gave their clients occurred under the judge's watchful eye, at the defense table some 15 feet from the bench. Should the defendant exhibit a facial grimace or utter a hostile response, Roger would raise the guilty plea offer and jail the defendant, while loudly repeating to those assembled the consequences that flow from such resistance. This display of force enabled Roberto Santiago and other defendants sitting in the courtroom to appreciate Roger's displeasure at recalcitrance and the power that the judge could bring to bear on any person who persisted in pleading not guilty (Dumm 1990).

On the day Santiago sat awaiting his turn, the first case conference involved two defendants, Hall and Powell. Both defendants had been released on money bail by another judge. The defendants were initially charged in a complaint of robbery and possession of a weapon. In Supreme Court, the robbery charges were dropped because the complaining witness had not appeared in the grand jury. This left the police as the witnesses to the sole remaining offense—possession of a weapon. As 18-B attorneys Graf and Novick entered the well of the courtroom, Roger stated: "This is the first time on; all of you come up." He began the "off-the-record" case conference:

Roger:	"I see there is a predicate felony statement[10] on Powell, and Hall has a pending King's County robbery. [Then loudly addressing himself to the court officers] Heads up on this fellas, please.[11] [Roger then reverted to addressing the lawyers in derisive tones] King's County set $200 bail!
	[Referring to a pending charge against Hall] Unbelievable! Of course there could have been a better write up on this . . ."
Graf:	"That [referring to the $200 bail] indicates that it wasn't much of a case."
Roger:	"Unbelievable! What's the offer?"
ADA:	"It's a 'D' to each.[12] Powell had the gun on him. We are asking $7,500 as to Powell and $2,500 as to Hall."
Roger:	[Reading from the prosecutor's summary]:
	"The complaining witness approaches a police officer and tells him that the defendants had harassed him, and robbed him in the past. The officer took him into the patrol car and the complainant pointed out the defendants. The officer recovered a gun from Powell. There's a dispute as to whose gun it is. Hall says 'Why can't you just charge me?' Powell says, 'I was simply keeping it.' Well, that puts both of them in it squarely. Now, let's see, Powell has a second violent felony. [Then addressing the whole courtroom] Bail is going up. It's going up."
Graf:	"What is the basis for the stop and search when . . ."
Roger:	"Look, make your motions but you have nothing to complain about, nothing to suppress. Nothing was seized from your guy . . ."

Graf:	"I think there is an issue . . ."
Roger:	"Make your motions. I'd like to see that. [Seeing the DA assigned to this case, Roger called out] There's Seifman; come up."
Roger [to	"What's going on? You told me [in prosecution summary]
Seifman]:	he has a second felony: In fact he is a second *violent* offender.[13] [Loudly] Let's arraign these defendants; they are going in."

The defendants were then arraigned on the indictment by the clerk's on-the-record reading of the charges and by asking the defendants how they pleaded: guilty or not guilty.

The Hall and Powell conference first demonstrates Roger's power to limit the opportunity for defendants to rely on an the assertion of rights (Casper 1972). Hall's statement "Why can't you just charge me?" may have been suppressible as the "fruits" of the illegal arrest (*Wong Sun vs. United States* 1963). (This was what Graf sought to determine when he awkwardly asked Roger about the basis for the "search," i.e., arrest.) Roger's response trivialized Graf's inquiry by informing Graf that "nothing was [actually] seized from your guy . . ." and by daring Graf to assert Hall's rights by making a motion to suppress. Should Graf have insisted on a hearing upon the grounds that the arrest violated his client's rights, Hall would have paid the price by remaining in jail until Roger conducted a hearing to determine whether Hall's statement should have been suppressed. Given Roger's admonition that Hall had "nothing to complain about, nothing to suppress," the time spent in detention and the likely denial of the motion to suppress would have served to reinforce the notion that reliance on formal legal rights was pointless. By contrast, Roger's substantive power to control the defendants' release through the pronouncement that "they are going in" was immediately effective, and it pre-empted any legal argument.

The case conference further demonstrates Roger's power to manipulate the bail of released defendants in pursuit of a guilty plea. Once Hall and Powell had entered not guilty pleas, Hall's lawyer made the following bail application "on the record:"

Roger:	"On Powell, I'm going to exonerate bail and fix it at $7,500/7,500. I'll hear your counsellor."
Novick:	"My client is 21. He has voluntarily returned to court. He has lived at the same address for 20 years and is currently employed with [a named business]. I would ask that bail be the same."
Roger:	"He has two violent felony convictions. He was found with the gun, and under these circumstances and having regard to the fact that he is facing a minimum of 2 years-5 years, $7,500 is, therefore, reasonable. With regard to Hall, bail is $2,500."
Graf:	"My client qualified for parole [release on his recognizance based upon verified community ties]. He was released and came back. He has no prior convictions. He is not facing any state

time. His record does not reflect he was arrested in King's County."

Roger: "But the detective was present [on a previous occasion when Hall appeared] to take him there."

ADA: "This will be confirmed on the NICIS [RAP] sheet."

Graf: "This is pending in Criminal Court in King's on $200 bail and the best person to set that was the judge who must have had all the facts . . ."

Roger: "I'm fixing bail . . ."

Graf: "He is not facing mandatory prison."

Roger: "The Gun Statute does contemplate one year but not in state prison. That is, after conviction. It is not mandatory until after conviction."

Graf: "He has returned here . . ."

Roger: "That's the second time you are telling me the purpose of bail. I understand you are frustrated . . ."

Graf: "I'm not frustrated. I'm trying to . . ."

Roger: "OK. $2,500/2,500. Ask the DA to get more facts on the King's County case."

Once Roger told the court officers to keep their "heads up," the judge indicated his intent to have the officers handcuff and remove the defendants to the court pens, even though both had previously appeared while on bail. This punitive rhetoric (Garland 1991) redefined the role of court personnel, from officers to jailers.

The next case demonstrated how respect for law became a function of the extent to which Roger was capable of instilling fear in the individual. Here, Roger threatened to increase the sentence to show defendants that law is "a compelling and powerful force" (Dumm 1990:30). As the court clerk called out the names of Leng, McBride, and Hervey, the defendants, who appeared to be about age 18, were escorted by officers from the court pen to stand behind the defense table. As they did so, three lawyers, Sherr, a Legal Aid attorney, and Gartenstein and Rucker, 18-B attorneys, entered the well of the courtroom and stood facing Roger. The ADA addressed Roger saying: "May we approach the bench?" Roger told all the lawyers to come up. The ADA then handed Roger a sheet that contained a short summary of the charges, the guilty plea and sentence offer, and a recommendation to continue to detain the defendants in lieu of $10,000 bail.

Roger read aloud the one-line statements of facts disclosed in the prosecutor's summary. As soon as the reading was completed, Roger glanced at the defendants' RAP sheets and made the following remark off the record: "Here's the offer." Before he said anything further, Gartenstein said: "Judge, he [Leng] said he made YO."[14]

Roger: "It is not so on the sheet."

Gartenstein: "He tells me he did or at least I think that's what he says."

Roger: "Check it out."

Gartenstein went to speak to Leng and returned a few seconds later saying: "I've checked and he did make YO." Roger continued: "Here's the offer. McBride 4 to 8 [years] [mandatory minimum sentence for a predicate felon], Leng and Hervey [not predicate felons] 1 to 4 and no YO." All three attorneys went back to inform their clients of the likely consequences of refusing Roger's guilty plea offer.

When Sherr told his client of Roger's offer, McBride recoiled, frowned, and made a dismissive gesture towards Sherr. Roger noticed this immediately and spoke in resonant off-the-record tones to the whole courtroom. Roger's speech enabled Roberto Santiago and others present to hear his contempt for the defendant's response, while it demonstrated that in Roger's court, a lawyer is little more than a formal appendage whose function is easily made redundant:

> McBride doesn't appear to like it. Tell him, Mr. Sherr, that I remember him and it's not good for a calendar judge to remember someone. Tell him it is going to go up next time, 6 to 12. It is not going to stay. It is going up. McBride is going to get 4- to 8 if he is smart, 6 to 12 if he is dumb. [McBride put his face into a nervous smile] I like his attitude. Tell McBride it is *now* 6 to 12 [Roger's emphasis]. If he wants to play hard ball, let's play hard ball. Tell the others it will go to 3 to 9 if they don't want the offer.

Within a few seconds, the lawyers returned to the bench and stated that the defendants were unwilling to accept the judge's offer. Thereafter, Roger showed everyone that the judge, as chief constable and jailor, was neither neutral with regard to the question of guilt or innocence nor powerless to ensure a guilty plea. Roger, speaking over the lawyers and directly to the defendants said: "All right, the offers are now 6 to 12 for McBride and 3 to 9 for Leng and Hervey." The effectiveness of Roger's actions was vividly demonstrated when Leng returned from the court pens moments later and pleaded guilty.

After the court officers had escorted the defendants to the court pen, Gartenstein had further opportunity to speak with Leng. He then asked the clerk to recall Leng's case so that Leng could accept Roger's initial offer of 1 to 4 years. Upon Gartenstein's statement that Leng was now willing to accept the offer, Roger spoke to Leng on the record, allowing him to waive his rights and to plead guilty. The transcript of this colloquy was quoted in the introduction to the article.

Santiago's Guilty Plea

Unknown to Roberto Santiago, Roger had decided to replace Emerson with another attorney, should Emerson appear again before him. Roger's decision was based upon Emerson's performance in an earlier case, when the lawyer had rejected, out-of-hand, Roger's guilty plea offer and had insisted that the defendant could not be convicted on the identification of a stranger. Roger later informed one of the authors that Emerson was an "incompetent lawyer" who acted "obstructively" when confronted with evidence which, in Roger's view, was sufficient to convict the defendant.

When the court clerk called out Roberto Santiago's name, Emerson entered the well of the courtroom along with the defendant. The clerk informed Santiago that he had been indicted for the sale of cocaine and asked Santiago: "How do you plead?" Santiago responded immediately and firmly: "Not guilty." Roger than asked Emerson to approach the bench and said: "I do not want you to appear again in my court. I am going to relieve you of this assignment." Emerson turned and left the courtroom, leaving Santiago standing alone at the defense table.

Roger's dismissal of Emerson demonized the only individual the court had earlier assigned to protect Santiago. Roger did this without consulting Santiago. To ensure the entry of Santiago's guilty plea, Roger continued the process without a moment's hesitation. He asked Richard Sartag to "accept the court's assignment" and to substitute for Emerson. Sartag, an 18-B regular who had positioned himself in the first row of the courtroom, nodded his assent. Thereafter, he approached the bench, after which Roger read the prosecution's summary of the case:

Roger: "The defendant is a first offender who was one of a group of people who sold drugs to an undercover officer over an 18-month period. The officer positively identified the defendant at the precinct after he was arrested."

Roger then turned to Sartag and stated the offer:

Roger: "Tell him in return for a plea to attempted criminal sale of a controlled substance in the third degree, I'll give him a split sentence [time already served and five years probation].[15] Tell him should he go to trial and be convicted of the sale, he would be facing at least 2 to 6 years."

Neither Roger nor Sartag said anything about whether the twenty-month delay in indictment had prejudiced the defendant's opportunity to receive a fair trial, the reliability of the undercover officer's identification, or the availability of any corroborative evidence to independently connect the defendant to the drug sale. No reference was made to the original allegation that the sale occurred six months before Roberto Santiago's arrest. Instead, Sartag conveyed Roger's offer to Santiago in a momentary conversation. Thereafter, Sartag advised Santiago to "plead guilty in return for a promise of probation." Santiago agreed, after which the formal guilty plea colloquy ensued, on the record. When Roger solicited Santiago's waiver of the rights associated with a jury trial, Santiago responded "yes" to each of the judge's inquiries. Thereafter, Roger asked Santiago two leading questions to provide a *prima facie* basis, in law, to legitimate the entry of the guilty plea:

Q: "Did you, on May 27 (past year), near the northeast corner of 106 Street and Amsterdam Ave., sell a controlled substance, to wit crack cocaine, to an individual then known to you?"

A: "Yes."

Q: "Did you, in exchange, receive $100 in U.S. currency?"

A: "Yes."

Roger directed the court clerk to enter Santiago's guilty plea and to adjourn the case for sentencing, while he rewarded Santiago by permitting him to remain free on bail. Sartag returned to the court benches.

After the court appearance, Santiago stood in the hallway of the courthouse visibly upset. When one of the authors asked him why he pleaded guilty, Santiago said he was "frightened" and that he feared he would have to "flee to Puerto Rico or some other island" to avoid "getting sent to prison." Santiago approached Emerson, who remained in the hallway, and asked: "What is going to happen next?" Emerson replied: "I am no longer your lawyer, and I don't know."

Conclusion: Legal and Social Order

Our research shows that guilty pleas in New York City are a part of a vertical process: What will happen later at the court stage influences what happens earlier at the police stage. (cf. Maynard 1984:69–75). Routine case processing in court, through guilty pleas, reinforces the actions and expectations of the police and defendants, thereby encouraging sweeps, dragnets and other non-individuated arrests. This integral feedback loop, in which facts are of little consequence and in which witnesses are not called at either hearings or trials (and the propriety of policing and the reliability of police evidence are untested), institutionalizes domination (Savelsberg 1994). Subordination and degradation (Garfinkel 1956; Freeman 1993) are thereafter employed to reinforce the substantive objectives of proactive policing.

Each stage of the criminal process, from arrest and court papers to arraignment and guilty plea court, displays the contrast between social discipline and a crime control system based upon factual or legal guilt. In a social disciplinary process, defendants charged with felonies, whom a judge has detained, may be released later because the setting of bail relates only to the initiating acts of the police and omits consideration of the sufficiency and persuasiveness of the evidence or the circumstances of the accused. Thereafter, while the subsequent entry of a guilty plea, even with the carrot of probation, may ensure social discipline, it is without any assurance that criminal activity occurred in the first instance or will cease thereafter.

In this setting, the judges, rather than the lawyers (Cain 1979, 1994), are the "conceptive ideologists" whose mission it is to translate the demands of social discipline into the language of the street—and to thereby persuade defendants, through their lawyers, of the desirability and inevitability of pleading guilty. If judges are key courtroom actors in securing guilty pleas, defense lawyers are structurally unable to exercise a meaningful influence on the process, except in relation to defendants. While it is the lawyer's task to convey to the defendant, in no uncertain terms, the wishes of the court (Blumberg 1967b), should the defendant reject the offer, the judge may speak directly to the defendant, further marginalizing the attorney. This hierarchy of power reduces what some commentators in other settings describe as a consensus model (Nardulli, Flemming, and Eisenstein 1985) to a formalistic canopy.

In New York City and other large urban settings, reliance on guilty pleas occurs because of three major structural features endemic to the justice system itself. First, judges proceeded on the assumption that their courtroom practices, while at variance with due process, were consonant with the perceived wishes of the wider society. While the general public observed guilty plea court at a distance, its impressions are created through accounts associated with the "common knowledge" (Garland 1991:206; Savelsberg 1994) that those arrested are guilty, and that when confronted with the moment of truth they will confess their guilt. Second, disciplinary practices regularly occurred in the presence of disempowered people, who expect nothing more from a system in which the objectives of policing define the process (Schur 1971; Taylor, Walton, and Young 1973). It is this audience that was first "taught . . . [the] lesson" (Garland 1991:202). Third, in employing domination, the actors exploited the political space provided by malleable legal rules in an attempt to validate the initiating acts of the police, and to thereby overcome law's perceived failure to arrive at a satisfactory strategy for social control (Simon 1993).

In achieving wider social disciplinary objectives, however, the actors discarded the criminal justice system's crime control objectives, except in so far as they happened to have been fulfilled by the police at the arrest stage. In guilty plea courts, law and legality took on a meaning separate from a crime control system based upon factual guilt or principles of proof associated with legal guilt. Law became redefined and reordered to validate substantive outcomes obtained through methods that subordinate and maintain order over groups society has labeled dangerous. Thus, even in guilty plea court, where the politics of social discipline were ascendant and a reality, order was not finally severed from law.

Notes

1. In the United States, more than 90 percent of state criminal cases and 85 percent of all federal cases are disposed of without trial, mostly through guilty pleas (United States Department of Justice 1990).

2. The leading question is directed to the definition of robbery in the second degree as contained in Penal Law Sec. 160.10 (1973). It tracks the elements of the offense and it provides a factual basis for the guilty plea. Upon the defendant's response, Judge Roger instructed the clerk to enter defendant Leng's guilty plea in the court record.

3. In New York City, between 1984 and 1990, guilty pleas accounted for between 76 and 84 percent of all dispositions. Trials account for between 7 and 10 percent and dismissals for between 8 and 10 percent (Office of Court Administration 1984–1990).

4. Under New York City's scheme, should a Legal Aid lawyer decline the assignment because of a professional conflict of interest, (usually involving representation of more than one defendant in the same case), a court officer would assign a private lawyer compensated by the city. These are known as "18-B attorneys" because of the law that provides for their appointment and compensation. (New York County Law Article 18-B [1972]; McConville and Mirsky 1986–87).

5. Before the case was called, the ADA reviewed the Navy warrant and determined, from a comparison of the physical descriptions, that Santiago and Santiageles were not the same person. Thereafter, no further mention was made of the warrant.

6. The section of the Criminal Procedure Law (1982) requires the prosecution to present the case to a grand jury within 120 hours of the time of arrest or, if witnesses were unavailable or memories unrefreshed, to release the defendant.

7. Monthly ratings are published that show the number of guilty plea dispositions for all judges over an equivalent number of judge work days, and all judges are compared against the judge with the highest disposition rate and the largest case load (New York State Supreme Court 1984–1994; Office of Court Administration 1986–1993).

8. Roger's use of the power to detain individuals, in lieu of money bail, occurred despite New York's statutory scheme (Criminal Procedure Law Sec. 530.40 [1971]), which first required a finding that the conditions of pre-trial release set by the arraignment judge were inadequate to secure the defendant's further appearance.

9. Off-the-record remarks were publicly uttered and audible to all but were not transcribed by the court stenographer, who waited for something official to occur before placing any words on the record.

10. The predicate felony statement notifies the defendant that the prosecutor will request that the defendant be sentenced as a second felony offender (Penal Law Sec. 70.06 [1987]).

11. "Heads up" is a term Roger used to inform the uniformed court officers that he was about to jail a defendant who had appeared in court on bail.

12. Possession of a weapon in the third degree is a D felony under the Penal Law Sec. 265.02 (1987).

13. A defendant who has been previously convicted of a violent felony offense is eligible for a more severe sentence than a defendant whose previous felony conviction was for a non-violent offense (Penal Law Sec. 70.04 [1987]). However, a judge is not bound to sentence a defendant as a second violent felony offender unless the prosecution serves notice that the defendant was previously convicted of such an offense (Criminal Procedure Law Sec. 240.20 [1982]).

14. People who are judged Youth Offenders (YO) have not been convicted of a crime despite the fact that they may have committed a criminal act. Hence, they may not be sentenced as predicate felons (Criminal Procedure Law 720.35 [1979]).

15. Criminal sale of a controlled substance is a class B felony with a maximum term of 81/3 to 25 years (Penal Law 70.02 [1979]). However, a defendant, like Santiago, pleading guilty to an attempt (a lesser class C felony) may receive a split sentence of imprisonment not in excess of 60 days followed by probation of 5 years (Penal Law Sec. 60.01, 60.05 [1979]).

References

Abel, Richard L. 1989. American Lawyers. New York: Oxford Press.

Alschuler, Albert W. 1976. "The trial judge's role in plea bargaining." Columbia Law Review 76:1059.

Assael, Shawn 1989. "18-B counsel made $17.5 million in '88." Manhattan Lawyer 49:1.

Blumberg, Abraham 1967a. Criminal Justice. Chicago: Quadrangle.

———1967b. "The practice of law as confidence game: Organizational cooptation of the profession." Law & Society Review 1:15.

Brereton, David, and Jonathan D. Caspar 1981. "Does it pay to plead guilty? Differential sentencing and the functioning of criminal courts." Law and Society Review 16:1.

Cain, Maureen 1979. "The general practice lawyer and the client: Towards a radical conception." International Journal of the Sociology of Law 7:331.

———1994. "The symbol traders." In Lawyers in a Postmodern World, eds. Maureen Cain and Christine B. Harrington, 15–48. New York: New York University Press.

Caspar, Jonathon 1972. American Criminal Justice. Englewood Cliffs, N.J.: Prentiss Hall.

Criminal Justice Agency 1984. Final Report. New York: Criminal Justice Agency.

———1985. Follow-Up Report. New York: Criminal Justice Agency.

Division of Criminal Justice Services 1989. Crime and Justice Annual Report. Albany: New York State.

Dumm, Thomas L. 1990. "Fear of law." In Studies in Law, Politics and Society, eds. Austin Sarat and Susan Silbey, 10:29. Greenwich, Conn.: JAI Press.

Feeley, Malcolm 1979. The Process Is The Punishment. New York: Russell Sage.

Freeman, Jody 1993. "The disciplinary function of race representation: Lessons from the Kennedy Smith and Tyson trials." Law and Social Inquiry 517-546.

Fritsch, Jane, and Matthew Purdy 1994. "Lawyers for New York poor: A program with no monitor." New York Times CXLIII:1.

Garfinkel, Harold 1956. "Conditions of successful degradation ceremonies." American Journal of Sociology 61:420.

Garland, David 1991. "Punishment in culture: The symbolic dimension of criminal justice." In Studies in Law, Politics and Society, eds. Austin Sarat and Susan Silbey, 11:191. Greenwich, Conn.: JAI Press.

Gilboy, Janet, and John R. Schmidt 1979. "Replacing lawyers: A case study of the sequential representation of criminal defendants." Journal of Criminal Law and Criminology 70:1.

Heumann, Milton 1978. Plea Bargaining: The Experiences of Prosecutors, Judges and Defense Attorneys. Chicago: University of Chicago Press.

Heydebrand, Wolf, and Carol Seron 1987. "The organizational structure of courts: Toward the technocratic administration of justice." International Review of Sociology 2:63.

Inciardi, James A. 1984. Criminal Justice. Oriando, Fla.: Academic Press.

Leo, Richard A. 1994. "Police interrogation and social control." Social and Legal Studies 3:93–120.

Luskin, Marie 1989. "Making sense of calendaring system: A reconsideration of concept and measurement." Justice System Journal 13:240.

Maynard, Douglas 1984. Inside Plea Bargaining: The Language of Negotiation. New York: Plenum Press.

McConville, Michael, and Chester L. Mirsky 1986–87. "Criminal defense of the poor in New York City." Review of Law and Social Change 15:582.

Miller, Herbert S., William F. McDonald, and James A. Cramer 1978. Plea Bargaining in the United States. Washington, D.C.: National Institute of Law Enforcement and Criminal Justice.

Mnookin, Robert H., and Lewis Kornhauser 1979. "Bargaining in the shadow of the law: The case of divorce." Yale Law Journal 88:950.

Nagel, Ilene 1983. "The legal/extra-legal controversy: Judicial decisions in pre-trial release." Law and Society Review 17:481-515.

Nardulli, Peter F., Roy B. Flemming, and James Eisenstein 1985. "Criminal courts and bureaucratic justice: Concessions and consensus in the guilty plea process." Criminal Law and Criminology 79:1103-1131.

Nardulli, Peter F., James Eisenstein, and Roy B. Flemming 1988. The Tenor of Justice. Chicago: University of Illinois Press.

National Minority Advisory Council on Criminal Justice 1980. The Inequality of Justice. Washington, D.C.: U.S. Department of Justice.

New York City Department of Corrections 1984. Admission Report. New York: New York.

New York State Supreme Court 1984–1994. New York County Criminal Term—The Weeks Summary of Judicial Proceedings. New York: New York.

Nonet, Philippe, and Phillip Seiznick 1978. Law and Society in Transition: Toward Responsive Law. New York: Octagon Books.

Office of Court Administration 1984–1990. Supreme Court Caseload Activity Reports. Albany: New York State.

———1984–1985. Supreme Court Criminal Term—Disposition Report. Albany: New York State.

———1986–1993. Report of Dispositions and Other Activity by Judge. Albany: New York State.

Pollner, Melvin 1979. "Explicative transactions: Making and managing meaning in traffic court." In Everyday Language: Studies in Ethnomethodology, ed. G. Pasathas, 227-255. New York: Irvington.

Resnick, Judith 1982. "Managerial judges." Harvard Law Review 96:374.

Rosett, Arthur, and Donald R. Cressey 1976. Justice By Consent, Philadelphia: J.B. Lippincott Co.

Savelsberg, Joachim J. 1992. "Law that does not fit society: Sentencing guidelines as a neoclassical reaction to the dilemmas of substantive law." The American Journal of Sociology 97:1346-1381.

———1994. "Knowledge, domination and criminal punishment." The American Journal of Sociology 99:911-943.

Schur, Edward 1971. Labeling Deviant Behavior. New York: Harper and Row.

Simon, Jonathan S. 1993. Poor Discipline: Parole and the Social Control of the Underclass. Chicago: University of Chicago Press.

Smith, Douglas A., and Christy A. Visher 1981. "Street level justice: Situational determinants of police arrest decisions." Social Problems 29:167–177.

Sudnow, David 1965. "Normal crimes: Sociological features of the penal code in a public defender's office." Social Problems 12:255.

Taylor, Ian, Paul Walton, and Jock Young 1973. The New Criminology. London: Routledge and Kegan Paul.

Teubner, Gunther 1987. "Juridification: Concepts, aspects, limits, solutions." In Juridification of Social Spheres: A Comparative Analysis in the Areas of Labor,

Corporate, Antitrust and Social Welfare Law, ed. Gunther Teubner, 3–48. Berlin/
N.Y.: Walter de Gruyter.

Uhlman, Thomas M., and N. Darlene Walker 1980. "He takes some of my time; I
take some of his: An analysis of sentencing patterns in jury cases." Law and Society Review 14:323.

Walker, Samuel 1993. Taming the System: The Control of Discretion in Criminal
Justice 1950-1990. New York: Oxford University Press.

Weber, Max 1968. Economy and Society. Berkeley: University of California Press.

Wice, Paul B. 1978. Criminal Lawyers. Beverly Hills, Calif.: Sage.

Wood, Arthur 1976. Criminal Lawyer, Connecticut: College and University Press.

POSTSCRIPT

Is Plea Bargaining Fair?

There is always a price to be paid to guarantee individual rights. The question for any society is how much it will pay. . . .

The U.S. Constitution guarantees, at least on its face, the right to a trial by jury. Has this been the reality? Can this be the reality?

The judicial system in the United States has maintained that while a jury trial is everyone's right, that right can be given up if one chooses to do so. A frequent method for doing so is to plead guilty. One dimension of the guilty pleas is "plea bargaining"—that is, pleading guilty in exchange for a reduced sentence. The assumption is that the guilty individual, rather than face "certain" conviction at the hands of a jury and suffer a stiffer sentence, would rather strike a deal with the prosecutor(s) and forego a trial. This certainly works in the interests of judicial efficiency by alleviating the burdens imposed upon the courts. But does plea bargaining result in justice? Is it possible that guilty parties might be receiving sentences that are "too light/lenient" for the harm they have perpetrated upon society? Even worse, isn't it possible that the innocent might be unjustly incarcerated, having pled guilty for fear of facing a guilty verdict at trial and a tougher sentence? Is it possible that those with lesser financial resources to mount a defense might be much more likely to plea bargain—even if innocent? If so, is this just? Is it fair?

Timothy Sandefur reviews some of the criticisms aimed at plea bargaining, but concludes that the practice is both constitutional and fair as long as the "terms" of "the contract" are clear. But therein lies the dilemma. If prosecutors are more savvy than defendants (and in the case of the indigent, this is typically so), is it likely that the defendant fully understands the consequences of his/her pleading? Just when does the process become abusive?

Mike McConville and Chester Mirsky believe the plea-bargaining process is inherently abusive because it follows a social disciplinary model wherein groups that a society has labeled "dangerous" are subordinated and do not receive the benefits of a factually based process.

Several works are particularly useful for further reading on this subject. In particular, see Arthur I. Rossett, *Justice by Consent: Plea Bargains in the American Courthouse*, Milton Henmann, *Plea Bargaining: The Experiences of Prosecutors, Judges, and Defense Attorneys,* and Jose A. Cabranes, *Fear of Judging: Sentencing Guidelines in the Federal Courts.*

ISSUE 4

Do Minorities Receive Tougher Sentencing?

YES: Norm R. Allen, Jr., from "Reforming the Incarceration System," *Free Inquiry* (Summer 2001)

NO: Stephen Klein, Joan Petersilia, and Susan Turner, from "Race and Imprisonment Decisions in California?" *Science* (February 16, 1990)

ISSUE SUMMARY

YES: Norm R. Allen argues that there are two standards of justice in the United States—legal and social—and that the disparity between the two works against minorities.

NO: Stephen Klein, Joan Petersilia, and Susan Turner argue that myths occur regarding racial discrimination because the word "discrimination" is mistakenly used in place of "disparity," and that the courts are not engaging in sentencing discrimination.

Returning to the notion of "blind justice," we must ask if sentences are meted out based on the crime committed without any consideration given to the demographics of the convicted. If justice is indeed blind, should it not also be uniformly applied?

Criminal sentencing has many nuances. What, for example, is its purpose? Is it to punish an individual for harms against society? Is it to rehabilitate? Is both?

Regardless of the answer to these questions, if particular individuals or groups in society receive longer sentences than do other groups, is justice being served? How can a society justify differential sentencing, if differential sentencing exists? And if those who are incarcerated—for whatever period of time—end up being disproportionately from one class, race, or group in society, what are the society's obligations to ameliorate the living conditions of that class, race, or group so that incarceration does not end up being their fate?

So, when we ask the question, Do minorities receive tougher sentencing?, we are asking broader questions about the nature of this society and its judicial system.

Some would argue, as does Norm R. Allen, that there is an extraordinary inequity in the sentencing meted out to racial minorities in the United States and that the system is in serious need of reform. Much as did Angela Davis, Allen discusses the "prison/industrial complex" and points out that there is a belief that a "conspiracy" exists to "oppress non-White and to further enrich the wealthy." Meanwhile, the opposing view that Allen points to is that there is a huge prison population that needs to be contained, and race has nothing to do with the necessity of containing these people.

Allen presents a poignant distinction between social and legal justice. Legal justice, of course, would simply concern itself with the results. Social justice would concern itself with the causes. As Allen notes, those concerned with each of these "types" of justice would have little concern for the other. Thus, there is an enduring dilemma.

How did we end up where we are now, with so many minorities incarcerated? Allen points out that this result is one of the spin-offs of a broader public policy, that of America's War on Drugs. During this "war," legislation was enacted that imposed more severe penalties upon those convicted of particular types of drug possession. It just so happened that the most severe penalties were imposed upon those who possess drugs used predominantly by African Americans. So, is this a law that is just at face value as well as just in its application?

Allen's exploration of the causes of crime and how to deal with them is an excellent synopsis of the problems facing this society. It should be well-heeded by policy makers as they assess the potentially inadvertent effects of a two- to three-decades-old public policy.

Stephen Klein, Joan Petersilia, and Susan Turner argue that the policy as enacted is even-handed. A key point they make is that

> the distinction between racial discrimination and racial disparity is too often glossed over in research and the debate on this issue. Discrimination occurs if officials of the justice system make ad hoc decisions based on an offender's race rather than on clearly defined, legitimate standards. In contrast, racial disparity occurs when fair standards are applied but the incident is different for racial groups.

Klein, Petersilia, and Turner present an excellent overview of recent research on the subject of racial minorities and sentencing as well as the finds of their own study on California. Their conclusion is that while there are racial disparities, there is not racial discrimination, and the "courts are making racially equitable sentencing decisions."

Norm R. Allen, Jr.

 **YES**

Reforming the Incarceration Nation

Can We Balance Social Justice With Legal Justice?

About two million people are currently incarcerated in the United States, a fact from which various observers have drawn widely varied inferences. Some believe that, because a disproportionately high number of prisoners are poor African Americans and Latinos, the "prison/industrial complex" is part of a racist conspiracy to oppress non-Whites and to further enrich the wealthy. Others, unconcerned about the huge prison population, simply accept that large numbers of criminals require large numbers of prisons to contain them—regardless of the criminals' background or color. People whose main concern is social justice often have little interest in—and may even oppose—efforts to bring about strictly legal justice. Meanwhile those who focus primarily on legal justice are often unconcerned with—and, in some cases, opposed to—social justice.

But why must legal justice and social justice be mutually exclusive? Why should people's politics determine the kinds of justice they will support or oppose? It is only fair—indeed, just—that people strive for a single standard of justice whenever the subject of justice arises.

Incarceration and Race

A principal consequence of America's War on Drugs has been a sharp increase in the U.S. prison population. During the Reagan and Bush administrations of the 1980s, Congress established harsher penalties for drug dealers and gave broader powers to law enforcement. The government spent billions to combat the drug scourge. In 1986, Congress mandated significantly longer prison sentences for people convicted of possessing crack cocaine than for those possessing cocaine in the powdered form. Because most crack users were Black, many within—and outside—the African American community believed the laws were part of a racist conspiracy to imprison Blacks. In truth, however, many Blacks supported these laws—including the Congressional Black Caucus. Black neighborhoods were being terrorized in violent crack wars nationwide. Lawmakers from all backgrounds felt extreme measures were needed to save Black neighborhoods.

From *Free Inquiry*, vol. 21, issue 3, Summer 2001, pp. 36. Copyright © 2001 by Council for Secular Humanism. Reprinted by permission.

The conclusion seems inescapable: Blacks and Whites have identified Blacks as the main targets of the War on Drugs. According to a report issued by Human Rights Watch, a non-governmental organization that monitors human rights abuses worldwide, Blacks account for 62.7 percent of all drug offenders sent to state prison. Whites account for just 36.7 percent. Yet according to the U.S. Department of Health and Human Services' Substance Abuse and Mental Health Services Administration (SAMHSA), there are five times as many White drug users as Black. Another SAMHSA survey found that drug users most often buy drugs from dealers of their own racial or ethnic group. Between 1991 and 1993, SAMHSA researchers found that 16 percent of admitted drug dealers were Black and 82 percent were White—a ratio radically at odds with the racial makeup of the population imprisoned on drug offenses. Clearly, the War on Drugs is largely a war on Blacks.

Social justice advocates argue that it is unfair to imprison vast numbers of poor, Black criminals, in part because such offenders cannot afford criminal lawyers capable of mounting a competent defense. Many liberals and radicals further maintain that poor Blacks who break the law are victims of an unjust, racist society that leaves them few viable options. On this view offenders from highly disadvantaged backgrounds should be viewed more as victims than as criminals.

But what does it mean for this view when the supposed victims become violent criminal victimizers? Are their victims entitled to legal justice? Or should society exonerate poor criminals in the name of social justice without regard to victims' plight? Should anyone other than the victim or the victim's loved ones have the right to forgive the victimizer?

To social justice advocates, rehabilitation, not retribution, should be the goal of the justice system. But these, too, need not be mutually exclusive alternatives. It is certainly important to guard against cruel and unusual punishment. To dispense with punishment altogether, however, would be an unwitting call for vigilante or "street" justice. Every society must give its citizens hope that they can turn to their legal system for justice.

The Causes of Crime

. . . The causes of crime are very complex and multidimensional. A partial list of the factors leading to crime would have to include all of the following: poverty, lack of opportunity, desperation, substance abuse, fear, greed, hatred, ambition, selfishness, loneliness, peer pressure, uncontrolled rage, lack of love, lack of ethical guidance, poor parenting skills, family dysfunction, child abuse, violence in the home, a crassly materialistic culture, the glamorization of violence in the popular culture, and easy access to guns.

Is Opportunity the Antidote?

Social justice advocates believe the best way to reduce crime is to bring about social and economic justice, primarily by reducing poverty and increasing opportunity. One way to reduce poverty is to create more jobs paying good wages. Yet most high-paying jobs supposedly require college degrees, which many poor Americans are unable to attain. Traditionally, only a minority of citizens throughout society has earned degrees. Moreover, if college education is not free, as it is in some nations, the college-educated minority may continue to shrink. This could cause the crime rate to rise.

Access to the workplace is an additional complication. Many more-desirable jobs are created in the suburbs rather than the inner cities. People from the inner cities often lack transportation. Making matters worse, suburban Whites frequently oppose public transport route expansions that would give inner-city non-Whites improved access to the suburbs.

Indeed, getting to and from work can be downright deadly for the inner-city poor. In 1995, Cynthia Wiggins, a Black teenage-mother from Buffalo, New York, was struck by a truck as she tried to cross a busy intersection. She later died of her injuries. Wiggins was trying to get to work at the Walden Galleria, a mall located in Cheektowaga, a Buffalo suburb. At the time, buses from the city were not allowed on mall property. After Wiggins's death, mall owners permitted buses to enter. (Since then, more blacks have been hired at the mall). Eventually, famed attorney Johnnie Cochran helped to win a multimillion-dollar wrongful death suit in favor of Wiggins's family.

The implications of all this for ex-convicts are stark. When reentering society, their first priority will be finding work. But employers often refuse to hire job applicants with criminal records. Yet, if ex-convicts cannot find employment, they are far more likely to return to crime. Hardliners may argue that former convicts should have thought about the consequences of their actions before they committed the criminal acts that caused their imprisonment. But if ex-cons cannot find gainful employment, society will continue to suffer under the burdens of spiraling crime and the taxes to pay for recidivists' re-imprisonment. . . .

Felons and Disenfranchisement

The U.S. prison system has numerous failings. One of its most reprehensible is the denial of the right to vote to millions of Americans. About four million people lack the right to vote because of felony convictions. Ex-felons may be disenfranchised even for minor offenses, or even if they had never been jailed or imprisoned. Many are disenfranchised for life—even after they have paid their debts to society.

The Sentencing Project is a nonprofit organization that fights for sentencing reform and engages in scholarly research in the area of criminal justice. With Human Rights Watch, the group published a report titled "Losing the Vote: The Impact of Felony Disenfranchisement Laws in the United States." The report—published in October 1998—pointed out many startling inequities, including:

- One and one-quarter million persons disenfranchised for a felony conviction are ex-offenders who have completed their criminal sentence. Another 1.4 million of the disenfranchised are on probation or parole. (Only 27 percent of the disenfranchised are in prison.)

- Thirty-six percent of the disenfranchised are Black men.
- Ten states disenfranchise more than one in five adult Black men; in seven of these states, one in four Black men are permanently disenfranchised.
- Given current rates of incarceration, three in ten of the next generation of Black men will be disenfranchised at some point in their lifetime. In states with the most restrictive voting laws, 40 percent of African American men are likely to be permanently disenfranchised.
- Many other countries let not only felons, but prisoners, vote—including France, Peru, Japan, Kenya, Israel, Norway, Sweden, Poland, Denmark, Zimbabwe, Romania, and the Czech Republic.

There is no good reason why prisoners should be forbidden to vote, unless they have been convicted of election fraud or a similar offense. Moreover, it is both irrational and unconscionable to deprive people of the right to vote after they have served their time. What better way to re-integrate ex-convicts into society than to grant them the internationally recognized right to vote?

A Plea for Justice Unskewed

At the same time, critics who complain about lax treatment of criminals are not always in the wrong. Too often criminals escape legal justice and rehabilitation by means of technicalities, plea bargains, light sentences, ineffective "anger management" programs, errors by incompetent jurors, and the like. The guilty are then free to commit other crimes and to victimize more innocent people. Law-abiding citizens richly deserve the right to live in safety a right that must never be jeopardized or abandoned in the name of social justice. The legitimate rights of victims must never be trampled upon in misguided efforts to rationalize the crimes of the guilty. Just as there is a need for prison reform, I would argue that there is a corresponding need to reform and punish the guilty.

Social justice activists generally oppose harsh prison sentences. But they will work doggedly to send certain alleged offenders to prison. For example, a civil rights worker might fight to imprison a cop charged with police brutality or a person or group charged with a hate crime. Yet this same civil rights advocate might work to defend a poor inner-city male caught in the act of murder. Similarly a radical feminist might work to free women convicted of violent crimes, yet work to imprison a man accused of rape or sexual assault. In these cases, social justice advocates often attempt to use the legal system to make a political point, rather than to seek true legal justice. In their eyes, "justice" simply means sending an accused member of a particular group to prison—regardless of whether the accused is innocent or guilty. An excellent example of this phenomenon was the Tawana Brawley rape hoax in New York in the 1980s. Despite all evidence to the contrary, civil rights advocates insisted that the teenager had been raped, and destroyed the reputations of innocent people in the process.

When people strive to realize a single standard of justice in every situation, such blunders are less likely. "No justice, no peace" is not mere politically loaded rhetoric. It represents a serious effort to be fair and to arrive at the truth.

A Hopeless Proposal

Angela Davis, Minister Louis Farrakhan of the Nation of Islam (NOI), and others have suggested that Black prisoners be summarily released from the U.S. prison system. Farrakhan has suggested that he could take large numbers under his wing and ensure their rehabilitation. This unrealistic and unworkable proposal strains credulity: NOI has a relatively small number of devotees (although it's said that no one knows the exact number, current estimates range from five to twenty thousand), nowhere near enough to assist the whole of the Black prison population. Further, the vast majority of American Blacks are non-Muslim. Finally, government has no business remanding ex-cons into an authoritarian, theocratic, patriarchal, and reactionary religious organization that influences anti-democratic leaders worldwide.

However, there must be ways in which the prison population can at least be greatly reduced. There is a clear correlation between unemployment and crime: the crime rate for employed Blacks is only slightly higher than that for employed whites. Yet the number of Black men attending college steadily declines. About half as many Black men attend college as Black women. Meanwhile, the prison/industrial complex continues to grow by leaps and bounds. Society would serve social justice and realize enlightened self-interest by making education, and consequently gainful employment, more equitably available to all citizens.

Crime Does Pay—for Some

Before this can happen, American society must come to terms with businesses that benefit from the prison/industrial complex and hope to preserve the status quo. Although businesses such as prison operating companies do not cause crime, it is at least problematic when correction systems form dubious partnerships with private enterprise. At the least, there is the appearance of impropriety that undermines faith in institutions when businesses thrive from and become dependent upon the incarceration of millions of citizens. It suggests that the government has decided to give up on serious efforts at crime prevention and rehabilitation, and settle for relying on the private sector to warehouse criminals to the end of their days. That is not the message that government should send to the citizenry. The government, not private industry, should run the nation's prisons.

An Issue of Life and Death

But should the government be responsible for putting criminals to death? Seventy countries worldwide outlaw capital punishment. So do twelve U.S. states and the District of Columbia. Across virtually the entire democratic world, the United States is regarded as incredibly reactionary where the death penalty is concerned. In February, Felix Rohatyn, U.S. ambassador to France from 1997 to 2000, wrote in the Washington Post: "There is a strong belief among our European allies that [the death penalty] has no place in a civilized society."

Capital punishment is illegal under European and Canadian law. European and Canadian authorities will not return alleged criminals to nations where they could face the death penalty. For this reason, convicted Pennsylvania killer Ira Einhorn remains a free man in France, four years after his capture. Likewise, James C. Kopp—who stands accused of killing abortion provider Barnett A. Slepian—probably will not be extradited by French authorities unless the death penalty is waived.

Near the time of Kopp's arrest, French President Jacques Chirac addressed the U.N. Human Rights Commission in Geneva and supported "the universal abolition of the death penalty, with a first step being a general moratorium." American lawyers and lawmakers have made similar calls.

There might be at least one good reason to administer the death penalty. If an unrepentant first-degree murderer kills again while in prison, one could persuasively argue that prison was not an effective deterrent for that murderer. Moreover, he might escape and kill again. It would not be right to give him more chances to kill. Generally, however, the death penalty is unnecessary. Killing the murderer will never bring closure to the victim's family. Indeed, nothing can. They will be in mourning as long as they are of sound mind. Life in prison with no chance of parole, however, is a very harsh, though fair and humane, punishment.

It is time to take a comprehensive look at proposed solutions to crime and poverty Social justice, economic justice, and legal justice are all important. It is time to develop what Robert Green Ingersoll called "a caring rationalism" in efforts to strive for true justice for every citizen in all the arenas of life.

Conflict resolution programs, early-child intervention programs, crime prevention programs, mentoring programs, stress management programs, moral education, parenting classes, parental support programs, drug prevention and rehabilitation programs, youth summits, and a host of other solutions have already demonstrated their effectiveness in reducing crime. Despite sensationalized media accounts of violence, juvenile arrests in most categories of violent crime have fallen in recent years. Moreover, psychologists, scholars, and law enforcement officials agree in predicting an even sharper crime rate decrease in the near future.

Positive and creative thinking wedded to activism can continue to make all the difference in the world. The role of the death penalty—if any—should be vanishingly small.

Stephen Klein, Joan Petersilia,
and Susan Turner

 **NO**

Race and Imprisonment Decisions in California

Race and Imprisonment Decisions in California

Crime has become an increasingly important element in American life. If the justice system is to operate fairly and efficiently, each of its aspects created to control crime deserves careful and objective scrutiny. Problems related to the speed of judgment, the appropriateness of sanctions, racial prejudice, and so on, should be analyzed to determine which components are operating correctly and which need improvement. One of the most controversial and frequently mentioned issues is the number of blacks in prison. Establishing the reason for that number—whether poverty, discrimination, failure of the justice system, or other causes—is essential for guiding those responsible for guaranteeing an equitable system.

Although blacks constitute less than 11% of the U.S. population, they make up nearly half of the national prison population. This startling disparity has prompted charges of racial discrimination. But are more blacks in prison because of racial bias in the criminal justice system or because they are more likely than whites to commit those crimes that lead to imprisonment? Young men are also overrepresented, but no one has yet suggested that this disparity is evidence of discrimination. The record clearly indicates that young men simply commit more serious crimes than women or older people do.

The distinction between racial discrimination and racial disparity is too often glossed over in research and the debate on this issue. Discrimination occurs if officials of the justice system make ad hoc decisions based on an offender's race rather than on clearly defined, legitimate standards. In contrast, racial disparity occurs when fair standards are applied but the incidence is different for racial groups.

Numerous studies have attempted to establish whether the racial disparity is due to discrimination in the criminal justice system or to other factors. The results have been mixed, largely because the analyses in most studies have failed to control for a range of variables related to imprisonment (for example, conviction crime, criminal record, and demographic factors) and for the possibility that many of these variables may be proxies for race.

From *Science*, Feb. 16, 1990, pp. 812–816. Copyright © 1990 by American Association for the Advancement of Science. Reprinted by permission. References omitted.

We conducted an analysis that controlled for these variables and examined the proxy issue, using data on California sentencing practices. The study focused only on sentencing (prison or probation and length of term) for offenders convicted of six felony offenses in California. Thus, it did not address issues of possible discrimination in arrests and prosecution or in capital sentencing, and its results may not apply to other states.

Research Background

Two recent studies have addressed the racial question by examining the correlation between imprisonment and crime committed, on the basis of two different measures of the latter. Blumstein[1] focused on arrests, controlling for number of offenders of each race arrested for each crime type and assuming there was no bias in processing these arrests. Under these conditions, he estimated that 43% of the prisoners in the United States would be black, an estimate 5 to 6 percentage points below the actual percentage of black prisoners.

Langan[2] examined racial disparities in imprisonment using data on victims' responses about the race of those who commit crime. His study used data from the National Crime Survey (NCS), conducted by the U.S. Census Bureau on a nationally representative sample of households. The NCS investigators inquired about crimes these households experienced (including crimes not reported to the police) and the race of the criminals who committed them. This approach frees the data from any racial bias that might stem from who reports crime or from police arrest or prosecution decisions. Langan found that the percentage of black prisoners was only 4 to 5% higher than would be expected on the basis of the NCS data.

Neither Blumstein nor Langan controlled for legitimate sentencing factors (such as the offender's prior record and victim injuries) that might explain the 4 to 6% difference their studies found. The need to control for such factors is illustrated in Kleck's[3] review of 57 studies that examined racial discrimination in sentencing (RDS). He found that 26 studies contradicted the RDS hypothesis, 16 had mixed results, and 15 found evidence of bias. For 13 of the studies that found evidence of bias, Kleck concludes that they:

> failed to include even the most rudimentary controls controls for the defendant's prior record and thus failed to eliminate the possibility that black defendants receive more severe sentences than whites because they generally have more serious official records of criminal behavior. Only two out of 24 studies which introduced such controls showed consistent evidence of RDS (and one of these two failed to control offense type) (4, p. 274). Kleck's and others' reviews of the racial disparity literature suggest that, in studies with control for factors legitimately considered in sentencing decisions, these factors often account for most or all of the observed racial disparities. This is especially true for studies that focus on offenders outside of the deep South.

An important exception to this trend was a study Petersilia[5] conducted on 1400 male prison inmates in California, Michigan, and Texas. Petersilia found that, in these states, courts typically imposed heavier sentences on Latinos and blacks than on whites who were convicted of the same crimes and who had similar criminal records. Further, the minority inmates also tended to receive and serve longer prison terms than their nonminority matched counterparts.

Petersilia expressed several concerns about the data in her study[5] and urged that it be replicated. These concerns ranged from the reliability of data sources to the lack of detailed information about the inmates' crimes and prior records. She also speculated that fuller implementation of determinate sentencing guidelines might change court and parole decisions markedly. These sentencing reforms were instituted, in part, to reduce judicial discretion and the influence of factors not legally relevant in criminal sentencing.

Our study examined racial bias controlling for the nature of crimes committed, prior record, other offender characteristics, and race. It used data on sentencing in California after the state implemented its 1977 Determinate Sentencing Act. Although previous studies are not directly comparable to the present one, some tentative support for reduced racial disparity after implementation of determinate sentencing is suggested by the present study.

Analyzing Sentencing Decisions

Overview   Our analyses focus on two sentencing decisions separately: (i) the decision to send an offender to prison or put him on probation and (ii) the length of term imposed on those imprisoned. We conducted three separate analyses for each decision: The first identifies by conviction crime what percentage of black, Latino, and white offenders received prison or probation sentences, and what the average lengths of their prison terms were. This step establishes whether there are racial disparities in sentencing based on conviction crime alone. The second analysis addresses two questions: First, controlling for offense and offender characteristics that legitimately enter judicial decisions, are there still unexplained racial disparities in sentencing? Second, does adding race to those factors add any explanatory power? The third analysis seeks to determine whether any of the other explanatory variables is a proxy for race—that is, does it mask racial effects?

Samples   Our samples of prisoners and probationers came from data collected by the California Board of Prison Terms (CBPT) on all offenders sentenced to prison in California in 1980 and on a sample of those sentenced to probation in Superior Court during that same year. This was a one-time collection effort underwritten by the legislature for purposes of analyzing consequences of implementing the Determinate Sentencing Act. To our knowledge, the resulting data base is unique: it contains the richest source of information in the country for analyzing imprisonment decisions, albeit for only 1 year.

The database contains detailed information on the offender's criminal, personal, and socioeconomic characteristics as well as important aspects of the case and details of court handling. From both the prisoner and probationer samples, we selected all the adult males who were convicted of assault, robbery, burglary, theft, forgery, or drug offences (that is, crimes that could result in either a prison or a probation sentence).

The CBPT drew its probationer sample from 17 highly populated urban counties. These counties account for 80% of the felony convictions in the state. Because the probability of being incarcerated differs among counties and crime types, we restricted the prisoner sample to offenders from these same 17 counties. We also weighted the prisoner and probationer samples to provide an accurate representation of the true proportions of prisoners and probationers in these countries. We have described the weighting procedures and their effect on sample size[6] (they had no impact on the percentage distribution of offenders by race).

Variables Racial bias in sentencing would be evidenced by disparities in the in/out decision (that is, whether the offender was sent to prison or granted probation) or the length of the prison term imposed, or both. We examined four groups of correlates of these two outcomes: (i) characteristics of the crime (for example, the use of a weapon by the criminal) and the offender's prior record, (ii) the offender's demographic characteristics (including age), (iii) process variables (such as whether the offender had a private attorney), and (iv) the offender's race.

Choice of statistical models We used different models for the in/out decision and the length-of-term decision.[7] For the in/out analyses, we used Fisher's linear discriminant function. For computational ease, this was done using OLS (ordinary least squares) multiple regression to fit a zero-one variable indicating this decision. If b is the vector of estimated regression coefficients from OLS, the maximum likelihood estimates of the coefficients for Fisher's linear discriminant function are given by kb, where k = n/SSE, n is the sample size, and SSE is the residual sum of squares from the zero-one regression. Thus, all significance probabilities are unaffected by the choice between OLS and discriminant function analyses. We used OLS for the analysis of the log of the length of prison term analyses because this outcome was a continuous variable.[8]

Prison or Probation:

In/Out Sentencing
In our 17-country sample of convicted felons, 44% of the blacks, 37% of the Latinos, but only 33% of the whites were sent to prison (10% of the whites were Asian, Indian, or other).

... These data show that black and Latino offenders were more likely to go to prison than white offenders, especially for assault and drug offenses. For example, 39% of those sent to prison for assault were black, whereas only 27% of those who received probation for this crime were black. [Data] also reveals proportional differences in racial representation across crime types. Latinos constituted more than half of those convicted of drug crimes, for example, but less than 25% of those convicted of theft or forgery.

Our analyses of the in/out decision sought to establish whether these disparities were explained by differences in sentencing variables besides crime type. . . .

This part of the analysis consisted of four steps. In step 1, we grouped the prisoners and probationers convicted of the same crime together, thereby reforming six offense groups. We then divided each group randomly into two subgroups, A and B, forming 12 subgroups (two for each of six crime types).

In step 2, we used the procedures we have described[6] to construct two discriminant rules to predict the in/out decision in each of the 12 subgroups. Rule 1 used all the prior record and crime characteristics, and all the offender demographic variables that had a statistically significant correlation with the in/out decision and/or added significantly to the overall prediction of this decision when used with other prior-record and offense variables. Rule 1 also used all the process variables. Rule 2 used all the foregoing variables plus race. . . .

In step 3, we applied rule 1 developed on subgroup A to all the offenders in subgroup B to predict whether they would go to prison, and applied rule 1 developed on subgroup B to all the offenders in subgroup A. These two subgroups were then recombined and a count was made of the number of offenders in each group whose predicted in/out status was the same as their actual in/or status (where the number predicted to be incarcerated was set equal to the number who were incarcerated). We then inserted these counts into the formula below to compute the percentage of case whose status was predicted accurately:

Percentage predicted accurately = 100 X [Number incarcerated who were predicted to be incarcerated + Number given probation who were predicted to be given probation / Total number of offenders]

Step 4 was the same as step 3, except that we used rule 2 rather than rule 1. The difference in the accuracy of the predictions between steps 3 and 4 is a good index of the effect of race on the in/out decision, because an offender's data were not considered in computing the equation used to predict this sentencing decision.

. . . For four of the six crimes, predictive accuracy does not improve when race is considered. The two exceptions are robbery and drugs. However, in both cases, the inclusion of race improved accuracy by only 1%. Moreover, racial disparities were not the same for the two crimes. For robbery, blacks had a relatively higher and Latinos a lower probability of going to prison, whereas for drugs, Latinos had a higher probability and white offenders had a lower probability.

The variables that were predictive of going to prison for one crime were generally the same as those for another crime. They were:

- Having multiple current conviction counts, prior prison terms, and juvenile incarcerations.
- Being on adult or juvenile probation or parole at the time of the current offense.
- Having been released from prison within 12 months of the current offense.
- Using a weapon in the current offense.

- Having a history of drug or alcohol addiction or both.
- Being over 21 years of age.
- Going to trial, as opposed to pleading guilty.
- Not being released before trial.
- Not being represented by a private attorney.

Across all crime types, we predicted with 80% accuracy which offenders would be sentenced to prison. Adding race to the prediction formulas did not improve this accuracy rate by even 1%.

These results suggest that, once we consider the other factors related to sentencing, knowing the offender's race does not improve our ability to predict who will be sentenced to prison or probation (the in/out decisions). This implies that, for our samples, any racial disparity in sentencing does not reflect racial discrimination. However, it is still possible that other variables may be proxies for race. In other words, the relation of these factors with race may hide racially biased decisions. To address this concern, we examined the relation between the in/out decision and offense and offender characteristics in two ways.

We first examined the extent to which race was correlated with each of the predictors used in rule 1. The results of this analysis showed again that a potentially high correlation between the predictors and race did not mask racial bias in the in/out decisions. For example, the best single predictor of going to prison was the number of conviction counts. "Counts" refers to the number of separate crimes the offender was convicted of during the current court proceedings. Within a given crime type, all three racial groups had about the same average number of counts (for example, the values for black, Latino, and white burglars were 1.3, 1.2, and 1.3, respectively). Similarly, the percentages of black, Latino, and white burglars whose cases went to trial (as opposed to being settled through plea bargaining) were 7, 7, and 5, respectively.

To pursue the matter further, we investigated whether race effects were hidden by measuring the degree to which race was related to the predicted probability of imprisonment generated by rule 1 in the analysis above. We found that with one exception, less than 1% of the variance in these predictions could be explained by offender race. The exception was drug crimes, where race accounted for 7% of the variance. Moreover, drug crimes were the only type for which race, by itself, explained more than 2% of the variance in the in/out decision.[9] Latinos convicted of drug crimes had a higher probability of imprisonment, even after the factors known to affect the in/out decision (and measured here) are statistically controlled. Taken together, these findings demonstrate that the variables most highly correlated with the in/out decision are not proxies for race.

Length of Prison Term Imposed

Under California's 1977 Determinate Sentencing Act, judges may assign one of three specified terms (short, middle, or long) for each conviction offense. The Act further instructs judges to impose the middle term unless there are aggravating or mitigating circumstances. If the short or long term is imposed, the judge must specify the circumstances that led to the selection of this term in the sentencing documentation. Enhancements for particular aggravating circumstances, such as prior record or weapon use, must be formally pled and adjudicated. The Act was designed to "eliminate disparity and provide uniform sentences throughout the State" [California Penal Code 1170.(a)(1)].

Petersilia[5] found that minority offenders sentenced to prison before this Act became law were likely to receive somewhat longer sentences than whites whose official criminal records showed them similarly culpable. The CBPT prisoner database let us examine whether this trend still held for offenders incarcerated after the Act became law.

The high degree of agreement in the average (mean) prison term imposed across racial groups [was also studied]. None of these means differed by more than 3 months. Moreover, an analysis of variance indicated that within a crime type, the means were not different from each other by a statistically significant (P[is less than]0.05) amount. Across crime types, the offenders in one racial group did not tend to receive shorter or longer sentences than those in another group.

We also used OLS regression to examine how well offender prior record, offense variables, offender characteristics, process variables, and race predicted the length of the prison term imposed. The dependent variable for these analyses was the log of the length of the term imposed. Again, we found that including offender race in the regression model did not improve predictive accuracy for any of the six crimes studied. Thus, offender race did not appear to influence prison sentence lengths.

The regression model and the percentage of variance explained for each crime . . . predicted with about 70 to 80% accuracy whether an offender received a sentence that was above or below the median sentence (which corresponds to a 40 to 60% improvement over chance).

Conclusions

Taken together, our findings indicate that California courts are making racially equitable sentencing decisions. The racial disparities apparent in the in/out decision are not evidence of discrimination in sentencing—once we control for relevant crime, prior record, and process variables. This finding held for five of the six of the crimes studied (assault, robbery, burglary, theft, and forgery). Drug crimes were the exceptions, where Latinos faced a higher probability of imprisonment. We found no evidence of racial discrimination in the length of prison term imposed for any of the crimes studied.

It is also clear that the other variables are not proxies for race—that is, they are not masking what are actually racially influenced decisions. Moreover, sentencing decisions were predictable, even though our database contained only some of the many variables that legally can be considered in imposing criminal sentences. For example, we did not know in multiple-offender robberies whether the defendant was the ringleader or just the driver of the getaway car, and we had no way of measuring the credibility of witnesses. Nevertheless, in more than 80% of the cases, we predicted accurately whether the offender would receive prison or probation; including offender race in the formulas did not increase predictive accuracy.

The current study did not examine decisions made at other justice system decision points (those made by the police and prosecutor) nor did it examine the more global relation between poverty and minority representation in the justice system. The present study does show, however, that two very important sentencing decisions do not show evidence of discrimination against minority offenders.

At this point we cannot tell why the present results differ from those of the earlier California results.[5] A tentative conclusion could be that California's Determinate Sentencing Act has contributed to racial equity in sentencing. However, because of differences between studies, this remains an open question.

References and Notes

1. A. Blumstein, J. Crim. Law Criminol. 73, 1259 (1982).
2. P. Langan, ibid. 76, 666 (1985).
3. G. Kleck, Am. Sociol. Rev. 46, 783 (1981).
4. G. Kleck, Law Hum. Behav. 9, 271 (1985).
5. J. Petersilia, Racial Disparities in the Criminal Justice System, R-2947-NIC (RAND, Santa Monica, CA, 1983).
6. S. Klein, S. Turner, J. Petersilia, Racial Equity in Sentencing, R-3599-RC (RAND, Santa, Monica, CA, 1988).
7. Some analysts consider the latter decision as conditionally dependent on the former and would therefore prefer to utilize Tobit or Heckman's sample-selection model [J. Heckman, Ann. Econ. Soc. Meas. 5, 475 (1976)]. This preference stems from concerns about models that do not directly correct for the correlation between outcomes. However, W. Manning et al. [J. Econometr. 35, 59 (1987)] have demonstrated that the overall prediction bias in two-part models (such as ours) is negligible if one does not know the true model specification and relies on the available data. These authors conclude, "In effect, picking a specification that fits the observed data largely eliminates the bias from 'ignoring' the selection effect. In the absence of a priori information (e.g., exclusions or the exact specification of the right-hand-side variables), these results raise the issue of whether the selection model can be distinguished from an empirically derived two-part model, even in a case favorable to the selection model" (p. 60).
8. G. Haggstrom, J. Bus. Econ. Stat. 1, 229 (1983).
9. Preliminary analyses indicated that adding interactions between race and predictor variables to the models would not produce a practical increase in the accuracy of these models to predict the in/out decision or sentence length. These analyses began by constructing two interaction terms for each independent variable: black X variable and Latino X variable. Thus, there were twice as many interaction terms as there were predictor variables. Given the large number of these terms, we did not test them individually (because several were likely to achieve statistical significance simply by chance). Instead, we examined whether predictive accuracy could be improved by using all of them together. This liberal omnibus test was run 12 times, once for each combination of the six crime types and two outcomes (in/out and sentence length). However, despite the large sample sizes and extensive number of

interaction terms considered, they produced very small F values (the only F greater than 2.0 was for the in/out decision on robbery, which was 2.16). These results indicate that adding race interaction terms to the model would not produce a meaningful increase in predictive accuracy and, thus, these terms were not included in subsequent analytic steps.

10.   The views expressed in this article are those of the authors and are not necessarily shared by the RAND Corporation or its research sponsors.

POSTSCRIPT

Do Minorities Receive Tougher Sentencing?

Norm R. Allen, Jr. maintains that social and legal justice are not mutually exclusive, and that we must work toward a single standard of justice, one that does not currently exist.

The overwhelming data tell us that non-whites have a higher incarceration rate and longer prison sentences than do whites. The Reagan and Bush administrations' War on Drugs resulted in an explosion in the U.S. prison population. In addition to committing greater financial resources to battling the war, Congress enacted legislation that required lengthier prison sentences for those possessing crack cocaine than for those possessing powdered cocaine. Since most crack cocaine users are black, Allen points out, blacks receive tougher sentencing. Allen makes the interesting point that both the both blacks and whites see blacks as the enemy in the war on drugs, and that Black legislators, concerned about black communities, supported the tough legislation. Yet, citing figures from the U.S. Department of Health and Human Services' Substance Abuse and Mental Health Administration, Allen points out that the number of white drug users is five times the number of black users. Yet, as social justice advocates argue, the War on Drugs continues to be a war on poor blacks who don't have the financial resources to engage a good criminal defense attorney.

Allen's question is an excellent one: If we see this part of the population as "victim," what about justice for the violent victim's victims? Norm Allen presents the argument that we can control crime at the same time we have to understand and treat the causes of crime.

Stephen Klein, Joan Petersilia, and Susan Turner argue that while blacks make up almost half of the prison population (a staggering figure in light of the fact that blacks comprise only 11 percent of the population in the country), they maintain that minorities do not receive tougher sentencing. Their conclusion is based on their careful and insightful distinction between racial discrimination versus racial disparity. Is there a disparity? Absolutely, but racial disparity is not the result of racial discrimination on the part of the courts. They warn against using other variables as "proxies" for race. They provide a useful list of the variables that are predictive of going to prison, including "multiple conviction counts, prior prison terms, juvenile incarcerations, . . . being on . . . adult or juvenile probation or parole . . . having been released from prison within 12 months of the current offense, using a weapon in the current offence, having a history of drug or alcohol addition or both, being over 21 years of age, going to trial as opposed to pleading guilty, not being released before trial, not being represented by a private attorney." They note that adding "race" to this list did not increase the prediction formulas.

Several significant readings on this subject include: R. Barri Flower, *Minorities and Criminality,* Tracy Brown, *Criminal Minded,* and Michael Tony, *Sentencing Matters.*

ISSUE 5

Are Mandatory Minimum Sentences Fair and Effective?

YES: David Risley, from "Mandatory Minimum Sentences: An Overview," *Drug Watch International* (May 2000)

NO: Carl M. Cannon, from "America: All Locked Up," *National Journal* (August 15, 1998)

ISSUE SUMMARY

YES: David Risley argues that the purpose of mandatory minimum sentences is to ensure that serious drug crimes are met with significant punishment and that they have been successful toward this end.

NO: Carl M. Cannon argues that, while increased prison sentences may make citizens feel safer, the damage done to prisoners' families is a high price for society to pay.

The judicial system is on the horns of a dilemma in determining whether sentences should be imposed regardless of any extenuating circumstances. At some point in all of our lives, we have read or seen Victor Hugo's nineteenth-century work *Les Miserables*. The protagonist, Jean Valjean, in an effort to help his starving sister and her children, steals a loaf of bread. For his "crime," he is punished by a lengthy sentence at hard labor.

Could we argue that Jean Valjean's "crime" was justified in the face of the alternative—the starvation of his family? If so, should the court have taken that circumstance into consideration when determining his fate? Once Valjean escapes, the "system"—in the personage of Inspector Javert, the policeman who pursues him—is relentless, representing the unrelenting insistence of the law to exact the punishment inflicted.

For Javert, it is irrelevant why Jean Valjean stole the loaf of bread. There are those who argue that a crime is a crime, and the sentencing for that crime should be consistent. This is an argument presented by David Risley, as he discusses mandatory minimum sentences. Risley argues that there should be consistency in sentences so that perpetrators will know the penalties they face. As he points out,

> Drug dealers are risk takers by nature. Lack of certainty of serious sentences for serious crimes encourages, rather than deters, such risk takers to elevate their level of criminal activity in the hope that, if caught, they will be lucky enough to draw a lenient judge and receive a lenient sentence. The only possible deterrent for people who are willing to take extreme risks is to take away their cause for hope.

Risley's position is a no-nonsense, no-compromise one similar to Inspector Javert.

Carl M. Cannon is much more sympathetic to the plight of those who are "all locked up." Cannon argues that

> Cities may be safer, many offenders who have committed three felonies have been sentenced to life in prison, and the prison population is growing. However, prisoners' families have been shattered, prison can be seen as a rite of passage for some communities, and the monetary expense is considerable.

Cannon points out that it is politically popular to come down hard on crime and criminals, since "voters have sent an unmistakable message that they don't really care about what causes crime, they just want something done to make them safer in their homes and on their streets." So the Jean Valjeans get "all locked up," regardless of the circumstances of their existence.

Cannon questions the "hidden social costs" of the policy of "locking them up and throwing away the key." If we were to think only in utilitarian terms, what is the cost to taxpayers of "warehousing" 1.5 million people annually? In humane terms, Cannon questions, "In trolling for culprits with such a fine net, is the criminal justice system catching people who are not dangerous and for whom lengthy prison sentences are a waste, if not an injustice?" Was Jean Valjean dangerous in his stealing a loaf of bread for his starving family?

YES

David Risley

Mandatory Minimum Sentences: An Overview

The purpose of mandatory minimum sentences is to prevent the judicial trivialization of serious drug crimes. They do that well, to which some protest. Because the federal sentencing system is the model most often cited, it will be used for illustration throughout the following discussion.

Before the advent of mandatory minimum sentences in serious drug cases, federal judges had unbridled discretion to impose whatever sentences they deemed appropriate, in their personal view, up to the statutory maximum. Because individual judges differ widely in their personal views about crime and sentencing, the sentences they imposed for similar offenses by similar defendants varied widely. What some judges treated as serious offenses, and punished accordingly, others minimized with much more lenient sentences.

Ironically, more lenient sentences became particularly prevalent in areas with high volumes of major drug crime, such as large metropolitan and drug importation centers. Perhaps the sheer volume of cases in such areas led to a certain degree of desensitization. When serious crime becomes routine, there is human tendency to treat it routinely, and sentences often drop accordingly. In some areas across the country, that phenomenon can even be seen with crimes such as murder.

While the ideal is that sentences be perfectly personalized by wise, prudent, and consistent judges to fit every individual defendant and crime, the reality is that judges are human, and their wide human differences and perspectives lead to widely different sentences, if given completely unbridled discretion.

Such wide disparity in sentencing is inherently unfair, at least to those who receive stiff sentences for crimes for which others are punished only lightly. But such inconsistency was welcomed by drug dealers, since it meant they could hope for a light sentence for serious drug crimes. That, of course, created a much bigger problem.

Drug dealers are risk takers by nature. Lack of certainty of serious sentences for serious crimes encourages, rather than deters, such risk takers to elevate their level of criminal activity in the hope that, if caught, they will be lucky enough to draw a lenient judge and receive a lenient sentence. The only possible deterrence for people who are willing to take extreme risks is to take away their cause for such hope.

Some counter that drug dealers are undeterrable by criminal sanctions because they sell drugs to support their own addictions, and so should be treated for their addictions rather than imprisoned. While there may be some merit to that argument for many low-level street dealers, it is generally untrue of their suppliers, and even many other street dealers. Most dealers and distributors at any substantial level do not use drugs themselves, or do so only infrequently. They are exploiters and predators, and users are their captive prey. Drug dealing is a business. As in any other business, drug addicts are unreliable and untrustworthy, especially around drugs, and so make poor business partners. Because drug dealers usually run their operations as high-risk businesses, they necessarily weigh those risks carefully, and so are deterrable when the risks become too high. Many dealers who used to carry firearms, for example, now avoid doing so when they are selling drugs due to the high mandatory federal penalties when guns and drugs are mixed.

However, drug dealers seldom view the risks as too high when they see reason to hope for a light sentence. Congress, however, can, and did, step in to take away that hope. By establishing mandatory minimum sentences for serious drug offenses, Congress sent a clear message to drug dealers: no matter who the judge is, serious crime will get you serious time.

To those who do not view crimes subject to mandatory minimum sentences as serious, including drug dealers and their support systems, that message is objectionable. To most, it is welcome. Mandatory minimum sentences put steel in the spine of our criminal justice system.

The natural question which follows is, what level of dealing must defendants reach before being subject to mandatory minimum sentences, and what are those sentences? The answer varies with the type of drug and whether the defendant is a repeat offender.

In the federal system, there are two levels of mandatory minimums, with each level doubling for defendants with prior convictions. The first tier requires a minimum sentence of imprisonment for five years (10 with a prior felony drug conviction), and the second tier requires a minimum of 10 years (20 with one prior felony drug conviction, and mandatory life with two such prior convictions). Of that, defendants can receive a reduction in the time they serve in prison of only 54 days per year as a reward for "good behavior," which means they must actually serve about 85% of their sentences.

For a prior drug offense to be considered a felony, it must be punishable by more than one year. In the federal system and most states, a drug offense is rarely classified as a felony unless it involves distribution of the drugs involved, or an intent to do so. For most practical purposes, therefore, a prior felony conviction for a drug such as marijuana can be read to mean a prior conviction for distribution. And, since most small distribution cases are reduced to misdemeanor simple possession (personal use) charges as part of plea bargains, especially for first-time offenders, a prior felony drug conviction for a drug such as marijuana usually means the prior conviction either involved a substantial amount of the drug or a repeat offender undeserving of another such break.

In the case of marijuana, those who oppose mandatory minimum sentencing on so-called "humanitarian" grounds seldom mention that, to be eligible for even a five-year minimum sentence, a defendant must be convicted of an offense involving at least 100 kilograms (220 pounds) of marijuana, or, in the case of a marijuana growing operation, at least 100 plants. Such defendants are not low-level offenders.

With marijuana available at the Mexican border in Texas for wholesale prices between $600 to $1100 per pound, and selling in most areas at a retail price of between $1200 to $2000 per pound, and with any reasonably healthy cultivated marijuana plant producing at least one and sometimes two pounds of finished product, eligibility for even the lowest mandatory minimum sentence requires conviction of an offense involving between $132,000 to $440,000 worth of marijuana, or plants capable of producing marijuana worth a bulk retail price of between $120,000 to $450,000.

To be eligible for the next, 10-year tier of minimum sentence, a defendant must be convicted of an offense involving 1000 kilograms (1.1 tons) of marijuana or 1000 marijuana plants. Even at a low wholesale price of $600 per pound, such offenses involve marijuana worth at least $1.3 million. One kilogram equals 2.2 pounds. Conversely, one pound equals 453.6 grams, and one ounce equals 28.35 grams.

It would be difficult to describe any offense involving between $120,000 to $450,000 worth of drugs as undeserving of even a five year prison sentence. Yet, those who oppose mandatory minimum sentences for marijuana and other drug offenses do just that, usually by attempting to convey the false impression the criminals they are attempting to protect are only low-level offenders.

In examining the deterrent potential of such mandatory minimum sentences, one must consider that the profit potential for marijuana offenses is relatively high, and the penalties relatively low, which makes marijuana an attractive drug in which to deal, as evidenced by its widespread availability. To illustrate, if a dealer bought 200 pounds of marijuana in Texas for $900 per pound for a total of $180,000, transported it to the Midwest and sold it for as low as $1400 per pound, for a total of $280,000 with minimal overhead, the profit for just one such trip would be $100,000. When the street-level price of between $125 to $300 per ounce is considered, or the lower acquisition costs if the marijuana is grown by the dealer himself, the profit potential for such a venture can be huge, and yet still not involve enough drugs to trigger even the lowest mandatory minimum penalty. Since the chance of getting caught for any single trip of that sort is relatively low, the prospect of a quick $100,000 profit lures plenty of eager dealers, even with the risk of spending close to five years in prison.

Of course, if drug dealers are undeterrable, as the actions of many demonstrate they are, the only realistic options left are to either give up and allow them to ply their predatory trade unhindered (the legalization "solution"), or incapacitate them with even longer sentences.

The debate, it would seem, should be about whether the mandatory minimum penalties for marijuana offenses are currently too lenient, not too harsh.

Mandatory Minimums as a Check on Sentencing Guidelines

The next question is whether the more recent advent of the federal sentencing guidelines, which also limit judicial sentencing discretion, made mandatory minimum penalties obsolete. The answer is definitely no. As a practical matter, only through mandatory minimum sentences can Congress maintain sentencing benchmarks for serious drug crimes which cannot be completely circumvented by the commission which establishes, and sometimes quietly alters, those guidelines. One of the best illustrations is that of the sentencing guidelines for marijuana growers, who have achieved favorable treatment under the sentencing guidelines, but fortunately not under Congress' statutory mandatory minimum sentences.

To appreciate the significance of that illustration, one must understand a little about the sentencing guideline system, and its relationship to mandatory minimum sentences. As part of the Sentencing Reform Act of 1984, Congress mandated the formation of the United States Sentencing Commission as an independent agency in the judicial branch composed of seven voting members, appointed by the President with the advice and consent of the Senate, at least three of whom must be federal judges, not more than four of whom may be from the same political party, serving staggered six-year terms. That Commission was charged with the formidable task of establishing binding sentencing guidelines to dramatically narrow judges' sentencing discretion, in order to provide reasonable uniformity in sentencing throughout the country, while at the same time taking into reasonable account the myriad of differences between the hundreds of federal crimes and limitless array of individual defendants.

The result of that enormous undertaking was the adoption, effective November 1987, of the United States Sentencing Guidelines. Using its provisions, contained in a book one inch thick, courts determine the seriousness of the offense and the extent of the defendant's past criminal history, and use that information to determine on a chart the relatively narrow sentencing range within which they have sentencing discretion. In drug cases, the seriousness of the offense (offense level) is determined mostly on the basis of the amount of drugs for which a defendant is accountable, with adjustments for factors such as role in the offense, whether a firearm was involved, and whether the defendant accepted responsibility for his or her actions through a candid guilty plea.

As part of its broad delegation of authority, Congress provided that changes promulgated by the Commission to the Sentencing Guidelines automatically become law unless Congress, within a 180-day waiting period, affirmatively acts to reject them. By that means Congress avoided a great deal of detailed work, but also created the possibility that changes to the Sentencing Guidelines to which they would object if carefully considered would become law if no one raises a sufficient alarm.

Because the Commission has only seven voting members, a change of only one member can result in the reversal of a previous 4–3 vote, sometimes with great consequences. Congress is ill-equipped to deal with the intricacies of the impact of many amendments to the Sentencing Guidelines, and is sometimes preoccupied with other, more pressing or "hot button" issues. Therefore, the only realistic check on the delegation of authority to the Commission to make changes in drug sentences is the trump card of mandatory minimums.

That is true because defendants receive the higher of whatever sentence is called for by the statutory mandatory minimums or the Sentencing Guidelines. If the Commission promulgates a change to the Sentencing Guidelines which calls for lower sentences than required by the statutory mandatory minimums, the mandatory minimums trump the Sentencing Guidelines. In other words, the mandatory minimums are mandatory, and are beyond the control of the Commission.

With that background, the vital importance of mandatory minimum sentences as at least a partial check over the Commission in drug sentences is dramatically illustrated by the changes the Commission made regarding sentences for marijuana growers. The mandatory minimum sentences for marijuana growers imposed by Congress, which kick in at 100 plants, equate one marijuana plant with one kilogram (2.2 pounds) of marijuana. Until November 1995, the Sentencing Guidelines used that same equivalency in calculating the offense level in cases involving 50 or more plants, but for cases involving less than 50 plants considered one plant as the equivalent of only 100 grams (3.5 ounces). That 10:1 ratio between the amount of marijuana to which plants were considered to represent was a major logical inconsistency, since marijuana plants do not produce significantly more or less marijuana just because they happen to be in the company of more or less than 49 other marijuana plants.

The Commission solved that inconsistency in early 1995 by promulgating an amendment to the Sentencing Guidelines which, instead of eliminating the unrealistically low 100 gram equivalency for smaller cases, eliminated the one kilogram equivalency for larger cases. Congress did nothing, so, as of November 1995, the Sentencing Guidelines treat all marijuana plants as if they were only capable of producing 3.5 ounces of marijuana.

In explanation, the Commission stated:

> In actuality, a marihuana plant does not produce a yield of one kilogram of marihuana. The one plant = 100 grams of marihuana equivalency used by the Commission for offenses involving fewer than 50 marihuana plants was selected as a reasonable approximation of the actual average yield of marihuana plants taking into account (1) studies reporting the actual yield of marihuana plants (37.5 to 412 grams depending on growing conditions); (2) that all plants regardless of size are counted for guideline purposes while, in actuality, not all plants will produce useable marihuana (e.g., some plants may die of disease before maturity, and when plants are grown outdoors some plants may be consumed by animals); and (3) that male plants, which are counted for guideline purposes, are frequently culled because they do not produce the same quality marihuana as do female plants. To enhance fairness and consistency, this amendment adopts the equivalency of 100 grams per marihuana plant for all guideline determinations.

Contrary to those claims, no self-respecting commercial marijuana grower would ever admit his plants produce no more than 412 grams (14.5 ounces) of marijuana, much less that they average only 100 grams. Based upon long experience with actual marijuana growing operations, it is widely accepted in law enforcement circles that cultivated marijuana plants typically produce about one pound of marijuana (453 grams), and sometimes two pounds (907 grams). While it is true that some growers cull out the male plants in order to produce the potent form of marijuana known as sinsemilla, derived from the unpollinated female plant, not all growers do so. And, the observations of the Commission completely ignore the fact that a marijuana plant is a renewable resource—the seeds from one plant can be used to grow several more plants. It is unrealistic, therefore, to treat one plant as representing only that amount of marijuana it can produce itself, and to require courts to assume all marijuana growers standing before them are incapable of producing more than 100 grams of marijuana per plant.

Fortunately, Congress was more realistic in establishing its mandatory minimum sentences. And, for cases involving 100 or more plants, those mandatory minimums trump the Sentencing Guidelines. The result, however, is still a boon to commercial marijuana growers who are informed enough to keep the number of plants in their operations under 100, or under 1000. That is because the interaction between the lenient Sentencing Guidelines and the stricter mandatory minimums produces a stair step effect on sentences at the 100 and 1000 plant marks.

If a marijuana grower is caught raising 99 marijuana plants, no mandatory minimum sentence is triggered. Under the Sentencing Guidelines, those plants would be treated as the equivalent of 9.9 kilograms of marijuana ($26,135 worth, using a conservative price of $1200 per pound), which, for an offender caught for the first time, would result in an unadjusted sentencing guideline range of only 15 to 21 months. With the normal adjustment to reward a candid guilty plea, that guideline range would drop to 10 to 16 months.

In contrast, if that same grower raised just one more plant, for a total of 100, the first tier of mandatory minimum sentences would be triggered, and the court would be required to impose a sentence of five years. The jump from a maximum sentence of 20 months for 99 plants up to five years for 100 plants is due solely to the overriding effect of the mandatory minimum sentence.

Not until that same grower was caught with 800 to 999 plants, treated as the equivalent of 80 to 99.9 kilograms of marijuana (at least $211,200 worth), would his unadjusted sentencing guideline range reach the 51 to 63 month mark, and even then a candid guilty plea would drop it to 37 to 46 months. Consequently, the five year mandatory minimum would probably still control the sentence. But, if the grower was caught with just one more plant, raising the total to 1000, the second tier of mandatory minimum sentences would be triggered, requiring a sentence of 10 years. Again, the jump from a maximum sentence of 63 months for 999 plants up to 10 years for 1000 plants is due solely to Congress' mandatory minimum sentence scheme.

Without those mandatory minimum sentences, the commission's view that marijuana plants should only be treated as the equivalent of 100 grams of marijuana would be controlling, which marijuana growers would doubtless applaud. Only because of the mandatory minimums does the more sensible view of Congress that each marijuana plant should be treated as the equivalent of one kilogram of marijuana impact growing operations involving 100 or more plants.

Ultimately, whether the effect of those mandatory minimum sentences is good or bad depends upon how seriously one views marijuana use. If a person believes a sentence of five years is too harsh for growing 100 marijuana plants conservatively capable of producing between $26,400 to $120,000 worth of marijuana, or distributing 220 pounds of marijuana worth at least $264,000, the mandatory minimum sentences for marijuana should be abolished. If, however, a five year sentence for such crimes seems reasonable, or even lenient, the mandatory minimums should be retained, and perhaps toughened.

There is no doubt about on which side of that question the marijuana growers, dealers, users, and their supporters stand. There is also little room to doubt on which side those who take marijuana crimes seriously should stand.

 **NO**

America: All Locked Up

Tough Sentencing Laws Are Putting Record Numbers of Americans Behind Bars. Supporters Say the Result Has Been Lower Crime Rates, But Critics Questions Whether We've Gone Too Far

In what has become a familiar ritual in federal courthouses, U.S. District Court Judge Joseph Goodwin peered at the young, small-time marijuana grower the kind who once would have qualified for an alternative-sentencing program and gave him five years in prison.

"This sentence seems unduly harsh," Goodwin told the defendant, 23-year-old Bobby Lee Sothen of Cabell County, W. Va. But there was not much Goodwin could do. In the mid-1980s, Congress took the responsibility for weighing the circumstances of drug cases out of the judiciary's hands. In federal courts nowadays, every sentence is the same if the amount of drugs involved is the same. If there is any discretion to be exercised, it belongs to prosecutors in deciding how defendants are charged. The U.S. Attorney's office in Huntington, W.Va., cut Bobby Lee Sothen no slack. He got the "mandatory minimum" sentence of 60 months.

That was in May. In June, a jury in Denton, Texas, deliberated all of 48 minutes before sentencing Eddie DeWayne Perot, a 34-year-old man with a full-time job, a fiancee and a new baby, to two life terms in prison for two cases of drunk driving. The convictions were his third and fourth for driving under the influence, which made them felonies. And because Perot had previously been convicted of two minor theft charges, prosecutors charged him under Texas' habitual offender statute—even though Perot had not injured anyone. He hadn't, in fact, even been in a car accident. But the prosecutor is running for a local judgeship, and, well, that's the way it goes in Texas these days.

"We incarcerate 'em by the truckload," says Ernest Tosh, Perot's lawyer. "We're known for the death penalty, but not only do we kill 'em, we also like to stack 'em deep."

In July, 19-year-old Andre Terial Wilks of North Hills, Calif., received a sentence of 25 years to life under California's "three strikes and you're out" law. His crime? Breaking a car window and stealing a cell phone. Wilks, who had two purse-snatching convictions on his record from when he was 16, had turned down a plea bargain, believing seven years in prison was too much time for a cell phone.

To Wilks' mother, Pamela Jones, her son's refusal to cop a plea revealed his immaturity, not his lack of contrition. It also showcased the capriciousness of the criminal justice system. "There are people doing attempted murders who don't get that much time," Jones complained bitterly. In an interview in early August, Eddie Perot's mom said the same thing. "I'm 61 years old, so I'll never see my son on the outside again," she said. "You've no idea how rough that is."

"An Orgy of Incarceration"

It is tempting to view such cases as aberrations, but they are more common than policy-makers might imagine. As hundreds of thousands of families have discovered in recent years, the United States, in the name of controlling crime, has embarked on a vast social experiment. It is an experiment with no name, only a theory, a huge price tag and droves of statistics.

The theory is that a substantial amount of the nation's street crime is committed by a small number of bad actors, and that putting them behind bars for exceedingly long stretches of time—maybe their whole lives—will make all of us safer. The statistics come in any form you like, from the falling national murder rate to the exorbitant estimates of how many crimes the average felon would have committed had he been out on the street.

The problem with the theory is that it may apply to only a small portion of those being incarcerated. Indeed, many of the statistics upon which the theory is based are myths. But with politicians and the public clamoring for safer streets, there appears to be no turning back. The upshot is that with few dissenting voices and, paradoxically, at a time of sustained economic prosperity that makes America the envy of the world, the authorities are incarcerating people at a rate approaching five times the historical norm.

If local jails are included, the United States will usher in the new century with something close to 2 million of its residents behind bars, twice as many as just 10 years ago. On any given day, one in three black men in several large American cities, including Washington, D.C., is either incarcerated or on probation or parole. Women inmates are the fastest-growing subpopulation in prison, and estimates of the number of minor children with one or both parents behind bars are as high as 1.5 million.

"It's an orgy of incarceration," says Marc Mauer, assistant director of the Sentencing Project, a liberal group that favors alternatives to lengthy prison terms. "It represents a societal commitment to imprisonment on a scale that would have been unthinkable a quarter of a century ago in this, or any other, country. Now, it's business as usual."

The government began compiling credible data on the number of people in prison in 1925. That year, 79 out of every 100,000 Americans served time in state or federal prisons. At the end of the Roaring '20s, the incarceration index had gone up slightly—to over 100. For 50 years, that is where it stayed, with only a few blips. The high point, 137 out of 100,000, came in 1939. A low period came in the late 1960s, when it dipped below 100 and stayed there for seven consecutive years, culminating in a low of 93 in 1972.

Then something happened.

In 1973, the incarceration number inched upward. It went up again in 1974 and in 1975. In fact, it kept climbing every year for the rest of the decade. By 1980, the percentage of Americans behind bars surpassed the record year of 1939. But it never went back down. It went up again every year in the 1980s as well. By 1985, the number topped 200—twice the historical norm. By 1995, the rate of Americans behind bars doubled again—to 411. At the beginning of August, Justice Department figures for 1997 showed yet another increase—to 445. If local jails are included, more than 1.7 million adults are currently incarcerated.

To accommodate all these inmates, the nation has embarked on a prison-building binge. Between 1990 and 1995, 168 state and 45 federal prisons were constructed. Rural counties covet them the way they once did Japanese auto plants. Private-sector prisons are all the rage. The largest private firm, the Corrections Corp. of America, runs 78 prisons in 25 states.

Behind the staggering increase in the incarceration rate are changes in the criminal statutes in Washington and the state capitals. These laws are not on the verge of being repealed, and in some cases, are only beginning to be felt. They include mandatory minimums for drug offenses; federal and state three-strikes statutes; and "truth-in-sentencing" laws, which require criminals to serve 85 percent of their terms before being eligible for parole.

"We've gone on this prison-building rampage," says Morgan Reynolds, a Texas A&M economics professor who is also director of the criminal justice department at the National Center for Policy Analysis, a Dallas-based conservative think tank. "But we've made an incontrovertible increase in public safety because of it."

Is Reynolds correct? Certainly most politicians think so. Or to be more precise, after decades of concern for the welfare of defendants, liberals have essentially thrown in the towel and have become indistinguishable from conservatives on the issue. "Stack 'em deep" has become national policy, and in the rush to incarcerate, profound questions have been getting short shrift:

- Is the increase in the prison population really a key reason that crime has been declining nationally for the past four years, or are there other, more salient, factors?
- What are the hidden social costs of the current policy, above and beyond the money it takes to warehouse upwards of 1.5 million people?
- In trolling for culprits with such a fine net, is the criminal justice system catching people who are not dangerous and for whom lengthy prison terms are a waste, if not an injustice?

"Let 'em Rot"

Violence has always been a defining trait of the American experience. So have the efforts of elected officials to control it. Discussions of deterrents invariably turn into discussions of the root causes of crime. Liberals tend to stress such factors as poverty, the cycle of domestic violence and a lack of gun control. Conservatives focus on such issues as violent Hollywood fare, the removal of school prayer and the degradation of family values. But in recent years, voters have sent an unmistakable message that they don't really care about what causes crime, they just want something done to make them safer in their homes and on their streets.

The prevailing public mood toward criminals was summed up in the headline over a 1994 essay written for *The Wall Street Journal* by Princeton University professor John J. DiIulio Jr. that said simply: "Let 'em rot." In the late 1980s and early 1990s, DiIulio was in the vanguard of a group of conservative scholars who challenged the nation's courts, parole boards and lawmakers to get tougher on convicted criminals. From 1960–80, they pointed out, the number of violent crimes in the United States almost quintupled, going from 288,000 to more than 1.3 million. Property crimes increased from some 8 million to 12 million. At the same time, the number of people in prison increased only from 213,000 to 316,000. Law-abiding Americans were far less safe in 1980 than in 1960, while criminals incurred only a marginally greater risk of going to prison.

"People got tired of that," former Attorney General Edwin Meese III says succinctly. Meese and other conservatives, determined to turn things around, began focusing on policing techniques and sentencing procedures, paying special attention to repeat offenders.

In time, catchphrases and statistics from their work became a kind of litany recited by politicians, especially conservatives, every time a crime bill was up for consideration: Only one out of 100 violent crimes results in a prison sentence. A rapist gets an average sentence of 60 days. Only 6 percent of the criminals commit 70 percent of the crimes. Juvenile crime is getting worse, with a generation of "superpredators" on the horizon. Prison does not rehabilitate. The average criminal commits between 187 and 287 crimes a year while out on the street. And those crimes cost society far more money than incarceration. In other words, prison pays for itself and makes society safer in the process. Locking more people up is not only the right thing to do, it is a good deal.

The lessons implicit in this mantra were obvious: The "medical model" of the 1960s and 1970s, which treated criminality almost as a disease and incarceration as a last resort, was utterly flawed. The solution was judges who would mete out longer prison sentences.

By the late 1980s, this view became a national consensus, and politicians who understood it fared better than those who did not. California Gov. George Deukmejian quipped in his 1986 campaign that when he promised criminals a "California cooler," he wasn't talking about a beverage. George Bush vowed to double spending on federal prisons when he campaigned for president, and criticized Massachusetts Gov. Michael S. Dukakis because a convicted killer named William Horton, while on furlough from a Massachusetts prison, raped a woman and stabbed her boyfriend. In 1992, then-Arkansas-Gov. Bill Clinton vowed to fund 100,000 more law enforcement officers. "We need to put more police on the street and more criminals behind bars," he said.

Funny Numbers

But here's a question often lost in the shuffle: Is the lore undergirding these get-tough policies even true?

- Sen. Phil Gramm, R-Texas, popularized the notion that a rapist can "expect" to serve 60 days behind bars. Gramm also said the average term for murder is 1.8 years in prison. These figures come from Morgan Reynolds, the Texas A&M economist, who arrived at them by dividing the average time served by rapists into the total number of rapes committed. Thus, those who never got arrested or convicted bring down the average. The real figures for homicide, including involuntary manslaughter, is more than 10 years, according to the U.S. Bureau of Justice Statistics. The Justice Department also says that seven years—not 60 days—is the average term for a convicted rapist.
- The statistic that only one out of 100 violent crimes is ever punished is a favorite of the conservative Council on Crime in America. It is also fanciful. The council took the number of violent crimes in a recent year—10 million—and divided it by the number of people sentenced to prison for crimes of violence—100,000. But a considerable number of the 100,000 are sentenced for more than one violent act. Second, half of the crimes in this category—simple assaults without injury—are not felonies at all and thus not punishable by prison terms. The council did not count those sentenced to jail, the common disposition in misdemeanor assaults, or to juvenile institutions. Third, the 10 million figure is derived from victimization surveys. Most of them are not even reported to the police. Finally, even in cases of serious violence, the main reason the perpetrator wouldn't go to prison is that he was never caught.
- The claim that the typical repeat offender commits between 187 and 287 crimes per year when on the street was made in the late 1970s by the Rand Corp. It was based on interviews with 2,190 inmates in California, Texas and Michigan. This study had problems, not the least of which was that it assumed that thieves admitting to burglaries at a rate of one every other day could go a whole year and not get caught. In 1994, Rand itself essentially disavowed the estimate in an extraordinary two-page document that received little or no coverage in the press. The fact sheet explains that in the 1970s study, 10 percent of the inmates were extremely active, committing more than 600 crimes apiece. The typical inmate—the median in the sample—reported committing 15 crimes a year. The fact sheet ends by citing the work of two University of California (Berkeley) researchers, Franklin E. Zimring and Gordon Hawkins, who estimate that California's recent prison buildup has prevented between three and four felonies per inmate per year—"primarily property offenses."

The most thorough study of recidivism, done in 1986 by the National Research Council, produced the estimate that "active violent offenders" probably commit two to four violent crimes a year, while "active nonviolent offenders" were responsible for five to 10 property crimes a year.

Nonetheless, the original Rand figure lives on and on. In 1988, a Justice Department economist named Edwin Zedlewski took the estimate of 187–287 annual crimes, assigned dollar costs to each of those crimes and concluded that the $8.6 billion spent on the nation's prisons and jails was a bargain. In Zedlewski's extrapolations, the cost to society of 187 crimes was $430,000 a year—ten times the cost of incarceration. In 1989, Justice Department official

Richard B. Abell used these figures to argue that "two good ideas" (fiscal conservatism and getting tough with criminals) were not really at odds. Amplifying Zedlewski's estimates, Abell contended that for every 100 offenders put behind bars, society could save about $40 million in costs associated with crime.

Noting that by 1989 the United States had recently incarcerated an additional half-million felons, Zimring and Hawkins responded caustically that if the original Rand study had been accurate, America would be crime-free.

- The claim that crime may be down but "the demographic fuses of America's ticking crime bomb are already burning" was John DiIulio's evocative warning that a generation of juvenile "superpredators" was just over the horizon. The next wave, DiIulio warned in a 1995 Weekly Standard article were younger, meaner and more likely to use guns than their predecessors. Elected officials seized on this dire scenario. Former Sen. Robert Dole featured "superpredators" in his 1996 presidential campaign. Rep. Bill McCollum, R-Fla., originally named his get-tough juvenile crime bill the Violent Juvenile Predator Act of 1996. A version of that bill is still pending in Congress, and Clinton has made several pitches in favor of it. There's just one nagging little problem, however. Juvenile crime has been plummeting almost since the moment DiIulio spoke.

"There's no proof whatsoever of a coming plague of superpredators. It's nonsense," scoffs Jerome G. Miller, president of the National Center on Institutions and Alternatives, a liberal group in Alexandria, Va. "DiIulio misuses statistics terribly."

To his credit, DiIulio has displayed some grace under fire, and an open mind as well. Last year, he conceded that "most kids"—notice he did not say superpredators—who get in serious trouble with the law need adult guidance. "And they won't find suitable role models in prison," he added. Earlier this year, he confessed to being puzzled by the drop in juvenile crime, adding, "This is a humbling time for all crime analysts." He has also broken with conservatives by opposing mandatory minimums for first-time drug offenders.

Fodder for Attack Ads

Historically, this is the way the endless debates about criminal justice work. Theories come in and out of vogue. If an approach proves to be based on faulty premises, well, laws can be changed. That once happened, in fact, with mandatory minimums in drug cases, which were passed in 1950 and repealed in 1970 when the federal prisons were filling up with minor drug offenders. That year, no less a law-and-order man than George Bush, then a congressman representing Houston, Texas, stood in the well of the House and noted that federal judges were almost unanimously opposed to the minimums. "Practicality requires a sentence structure which is generally acceptable to the courts, to prosecutors and to the general public," Bush said.

But in the current contentious political climate, the political system seems locked in place. "The reason is, the most inexperienced political campaign consultant can write a 30-second ad that says, 'Congressman Smith voted to let hundreds of crack dealers out of federal prison,'" says Eric E. Sterling, president of the Criminal Justice Policy Foundation, which is seeking to overturn mandatory minimums. "That can be the end of a campaign."

It happened barely three weeks ago in Georgia. Gubernatorial candidate Roy Barnes, a Democrat, found himself on the receiving end of just such an attack ad from Republican candidate Guy Millner over the issue of crime. Millner's campaign unearthed a 1981 state Senate vote in which Barnes supported a measure designed to streamline parole procedures. The ad does not point out that the measure was in response to a federal court order to reduce prison overcrowding, that it involved only first-time offenders—or that it passed the state Senate 48–0. It just says, "Roy Barnes is soft on crime. And he's too liberal for Georgia."

Such casual demagoguing about crime helps explain why in 1995, after the U.S. Sentencing Commission recommended that crack cocaine and powder cocaine be treated the same under the law, Congress refused to act—despite overwhelming evidence that the impact of the differential has been borne almost exclusively by black defendants. (The 1986 crime bill, voted into law, called for treating crimes involving crack as 100 times more serious than those involving powder cocaine.)

In response to similar complaints about three-strikes laws, law-and-order advocates insist that they have made our streets safe. Earlier this summer, while announcing that California's crime rate plunged to a 30-year low, California Attorney General Dan Lungren, a Republican candidate for governor, estimated that the steady, four-year decline in crime has resulted in 800,000 fewer crimes, including 6,000 rapes and 4,000 murders—and gave credit to three-strikes.

Surely, Lungren is overselling the deterrent effects of three-strikes. But just as surely, increased incarceration must have some impact on lowering the nation's crime rates, as even many liberal academics concede. But how much? Criminologists from across the ideological spectrum often cite two other factors that may have more to do with the downward trend of crime in America. The first is the favorable demographic trend in the country. Overall, the population is getting older. Gall it the geezer factor, but as the proportion of older Americans has increased and the baby boomers have moved into middle age, the segment of 15- to 29-year-olds—the prime years of criminality—has shrunk from 23 percent in 1990 to 21 percent today.

A second, and perhaps more important, factor is the revolution in policing techniques. Clinton often refers to improved policing by the shorthand expression "community policing," which evokes neighborhood-watch programs, uniformed cops playing midnight basketball, officers patrolling parks on bicycles and various other outreach programs designed to make officers a welcome presence in the community. In truth, the greatest success stories in policing during the 1990s have come in cities using nearly the opposite technique, known in law enforcement as "proactive" policing. Proactive policing entails rousting a lot of suspicious-looking characters, holding watch commanders responsible for their precincts and vigorously arresting and prosecuting every crime, no matter how small.

What the two approaches have in common is that they get cops out of patrol cars and station houses and into the community. Both have met with success. Los Angeles, which pioneered proactive policing, has, in the wake of the 1991 Rodney King case, embraced a community approach. So have St. Louis and Denver. New York and Houston, to cite the two most successful examples, have embraced an aggressive proactive policing strategy.

"You have had major increases in incarceration and clearly that helps," says Meese. "But I believe the changes in policing are the most important factor in lowering the crime rate."

If so, then Bill Clinton deserves some of the credit because, whatever he wants to call it, he is responsible for helping the communities of this country get another 100,000 officers out on the street as part of the Community-Oriented Policing Services program he insisted on in the 1994 crime bill.

By that year, Congress was in a well-established pattern of passing a crime bill every two years—every election year. This trend began in 1986, with a tragedy that everyone who was in Washington at the time remembers well, the death of University of Maryland basketball star Len Bias.

From Len Bias to Polly Klaas

In June 1986, Bias was drafted by the Boston Celtics and was poised to make millions of dollars to play with Larry Bird and other legends in Boston Garden. The next day, he was dead of a cocaine overdose. That summer, crack cocaine and its associated violence and health risks exploded on the public consciousness. New York City reported a sharp increase in murder, robbery and assault in neighborhoods where crack had taken hold. On June 27, a week after Len Bias was buried, cocaine killed Don Rogers, a defensive back for the Cleveland Browns. Over the July 4 recess, all Democratic House Speaker Thomas P. "Tip" O'Neill Jr. and Majority Leader Jim Wright heard back home was drugs, guns and cocaine.

"The chemistry to create an issue was there—and Bias lit it," former Rep. Tony Coelho, D-Calif., later recalled.

Back in Washington, O'Neill convened a July 23 meeting with the chairmen of 11 House committees. He told them to fashion a sweeping bipartisan bill aimed at drug control and to bring it to the floor for a vote by September. The $1.7 billion plan passed the House 392–16 and the Senate by a voice vote. The media coverage scarcely mentioned the feature that would be the law's enduring and controversial legacy: the "mandatory minimums" that would fill the federal prisons with small-time dealers, especially those who dealt crack. A crack dealer caught with 5 grams—a handful of "rocks" worth roughly $500— automatically gets five years in federal prison, the same as someone selling 500 grams of powder cocaine.

When Clinton was first elected president, groups such as the Families Against Mandatory Minimums Foundation had high hopes he would champion their cause. They knew Clinton's brother, Roger, had done a short stretch behind bars for cocaine—before mandatory minimums were in vogue—and they noted that Attorney General Janet Reno openly questioned the need for mandatory prison terms for small, first-time dealers. But these would-be reformers did not really know their man: Bill Clinton was keenly aware that for decades Democrats had sounded more concerned about criminals than victims. Clinton thought this was stupid politics; moreover, it was not where his sympathies were. As governor of Arkansas, he had twice been burned by granting parole to lifers—only to see them murder again.

On Oct. 1, 1993, a terrible event in Petaluma, Calif., only solidified Clinton's stance on crime. At 10:30 P.M., a tattooed, bearded stranger walked through an unlocked door into the house where a 12-year-old named Polly Klaas was having a slumber party with three of her girlfriends. The intruder, armed with a knife, tied up the other three girls and took Polly into the Northern California night. It was not until Nov. 30, when a parolee named Richard Allen Davis led police to the murder scene, that Polly's body was found. When it turned out that Davis had a lifelong history of crime, especially sexual assaults against women, grief hardened into anger. Polly's father, Marc Klaas, asked a simple question: Why was this monster ever let out of prison?

The answer was that each time he'd committed a crime, Davis had quietly done his time in prison, been released and offended again in an escalating pattern of violence. Klaas devoted his life to passing three-strikes legislation, modeled after a law passed by referendum in Washington state. He found a willing audience not just in California but across the nation. Five days before Christmas 1993, Klaas met for 30 minutes with Clinton in a session that left both men emotionally drained. "Mr. President," Klaas addressed the father of a girl not much older than Polly, "let me tell you about my daughter. . . ."

A month later, during his State of the Union address, Clinton told the nation: "Those who commit crimes should be punished. And those who commit repeated, violent crimes should be told, 'When you commit a third violent crime, you will be put away, and put away for good. Three strikes, and you are out!'" It was the biggest applause line of the night. But in the end, the law signed by Clinton later that year doesn't require that all three felonies be violent crimes for the perpetrator to be put away for life. Sometimes, one will suffice. This is the great problem with sweeping laws passed in the heat of anger: There's no room for mercy or extenuating circumstances.

In 1988, for example, the mandatory minimums requirement was amended, again without much debate, to include co-conspirators or those who attempt to traffic drugs. Advertised as a tool that would help federal drug agents nab ranking members of the Medellin cartel, it has been used in practice to nab the girlfriends of petty drug dealers, occasionally for doing nothing more than telling an informant they thought was a friend where to go to meet the boyfriend-dealer.

That's what happened in 1992 to Nicole Richardson, a 19-year-old college freshman from Mobile, Ala., whose boyfriend, Jeff Thompson, was dealing LSD when Drug Enforcement Administration agents busted one of his suppliers. When a DEA informer posing as a drug buyer called his house to set up a sting, Nicole Richardson told him where Thompson could be found to pay him for the drugs. That conversation earned her a 10-year federal prison term. Her boyfriend had information of value, cooperated with authorities, got a five-year term and today is a free man. Richardson, because she knew nothing, is still inside.

Even more perverse is the way the gun "enhancements" are being used. In 1994, Monica Clyburn, a Florida welfare mom with a previous history of drug use, three small children and a baby on the way, accompanied her boyfriend to a pawnshop so they could peddle a .22-caliber pistol. Her testimony, uncontroverted by the government, was that the gun was not hers and she only filled out the required federal forms because her boyfriend did not bring his identification. Months later, when agents from the Bureau of Alcohol, Tobacco and Firearms did a routine check of records, Clyburn, who had several previous convictions on minor theft and drug charges, was arrested for being a felon in possession of a firearm. She was indicted and pleaded guilty—and received the mandatory minimum of 15 years in prison. She did not use the gun to commit a crime, never even redeemed the pawnshop ticket. In other words, Clyburn had gotten rid of a gun—and went to prison for it.

"Everyone I've described this case to says, 'This can't be happening,'" says H. Jay Stevens, the chief federal public defender for the middle district of Florida. "The reality is that it's happening five days a week all over this country."

Second Thoughts

Such cases serve as reminders of the huge social costs associated with a policy of incarcerating 1.7 million people. One obvious cost is the burden society is incurring by tearing so many families apart. In early August, Phillip Sanders, a 43-year-old ex-con from West Palm Beach, Fla., was sentenced to life in prison under Florida's three-strikes law. His crime was shoplifting—$49.73 worth of boxer shorts and cigarette lighters, to be exact. He used a knife to cut open the packages before stuffing them down his pants and then apparently showed the knife to store employees when they confronted him in the parking lot. The local paper wrote about the case, but no one bothered to interview Sanders' two children, who will never be taken on outings with their father again.

Likewise, Monica Clyburn's four children live with their grandmother, an hour-and-45-minute drive from their mother's prison. They see her once or twice a month, and have no father who is present in their lives. Their grandmother, Naomi Ivery, 44, of Sarasota, has high blood pressure and a family medical history that suggests this condition is a serious health risk for her. Monica's two youngest children have no memory of their mother not being behind bars. The oldest is a bright 10-year-old named Crystal, who sometimes admonishes her siblings to behave by telling them, "If Grandma dies, where will we go?" Ivery says Crystal is an A and B student who perhaps is too bright for her own good. "She's afraid of having to go into foster care," Ivery says. "She asks me about it all the time. I also hear her cry herself to sleep some nights; she tells me it's because she doesn't have a mother or a father here for her. God has been good to us, but I do know that these children need their mom."

The $30 billion crime bill passed in 1994 contained money for a pilot prison so that nonviolent female offenders with infants and toddlers can be housed with their children. Like most of the other prevention programs in the law, the pilot prison has not been funded, however, and the facility has never been built. In 1991, a Justice Department survey concluded that 825,000 American youths had one or both parents in prison. No research has been done since, even to determine the up-to-date number, and little is done to study these children or to help them.

Another well-documented cost is the alienation of innercity blacks from the society at large. This can be measured in myriad ways, from chronic unemployment rates to the crisis of family formation in the black community. Often, the signs are subtle: According to the Sentencing Project, out of a total voting-age population of 10.4 million black men nationwide, nearly 1.5 million have lost the right to vote. "Voting is what makes you a citizen," observed Brenda Wright, managing attorney for the Boston-based National Voting Rights Institute.

Perhaps most ominous, as more and more young people are incarcerated, prison loses its stigma and, in fact, becomes a rite of passage in certain tough communities. "I've talked to many kids, and they tell me that going to prison is like going into the Army was for the previous generation," says Barry Krisberg, president of the San Francisco-based National Council on Crime and Delinquency. "Prison doesn't scare them because almost everyone they know has been to prison."

Finally, there is the issue of money. In California, 10,000 jobs have been created in the prison system during Gov. Pete Wilson's tenure. That figure corresponds almost exactly to the number of jobs cut in the field of higher education, and punctuates one of the Rev. Jesse Jackson's more memorable rhymes: "Yale is cheaper than jail."

It's not an isolated example. According to the San Francisco-based Justice Policy Institute, state bond expenditures on prison construction in the United States surpassed those for higher education for the first time in 1995. The institute said that from 1984–92, spending per $1,000 of personal income increased less than 1 percent for higher education, while the increase for prisons was 47 percent.

In the last five years, the pressures on states to continue this trend have only mounted. Most of the billions of dollars earmarked for prison construction in the 1994 crime bill are designated only for states that require inmates to serve 85 percent of their sentences.

"We rely more on prison than we rely on early prevention, and it's a very expensive policy," says Lawrence W. Sherman, chairman of the criminal justice department at the University of Maryland. "For every piranha we're getting off the street, we're getting a lot of tuna . . . and may be turning them into piranha."

Prevention or Punishment?

Meanwhile, an increasing body of social science, rarely mentioned in Washington, is emerging that shows it's more efficient by far for government to spend money on a variety of prevention programs than on incarceration. These alternatives include after-school programs for juveniles who are unsupervised in the afternoons, family therapy for children who've exhibited aggressive behavior in school and home visits by social workers or mental health professionals to young mothers who fit various "atrisk" profiles.

Ironically, the most conclusive of the studies showing that prevention programs pack more bang for the buck than incarceration was produced by Rand, the think tank cited as the source for the conventional wisdom that prison terms needed to be longer. Citing the recent Rand work, virtually every major law enforcement organization in the nation has called upon government to spend more for child care and after-school programs. "Political leaders are competing with each other to see who can build more prisons, but the officers who are actually putting people into those prisons are saying, 'We won't win this war unless we cut off the supply line,'" said Sanford A. Newman, president of a group called Fight Crime: Invest in Kids.

One has to look hard, but there are a few signs that policy-makers might be willing to re-examine what they have done. The other day, John DiIulio and former Rep. Floyd H. Flake, D-N.Y., were among a bipartisan group of leaders calling for the repeal of New York state's drug minimum statutes, known as the Rockefeller laws.

In an interview with *National Journal,* even the venerable Ed Meese, a defender of tough sentencing, conceded that the mandatories rob judges of the needed ability to temper justice with mercy in unusual cases. "It would be worthwhile to review the mandatory minimums to see if these `horror stories' are representative or if they are very rare," Meese said. "There is very little analysis of sentencing, and that is unfortunate. I feel that any mandatory minimum needs an escape clause for use in the extraordinary case. You don't want to take all the power from the judge. . . ."

And finally, there is the testimonial of former Democratic Rep. Dan Rostenkowski of Illinois, who truly learned what he'd been voting for only after he saw the inside of prison himself after being convicted on corruption charges. He was stunned by how many low-level drug offenders were doing 15- and 20-year stretches.

"The waste of these lives is a loss to the entire community," Rostenkowski said in a May speech. "That's not a problem many people spend much time thinking about. . . . Certainly, I didn't give these issues a lot of thought when I was a member of the civilian population."

The former Ways and Means chairman went on to express guilt for voting for these "misguided" policies. "I was swept along by the rhetoric about getting tough on crime," he said. "Frankly, I lacked both expertise and perspective on these issues. So I deferred to my colleagues who had stronger opinions but little more expertise." . . .

POSTSCRIPT

Are Mandatory Minimum Sentences Fair and Effective?

The question of whether mandatory minimum sentences are fair and effective intentionally invites mixed reactions. The effectiveness of a policy does not mean that it is fair. If by "fair" we mean uniform, then consistency of sentencing is indeed fair. But if "fair" is to include a consideration of the totality of circumstances of those who commit crime, the answer cannot be as clear. Carl M. Cannon and David Risley present us with some of the dilemmas in answering this question.

Carl M. Cannon provides a thorough and succinct discussion of the purpose, process, and effects of mandatory minimum sentences. By removing a judge's discretion, sentences are proportionate to the crime committed. This results in consistency. As Cannon points out, however, minorities are nonetheless spending more time in prison. But the reason for this is that the types of crime committed by minorities carry longer sentences.

David Risley also discusses federal mandatory minimum sentences, with a very useful discussion of the effects of the federal sentencing guidelines. As Risley points out, because sentencing guidelines limit judicial discretion, they are a form of mandatory sentencing. Judges are not permitted to take into account any of the personal attributes of the defendant. Risley notes,

> While the ideal is that sentences be perfectly personalized by wise, prudent, and consistent judges to fit every individual defendant and crime, the reality is that judges are human, and their wide human differences and perspectives lead to widely different sentences, if given completely unbridled discretion.

Such wide disparity in sentencing is inherently unfair, at least to those who receive stiff sentences for crimes for which others are punished only lightly. But inconsistency was welcomed by drug dealers, since it meant they could hope for a light sentence for serious crimes. That, of course, created a much bigger problem.

Why? Risley points out that drug dealers, as inherent risk takers, gambled on the sentence they might receive from a potentially lenient judge. With judicial discretion removed, what has been the result?

The overwhelming data tell us that minorities are more likely than whites to be convicted under mandatory minimum provisions and to be sentenced at or above the mandatory minimum. This is the result of the more severe penalties upon those who use crack cocaine. Risley provides a useful discussion of the different levels of mandatory sentencing accompanying particular types of drug offense.

So, we have achieved consistency and have once again "controlled crime," but minorities still suffer the consequences of their demographics. And their plight is all the worse because those demographics cannot factor into how they are treated by the judicial system.

A particularly useful work for further reading is Walter Dickey, *Evaluating Mandatory Minimum Sentences.*

Public Agenda Online

Public Agenda Online provides access to public policy research on a wide range of issues, including Social Security.

http://www.publicagenda.org

Library of Congress

The Library of Congress is the paramount resource for public policy and governmental studies.

http://www.loc.gov

United States Senate

The United States Senate provides a useful link to such key issues as committee activity and public policy and legislative issues.

http://www.senate.gov

United States House of Representatives

The U.S. House of Representatives provides a useful link to such key issues as committee activity and public policy and legislative issues.

http://www.house.gov

PART 2

Gender

If we accept the fact that the dominant culture has been shaped by white male–dominated institutions, women, too, although a numerical majority, are a minority. One of the problems that minorities, collectively, face is the tendency to not see themselves as having more in common than that which separates them. The problems of racial and ethnic minorities are often problems shared by women as a minority. And the problems of women from all walks of life are often very similar. Yet women of different racial and ethnic groups, women of different age groups, and women of vastly differing socioeconomic status often don't see their similarities.

There are, of course, forces that exacerbate the plight of some groups of women more than others. So, for example, women living in poverty are more likely to be incarcerated than those who are middle or upper class. Yet all women in this country face the threat of being poor, especially in their old age. All women have had to fight a battle for economic, political, and social achievement. All women face the risk of being abused at some point in their lives. In this section, we address public policy, justice, and legal issues that affect all women as well as issues that disproportionately affect some women. With the exception of social security privatization, particular attention is paid here to the judicial system. Take note, too, that some of the issues in this section could easily be discussed in other sections.

- Is Affirmative Action Reverse Discrimination?

- Is Mandatory Minimum Sentencing Fair to Women?

- Would Privatization of Social Security Be Detrimental to Women?

- Does Gender Affect Criminal Sentencing?

ISSUE 6

Is Affirmative Action
Reverse Discrimination?

YES: Fred L. Pincus, from "The Social Construction of Reverse Discrimination: The Impact of Affirmative Action on Whites," *Journal of Intergroup Relations* (Winter 2001/2002)

NO: Charles Murray, from "Affirmative Racism: How Preferential Treatment Works Against Blacks," *The New Republic* (December 31, 1984)

ISSUE SUMMARY

YES: Professor Fred L. Pincus argues that "reverse discrimination" (i.e., discrimination against whites and especially white males) is the result of affirmative action because affirmative action gives them fewer *opportunities*.

NO: Charles Murray argues that whites are not adversely affected by affirmative action because those minorities who are hired are qualified and would be hired even if affirmative action programs were not in existence.

Perhaps no other issue other than busing has been as racially divisive as the affirmative action program. With its roots in Title VII of the Civil Rights Act of 1964 Equal Employment Opportunity as law, equal protection clause of the Fourteenth Amendment to the Constitution of the United States, and the due process clause of the Fifth Amendment (at the federal level), affirmative action looks to right past wrongs. Its very wording argues for not only the elimination of discrimination in the workplace and education, but a proactive approach in remedying the ill effects of past discrimination and under-representation of groups in the past. This remedial action applied not only to racial minorities, but to women as well.

Keeping in mind, once again, that public policy involves both benefiting and burdening, it is obvious that pro-active efforts to provide opportunities for racial minorities and women would have to be at someone else's expense. Typically, it was the white male who suffered when people of color and women were given preferential treatment. Many opponents of affirmative action, especially white males, have termed this "preferential treatment," "affirmative discrimination, "discrimination in reverse," or "reverse discrimination."

This certainly points to the power of words in depicting the virtues or vices of a program. How can one be opposed to programs that are "affirmative" and help people who have suffered in the past? On the other hand, label the same programs as any kind of "discrimination," and one begins to wonder. Is it *just* to address past discrimination with present discrimination?

Fred L. Pincus poses a related hypothetical.

> Consider the case of previously all white, male agency that is under a consent decree to hire people of color and women. By the logic of reverse discrimination, a qualified white male who did not get the position is just as harmed as the dozens or hundreds of qualified people of color and women that have been denied employment in this agency in the past.

Charles Murray argues that affirmative action is not reverse discrimination. In fact, suggests Murray, affirmative action may be "affirmative racism." We could probably add to this observation that affirmative action may also be "affirmative sexism." How can programs that give "preferential treatment" to people of color and women hurt them?

Murray suggests the possibility of these negative results because stereotypes begin to develop around those minorities and women who "get the job," or "get into the school." The stereotype is that they wouldn't be where they are in the absence of affirmative action. The reality, of course, is that they are likely qualified to be where they are, but perception becomes reality. "New racists" have emerged, argues Murray. These racists are not the racists of the past. In fact, argues Murray, "They are typically longtime supporters of civil rights. But they exhibit the classic behavioral symptom of racism: they treat blacks differently from whites, because of their race. The results can be as concretely bad and unjust as any that the old racism produces."

So here we have another dilemma surrounding public policy, law, and justice. What do we do if a well-intentioned public policy or law, while attempting to achieve one form of justice, inadvertently creates another, perhaps more insidious, form of injustice?

Fred L. Pincus

 **YES**

The Social Construction of Reverse Discrimination: The Impact of Affirmative Action on Whites

One of the most controversial issues in the affirmative action debate is its perceived negative impact on large numbers of whites, especially white males. Public opinion polls show that between half and three-fourths of whites believe that, as a group, they are routinely discriminated against. A 1999 poll, commissioned by the Seattle Times, found that 75% of whites agreed with the statement saying that 'Unqualified minorities get hired over qualified whites' most of the time or some of the time. Two-thirds said the same about promotion and 63% said the same about college admission (Seattle Times, 1999; Steeh & Krysan, 1996).

This phenomenon, where whites believe that they have less opportunity because of affirmative action, goes by a variety of names including 'affirmative discrimination' (Glazer, 1975), 'discrimination in reverse' (Gross, 1978) and 'preferential treatment.' The most popular term, however, is 'reverse discrimination.' The earliest use of this term dates back to the late 1960s and it has been employed by critics of affirmative action ever since. The Internet has numerous reverse discrimination sites, the most sophisticated of which is http://www.adversity.net....

❦

Reverse discrimination is usually discussed only as a racial issue although evidence suggests that gender is at least as important. Studies of reverse discrimination lawsuits show that there are more gender-related complaints (men saying they were discriminated against because of their gender) than race-related complaints (Burstein, 1991). Frederick Lynch (1989), an affirmative action critic, says that he is more concerned with racial issues because "Quotas for minorities have more emotional and political bite than [quotas for women]." If the true role of gender were understood, would the whole concept of reverse discrimination would have less "emotional and political bite?"

From *Journal of Intergroup Relations*, Vol. XXXVIII. No. 4, Winter 2001/2002, pp. 33–44. Copyright © 2001 by National Association of Human Rights Workers. Reprinted by permission.

In short, reverse discrimination is more than just a description of whites being harmed by affirmative action. It is a socially constructed, ideological package that contains an entire set of conservative attitudes about the state of race and gender relations today. It is a codeword for those angry whites who feel threatened by increased competition from people of color and women. Although reverse discrimination is seen as something real, it is actually a socially constructed interpretation of reality that exaggerates and misinterprets the problems that whites genuinely have.

Reduced (Balanced) Opportunity

Dispensing with the concept of reverse discrimination does not mean that some whites, especially white males, may have fewer opportunities for jobs, promotions, college seats or government contracts as a result of affirmative action. In a zero-sum competitive society, if one group receives more opportunities, other groups will receive less. While affirmative action critics view this

Incidents of Reduced Opportunity

Earlier I alluded to how half to two-thirds of whites and males believe that reverse discrimination is common. Some of the polls asked respondents whether they, personally, had lost a job, promotion, college seat, etc. because of affirmative action. When the question is phrased this way, the number of whites and males who respond 'yes' drops significantly to between 2% and 13% (Steeh & Krysan, 1996). These numbers are also considerably lower than the percentage of people of color and women that respond 'yes' to similar questions. In a recent survey by the National Conference for Community and Justice (2000), for example, 13% of whites said that they had been discriminated against in the past month at restaurants, while shopping, during worship, at work or in other situations. On the other hand, 16% of Latinos, 31% of Asians and 42% of blacks said 'yes' to the same question.

Several studies of court cases also show that the number of racial discrimination cases filed by whites and sex discrimination cases filed by men ranges from 2% to 5% of all discrimination cases. The remaining cases involve charges of discrimination by people of color, women, the elderly, the handicapped, etc. (Burstein, 1991; "Reverse discrimination against whites is rare," 1995). Another study of complaints filed with the Equal Employment Opportunities Commission between 1987 and 1994 revealed that only 4% involved changes of reverse discrimination (Reskin, 1998).

Both the opinion surveys and the court cases show relatively few whites feel that they have been discriminated against. Equally important is the fact that not all the perceived discrimination is due to affirmative action. Many whites and men feel that they were mistreated by prejudiced supervisors and co-workers which often has nothing to do with affirmative action programs.

The next question is whether or not the charges of discrimination are actually valid. Just because someone, whether they are white or a person of color, reports that they have been discriminated against does not mean that they actually have. Unfortunately, we can not say anything about the 2%–13% of whites and males in public opinion polls who answered 'yes' to the discrimination question. The pollsters did not get any additional information to evaluate.

We can, however, come to some tentative conclusions from the court and EEOC cases. In one study (Burstein, 1991), one-third of the reverse discrimination cases were decided in favor of the plaintiff, compared to 58% of the "regular" discrimination cases being decided in favor of the plaintiff. In another study ("Reverse discrimination against whites is rare," 1995), only 6% of the reverse discrimination cases were decided in favor of the plaintiff. In a third study (as cited in Reskin, 1998), less than 1% of the reverse discrimination EEOC complaints filed in 1994 were deemed credible. These studies suggest that relatively few reverse discrimination court cases and EEOC complaints have legal merit.

Another question involves the extent to which people who were discriminated against were harmed economically. Herring et al. (1998) compared the incomes of those who said they were discriminated against with those who said they were not discriminated against in different groups. Using a multi-variate statistical technique which controlled for a number of factors simultaneously, they found that the incomes of blacks who said they were discriminated against were $6200 smaller than those blacks who said that they were not discriminated against. Hispanics who were discriminated against had an $11,000 disadvantage over Hispanics who were not discriminated against. On the other hand, whites and women who said they were discriminated against had much smaller disadvantages relative to whites and women who said they were not discriminated against; indeed, the income differences were so small that they did not reach the level of statistical significance. These findings suggest that blacks and Hispanics who are discriminated against suffer greater economic harm than whites and women. Unfortunately, no data were provided for men.

Consequently, we can conclude that affirmative action does result in reduced opportunities for a small number of whites and males. From the data discussed earlier, my guess is that we are talking about less than 5% of the white male populations and possibly as low as 1–2%. This is much lower than affirmative action critics allege. Much of this reduced opportunity is legal, either a result of increased competition or of other legal government policies; whites and males have little legal recourse. Yet, some of the reduced opportunity is illegal and whites could make use of various antidiscrimination policies and laws in order to seek justice.

Conclusion

Why is it important to distinguish between reverse discrimination and reduced opportunity? First, it is important to discredit the entire reverse discrimination discourse with its empirical and theoretical exaggerations and distortions. Discrimination against people of color and women is still the major problem according to the self-report data in the polls as well as the studies of formal complaints. Color-blind policies may resonate as powerful political symbols but they will not solve the existing problems. Preferences and quotas only account for a small portion of affirmative action policies. Using the term reverse discrimination, and others associated with this package, needlessly fans the flames of racism and sexism.

Second, it is much easier to talk to affirmative action skeptics when using the concept of reduced opportunity. Skeptics may be more likely to accept the small degree of reduced opportunity that results from goals and timetables if they understand that it is a result of increased competition rather than quotas. The empirical evidence showing that only a small number of whites and males are negatively affected by affirmative action may ease some of the hysteria caused by the reverse discrimination discourse.

Third, it is easier to talk about the effects of affirmative action on whites to affirmative action supporters. It is important that they not deny that a small number of whites males and an even smaller number of white females are, in fact, negatively effected. It is important to address the issue of what, if anything, should be done about this small group of whites. Those who have been discriminated against in the legal sense have recourse to the legal system. They can file complaints with the EEOC; they can sue universities like Alan Bakke did when he was denied admission to medical school; or they can sue the federal government like Randy Pech did in the Adarand case when he was not granted a government contract due to set-aside policies. If they can prove their case, they can get compensation.

However, what about those whites who have experienced reduced opportunity because of legal affirmative action programs? Hill (1995) offers the following message to white males in terms of admission to selective institutions of higher education:

> These are the concerns that we felt made necessary the policy under which the university is temporarily giving special attention to women and minorities. We respect your rights to formal justice and to a policy guided by the university's educational and research mission as well as its social responsibilities. Our policy in no way implies the view that your opportunities are less important than others', but we estimate (roughly, as we must) that as a white male you have probably had advantages and encouragement that for a long time have been systematically, unfairly, insultingly unavailable to most women and minorities. We deplore invidious race and gender distinctions; we hope that no misunderstanding of our program will prolong them. Unfortunately, nearly all blacks and women have been disadvantaged to some degree by bias against their groups, and it is impractical for universities to undertake the detailed investigations that would be needed to assess how much particular individuals have suffered or gained from racism and sexism. We appeal to you to share the historical values of fair opportunity and mutual respect that underlie this policy and hope that, even though its effects may be personally disappointing, you can see the policy as an appropriate response to the current situation. (p. 190)

Hill is not under the illusion that this type of message will automatically be embraced by anti-affirmative action whites. Educating whites about affirmative action is part of a larger process of educating whites about the realities of race and gender relations in the 21st century.

Ezorsky (1991) has a more concrete proposal. Whites and males who can prove that they have been negatively impacted by legal affirmative action policies should receive some sort of financial compensation from a special program that is funded by a progressive tax on the wealthy. In effect, this would be compensation for sacrificing their own opportunities for the public good.

Neither Hills message, nor Ezorsky's proposal, may contribute to solving the problem of reduced opportunity. However, this is certainly a more constructive way to begin a conversation with skeptical whites than by invoking an abstract, ahistorical call for color-blind, meritocratic decision making. It is certainly better than employing the conservative, misleading discourse of reverse discrimination.

References

Burstein, P. (1991). "Reverse discrimination" cases in federal courts: Legal mobilization by a countermovement. *Sociological Quarterly, 32,* 511–528.

Ezorsky, G. (1991). *Racism and justice: The case for affirmative action.* Ithaca, NY: Cornell University Press.

Feagin, J, & Imani, N. (1994). Racial barriers to African American entrepreneurship: An exploratory study. *Social Problems, 4,* 562–584.

Glazer, N. (1975). *Affirmative discrimination: Ethnic inequality and public policy.* New York: Basic Books.

Gross, B. R. (1978). *Discrimination in reverse: Is turnabout fair play.* New York: New York University Press.

Herring, C., Thomas, M. E., Durr, M., & Horton, H. D. (1998). Does race matter?: The determinants and consequences of self-reports of discrimination victimization. *Race and Society, 1,* 109–123.

Hill, T. E., Jr. (1995). The message of affirmative action. In S. M. Cahn (Ed.), *The afermative action debate* (pp. 169–191). New York: Routledge.

Kane, T. J. (1998). Misconceptions in the debate over affirmative action in college admissions. In G. Orfield & E. Miller (Eds.), *Chilling admissions: The affirmative action crisis and the search for alternatives* (pp. 17–32). Cambridge, MA: The Harvard University Civil Rights Project.

National Conference for Community and Justice (2000). Taking America's Pulse II. http://www.nccj.orenccj3.nsf/Organization/Spotlight.

Reskin, B. (1998). *The realities of affirmative action in employment.* Washington, DC: American Sociological Association.

Reverse Discrimination of Whites Is Rare, Labor Study Finds. (1995, March 24). *New York Times,* p. A23.

Seattle Times. (1999) Affirmative Action National Opinion Survey. Seattle, WA. Elway Research Associates.

Steeh, C., & Krysan, M. (1996). Affirmative action and the public: 1970–1995. *Public Opinion Quarterly, 60,* 128–158.

Wilcher, S. J. (1995). Statement of Shirley J. Wilcher, Deputy Assistant Secretary for Federal Contract Compliance, Employment Standards Administration, U.S. Department of Labor, before the House Committee on Economic and Educational Opportunities, Subcommittee on Employer and Employee Relations, June 21 1995.

NO

Charles Murray

Affirmative Racism: How Preferential Treatment Works Against Blacks

A few years ago, I got into an argument with a lawyer friend who is a partner in a New York firm. I was being the conservative, arguing that preferential treatment of blacks was immoral; he was being the liberal, urging that it was the only way to bring blacks to full equality. In the middle of all this he abruptly said, "But you know, let's face it. We must have hired at least ten blacks in the last few years, and none of them has really worked out." He then returned to his case for still stronger affirmative action, while I wondered what it had been like for those ten blacks. And if he could make a remark like that so casually, what remarks would he be able to make some years down the road, if by that time it had been fifty blacks who hadn't "really worked out"?

My friend's comment was an outcropping of a new racism that is emerging to take its place alongside the old. It grows out of preferential treatment for blacks, and it is not just the much-publicized reactions, for example, of the white policemen or firemen who are passed over for promotion because of an affirmative action court order. The new racism that is potentially most damaging is located among the white elites—educated, affluent, and occupying the positions in education, business, and government from which this country is run. It currently focuses on blacks; whether it will eventuall extend to include Hispanics and other minorities remains to be seen.

The new racists do not think blacks are inferior. They are typically long-time supporters of civil rights. But they exhibit the classic behavioral symptom of racism: they treat blacks differently from whites, because of their race. The results can be as concretely bad and unjust as any that the old racism produces. Sometimes the effect is that blacks are refused an education they otherwise could have gotten. Sometimes blacks are shunted into dead-end jobs. Always, blacks are denied the right to compete as equals.

The new racists also exhibit another characteristic of racism: they think about blacks differently from the way they think about whites. Their global view of blacks and civil rights is impeccable, blacks must be enabled to achieve full equality. They are still unequal, through no fault of their own (it is the fault of racism, it is the fault of inadequate opportunity, it is the legacy of history). But the new racists' local view is that the blacks they run across professionally are not, on the average, up to the white standard. Among the new racists, lawyers have gotten used to the idea that the brief a black colleague turns in will be a little less well-rehearsed and argued than the one they would have done. Businessmen expect that a black colleague will not read a balance sheet as subtly as they do. Teachers expect black students to wind up toward the bottom of the class.

The new racists also tend to think of blacks as a commodity. The office must have a sufficient supply of blacks, who must be treated with special delicacy. The personnel problems this creates are more difficult than most because whites barely admit to themselves what's going on. . . .

As in so many of the crusades of the 1960s, the nation began with a good idea. It was called "affirmative action," initiated by Lyndon Johnson through Executive Order 11246 in September 1965. It was an attractive label and a natural corrective to past racism: actively seek out black candidates for jobs, college, or promotions, without treating them differently in the actual decision to hire, admit, or promote. The term originally evoked both the letter and the spirit of the order.

Then, gradually, affirmative action came to mean something quite different. In 1970 federal court established the legitimacy of quotas as a means of implementing Johnson's executive orders. In 1971 the Supreme Court ruled that an employer could not use minimum credentials as a prerequisite for hiring if the credential acted as a "built-in headwind" for minority groups—even when there was no discriminatory intent and even when the hiring procedures were "fair in form." In 1972 the Equal Employment Opportunity Commission acquired broad, independent enforcement powers.

Thus by the early 1970s it had become generally recognized that a good-faith effort to recruit qualified blacks was not enough—especially if one's school depended on federal grants or one's business depended on federal contracts. Even for businesses and schools not directly dependent on the government, the simplest way to withstand an accusation of violating Title VII of the Civil Rights Act of 1964 was to make sure not that they had not just interviewed enough minority candidates, but that they had actually hired or admitted enough of them. Employers and admissions committees arrived at a rule of thumb: if the blacks who are available happen to be the best candidates, fine; if not, the best available black candidates will be given some sort of edge in the selection process. Sometimes the edge will be small; sometimes it will be predetermined that a black candidate is essential, and the edge will be very large.

Perhaps the first crucial place where the edge applies is in admission to college. Consider the cases of the following three students: John, William, and Carol, 17 years old and applying to college, are all equal on paper. Each has a score of 520 in the mathematics section of the Scholastic Aptitude Test, which puts them in the top third—at the 67th percentile—of all students who took the test. (Figures are based on 1983 data.)

John is white. A score of 520 gets him into the state university. Against the advice of his high school counselor, he applies to prestigious school, Ivy U, where his application is rejected in the first cut—its average white applicant has math scores in the high 600s.

William is black, from a middle-class family who sent him to good schools. His score of 520 puts him at the 95th percentile of all blacks who took the test. William's high school counselor points out that he could probably get into Ivy U. William applies and is admitted—Ivy U. uses separate standards for admission of whites and blacks, and William is among the top blacks who applied.

Carol is black, educated at an inner-city school, and her score of 520 represents an extraordinary achievement in the face of terrible schooling. An alumnus of Ivy U. who regularly looks for promising inner-city candidates finds her, recruits her, and sends her off with a full scholarship to Ivy U.

◆

When American universities embarked on policies of preferential admissions by race, they had the Carols in mind. They had good reason to be optimistic that preferential treatment would work—for many years, the best universities had been weighting the test scores of applicants from small-town public schools when they were compared against those of applicants from the top private schools, and had been giving special breaks to students from distant states to ensure geographic distribution. The differences in preparation tended to even out after the first year or so. Blacks were being brought into a long-standing and successful tradition of preferential treatment.

In the case of blacks, however, preferential treatment ran up against a large black-white gap in academic performance combined with ambitious goals for proportional representation. This gap has been the hardest for whites to confront. But though it is not necessary or even plausible to believe that such differences are innate, it is necessary to recognize openly that the differences exist. By pretending they don't, we begin the process whereby both the real differences and the racial factor are exaggerated.

The black-white gap that applies most directly to this discussion is the one that separates blacks and whites who go to college. In 1983, for example, the mean Scholastic Aptitude Test score for all blacks who took the examination was more than 100 points below the white score on both the verbal and the math sections. Statistically, it is an extremely wide gap. To convert the gap into more concrete terms, think of it this way: in 1983, the same Scholastic Aptitude Test math score that put a black at the 50th percentile of all blacks who took the test put him at the 16th percentile of all whites who took the test.

These results clearly mean we ought to be making an allout effort to improve elementary and secondary education for blacks. But that doesn't help much now, when an academic discrepancy of this magnitude is fed into a preferential admissions process. As universities scramble to make sure they are admitting enough blacks, the results feed the new racism. Here's how it works:

In 1983, only 66 black students nationwide scored above 700 in the verbal section of the Scholastic Aptitude Test, and only 205 scored above 700 in the mathematics section. This handful of students cannot begin to meet the demand for blacks with such scores. For example, Harvard, Yale, and Princeton have in recent years been bringing an aggregate of about 270 blacks into each entering class. If the black students entering these schools had the same distribution of scores as that of the freshman class as a whole, then every black student in the nation with a verbal score in the 700s, and roughly 70 percent of the ones with a math score in the 700s, would be in their freshman classes.

The main problem is not that a few schools monopolize the very top black applicants, but that these same schools have much larger implicit quotas than they can fill with those applicants. They fill out the rest with the next students in line—students who would not have gotten into these schools if they were not black, who otherwise would have been showing up in the classrooms of the nation's less glamorous colleges and universities. But the size of the black pool does not expand appreciably at the next levels. The number of blacks scoring in the 600s on the math section in 1983, for example, was 1,531. Meanwhile, 31,704 nonblack students in 1983 scored in the 700s on the math section and 121,640 scored in the 600s. The prestige schools cannot begin to absorb these numbers of other highly qualified freshman, and they are perfore spread widely throughout the system.

◦◦◦

At schools that draw most broadly from the student population, such as the large state universities, the effects of this skimming produce a situation that confirms the old racists in everything they want most to believe. There are plenty of outstanding students in such student bodies (at the University of Colorado, for example, 6 percent of the freshmen in 1981 had math scores in the 700s and 28 percent had scores in the 600s), but the skimming process combined with the very small raw numbers means that almost none of them are black. What students and instructors see i their day-to-day experience in the classroom is a disproportionate number of blacks who are below the white average, relatively few blacks who are at the white average, and virtually none who are in the first rank. The image that the white student carries away is that blacks are less able than whites. . . .

They do not talk openly about such matters. One characteristic of the new racism is that whites deny in public but acknowledge in private that there are significant differences in black and white academic performance. Another is that they dismiss the importance of tests when black scores are at issue, blaming cultural bias and saying that test scores are not good predictors of college performance. At the same time, they watch anxiously over their own children's test scores.

The differences in academic performance do not disappear by the end of college. Far from narrowing, the gap separating black and white academic achievement appears to get larger. Various studies, most recently at Harvard, have found that during the 1970s blacks did worse in college (as measured by grade point average) than their test scores would have predicted. Moreover, the blackwhite gap in the Graduate Record Examination is larger than the gap in the Scholastic Aptitude Test. The gap between black and white freshmen is a bit less than one standard deviation (the technical measure for comparing scores). Black and white seniors who take the Graduate Record Examination reveal a gap of about one and a quarter standard deviations.

Why should the gap grow wider? Perhaps it is an illusion—for example, perhaps a disproportionate number of the best black students never take the examination. But there are also reasons for suspecting that in fact blacks get a worse education in college than whites do. Here are a few of the hypotheses that deserve full exploration.

❧⊙❧

Take the situation of William—a slightly above average student who, because he is black, gets into a highly competitive school. William studies very hard during the first year. He nonetheless gets mediocre grades. He has a choice. He can continue to study hard and continue to get mediocre grades, and be seen by his classmates as a black who cannot do very well. Or he can explicitly refuse to engage in the academic game. He decides to opt out, and his performance gets worse as time goes on. He emerges from college with a poor education and is further behind the whites than he was as a freshman.

If large numbers of other black students at the institution are in the same situation as William, the result can be group pressure not to compete academically. (At Harvard, it is said, the current term among black students for a black who studies like a white is "incognegro.") The response is not hard to understand. If one subpopulation of students is conspicuously behind another population and is visibly identifiable, then the population that is behind must come up with a good excuse for doing poorly. "Not wanting to do better" is as good as any.

But there is another crucial reason why blacks might not close the gap with whites during college: they are not taught as well as whites are. Racist teachers impeding the progress of student? Perhaps, but most college faculty members I know tend to bend over backward to be "fair" to black students—and that may be the problem. I suggest that inferior instruction is more likely to be a manifestation of the new racism than the old.

Consider the case of Carol, with outstanding abilities but deprived of decent prior schooling: she struggles the first year, but she gets by. Her academic skills still show the aftereffects of her inferior preparation. Her instructors diplomatically point out the more flagrant mistakes, but they ignore minor lapses, and never push her in the aggressive way they push white students who have her intellectual capacity. Some of them are being patronizing (she is doing quite well, considering). Other are being prudent: teachers who criticize black students can find themselves being called racists in the classroom, in the campus newspaper, or in complaints to the administration.

The same process continues in graduate school. Indeed, because there are even fewer blacks in graduate schools than in undergraduate schools, the pressures to get black students through to the degree, no matter what, can be still greater. But apart from differences in preparation and ability that have accumulated by the end of schooling, the process whereby we foster the appearance of black inferiority continues. Let's assume that William did not give up during college. He goes to business school, where he gets his Masters degree. He signs up for interviews with the corporate recruiters. There are 100 persons in his class, and William is ranked near the middle. But of the 5 blacks in his class, he ranks first (remember that he was at the 95th percentile of blacks taking the Scholastic Aptitude Test). He is hired on his first interview by his first-choice company, which also attracted the very best of the white students. He is hired alongside 5 of the top-ranking white members of the class.

William's situation as one of 5 blacks in a class of 100 illustrates the proportions that rrevail in business schools, and business schools are by no means one of the more extreme examples. The pool of black candidates for any given profession is a small fraction of the white pool. This works out to a 20-to-1 edge in business; it is even greater in most of the other professions. The result, when many hiring institutions are competing, is that a major gap between the abilities of new black and white employees in any given workplace is highly likely. Everyone needs to hire a few blacks, and the edge that "being black" confers in the hiring decision warps the sequence of hiring in such a way that a scarce resource (the blacks with a given set of qualifications) is exhausted at an artificially high rate, producing a widening gap in comparison with the remaining whities from which an employer can choose.

The more aggresively affirmative action is enforced, the greater the imbalance. In general, the first companies to hire can pursue strategies that minimize or even eliminate the difference in ability between the new black and white employees. IBM and Park Avenue law firms can do very well, just as Harvard does quite well in attracting the top black students. But the more effectively they pursue these strategies, the more quickly they strip the population of the best black candidates. . . .

⌇⊙⌇

Even if a black is hired under terms that put him on a par with his white peers, the subtler forms of differential treatment work against him. Particularly for any corporation that does business with the government, the new employee has a specific, immediate value purely because he is black. There are a variety of requirements to be met and rituals to be observed for which a black face is helpful. These have very little to do with the long-term career interests of the new employee; on the contrary, they often lead to a dead end as head of the minority-relations section of the personnel department.

Added to this is another problem that has nothing to do with the government. When the old racism was at fault (as it often still is), the newly hired black employee was excluded from the socialization process because the whites did not want him to become part of the group. When the new racism is at fault, it is because many whites are embarrassed to treat black employees as badly as they are willing to treat whites. Hence another reason that whites get on-the-job training that blacks do not: much of the early training of an employee is intertwined with menial assignments and mild hazing. Blacks who are put through these routines often see themselves as racially abused (and when a black is involved, old-racist responses may well have crept in). But even it the black is not unhappy about the process, the whites are afraid that he is, and so protect him from it. There are many variations, all havin the same effect: the black is denied an apprenticeship that the white has no way of escaping. Without serving the apprenticeship, there is no way of becoming part of the team. . . .

〜◎〜

The most obvious consequence of preferential treatment is that every black professional, no matter how able, is tainted. Every black who is hired by a white-run organization that hires blacks preferentially has to put with the knowledge that many of his co-workers believe he was hired because of his race; and he has to put up with the suspicion in his own mind that they might be right.

Whites are curiously reluctant to consider this a real problem—it is an abstraction, I am told, much less important than the problem that blacks face in getting a job in the first place. But black professionals talk about it, and they tell stories of mental breakdowns; of people who had to leave the job altogether; of long-term professional paralysis. What white would want to be put in such a situation? Of course it would be a constant humiliation to be resented by some of your co-workers and condescended to by others. Of course it would affect your perceptions of yourself and your self-confidence. No system that produces such side effects—as preferential treatment must do—can be defended unless it is producing some extremely important benefits.

〜◎〜

And that brings us to the decisive question. If the alternative were no job at all, as it was for so many blacks for so long, the resentment and condescension are part of the price of getting black into the positions they deserve. But is that the alternative today? If the institutions of this country were left to their own devices now, to what extent would refuse to admit, hire, and promote people because they were black? To what extent are American institutions kept from being racist by the government's intervention?

It is another one of those questions that are seldom investigated aggressively, and I have no evidence. Let me suggest a hypothesis that bears looking into: that the signal event in the struggle for black equality during the last thirty years, the one with real impact, was not the Civil Rights Act of 1964 or Executive Order 11246 or any other government act. It was the civil rights movement itself. It raised to a pitch acute and lasting discomfort the racial consciousness of the generations of white Americans who are now running the country. I will not argue that the old racism is dead at any level of society. I will argue, however, that in the typical corporation or in the typical admissions office, there is an abiding desire to be not-racist. This need no be construed as brotherly love. Guilt will do as well. But the civil rights movement did its job. I suggest that the laws and the court decisions and the continuing intellectual respectability behind preferential treatment are not holding many doors open to qualified blacks that would otherwise be closed.

Suppose for a moment that I am right. Suppose that, for practical purposes, racism would not get in the way of blacks if preferential treatment were abandoned. How, in my most optimistic view, would the world look different?

There would be fewer blacks at Harvard and Yale; but they would all be fully competitive with the whites who were there. White students at the state university would encounter a cross-section of blacks who span the full range of ability, including the top levels, just as whites do. College remedial courses would no longer be disproportionately black. Whites rejected by the school they wanted would quit assuming they were kept out because a less-qualified black was admitted in their place. Blacks in big corporations would no longer be shunted off to personnel-relations positions, but would be left on the main-line tracks toward becoming comptrollers and sales managers and chief executive officers. Whites would quit assuming that black colleagues had been hired because they were black. Blacks would quit worrying that they had been hired because they were black.

Would blacks still lag behind? As a population, yes, for a time, and the nation should be mounting a far more effective program to improve elementary and secondary education for blacks than it has mounted in the last few decades. But in years past virtually every ethnic group in America has at one time or another lagged behind as a population, and has eventually caught up. In the process of catching up, the ones who breached the barriers were evidence of the success of that group. Now blacks who breach the barriers tend to be seen as evidence of the inferiority of that group.

❧❦❧

And that is the evil of preferential treatment. It perpetuates an impression of inferiority. The system segments whites and blacks who come in contact with each other so as to maximize the likelihood that whites have the advantage in experience and ability. The system then encourages both whites and blacks to behave in ways that create self-fulfilling prophecies even when no real differences exist.

It is here that the new racism links up with the old. The old racism has always openly held that blacks are permanently less competent than whites. The new racism tacitly accepts that, in the course of overcoming the legacy of the old racism, blacks are temporarily less competent than whites. It is an extremely fine distinction. As time goes on, fine distinctions tend to be lost. Preferential treatment is providing persuasive evidence for the old racists, and we can already hear it sotto voce: "We gave you your chance, we let you educate them and push them into jubs they couldn't have gotten on their own and coddle them every way you could. And see: they still aren't as good as whites, and you are beginning to admit it yourselves." Sooner or later this message is going to be heard by a white elite that needs to excuse its failure to achieve black equality.

The only happy aspect of the new racism is that the corrective—to get rid of the policies encouraging preferential treatment—is so natural. Deliberate preferential treatment by race has sat as uneasily with America's equal-opportunity ideal during the post-1965 period as it did during the days of legalized segregation. We had to construct tortuous rationalizations when we permitted blacks to be kept on the back of the bus—and the rationalizations to justify sending blacks to the head of the line have been just as tortuous. Both kinds of rationalization say that sometimes it is all right to treat people of different races in different ways. For years, we have instinctively sensed this was wrong in principle but intellectualized our support for it as an expedient. I submit that our instincts were right. There is no such thing as good racial discrimination.

POSTSCRIPT

Is Affirmative Action Reverse Discrimination?

The debate over whether affirmative action is "reverse discrimination" (the most popular term used for the concept of disadvantaging non-minorities to compensate minorities for past injustices), "affirmative discrimination," "discrimination in reverse," or "preferential treatment" has been raging since the 1960s, as Fred L. Pincus points out. Regardless of what it is called or whether any of these terms is true, the overwhelming majority of whites *believe* they are being shortchanged in favor of minorities. White males are especially enraged by this belief, since they would also see themselves as being passed over in favor of women, even though, as Pincus points out, "reverse discrimination" is usually seen in terms of race.

Pincus notes that since there are a finite number of jobs, job opportunities, or seats in a classroom, if affirmative action gives those positions to groups who have suffered past injustices, it is only obvious that the formerly "favored" group—whites or white males—are going to "lose out" in the present. The reality according to Pincus, is that whites and males *do* suffer from reverse discrimination, with reduced opportunity critical. The constant cry of whites and the white male is why they should be responsible for what people did in the past. Why should they be the ones to suffer?

Charles Murray provides us with a succinct history of affirmative action and its various phases and nuances. Through hypothetical individuals, Murray brings us the message of how affirmative action has been applied. In the early phases of recognizing that something had to be done to increase minority numbers in education, business, and government, the recruitment effort was the mode of operation. But this seemed to yield insufficient numbers. To avoid suspicion of not being in compliance with Title VII of the Civil Rights Act of 1964, Murray argues, employers and admissions committees made sure that they not only interviewed sufficient numbers of minority candidates, they often gave them the edge.

Murray argues that blacks (and by logical extension, we can add all minorities) actually *suffer* from affirmative action because the white elite assumes that minorities in prestigious positions in business, academe, and government have gotten there not through merit but because of affirmative action. Moreover, referring to "the new racists," Murray argues that there is a tendency to think of minorities as a "commodity" in the sense that a requisite number must be present and treated differently—gently. He argues that "subtler forms of differential treatment" work against minorities. Typically, he says, the minority who has satisfied the quota has little hopes of long-term career interests. Murray also argues that the minority is "left out" of the in-group.

Beyond this, the qualified minority is constantly haunted with being perceived as unqualified. S/he is also subjected to both resentment and humiliation at the hands of co-workers. Minorities seem to end up in a no-win situation.

Three works particularly worth reading on this subject are Terry H. Anderson, *The Pursuit of Fairness: A History of Affirmative;* George E. Curry, ed., *The Affirmative Action Debate;* and Terry Eastland, *Ending Affirmative Action: The Case for Colorblind Justice.*

ISSUE 7

Is Mandatory Minimum Sentencing Fair to Women?

YES: Ilene H. Nagel and Barry L. Johnson, from "The Role of Gender in a Structured Sentencing System: Equal Treatment, Policy Choices, and the Sentencing of Female Offenders Under the United States Sentencing Guidelines," *Journal of Criminal Law and Criminology* (Summer 1994)

NO: Shimica Gaskins, from "'Women of Circumstance'—The Effects of Mandatory Minimum Sentencing on Women Minimally Involved in Drug Crimes," *American Criminal Law Review* (Fall 2004)

ISSUE SUMMARY

YES: Nagel and Johnson argue that recent social and historical events have resulted in race, gender, and class discrimination. They argue that the current emphasis is on the crime committed, rather than on who committed the crime.

NO: Gaskins argues that women suffer disproportionately by virtue of being caught in the circumstance of serving as conspirators to males in drug conspiracy. She further argues that such "trapped" women should be given preferential treatment because of their role as mothers.

Recall the maxim: "Be careful what you wish for, because you may get it." Any group that has been discriminated against and has fought for equality will eventually and inevitably find itself in a situation where having achieved equality works against it.

Is this the case when it comes to mandatory minimum sentencing for women? Is being treated equally under the law equivalent to being treated fairly? Can the strident feminist ever argue for differential treatment? The classic law school answer is, "It depends."

Mandatory minimum sentencing and sentencing guidelines are major judicial reforms. There has long been a concern that a sentencing is a "roll of the dice" because of judicial discretion. Two different judges may impose dramatically different sentences for the same crime. Ilene H. Nagel and Barry L. Johnson cited Willard Gaylin's observation that "each [judge] has a point of view, a set of standards and values, a bias, if you will, which will color, influence, and the direct the nature of . . . verdicts independently of the specific condition of the criminal being charged. . . . These sets of values constitute bias in a non-pejorative sense—but bias nonetheless, and a bias that will influence equity and fairness in exactly the same way as naked bigotry does." In the interests of a more equitable judicial system, the answer seemed to be to remove judicial discretion.

As Nagel and Johnson point out, "These reforms were designed to substantially reduce judicial sentencing discretion, to reduce unwarranted disparities, and to reduce race, gender and class discrimination." Such reforms would thus be viewed as just because of their even application.

But are there ever any extenuating circumstances in which it might be desirable to have judicial discretion? Are women in a different position than men? Should women be dealt with differently because they are often the only parent available, or because they are more likely to live in poverty (and tempted to criminal activity), or because they live in an abusive household, or because they might commit crimes because the male in their life forces them to do so? There is a French saying, "La loi est la loi," meaning "the law is the law." There are no ifs, ands, and buts. But should there be?

Nagel and Johnson argue that mandatory minimum sentencing is indeed fair to women. They also argue that despite the reforms and the adoption of guidelines, women continue to be given special treatment, raising the specter of the difficulty in achieving true uniformity in the system.

Shimica Gaskins picks up the gauntlet for women, arguing that mandatory minimum sentences are unfair to "women of circumstance." She describes a "triangle of women, drugs, and male dealers" who are forced or dragged into situations not of their choosing. Yet, under sentencing reforms, particularly for drugs, these women face long incarcerations under federal conspiracy laws.

In assessing the effectiveness and justness of mandatory minimums, it is important to view their long-term effects on society. Many within the judicial community, including Supreme Court Justices Anthony Kennedy, Stephen Breyer, and Chief Justice William Rehnquist oppose mandatory minimum sentencing. Gaskins cites the views of Justices Kennedy, Breyer, and Rehnquist. Noted Kennedy, "I accept neither the wisdom, the justice nor the necessity of mandatory minimums. In all too many cases they are *unjust*." (Italics added.) And Breyer observed that mandatory minimum sentences are "not going to advance the cause of law enforcement in my opinion and it's going to set back the course in *fairness* in sentence." (Italics added.) And as far as the Chief Justice is concerned, "[o]ur resources are misspent, our punishments too severe, our sentences too long." If such learned legal minds can see the flaws in the well-intentioned reforms, society must re-visit the issue.

Ilene H. Nagel and
Barry L. Johnson

 **YES**

The Role of Gender in a Structured Sentencing System: Equal Treatment, Policy Choices, and the Sentencing of Female Offenders Under the United States Sentencing Guidelines

Introduction

Historically, female offenders have been at the margins of the criminal justice system. Theories of criminal behavior, as well as studies of arrest, pre-trial, prosecution, and sentencing outcomes, have tended to focus on patterns of criminality derived from studying male offenders. This does not reflect a lack of interest in female offenders, but rather the empirical fact that the vast majority of criminal offenders, especially violent criminal offenders, have been male. In other words, the traditional preoccupation of theorists, researchers, and criminal justice professionals with male offenders derives from the gender-skewed demographics of criminal behavior.

Recently, however, the combination of the women's rights movement, the rise of feminist scholarship, and the noted increase in female criminality, has begun to reverse this long-standing neglect of female criminality and inattention to the outcome of decisions involving females in the criminal justice system. And, "a rich and complex literature . . . devoted to the issues of gender and crime" has emerged. A good deal of this literature examines the treatment of women by key criminal justice decisionmakers, such as police, prosecutors, and judges. One commonly tested hypothesis is that when these decision-makers are free to exercise discretion, they systematically favor female offenders over similarly situated male offenders. This pattern of gender-based leniency is particularly evident at the sentencing phase. Female offenders tend to benefit at sentencing from what many presume to be a benign form of reverse discrimination.

From *Journal of Criminal Law & Criminology*, vol. 85, no. 1, Summer 1994, pp. 2–3, 7–9. Copyright © 1994 by Northwestern University School of Law. Reprinted by permission. References omitted.

Despite the recency of the "women and crime" literature, it may describe sentencing patterns that no longer exist. Much of the research contained in these works is based on data collected in the 1960s and 1970s. In the 1980s, however, significant efforts were made to reform sentencing systems at both the state and federal levels. These reforms were designed to substantially reduce judicial 'sentencing discretion, to reduce unwarranted sentencing disparities, and to reduce race, gender, and class discrimination. Moreover, these reforms, at least at the federal level, shifted the focus of sentencing from "offender" characteristics, such as family and community ties, education, and employment, to "offense" characteristics and the offender's criminal history. If successful, these reforms will reduce the favorable treatment previously afforded female offenders, by increasing both their incarceration rate and the length of their sentences. . . .

Neutrality and the Guidelines Scheme

The Sentencing Reform Act embodies Congress' rejection of traditional penal rehabilitationism. The Act: (1) abolishes parole and adopts a determinate, "real time" sentencing scheme; and (2) structures and narrows judicial sentencing discretion through the creation of a single administrative agency—the United States Sentencing Commission—empowered to promulgate presumptively binding sentencing guidelines. The Act's legislative history clearly establishes that Congress' "primary goal" in undertaking sentencing reform was the elimination of unwarranted sentencing disparity. Advocates of sentencing reform repeatedly emphasized the unfairness of the fact that offenders convicted of the same crime and possessing similar criminal histories, received vastly different sentences. Moreover, Congress was especially sensitive to the need to reduce disparities associated with such factors as the defendant's race, gender, and socioeconomic status. Thus, Congress instructed the Commission to "assure that the guidelines and policy statements are entirely neutral as to the race, sex, national origin, creed, and socioeconomic status of offenders." Furthermore, Congress instructed the Commission to de-emphasize the traditional "individualizing" factors which predominated in rehabilitative sentencing—e.g., family and community ties, occupation, and education—as part of the overall mandate to shift from a rehabilitative sentencing system focused on the offender to a system emphasizing the seriousness of the offense.

Rather than articulating a single purpose of sentencing, Congress chose an amalgam of goals it wanted the Sentencing Reform Act to meet. It is clear, however, that the dual purposes of "just punishment" for the offense and "crime control," are of primary importance. The principal evil Congress sought to remedy—unwarranted sentencing disparity—implicidy rests on notions of deserved or "just" punishment.

Crime control concerns—deterrence and incapacitation of offenders— were also important to Congress. Indeed, the Sentencing Reform Act is merely one aspect of Congress' rejection of indeterminate, rehabilitation-based sentencing in favor of a sentencing philosophy emphasizing punishment and crime control. Throughout the 1980s Congress increasingly adopted mandatory minimum sentencing schemes, which completely eliminate the consideration of the individual offender characteristics that were the staple of traditional rehabilitative sentencing. Instead, single offense characteristics are the bases for imposing punishment and controlling crime.

Consistent with the statutory mandate, the Commission promulgated guidelines embodying the dual purposes of "just punishment" and "crime control." The guidelines establish sentencing ranges beised on the offense, the presence of certain enumerated aggravating and mitigating factors related to the offense, and the offender's criminal history. Other potentially aggravating or mitigating circumstances may allow judges to depart from the guidelines' range, but only if they involve factors "not adequately taken into consideration by the Sentencing Commission in formulating the guidelines" and demand a sentence outside the guidelines' range. Further, these departures are subject to appellate review.

In addition to the sentencing guidelines submitted to Congress, the Commission promulgated a series of policy statements which provide that an offender's age, physical condition, mental or emotional condition, and family and community ties are not ordinarily relevant in decisions to depart from the guidelines. The Commission chose the words "not ordinarily relevant" to make it clear that these factors may be relevant only in extraordinary cases. In marked contrast, gender, like race, national origin, creed, and socioeconomic status, is never relevant.

Finally, the guidelines emphasize offense characteristics and culpability factors such as the offender's role in the offense, the level of planning involved in the offense, and whether a weapon was used. This focus is consistent with the goal of "just punishment" for the offense.

The Commission sought to incorporate crime control considerations through provisions requiring sentences at or near the statutory maximum for repeat, violent offenders. The importance of deterrence is evident in the Commission's decision (at Congress' urging) to impose incarcerative sentences for white collar crimes, which many have argued are more easily deterred than typical street crimes.

In short, the 1980s marked a period of increased concern for more equal treatment of similarly situated offenders. Reflecting this concern, the Sentencing Reform Act and the resulting sentencing guidelines embody aspirations of gender-neutral sentencing. One potential consequence of this neutrality, however, is the elimination, or at least reduction, of the traditional leniency afforded female offenders described in section I, above. It is unclear whether Congress specifically intended this result. While Congress was clear in its prescription of gender neutrality, the legislative history contains no discussion of the potential consequences of this neutrality for the overall severity of the sentences of female offenders. As more women are subject to this facially gender-neutral system, the question increasingly asked is whether strict gender neutrality is desirable in the sentencing context. It is here that those favoring leniency come into conflict with those who, for the sake of feminist equality, are willing to forego leniency if it derives from inappropriate values or from gender stereotypes. The next section examines this tension between formal equality and leniency.

The Feminist Dilemma: Equal Treatment v. Special Treatment of Female Offenders

Feminist legal theorists have vigorously debated whether to advocate formal, legal equality with men, or to support special treatment, recognizing pertinent gender differences. Advocates of an "equal treatment" approach recognize that although men and women differ in many important respects (especially with respect to reproduction), special treatment of women entails significant risks, because the laws meant to protect women have oppressed them. As one commentator noted: "[e]xperience with protective-labor legislation, preferential-welfare statutes, child-custody presumptions, and maternity policies makes clear that benign discrimination' is a mixed blessing." The early wave of feminist litigators, such as Supreme Court Justice Ruth Bader Ginsburg, successfully emphasized formal, legal, equal treatment in their efforts to break down the gender-based classifications which acted as barriers to women's participation in social and economic institutions.

In contrast to the equal treatment model, special treatment models of gender equality emphasize the cultural and biological differences between men and women and advocate the need for special protection of women's interests based on those differences. Elizabeth Wolgast, one proponent of special rights, contends that women cannot be men's "equals" because equality requires sameness. Instead, she suggests seeking "justice," which in her view requires special treatment of women in light of their special circumstances.

Ultimately, both "equal treatment" and "special treatment" models provide valuable insights into the public policy debate about the role of gender in sentencing. However, a monolithic approach to accounting for gender is insufficiently sensitive to the contexts in which gender equity is evaluated. That is, whether equal treatment or special treatment is appropriate depends largely on the specific legal issues and underlying factual circumstances involved. In addressing the issue of pregnancy in the employment context, Wendy Williams makes a similar point:

> The question is not whether pregnancy is different (it is, of course—it has its own specific physical manifestations, course of development, risks, and a different, usually desirable and certainly life altering outcome), but how it is different. . . . The focus of the pregnancy debate, as with men and women or blacks and whites, should be on whether the differences should be deemed relevant in the context of particular employment rules.

Similarly, broader questions of gender equity turn on whether differences between men and women are pertinent in the context of the particular legal and policy issues addressed. The values underlying criminal sentencing suggest that it is an area in which the need for formal gender neutrality has special resonance.

Divergence from principles of equal treatment is potentially inconsistent with deeply held notions of fairness in a broad range of contexts. As Justice Scalia has remarked:

> As a motivating force of the human spirit, that value [the appearance of equal treatment] cannot be overestimated. Parents know that children

will accept quite readily all sorts of arbitrary substantive dispositions—no television in the afternoon, or no television in the evening, or even no television at all. But try to let one brother or sister watch television when the others do not, and you will feel the fury of the fundamental sense of justice unleashed.

This fundamental appeal of equal treatment is heightened by the special characteristics of criminal punishment.

Criminal punishment is distinctive in the law because of its condemnatory character. Unlike other legal sanctions (e.g., for breach of contract), criminal sentencing imparts blame on the offender. The extent of reprobation is represented, in part, by the severity of the punishment imposed. Punishing offenders to a degree inconsistent with the nature of their crimes and the level of their culpability is unjust, because it imparts more or less blame than the offender deserves. And sentencing offenders found guilty of identical crimes to vastly different terms of imprisonment seems inconsistent with common-sense notions of justice.

Moreover, the injustice of unequal treatment in sentencing is highlighted by the stakes involved. Criminal sentencing, which involves drastic deprivations of freedom and associated moral stigma, affects fundamental liberty interests. Congress recognized that the very legitimacy of the criminal justice system is at risk if the appearance of equal treatment is breached.

Special treatment of women in sentencing potentially undermines the strong principles of justice and equity that animate contemporary notions of blameworthiness and proportionality. Moreover, a special treatment approach to criminal sentencing should trouble feminists, because it perpetuates damaging stereotypes of female weakness, implying a moral inferiority that undermines claims to full citizenship and even personhood. The blameworthiness that supports notions of proportional punishment implies a recognition of the full moral agency of the offender. Society believes that it is inappropriate to punish the very young or the insane, because, unlike responsible adults, they cannot be expected to conform their behavior to the norms of the law. Only those fully capable of understanding criminal norms and conforming their behavior to those norms are fit subjects for punishment. Thus, when women are granted special treatment, they are reduced to the moral status of infants.

In short, formal equal treatment under the criminal justice system, and questions of the allocation of criminal sentences, touch on fundamental notions of moral autonomy in a way that questions of formal equal treatment in employment rules or insurance benefits do not. In the context of criminal sentencing, those who advocate special treatment of any particular group, or ostensibly neutral rules designed to benefit a particular group, bear the burden of justifying departure from the traditionally accepted norms governing allocation of criminal sentences. . . .

NO

Shimica Gaskins

"Women of Circumstance"—The Effects of Mandatory Minimum Sentencing on Women Minimally Involved in Drug Crimes

Introduction

In recent years, federal courts around the country have seen an emergence of a new type of drug offender—women who are minimally involved in drug crime, but are disparately punished by the existing criminal justice system. These women are the wives, mothers, sisters, daughters, girlfriends, and nieces, who become involved in crime because of their financial dependence on, fear of, or romantic attachment to a male drug trafficker. These "women of circumstance" find themselves incarcerated and subject to draconian sentences because the men in their lives persuade, force, or trick them into carrying drugs.

Between 1980 and 2002, the number of women in state and federal prisons has increased from 12,300 to more than 96,000. The number of women incarcerated for drug trafficking reached a record high of 6.8% of all offenders in 2002. While these numbers are the product of many factors, the "war on drugs" together with the enactment of mandatory minimum sentencing guidelines are the two most significant. National mandatory sentencing policies disparately affect women who tend to play marginal roles in drug trafficking crimes by tying sanctions to the quantity of drugs involved in the transaction and limiting judicial discretion in considering prior criminal history and family responsibilities.

The concern that criminal drug laws—specifically drug conspiracy laws—have a disparate impact on low-level, non-violent offenders has been discussed only peripherally in legal scholarship. Law review articles have given limited attention to a gendered analysis of drug conspiracy laws. In 2000, discussions concerning the participation of women in drug activities received national attention when President Clinton pardoned several women of circumstance. Kemba Smith, one of the women pardoned, received a twenty-four year

From *American Criminal Law Review*, vol. 41, no. 4, Fall 2004, pp. 1533–1553. Copyright © 2004 by American Criminal Law Review. Reprinted by permission. References omitted.

sentence for conspiracy to distribute cocaine. She was twenty-four years old and a college student with no prior criminal record. As a student at Hampton University, she met Peter Hall, a man eight years her senior and the ringleader of a cocaine enterprise. By the time Kemba realized Hall was a drug dealer, she was already a victim of physical abuse. In addition, she was fearful of Hall, who eventually killed his best friend for informing on him. According to the prosecution, Kemba never actually handled or used any of the drugs but was still subject to the harsh penalties of mandatory minimum sentencing. Pardoned after six years of incarceration and a mass media campaign, Kemba is now seen as the paradigmatic example for a failed and unjust "war on drugs."

Drug conspiracy laws have a discriminatory effect upon women like Kemba who play a minimal role, if any, in drug conspiracies. Supreme Court case law permits these women to be charged with the same offense as the principal conspirators and to, therefore, be subject to the mandatory minimum sentencing regime for drug trafficking. As a result, such women often serve lengthy sentences when they might otherwise have received a more modest sentence or even probation. The application of mandatory minimum sentencing makes it highly unlikely that the women who have peripheral roles in the conspiracy will be able to receive a reduction in their sentence. In many instances, they lack the necessary knowledge about the drug conspiracy to provide "substantial assistance" to prosecutors and thereby qualify for a lesser sentence. This Note will address how mandatory minimum sentencing, as applied to women of circumstance, is unduly harsh, fails to adequately meet the goals of punishment, and undervalues the role of mitigating factors by circumventing the discretion of the judiciary. A better and more rational way to fight the "war on drugs" and preserve justice for such women is to return to individualized sentencing under the United States Sentencing Guidelines. . . .

Women, Drugs, and Sentencing

Federal Sentencing Guidelines and Mandatory Minimums

Federal sentencing guidelines and mandatory minimum sentencing laws are reforms designed to reduce judicial sentencing discretion and unwarranted sentencing disparities—specifically pertaining to race, gender and class discrimination. Their enactment shifted the focus of sentencing from the traditional notion of "'offender' characteristics, such as family, community ties, education, and employment, to 'offense' characteristics and the offender's criminal history." Mandatory minimum sentences "trump the guideline ranges" and force the courts to impose specific criminal penalties for certain drug-related crimes. The sentencing guidelines assign a sentence; however, even if the guidelines require a sentence that is less than that which is required by mandatory minimum laws, the court must impose the mandatory minimum sentence.

The Sentencing Reform Act of 1984 was enacted to eliminate unwarranted sentencing disparity by establishing a consistent system of federal sentencing. Under the Guidelines, a sentencing judge can consider various facts about the crime and the defendant. After evaluating the facts, the judge decides a guideline range, for example eighteen to twenty-four months. Generally judges must impose a sentence within the range, however, the guidelines do allow for limited judicial discretion. Thus, in unusual cases, if the judge provides an explanation he may choose a sentence anywhere above or below the range. In order to eliminate judicial paternalism, the protection of women by the court because they are the weaker sex, the Guidelines deliberately take a facially gender-neutral approach to sentencing. Some legal theorists contend that the absence of judicial paternalism results in harsher sentences for women because familial obligations and other factors are no longer taken into account. The absence of judicial paternalism, however, does not disadvantage women of circumstance as much as the law failing to consider the circumstances under which they become peripherally involved in drug conspiracies does.

Mandatory Minimum Sentencing and Female Drug Offenders

Mandatory minimum sentencing laws, established by Congress in 1986, set the minimum punishment for crimes. The idea behind them is simple, but the consequences for certain offenders compromise the basic fairness and integrity of the federal criminal justice system. If a defendant commits a crime involving more than a certain threshold quantity of drugs, the "judge must impose a prison term of five years, ten years, thirty years, or even life imprisonment, without the possibility of parole." The judge must impose the minimum punishment on every offender who satisfies the statutory criteria almost regardless of the facts surrounding the case. Mandatory minimum sentencing "effectively eliminated the ability of judges to apply mitigating factors that would normally reduce sentences for less culpable offenders under the Federal Sentencing Guidelines' system of calculating sentences." As a result, low-level offenders receive mandatory minimum sentences regardless of their level of culpability.

Brenda Valencia's story provides a poignant example of how mandatory minimums do not provide sufficient flexibility to permit individualized sentencing when warranted by mitigating or aggravating factors.

> Brenda Valencia's aunt did not have a driver's license, so Brenda gave her a ride. Unfortunately, it was to a house where the aunt sold seven kilos of cocaine. Though Brenda knew nothing of the sale, a cocaine dealer cooperating with the prosecution for a lower sentence testified that she did. She received a 10-year mandatory sentence, plus two years because her aunt had carded a concealed weapon. The sentencing judge said, "This case is the perfect example of why the minimum mandatory sentences and the sentencing guidelines are not only absurd, but an insult to justice. This young lady does not need to be sentenced to 151 months without parole; however, the law is the law, and we're all bound to obey it. But it's absolutely ridiculous to impose this sentence in this case, considering the degree of participation that this defendant had in the crime."

Tough mandatory minimum sentences for participation in drug conspiracies hold minor participants, like Brenda, accountable for the offense as if they were the principal conspirators. Mandatory minimums require the courts to determine the sentences by the quantity of drugs and the size of the conspiracy, rather than the offender's role in the conspiracy. If a young woman with no prior criminal history is arrested for delivering to an undercover officer forty-eight bags of cocaine base totaling 6.854 grams, the Sentencing Guidelines imprisonment range would be anywhere from fifty-one to sixty-three months, which can be reduced by the judge. However, mandatory minimum sentencing would subject that young woman to a minimum term of five years because the weight of the drugs serves as the basis for computing the sentence. Under the Sentencing Guidelines, Tammi, who was convicted of conspiracy to distribute 2.41 kilograms of cocaine and 510.05 grams of cocaine base, obtained an offense level of thirty-six. She received a two-level enhancement for the firearms found in the search, a two-level reduction for being a minor participant in the conspiracy and a two-level obstruction of justice enhancement for testifying to her innocence at trial. While her husband, Ronald, received 210 months (17.5 years), his mistress received 78 months (6.5 years), and his drug associate in Ocala received 168 months (14 years), Tammi received the longest sentence of anyone convicted in the conspiracy, 235 months (19.6 years).

Mandatory minimums are inappropriate for women of circumstance who associate with male drug dealers because they are involved in intimate or familial relationships and gain economic support from the crime. "Receiving a mandatory sentence for trusting, acquiescing, submitting to, [or being economically dependent upon] the dominance of a boyfriend or husband involved in the drug trade is grossly disproportionate to the crime committed." Recall the cases of Monica and Lisa. Due to mandatory minimum sentencing, the judge was forced to sentence Monica to ten years for a conspiracy to distribute crack cocaine. Lisa's estranged husband reduced his sentence by portraying her as the most culpable member of the conspiracy. Facing a longer sentence, Lisa entered a plea bargain for a nineteen-year sentence, the longest of anyone in the conspiracy. The original partner received nine years and two months, half of Lisa's sentence; her estranged husband received seven years and three months; the twelve other conspirators received sentences that ranged from two years and nine months to seven years and three months.

Thus, women of circumstance who might otherwise receive more modest sentences, intermediate sentences, or even probation, have to serve lengthy sentences for their minimal involvement in trafficking drugs. As stated by the Honorable J. Spencer Letts, U.S. District Judge, Central District of California:

> Statutory mandatory minimum sentences create injustice because the sentence is determined without looking at the particular defendant. . . . It can make no difference whether he is a lifetime criminal or a first-time offender. Indeed, under this sledgehammer approach, it could make no difference if the day before making this one slip in an otherwise unblemished life the defendant had rescued 15 children from a burning building or had won the Congressional Medal of Honor while defending his country.

The problem raised by Judge Letts should be the concern of the entire legal community. In 1994, 42.3% of federal drug offenders were comprised of drug couriers or those who played peripheral roles in drug trafficking, who are mostly serving mandatory minimum sentences.

Avoiding the Guidelines and the Mandatory Minimum Sentencing Regime

1. Substantial Assistance Downward Departure: Unavailable to Women of Circumstance

One way to avoid a mandatory minimum sentence is to provide substantial assistance, as defined by the Sentencing Reform Act, to the government. The Sentencing Reform Act grants a downward departure in the Sentencing Guidelines to defendants who assist the authorities in the prosecution of others. Many high-level offenders are able to avoid mandatory minimum sentences by providing substantial assistance, while low-level offenders generally lack the requisite knowledge. A defendant may be eligible for a substantial assistance departure if he is able and willing to provide the government with information in an investigation. Only those with significant knowledge in drug conspiracies, however, are able to provide information that prosecutors most often deem valuable enough to substantially assist them in prosecuting others. Consequently, in a drug conspiracy, "the drug offenders who are eligible for substantial assistance downward departures are those offenders who have substantial, useful knowledge that will aid the government in the investigation or prosecution of another person who has committed an offense." As many commentators have noted, only high-level, more culpable drug offenders are able to take advantage of this exemption because they have the sort of knowledge for which a prosecutor is willing to bargain. Ironically, substantial assistance departures coupled with mandatory minimums result in sentences that are more lenient for high-level drug offenders and harsher for low-level drug offenders. Professor Stephen Schulhofer describes this as the "cooperation paradox:" "[O]ffenders who are more involved in the drug network and have more valuable information to provide are in a better position to receive a reduced sentence than are less culpable offenders who are less informed."

The "cooperation paradox" is particularly visible in drug conspiracy cases. Low-level co-conspirators have little or no information to provide the government, while leaders of conspiracies run the operations and know the other participants. The highly culpable leaders receive the benefit of the substantial assistance departure by cooperating with the prosecution. Thus, the defendants most knowledgeable are best placed to negotiate sentences while those who play minor roles with little knowledge or responsibility end up with far more severe sentences. The "cooperation paradox" has a disparate impact upon women in these peripheral roles because they usually do not know enough information about the drug conspiracies, thereby placing them at a distinct disadvantage in obtaining a sentence departure. Consider Monica's case: "Two of her co-defendants were crack suppliers and heavily involved in the drug ring . . .; one had even been a violent gang member. By cooperating with the government, they were able to reduce their sentences so that they are serving about the same amount of time in prison as Monica."

In addition, women that do offer assistance are not guaranteed that the prosecution will consider their information sufficient to qualify as "substantial assistance." Stephaney Roberts, indicted for distribution of cocaine base and use of a firearm, agreed to assist law enforcement authorities. Roberts met with and gave information to the Federal Bureau of Investigation, the Drug Enforcement Administration, and several Assistant U.S. Attorneys.

> According to [her] counsel, notwithstanding her significant assistance and the fact that an understanding had been reached that substantial leniency would be accorded to her on account of that assistance, the prosecution ultimately agreed only to permit her to plead guilty to the drug distribution charge which carries a mandatory minimum sentence of ten years, the theory being that her cooperation was insubstantial.

While some argue that a disproportionate share of departures are received by female drug offenders, it is not at all evident that female offenders, who play minor roles in drug offenses and often lack significant information about the crime, are able to provide adequate substantial assistance. The prosecutor and sentencing judge have considerable discretion in filing for and granting a reduction of the sentence, which is often based on their individual view of the defendant. The Guidelines give prosecutors authority to file a substantial-assistance motion; however, prosecutors should have a duty to file a motion when a defendant has provided information that substantially assists the government in making arrests or preventing future crimes.

2. Statutory Safety Valve

In 1994, Congress responded to the concerns about the effects of mandatory minimum sentencing on low-level offenders by passing the "safety valve," [section] 80001 of the Violent Crime Control and Law Enforcement Act. The safety valve creates a narrow exemption from mandatory minimum sentencing for certain nonviolent, low-level drug offenders. The exemption requires the sentencing judge to waive the mandatory minimum sentence and impose a strictly regulated reduction in the sentence if the offender falls within the safety valve provision. In order to fall within the provision a defendant must (1) not have more than one criminal history point, as determined under the Sentencing Guidelines; (2) not have possessed a firearm in connection with the offense; (3) not have participated in an offense that resulted in death or serious bodily injury to any person; (4) not be a leader, organizer, or supervisor of others in the offense; and (5) truthfully provide to the government all information the defendant has concerning the offense or offenses that were part of the same course of conduct no later than the time of the sentencing hearing.

The safety valve's first three requirements—criminal history, possession of a dangerous weapon, and the death or serious injury of another person—usually render the exception inapplicable to women who have minor roles in drug conspiracies. If a woman has any criminal history, she does not qualify, regardless of the nature of her past conduct. This may help to explain why a 1994 study found that women were over-represented among those convicted of low-level drug crimes, despite having no prior criminal histories. Moreover, the Pinkerton rule and the constructive possession theory of conspiracy laws allow for any involvement with a firearm or the death of an individual to be imputed to a woman of circumstance.

Even though women of circumstance, by definition, meet the fourth requirement, they are still required to satisfy the fifth element of knowledge. In order to be considered a low-level offender it must be determined that the defendant has "truthfully provided to the government all information and evidence that the defendant has concerning [the] offense." Thus, the safety valve provision requires defendants to cooperate with the government without taking into consideration the defendant's status as a low-level offender or on traditional factors that have been considered in assessing a defendant's threat to society. In addition, women of circumstance have the increased risk of putting themselves and families in danger by revealing information. For example, Kemba Smith was too afraid to even leave her abusive kingpin boyfriend let alone reveal any of the little information she may have known concerning his drug business. These situations are further compounded by the fact that the burden is on the defendant to prove that the information is truthful and arguably on many occasions the defendant simply cannot overcome the court's credibility determination. The requirement of such assistance as part of a determination regarding whether one is a low-level offender "frustrates the purpose of allowing low-level offenders access through the safety valve to the benefits of the Sentencing Guidelines." . . .

"Is Anyone Out there Listening?"

Federal judges have spoken out against the harshness of mandatory minimum sentences and their effect of significantly eviscerating judicial discretion. Judge John S. Martin resigned from the federal bench in the Southern District of New York in June 2003 calling the criminal justice system unjust because it advocates for lengthy prison sentences for low-level drug offenders "who society failed at every step." Most significantly, U.S. Supreme Court Justices Anthony Kennedy, Stephen Breyer and Chief Justice William Rehnquist have spoken unfavorably about mandatory minimum sentencing guidelines. At the 2003 Annual American Bar Association meeting, Justice Kennedy specifically criticized the length of the sentences, the transfer of sentencing discretion from judges to prosecutors, the racial disparity and the human toll the laws take on men and women sentenced to decades behind bars. Justice Kennedy stated, "While I accept and endorse the necessity and the fairness of the guidelines, if revised downward, I accept neither the wisdom, the justice nor the necessity of mandatory minimums. In all too many cases they are unjust." Justice Breyer stated that the passage of more mandatory minimum statues by Congress is "not going to advance the cause of law enforcement in my opinion and it's going to set back the course in fairness in sentencing." In addition, Chief Justice Rehnquist also stated at the 2003 annual meeting of the American Bar Association that "[o]ur resources are misspent, our punishments too severe, our sentences too long."

The current system is unfair to defendants, victims and society as a whole. In reality, mandatory minimum sentencing is needlessly filling the nation's prisons with nonviolent offenders at taxpayers' expense while offenders that are more dangerous too often escape harsh punishment. In a 2000 opinion, Judge Myron Bright, a 35-year veteran of the Eighth Circuit Court of Appeals, argued that the time has come for major reform in the system and pointedly inquired, "Is anyone out there listening?"

Forgotten Victims: Children of Women of Circumstance

In the end, the harsh consequences of mandatory minimums are mostly felt by the children of women of circumstance. In federal prisons, approximately fifty-nine percent of women have minor children. Although no statistics reveal the exact number of women of circumstance who have children, it is estimated that 126,100 children had a mother in prison in 1999, up from 63,700 in 1991. The increasing rate of incarceration of adult women is particularly worrisome because it undoubtedly involves the incarceration of more mothers.

The impact of a mother's arrest and incarceration on a family is often more disruptive than that of a father's arrest and incarceration because mothers are often the sole caregivers and providers of their children. "The children may suffer from multiple psychological problems, including trauma, anxiety, guilt, shame, and fear. Negative behavioral manifestations can include sadness, withdrawal, low self-esteem, decline in school performance, truancy and use of drugs or alcohol and aggression." Researchers have concluded that the risks of these problems are heightened when parents are imprisoned for multiple periods. Because of stricter sentences like mandatory minimums, federal drug offenders in particular are now serving terms fifty-four percent longer than the terms they would have served ten years ago. It becomes more difficult to maintain consistent contact with a child when the parent is imprisoned for a long time. Studies have shown that mothers experience a significant disadvantage compared to male prisoners because incarcerated women are usually places farther from their homes than men because there are few prisons for women in most states. Moreover, many women whose children are in non-relative foster care may face the possibility of losing their parental rights.

According to a recent study by the Urban Institute, "the long-term effects [on children of imprisoned parents serving lengthy sentences] can range from the questioning of parental authority, negative perceptions of police and the legal system, and increased dependency or maturational regression to impaired ability to cope with future stress or trauma, disruption of development, and intergenerational patterns of criminal behavior." Long-term societal implications militate against the perpetuation of such familial cycles of incarceration. The first step is not subjecting women of circumstance to draconian sentences for their minimal involvement in criminal activity.

Conclusion

It is difficult to draw a firm, yet principled line demarcating how women of circumstance should be sentenced in drug conspiracies because their roles are frequently based on their indigence, dependence, interpersonal connections, and concern for their children. Although these women may have had some knowledge of the ongoing drug conspiracy, in many cases there is little doubt that their involvement in the crime revolves around their relationships with male drug dealers. While the overall crime rate has dropped, the number of low-level female drug offenders has increased. Today, "drug offenders make up more than half of the federal prisoners and account for 48% of prison growth increase from 1995 to 2001."

Federal prisons can barely handle this growth. Moreover, the lack of judicial discretion in sentencing is likely to continue this increase. The Federal Sentencing Guidelines and mandatory minimum sentencing laws are both ways to limit judicial discretion, but the Guidelines are preferable because unlike harsh mandatory minimums, the Guidelines permit a judge to consider more relevant facts. The Sentencing Guidelines, though far from perfect, offer a better way to balance justice by taking into account more factors—including some adjustments for role, acceptance of responsibility, and "extraordinary" family responsibilities. The Guidelines avoid the sentencing cliffs inherent in the mandatory minimums by calibrating drug amounts and prior record more finely, and providing for overlapping guideline ranges.

Most importantly judges should not be deprived of their ability to consider all of the factors that go into formulating a just sentence. There is an increased societal harm from mandatory minimum sentencing because of the heightened problems of having parents imprisoned for long periods. As stated by Judge John S. Martin, Jr., "every sentence imposed affects a human life and, in most cases, the lives of several innocent family members who suffer as a result of a defendant's incarceration." It is "completely at odds with the sentencing philosophy that has been a hallmark of the American system of justice" to allow women of circumstance to be subject to mandatory minimum sentencing.

POSTSCRIPT

Is Mandatory Minimum Sentencing Fair to Women?

The U.S. judicial system, in response to cries to have truth-in-sentencing and definitive guidelines, began significant reform in the 1980s. As Ilene H. Nagel and Barry L. Johnson note, "These reforms were designed to substantially reduce judicial sentencing discretion, to reduce unwarranted sentencing disparities, and to reduce race, gender, and class discrimination." The result has largely been a transference from personal characteristics to "offense" characteristics.

One of the effects of this has been a dramatic change in the way female offenders fare in the judicial system. Formerly, women were afforded more favorable treatment. The assumption was that women were more likely to rehabilitate, that women had children for whom to care, and that on the whole women were more likely to suffer disproportionately if incarcerated.

The irony is that in a society where women's advocate groups have been calling for gender equality and equity, now that the sentencing guidelines are gender-blind, there is a hue and cry that women should be treated differently by the judicial system. If women are to be equal to their male counterparts, how can it be argued that the jurisprudential system should deviate from this goal? They cannot—and that is what the sentencing guidelines are all about.

Shimica Gaskins argues that women who commit crimes are largely victims themselves and that the sentencing guidelines should take this demographic into consideration. Since the Federal Sentencing Guidelines impose heavy sentences for drug trafficking and drug conspiracy and women are often forced by the male(s) in their life to partake in this crime, the woman who gets caught suffers from usually having played a minimal role in the offense. Gaskins relates the story of "Kemba Smith . . . [who] received a twenty-four year sentence for conspiracy to distribute cocaine. She was twenty-four years old and a college student with no criminal record. As a student at Hampton University, she met Peter Hall, a man eight years her senior and the ringleader of a cocaine enterprise. By the time Kemba realized Hall was a drug dealer, she was already a victim of physical abuse. In addition, she was fearful of Hall," and the reader can complete the rest of the story.

Gaskins argues that because women who "commit" a crime are typically involved in intimate and economically dependent relationships with male offenders, they should not be subjected to the mandatory minimums imposed by the Federal Sentencing Guidelines. Gaskins looks to the Sentencing Reform Act, which reduces sentences for those who assist in the prosecution of perpetrators.

Gaskins further argues that mandatory minimum sentences worsen the plight of primarily low-income women who find themselves in the sorry situation of "indigence, dependence, interpersonal connections, and concern for their children." Sending these women to prison, she argues, does little to serve society. Indeed, she argues, society is worse off when children lose their mothers to prison. Gaskins would return to judicial discretion and the ability to view the totality of circumstances.

There are numerous works on the subject of mandatory minimum sentences. Further reading might include Laura Sager, *Let the Punishment Fit the Crime;* Jonathan P. Caulins, C. Peter Rydell, and J. Chiesta, *Mandatory Minimums Drug Sentences: Throwing Away the Key or the Taxpayers' Money?;* and Walter J. Dickey, *Mandatory Minimum Sentences.*

ISSUE 8

Would Privatization of Social Security Be Detrimental to Women?

YES: National Organization for Women (NOW), from "Viewpoint: A Foolish Bargain for Women," *National NOW Times* (Spring 2005)

NO: Ekaterina Shirley and Peter Spiegler, from "The Benefits of Social Security Privatization for Women," *Cato Institute* (July 12, 2005)

ISSUE SUMMARY

YES: The National Organization for Women (NOW) argues that the privatization of Social Security will be detrimental to women. Women rely upon current Social Security benefits and would fare poorly under privatization.

NO: Authors Shirley and Spiegler argue that women will do very well under the privatization of Social Security because the current Social Security system is detrimental to women.

The current state and future of the U.S. Social Security system are hot button issues. Is the system really in trouble? Will it be depleted as the "baby boomers" move into retirement, leaving fewer workers behind to fuel the system? Or is it that the problem with Social Security is the way in which government has handled it? Does a crisis exist, or is it merely a problem, if even that? And if so, would "privatization" of the system protect its future? What, if any, differential effects might this have on those already differentially affected by the system—women?

The National Organization for Women (NOW) adamantly opposes privatization of the Social Security system, arguing that women will be financially devastated by it. As it is, women are dependent upon benefits from the existing system, be they generally inadequate and uneven as a result of the manner in which the system was constructed. That construction is an excellent example of a public policy that became unjust for failure to see the unintended consequences of its provisions. Women generally spend less time in the workforce, since they often take time out to raise a family. Women are also generally paid less than men. Combine the two and factor in the provision of Social Security that one's benefits are based upon amount paid into the system and wages, and women come up short. NOW is concerned that things will only get worse if we were to follow the privatization route. They further argue that those who are advocating privatization are "selling panic and trying to create a crisis to convince people to do something they wouldn't do if they had full information and knew the true consequences of their actions."

NOW's view is that since women still earn less than men, have less money to invest in annuities and are therefore less likely to do so, the end result will be financially negative, especially given the vagaries of the stock market.

Proponents of privatization, such as authors Elizabeth Shirley and Peter Spiegler, believe that women can only benefit from privatization of the Social Security system. Their view is that "[a]lthough the Social Security system is gender neutral on its face, it produces some financial outcomes that place women at a disadvantage in retirement compared with men," and that "Social Security provides less protection against poverty for elderly women than for men because women tend to outlive their husbands." The Shirley-Spiegel article presents an excellent synopsis of how the Social Security system works, and very specifically, how it works against women. Recall, if you will, Rev. Martin Luther King's view concerning laws or policies that are just on their face, but unjust in their application.

The Social Security debate is one that will undoubtedly continue. In moving toward reform, policymakers must seriously consider all of the unintended consequences that may come out of reform, so that greater inequities and injustices are not created or perpetuated.

 **YES**

Viewpoint: A Foolish Bargain for Women

Using a combination of shell-game math and "the sky is falling" rhetoric, proponents of Social Security privatization to frighten us into giving up the only guaranteed family safety and retirement insurance this country provides, while wooing our support for private accounts with visions of big bucks from playing the stock market.

This well-orchestrated media extravaganza has all the bells and whistles of a political rock concert, complete with a 60-day campaign tour by George W. Bush. The president wraps himself in the flag and packs arenas with audiences of the faithful—by invitation only, natch—cheering the carefully scripted stories from "real people." But those rose-colored glasses just make me see red.

Make no mistake. Privatizing Social Security will be financially devastating for women. Without this essential social insurance program, more than half of women over 65 would be living in poverty. It provides a monthly income to retired workers, to workers who become disabled and to survivors of deceased workers. It is time-tested, extremely cost-efficient and, most importantly, it works. Fortunately, the public is becoming more skeptical, not less.

Make no mistake. Privatizing Social Security will be financially devastating for women. Without this essential social insurance program, more than half of women over 65 would be living in poverty. It provides a monthly income to retired workers, to workers who become disabled and to survivors of deceased workers. It is time-tested, extremely cost-efficient and, most importantly, it works. Fortunately, the public is becoming more skeptical, not less.

Just What Are Privatizers Selling?

They are selling panic and trying to create a sense of crisis to convince people to do something they wouldn't do if they had full information and knew the true consequences of their actions (think: weapons of mass destruction).

In selling a vaguely defined "plan," President Bush and other administration representatives gloss over their own fiscally irresponsible decisions, like the

Medicare prescription drug boondoggle and the administration's tax-cuts, not to mention the Iraq war, and how those decisions have helped run up the largest deficit in history. Then they want to use the very deficit they've created as an excuse to undermine Social Security.

Bush's rather fuzzy plan, which is difficult to separate from the spin, seems to be based on these ideas:

Drastically cut Social Security's promised benefits for workers under age 55—cuts of 30 percent by 2045, 45 percent by 2065—and trust that workers will be able to make up the difference by putting a portion of their payroll taxes into private accounts to be invested in Wall Street.

When a worker retires, she or he will be required to pay back the government some portion of that money and use the rest to purchase a private annuity with a monthly payout—hopefully enough to supplement the reduced Social Security check if the market hasn't crashed lately.

Those under age 55 who choose not to participate will still have their Social Security benefits cut—so the "opt out" is really not a choice at all.

Bush's most recent proposal includes reducing benefits to workers making $25,000 or more a year in 2012 dollars ($20,000 in today's dollars). Workers earning below that would receive the same level of benefits promised under the current system—not an increase as has been reported.

Does Privatization Work?

Not for workers, and not for women. I was a math major in college and my first job was in forecasting and statistics—so I've looked at the numbers carefully. And it's clear to me that Bush's rhetoric about Social Security just doesn't add up. It was enough to get me to pull out my old paper-back of the classic book "Lies, Damned Lies, and Statistics." Here are just a few of the important points to consider:

The cost of managing private accounts cuts deeply into any profit that might come from them. Management fees for private accounts will be 20 to 30 times higher than the modest cost of Social Security management.

Currently Social Security provides a guaranteed, inflation-adjusted income for the worker's entire retirement. When workers divert a significant part of their Social Security tax into a private account, their monthly check from Social Security will be substantially reduced. In order for private accounts to supplement those reduced benefits, workers would have to buy a lifetime annuity with their private accounts when they retire.

Annuities discriminate against women. Because women statistically live longer than men, private annuities provide less annual income for women. In fact, most women don't actually live longer than men—only about 15 percent do—but the other 85 percent of women (whose life expectancies are similar to men's) still pay the price with lower annuities and pensions based on the longevity of a few.

The stock market is inherently risky. Should the stock market take a nosedive—as it always does from time to time—there will be no way to take so much private retirement account money out of the market. And if a worker is unfortunate enough to retire during a downturn, her account will be worth much less than expected.

Not only does privatization put workers' retirement funds at the mercy of the market, but it will take $2 to $5 trillion to implement this plan—that's right, $2 trillion or more just for the transition costs! Bush's domestic and international policies have drained U.S. coffers and our government simply does not have a few trillion "to spare." We'll have to borrow it—increasing our debt and cutting social programs to pay the price.

So Who Does Privatization Benefit?

It certainly works for Wall Street. That $2 trillion or more would go directly into the pockets of private companies who will provide the management of the private accounts.

It also works for large corporations favored by the government. In some privatization plans that have been suggested, workers would have the choice of four to five government-chosen funds to invest in. The government would decide which funds get this huge windfall of private investment capital, a situation that is rife with possibilities for corruption.

The bottom line is this: women depend on Social Security more than men do. Women are less likely to receive pensions from employers—the average pension for a woman is less than half of the average pension for a man. Wage discrimination—women still make only 76 cents to every man's dollar—and time out of the workforce for care giving make it more difficult to save an adequate amount of money for retirement. Social Security is simply vital for women's financial stability in their golden years.

Social Security is a progressive program and this is particularly important to women. People who make less money over their lifetimes get a higher percentage of their earnings in a monthly check when they retire. This works entirely to women's advantage and the advantage would be lost in a program of private accounts.

Privatization of Social Security is foolish and irresponsible, and women aren't buying it. We weren't born Democratic, Republican or yesterday.

NO

Ekaterina Shirley and
Peter Spiegler

The Benefits of Social Security Privatization for Women

Executive Summary

The economic case for privatization as a response to Social Security's insolvency problems has been made extensively in the academic and policy literature. How privatization would affect various social groups, however, has remained largely unaddressed. There are reasons to be especially concerned about the impact of reform on women. Women are known to be disproportionately dependent on Social Security benefits in their old age and because of longer life expectancy and employment patterns, an elderly woman is twice as likely to be living in poverty as is an elderly man.

Although the Social Security system is gender neutral on its face, it produces some financial outcomes that place women at a disadvantage in retirement compared with men.

- The employment patterns of women, characterized by fewer years in the labor force, lower earnings, and more frequent job changes, translate into lower Social Security benefits.
- The dual-entitlement rules of the system often impose a penalty on wives and widows of two-earner couples.
- The loss of up to 50 percent of a couple's benefit at the husband's death throws every fifth widow into poverty.

Those outcomes are exacerbated by women's disproportionate dependence on Social Security benefits. As a result of low private asset accumulation and inadequate or absent supplementary pension coverage, on average, nonmarried women over 65 rely on Social Security for 72 percent of their retirement income. Forty percent of that group rely on Social Security for 90 percent or more of their retirement income.

Contrary to some criticisms raised in the course of the Social Security reform debate, our analysis demonstrated that privatization of Social Security in fact would offer tangible financial benefits to women. If higher rates of return are realized on investments in the private capital markets, privatization is likely to boost the retirement savings of both men and women. Indeed, this study finds that

- Virtually all women would be better off (most *significantly*) under a system of individually owned, privately invested accounts than under the current Social Security system.
- A fully privatized Social Security system with earnings sharing between spouses provides greater benefits to women than does a partially privatized, two-tiered system.
- Contributions to personal accounts could be reduced to as little as 7 percent of covered earnings and still provide all categories of women (single, divorced, married, widowed) with significantly higher retirement benefits than does Social Security. That would allow the remaining 5.4 percent of the current payroll tax to be used to provide disability benefits, help finance transition costs, protect against market risk, or even provide a tax cut at some point in the future.

Introduction

As a result of the pressing need for Social Security reform, there is an unprecedented opportunity to make comprehensive changes to the current system. Privatization, in some form, has attracted much support because of its potential to effectively address the system's solvency issues while providing higher rates of return to retirees.

In assessing the merits of privatization as a reform tool, it is important to recognize that it would affect different groups in society differently. There are reasons to be especially concerned about the impact of reform on women. Women are known to be disproportionately dependent on Social Security benefits in their old age; and because of longer life expectancy and gender differences in employment patterns, an elderly woman is twice as likely to be living in poverty as is an elderly man. The poverty rates are especially high among widows (20.2 percent) and divorced, separated, or never-married women over 65 (27.4 percent) compared with those in corresponding groups of men, 12.1 and 18.7 percent respectively. The rules of the current system exacerbate those difficulties. Although Social Security does not penalize women explicitly, because of demographic factors and the different roles of men and women in families, women ultimately are economically disadvantaged by the system.

As the country moves toward a policy choice on Social Security reform, it is crucially important to understand how the proposed alternatives, and privatization in particular, would affect women's well-being. We have assessed the potential benefits of privatization for women by focusing on two groups of questions: First, what are the flaws of the existing system in its treatment of women, and how do the privatization proposals address those flaws? Second, what features should a private system incorporate in order to take account of the special needs of female participants—needs associated with their earnings, employment patterns, family roles, and longevity—and to guarantee adequate and equitable protection to women?

Social Security's Unfair Treatment of Women

Social Security's provisions are "gender neutral" in that benefits for women are calculated using exactly the same rules that are used to calculate benefits for men. That legal equality, however, has led to de facto inequality due to differences between men and women in wages, employment patterns, family roles, and longevity. On average, women earn less and change jobs more frequently than do men. They take more time out of the labor force for childbearing and childrearing and for managing a wide range of family emergencies. In addition, living longer than men, on average, makes women more dependent on retirement benefits for a longer period of time. As a result of those gender-driven differences, the Social Security program produces some negative outcomes for women. Some of the most serious effects are the following:

- **Women receive lower benefits than men.** As a result of lower earnings and fewer years of work, women, on average, earn fewer Social Security benefits than do men. For instance, in 1995 a retired male worker received $810 in monthly benefits, while a retired female worker received only $621, on average.
- **Divorcée benefits may be inadequate.** Benefits for divorced spouses, which comprise only 50 percent of the former spouse's worker benefit, may not be adequate to support a woman living alone. The average monthly benefit for a divorced spouse in 1995 was only $372.
- **Two-earner couples and widows of two-earner couples are penalized.** Due to lower (or absent) spousal benefits received by some working wives under current "dual-entitlement" rules, combined benefits for some two-earner couples can be lower by as much as one-third than are those for one-earner couples with identical average lifetime earnings (and other relevant characteristics such as age). The widow's benefit for the survivor of a two-earner couple may be as little as one-half of what the couple had been receiving.
- **Social Security may discourage work.** A married woman who works and pays Social Security taxes might not receive more benefits than she would if she had never worked and received only a spousal benefit.

Those aspects of the current system are especially damaging for women, because they are disproportionately dependent on Social Security for their retirement income for the following reasons:

- **Women are less likely to have independent private savings.** Lower earnings impair women's ability to accumulate individual, private savings for retirement.
- **Women are less likely to have supplementary private pensions.** Women are less likely than men both to qualify for employer-provided pension plans and to work for employers who offer those retirement plans.
- **Women's longer life expectancy requires more retirement income.** Given amounts of individual retirement savings might be sufficient for men but not for women who tend to live longer and, thus, incur more postretirement living expenses.

Those factors result in an alarmingly high incidence of poverty among elderly women. Poverty rates for women aged 65 and over (14.9 percent) are twice as high as for elderly men (7.2 percent). In addition, the female poverty rate increases with age—20.2 percent of women over 85 are poor.

Women Receive Lower Retirement Benefits

The tendency of women to take more time out of the workforce and to seek part-time work results in lower lifetime earnings and incomplete lifetime earnings records, which translate into lower Social Security benefits. Although female labor force participation rates have grown and the gender gap between earnings of men and women has narrowed in recent decades, the gender differences remain significant. . . .

An important link between those labor force trends and lower Social Security benefits is the manner in which benefits are calculated. Currently, a worker's 35 years of highest annual earnings are used for benefit computation. Clearly, lower lifetime earnings will lead to lower benefits. Lower benefits also result from incomplete earnings records, however, which are the result of years spend out of the official workforce. Benefits are computed on the basis of the worker's 35 years of highest earnings, and any years short of 35 count as zero. That affects women disproportionately. The median number of years with zero earnings for workers turning 62 and 1993 was 4 for men and 15 for women. Some of the currently debated proposals for reforming Social Security argue for further extending the computation period to 38 years. Although women's labor force participation is increasing, the Social Security Administration forecasts that fewer than 30 percent of women retiring in 2020 will have 38 years of covered earnings, compared with almost 60 percent of men.

The tendency to earn lower benefits is especially problematic because many retired women (38 percent in 1993) draw Social Security benefits based only on their own employment records. Of particular concern is the group of unmarried women who either never married or were divorced after one or more marriages that lasted for less than 10 years, the minimum term required for divorcées to qualify for spousal or survivor benefits. It is important to note that divorced wives are entitled to a benefit of only 50 percent of their ex-husbands' worker benefit amount. The poverty rate observed in the group of elderly divorced, separated, or never-married women (27.4 percent) is the highest of all demographic groups.

Social Security Penalizes Two-Earner Couples

The provisions of the 1935 Social Security Act were based on the principle of "individual equity": only those who contribute to the program should receive benefits, and individual benefit levels should relate to individual earnings levels. Since then, Congress has sought to support families of covered workers also. The 1939 amendments extended benefits to workers' wives, widows, eligible children, and, in a few instances, parents.

As a result of those amendments, some individuals became "dually entitled"—that is, entitled to benefits both as a retired worker and as the spouse (or surviving spouse) of another worker. Dually entitled beneficiaries, however, do not receive the sum of those two benefits. Rather, they receive (1) the retired worker benefit they earned, and (2) the difference, if any, between that benefit and the benefit they would receive as a spouse or survivor. In effect, they receive either their own earned benefit or their spousal (or survivor) benefit, whichever is greater. The spousal benefit is currently 50 percent of the spouse's worker benefit, while the survivor's benefit is 100 percent of the deceased worker's benefit.

As more and more women have entered the labor force, it has become increasingly apparent that the dual-entitlement rule produces many unintended negative results. For example:

- Couples with only one worker may receive more benefits than couples with the same total earnings earned by two workers.
- Wives may not receive more benefits as a result of working than they receive on the basis of their husband's earnings. . . .

Because women tend to have lower lifetime earnings and longer life expectancies than men, they are much more likely than men to qualify for spousal and survivor benefits and, thus, to be affected by the dual-entitlement classification. Women at present account for 99 percent of beneficiaries who receive spousal or survivor benefits. As a result, the program's treatment of two-earner couples is generally perceived as a women's issue.

Poverty among Elderly Women

About 64 percent of all elderly women who live in poverty are widows. Although poverty rates are higher for divorced, separated, or never-married women (27.4 percent), those groups make up a small proportion of the elderly population.

Social Security provides less protection against poverty for elderly women than for men because women tend to outlive their husbands and Social Security's survivor benefit rules can leave widows with up to 50 percent less income than the couple was receiving when the husband was alive. That is one reason why the poverty rate for widows is 20.2 percent, 1.7 times greater than for widowers (12.1 percent) and four times greater than for married couples (5 percent).

The amount a widow receives from Social Security depends on how earnings were split between husband and wife. Generally, the more of the couple's earnings the widow earned, the smaller the share of the couple's retirement benefit she receives after he dies. . . . [The] wife who did not work (couple A) will receive two-thirds of the couple's retirement benefit when she becomes a widow. The wife who worked and earned half the couple's earnings (couple C) will get only half the couple's benefits as a widow. Moreover, of the three couples, the one-earner couple A was not only receiving the highest retirement benefits when the husband was alive ($860), but also the surviving wife receives the highest widow benefit in absolute terms. . . .

Thus, a widow's benefit may be as little as one-half of what the couple had been receiving, but living expenses do not drop by half when a husband dies. That is seen clearly by the fact that the poverty line for couples age 65 and older was $9,219 (in 1995), while that for an individual age 65 and older was $7,309—only about 20 percent less than that for couples. The substantial decrease in Social Security income constitutes one of the major causes of poverty among elderly widows.

The Social Security program, as it was enacted in 1935, was intended to provide some "floor protection" in retirement that would be supplemented by personal savings and private pensions. Many elderly women rely on Social Security as their primary source of retirement income, however. Nonmarried women over 65 rely on Social Security for 72 percent of their retirement income, on average (men for 65 percent and married couples for 55 percent). Forty percent of nonmarried women over 65 rely on Social Security for 90 percent or more of their retirement income (29 percent of men and 18 percent of married couples).

There are two main reasons for that dependence. First, elderly women, on average, do not have sufficient private savings to support themselves. Earning less money makes it more difficult for women to save for anything, including retirement. A telephone survey by Merrill Lynch Consulting in 1993 found that only 30 percent of women, compared with 47 percent of men, between ages 25 and 65 are saving for retirement. The female respondents' average total personal savings were $25,700 compared with $52,500 for men. One study found that in 1994 the median annual income from assets for nonmarried women age 65 and over was only $860, compared with $1,249 for nonmarried men and $2,039 for married couples. Second, only a small percentage of elderly women (18 percent, compared with 34 percent of men) received private pensions or annuities. The median annual private pension and annuity income of women was only $2,682 compared with $5,731 for men. Moreover, women who do receive private pensions find their income streams more susceptible to the effects of inflation. Fewer than 5 percent of participants receiving retirement payments from defined benefit plans have those benefits adjusted for inflation through periodic "cost of living adjustments," or COLAs. Because women live longer than men, the impact of inflation is greater for them.

Despite the dramatic increase in women's workforce participation, their access to and participation in pension plans have not increased at the same rate. More than half of American women working full-time, and almost all of those working in part-time or temporary jobs, work for employers who do not provide retirement benefits over and above Social Security. The major reason is that women are concentrated in low-wage, service, part-time, nonunion, and small-firm jobs where pension coverage is less common.

Most employer-provided (defined-benefit) retirement plans require an employee to work for the firm for at least five years for at least 1,000 hours a year before the employee is legally entitled to any pension benefit, regardless of further attachment to the company. In addition, many employers require that an employee work a full year before being eligible to join a retirement plan. Ironically, women over 25 stay with an employer an average of only 4.8 years, compared with an average of 6.6 years for men. Thus, a female employee who in her lifetime held five different jobs could lose not only five years of benefits built up over her career but also the benefits accrued for jobs held for fewer than five years. Therefore, working part-time, changing jobs, and taking time out of the workforce—typical in women's careers—have a dramatic and disproportionate effect on employer-provided retirement benefits and ultimately contribute to female dependence on Social Security income.

The Benefits of Privatization for Women

Given the shortcomings of the current system, it is crucial that the debate over reform of Social Security take into account the likely impact of any Social Security reform on women. That is particularly true of fundamental changes to the system such as privatization, which would transform Social Security into a system of individually owned, privately invested accounts, similar to individual retirement accounts or 401(k) plans.

An example of a straightforward privatization model is the Mandatory Individual Retirement Account (MIRA) proposed by Harvard University's Martin Feldstein and Dartmouth University's Andrew Samwick. Under that plan, each individual would contribute a mandatory amount of payroll into a private account, would have some degree of choice about how it could be invested, and would own the account at retirement. The plan is attractive for two reasons. First, moving the retirement benefit system from a pay-as-you-go basis to a fully funded basis would in effect release an enormous amount of previously unproductive capital for productive investment. Second, it would entail a much higher rate of return on retirement savings, which would greatly enhance the well-being of average workers. As MIT's Peter Diamond explains, "In a steady state the rate of return to participants in a strictly pay-as-you-go Social Security system is the rate of growth of the economy, while the rate of return in a fully funded system is the rate of interest." Between 1960 and 1995 the average rate of growth of the economy was 2.5 percent, whereas the pretax return on private capital (the relevant interest rate for purposes of invested MIRA funds) averaged 9.3 percent for the period from 1960 to 1994 and is currently estimated to be 6.2 percent. For a given average level of retirement benefits, then, the contribution rate could be much lower. Feldstein and Samwick estimate that a payroll tax of approximately 2 percent under a MIRA plan would provide the same average level of benefits currently provided under Social Security.

Despite those potential benefits, however, the MIRA raises questions about privatization's impact on women. First, because women generally have lower earnings than men, and since an individual's retirement income would be determined almost entirely by the amount contributed over one's lifetime, women may receive relatively lower benefits than men. Second, depending on how much freedom an individual has to choose how to invest her MIRA, her investment behavior could become a key determinant of her retirement benefits. Women tend to be more conservative investors than men, so, on average, women might see lower returns to their investments, exacerbating the disadvantage of lower lifetime income. Third, because an individual's retirement income is generated entirely from personal contributions that are personal property, married women who interrupt or curtail their careers may find themselves largely or completely dependent in retirement on their husbands' retirement savings and spending behavior.

Whether those problems outweigh the benefits of privatization for women is debatable. It is possible, however, to design a privatized Social Security system with safeguards to protect lower wage earners, to ensure that married women's welfare in retirement is not vulnerable to their husbands' spending habits, and to mitigate the penalty for time taken away from work for family reasons. Two possible ways to address those concerns are the "double-decker" and "earnings sharing" approaches. . . .

POSTSCRIPT

Would Privatization of Social Security Be Detrimental to Women?

President George W. Bush's efforts to privatize Social Security may affect various groups in society in different ways. Some argue that women as a whole may fare poorly as a result of privatization. Others view women as being substantially better off if privatization were to take place.

The first view is one held by the National Organization for Women (NOW). The organization's position is that Social Security as it stands provides women with "guaranteed family safety and retirement insurance," and that "women depend more upon Social Security than do men." They argue that the Bush privatization initiative "has all the bells and whistles of a political rock concert" with the President leading the band. They also argue that advocates of privatization are using panic and scare tactics "to create a sense of crisis."

The reality, they argue, is that women would be "devastated" through privatization. Indeed, the figure NOW presents is that more than half the women over 65 would end up living in poverty. Besides the vagaries of the stock market (to which private annuities would be subject), NOW argues that since statistically women live longer than men, they would receive less annual income. The organization's bottom line is that privatization will benefit Wall Street and private management companies.

Ekaterina Shirley and Peter Spiegler, writing for the Cato Institute, dispute the notion that women will be harmed by privatization of social security. They argue that because of women's employment patterns of fewer years in the labor force and lower earnings, women receive lower Social Security benefits. They also argue that Social Security's "dual-entitlement" rules (i.e., entitlement as a retired worker and as the spouse/surviving spouse of another worker, which can impose a penalty on women under certain circumstances) and the 50 percent loss upon a husband's death are what truly devastate women in their elder years. The authors point out that approximately 64 percent of elderly women living in poverty are widows. In addition to the impact of Social Security policies, women on the whole have insufficient private savings. As Shirley and Spiegler note, "Earning less money makes it more difficult for women to save for anything, including retirement," and that "only 30 percent of women, compared with 47 percent of men between ages 25 and 65 are saving for retirement." Moreover, only 18 percent of elderly women receive private pensions or annuities—versus 34 percent of men.

Shirley and Spiegler argue that women would benefit substantially from the privatization of the system. While they admit that women's lower wages and their more conservative investment strategies could yield lower retirements investments, they further argue that a system could be designed with "safeguards" for lower wage earners.

For those readers who are unfamiliar with the complexities of the Social Security system in the United States, *The Real Deal: The History and Future of Social Security* by Sylvester Schreiber and John Shoven will be immensely useful reading. Schreiber and Shoven provide a useful history of the program in a format that is readily understandable. They support the notion that the system is in serious trouble. By contrast, Dean Baker and Mark Weisbrot, in *Social Security: The Phony Crisis,* argue that the public is being besieged by misinformation designed to convince us that only through privatization of the system will the future be protected.

ISSUE 9

Does Gender Affect Criminal Sentencing?

YES: Cathy Young, from "License to Kill: Men and Women, Crime and Punishment," *Reason Foundation* (July 2004)

NO: Barbara Cruikshank, from "Feminism and Punishment," *Signs* (Summer 1999)

ISSUE SUMMARY

YES: Cathy Young cites judicial leniency toward women, arguing that women do indeed receive lesser sentences for the same crime.

NO: Through the issue of capital punishment, Barbara Cruikshank explores the dilemmas posed by feminist thinking that would argue for equality vs. special consideration for women. If there is to be equality of the sexes, gender cannot be considered in sentencing.

The subject of potentially preferential treatment of women by the criminal justice system raises myriad issues. What is the purpose of the system? Is it to exclusively protect society from further harm? Is it to inflict the wrath of society upon a wrongdoer? Is it to deter potential future wrongdoing on the part of the individual perpetrator as well as would-be perpetrators? Is it to exact retribution? Is it to rehabilitate?

The answers to these questions will help society determine how to treat those who become embroiled in the criminal justice system. All too often, policies are created without a clear-cut understanding of their ultimate goal. Relatedly, policies tend to remain in place because they happen to be there. The just society is one that scrutinizes the implications of policies prior to their creation. The just society is also one that periodically reviews the validity of its policies. This ranges from public transit to penal institutions.

Data tell us that women have received differential—indeed, preferential—treatment in the U.S. judicial system. Aspects of this subject were discussed in Issue 7, which dealt with mandatory minimum sentencing. Here, we explore the issue of the whether there is preferential treatment of women in criminal sentencing.

Cathy Young presents a very convincing case that women do, indeed, still benefit from their gender. From the case examples she discusses, it is clear that but for gender, the sentence would have been far more severe. Indeed, she points out that many cases never go to trial. Young makes the argument that feminists defend leniency toward women in the criminal justice system because of their pervasive view that women commit crimes only because of the yoke of a patriarchal society. In no way is Cathy Young defending the differential and preferential treatment of women. She is merely describing the system as she sees it.

Barbara Cruikshank explores the role of gender as related to the specific topic of capital punishment. Citing real-life cases, Cruikshank questions how gender has been used to strategize appeals on death row. An interesting dimension of death row gender politics is the trend toward prisoners telling their stories. Cruikshank points out that "virtually any case can be transformed into a feminist narrative."

Is it just to see and treat women criminal offenders differently than their male counterparts? Those who would answer yes would argue that there are no male "counterparts" because women commit crimes for different reasons than do men. They would also argue that women have responsibilities toward children and families, and the broader implications of their sentencing should be considered, even if it is for a capital offense. Those who would answer no would undoubtedly do so because the commission of a crime, regardless of by whom, is still a crime. This is not to say that a society should not pursue paths to deter both men and women from criminal activity. As Henry David Thoreau once observed, "There are a thousand hacking at the branches of evil to one who is striking at the root."

YES

Cathy Young

License to Kill: Men and Women, Crime and Punishment

Late one night in August 1997, a Tacoma, Washington, woman named Brenda Lee Working called her estranged husband, Michael, and told him that her car had broken down, stranding her and their two preschool daughters in a wooded area on a military base. When Michael Working came to her aid, it turned out to be an ambush. Brenda shot him several times, hitting him in the arm and the shoulder. Then she beat him in the face with the handgun as he tried to wrench it from her hands and stalked him through the woods for hours after he managed to get away.

Brenda Working's sentence for the attempted murder of her husband: one day in jail.

Admittedly, this was not the full extent of Working's punishment: She received a separate five-year sentence for using a gun in the commission of a crime. Yet the sentencing judge, U.S. District Judge Jack Tanner, openly stated that he would have suspended that sentence too if it had not been mandatory under federal law. His reasoning was that Working had been depressed and fearful that her estranged husband would take away her children in a custody battle.

In April the U.S. Court of Appeals for the 9th Circuit overturned the sentence, ruling that Tanner had improperly departed from the sentencing guidelines without adequate reasons. The case was sent back to the lower court and reassigned to another judge. The 9th Circuit's ruling made an unusual explicit reference to gender bias, stating that Tanner "would be unlikely to set aside considerations of Working's sex."

Despite the eventual outcome, many would say the Working case illustrates a pervasive pattern in the criminal justice system of gender-based leniency toward women. This has become an article of faith among men's rights activists. In his 1993 book *The Myth of Male Power*, Warren Farrell asserts that "twelve distinct female-only defenses allow a woman who commits a premeditated murder to have the charges dropped or significantly reduced."

This sensational claim is seriously exaggerated. Of the 12 items listed by Farrell, only three—insanity pleas based on premenstrual syndrome or postpartum depression and self-defense or insanity pleas based on battered woman

From *Reason*, vol. 34, issue 3, July 2004, pp. 22. Copyright © 2004 by Reason Foundation. Reprinted by permission.

syndrome—can accurately be called "female-only defenses." (And even these defenses rarely succeed.)

The rest of Farrell's list consists of factors that contribute to more-lenient treatment of women, from stereotypes that make women less likely suspects to protective husbands standing by wives who have committed violence against them or their children.

Nonetheless, the pattern does exist. Two Justice Department studies in the late 1980s found that male offenders were more than twice as likely as women charged with similar crimes to be incarcerated for more than a year, and that even allowing for other factors, such as prior convictions, women were more likely to receive a light sentence.

The disparities are especially striking in family murders, the primary form of homicide committed by women. A Justice Department study of domestic homicides in 1988 found that 94 percent of men who were convicted of (or pled guilty to) killing their spouses received prison sentences, but only 81 percent of the women did. The average sentence was 16.5 years for husbands and a mere six years for wives.

Some of the difference was due to the fact that more of the women had been "provoked"—that is, assaulted or threatened prior to the killing. But when there had been no provocation, the average prison sentence was seven years for killer wives and 17 years for killer husbands.

Beyond the numbers, the contrast between the treatment of male and female defendants can be shocking in individual cases.

In 1995 Texas executed Jesse Dewayne Jacobs for a murder that, by the prosecutors' admission, was committed by his sister, Bobbie Jean Hogan. Hogan-who had gotten Jacobs to help her abduct her boyfriend's ex-wife and had actually pulled the trigger-served 10 years in prison.

She was convicted only of involuntary manslaughter after her lawyers managed to persuade the jury that the gun went off accidentally.

Old-fashioned chivalry undoubtedly plays a role. "Women and men do occupy separate places in the collective psyche of society," Jonathan Last wrote approvingly in The Weekly Standard in 1998, shortly after the execution of ax murderer Karla Faye Tucker. "Because society has a low tolerance for seeing them harmed, women-even criminals-have traditionally been treated differently by the justice system. Differently, but still, at least possibly, with justice."

In recent years, this chivalry has declined. Yet while it is no longer acceptable to argue that female criminals are due special consideration because they're women, many feminists' insistence on seeing women as victims of patriarchy sometimes has the same effect.

Most anti-domestic violence activists, for instance, cling to the dogma that women kill only in response to male violence. The battered women's clemency movement has obtained pardons for female murderers who, as subsequent investigations found, had very flimsy claims of abuse and probably had been driven by "masculine" motives, such as jealousy.

Other cases never go to trial. In Brooklyn in 1987, Marlene Wagshall shot her sleeping husband, Joshua, in the stomach, crippling him for life, after finding a photo of him with a scantily clad woman. Wagshall was charged with attempted murder, but on the basis of her uncorroborated assertion that her husband had beaten her, District Attorney Elizabeth Holtzman, a strong champion of women's rights, let her plead guilty to assault with a sentence of one day in jail and five years' probation.

Even when feminists do not actively defend violent women, they hardly ever speak up against inappropriate leniency toward female defendants. Mostly, they refuse to admit that such leniency exists—perhaps because it would be heresy to concede that "patriarchy" has sometimes worked in women's favor—and prefer to focus on real or mythical instances in which the justice system treats women more harshly. (Battered women's advocates have promoted the wholly fictional factoid that a woman who kills her mate is sentenced to an average of 15 to 20 years in prison, while a man gets two to six years.)

As a result, if a man commits a violent crime against a woman and gets off lightly, an outcry from women's groups often follows. If it's the other way round, the only vocal protests are likely to come from the victim's family and from prosecutors.

The Working case, like the Wagshall case, received minimal publicity. Imagine the reaction if a judge had said publicly that a man who had ambushed and shot his estranged wife should have been spared prison because he was depressed over the divorce.

There are feminists, such as Patricia Pearson, author of the 1997 book *When She Was Bad: Violent Women and the Myth of Innocence,* who find feminist paternalism toward women no less distasteful than the traditional kind. They argue that in the long run, excusing women's violence on the grounds of emotional problems may undercut women's ability to be seen as capable workers and leaders.

That may or may not happen. But even if women stand to lose nothing from the new double standards, any self-respecting feminist should still oppose them in the name of equal justice.

Barbara Cruikshank  **NO**

Feminism and Punishment

> If you believe in [capital punishment] for one, you believe in it for
> everybody. If you don't believe in it, don't believe in it for anybody.
>
> —Karla Faye Tucker, December 1997 (quoted in Verhovek 1998)

Karla Faye Tucker's statement, made shortly before she was killed by the
state of Texas in 1998, undercuts the liberal feminist argument that one can be
opposed to the death penalty and yet continue to hold that so long as the
death penalty is imposed, it should be imposed equally on men and women.
However, the target of Tucker's statement was not feminism, as we will see,
but the one person who held her life in his hands, Governor George W. Bush.
Tucker is making a case not for liberal equality before the law but against capital
punishment, her own in particular. Neither is she calling the state's legitimacy
into question; to my knowledge, interviews with Tucker did not disclose any
explicitly political claim against the state or any political motivations for her
crime. While her comments were not explicitly political, I suggest that they
were strategically aimed at Bush in the final contest over Karla Faye Tucker's life.

In these brief comments, I consider gender as it bears in the strategic
contest over the life of the condemned. It is impossible here to fully defend
either treating capital punishment as a strategic contest or treating the significance of gender only within that contest. However, it is enough, I think, to
realize that capital punishment is a contest in which the condemned often
believe they have a chance to win. Moreover, like both Renee Heberle and
Timothy Kaufman-Osborn, I understand capital punishment to be a discretionary system of decisions, conflicts, contests, and trials. That means there is
always a chance to intervene in the process leading up to death. The condemned are vying for their lives; that is why law books are worth fighting for
on the inside.[1] From death row, Mumia Abu-Jamal explains that jailhouse
lawyers make up the largest group in disciplinary units because they are capable of using the law to alter prison conditions as well as to affect the outcomes
of their own cases. When prisons single out jailhouse lawyers, they too are acting strategically in a contest over the lives and bodies of prisoners. If feminists
treat each case as a strategic contest, there is always room for gender to matter
differently.

From *Signs: Journal of Women in Culture and Society*, vol. 24, issue 4, Summer 1999, pp. 1113.
Copyright © 1999 by University of Chicago Press. Reprinted by permission.

For these reasons, understanding capital punishment as a strategic contest is not cynical. To the contrary, it is optimistic to think that feminists might intervene at any point in a capital punishment case. By considering gender here only as it plays a part in that strategic contest, I do not mean to imply that gender has no deeper meaning or significance. Rather, my point is that, at least as far as feminism is concerned, it is important to concentrate on how gender figures as a part of the strategic contest in which the condemned find themselves. Most important, it is possible that gender could figure at every strategic point, and so it is crucial that the meaning or significance of gender not be fixed in advance.

The strategy that Tucker pursued was to deny the significance of gender in her own case and in relation to her crime: "When we are talking about the crime I committed, gender has no place as an issue" (Verhovek 1998, 3). Yet, given all the publicity that surrounded her execution because she was a woman, how could she say that gender had no place? Moreover, why did she say it? I believe her claims were made to escape death, not to express an article of faith or a principle. Her only chance for salvation in this world was to make an argument that would convince Governor Bush to grant her clemency. Bush claimed that her gender would not figure in his decision because he was determined to apply the law in a liberal way, to the individual qua individual. Gender, or the denial of gender, was a point of resistance for Tucker in the sense that her refusal to see her case as exceptional undercut any justification of her execution that Bush could make based on treating women the same as men. By making her own case against the significance of gender, Tucker was trying to steal Bush's bluster. She knew that if she tried to make the case that women should not be killed, Governor Bush would let her die to demonstrate his own gender-blindness. The two parties denied the significance of gender for opposite reasons. They did so not because either held strongly feminist or antifeminist views but because they were caught up together in a contest that neither could win so long as gender was seen to play a part.

Tucker and other notable fundamentalists made the case that she was saved in the eyes of God. As a born-again believer, she would supposedly no longer be capable of murder and mayhem. This defense, however, depended on overcoming the dominant media interpretation of her case as gendered. Unable to do so, it could be said, Tucker was executed. Despite Tucker's salvation in the eyes of God and her redemption within a community of notable fundamentalists, she faced the ultimate condemnation in this life. The dissonance between the saved Tucker and the condemned Tucker did not work to offer Bush an alternative to gender as grounds for a stay of execution. (Perhaps only a religious fundamentalist could think it was possible to redeem Tucker and erase the public significance of her gender by restoring her to the community of the faithful.) Though her strategy failed, it makes clear that gender does not matter systematically but that it does matter strategically.

Instead of arguing as Heberle does that women are "embodiments of sex" or that gender is solidified "on the outside" I hold (as does Kaufman-Osborn) that gender confusion reigns in all kinds of contests that are ongoing within the liberal state. Gender is not something that we inhabit or embody so much as something we negotiate on an ongoing basis within the context of power relations. While systems of control on the outside subject women in particular ways, I suspect that gender, far from being stabilized by extralegal social hierarchies, continues to undergo radically destabilizing conflicts. That makes gender available to all sides in any contest, which, in turn, means that the variability of gender presents both dangers and powerful possibilities to the strategies of the condemned and of the state.

Gender should not be expected to matter strategically in the same way again. For example, the execution of Judy Buenoano in Florida followed shortly after that of Tucker, yet none of the same kinds of contests over gender made her execution debatable. Nevertheless, it seems to me that Buenoano was not "divested" of her gender identity when she was killed, as Kaufman-Osborn puts it, so much as she was never vested in the first place. Signs readers will understand what I mean when I say that not all women are "women" Nor should gender be expected to matter only in the context of political posturing and media discourses. In the strategic contest over the life of the condemned, gender could figure in any number of possible terrains of action. In their isolation, especially in lock-down units, the condemned tend to focus their strategies on the law. Yet, in addition to the law and to the possibility of physical resistance such as riots, hunger strikes, and labor strikes, there are several terrains of contestation open to the condemned. Although none can offer stable ground to the condemned, these avenues do suggest strategies in which gender could possibly make the difference between life and death.

First, prisoners have their bodies. While both men's and women's bodies and sexualities are commodities in the political economy of power and desire on the inside, women's prisons are famous for recreating ties of kinship and sustaining sexual relationships among women. Tucker was exceptional in that she married the prison minister, which no doubt limited her relationships with other prisoners. Women are condemned to death or to life in prison most often for the murder of their own children, lovers, and husbands, and they recreate those types of relations in prison. If same-sex marriage were legalized, for example, partnerships in prisons could become significant in capital punishment cases. Also, if a woman on death row could somehow become pregnant, it is possible that she could avert any immediate attempts on her life. Nevertheless, women's bodies are not uniformly gendered. The genders of masculine women and lesbian butches, for example, would have significantly different strategic value than more traditionally feminine genders. While sexual, kinship, and gang relationships on the inside might possibly have strategic value, there are certainly grounds to think that they are as likely to be liabilities as they are on the outside.

Contacts on the outside also present the possibility of wielding influence in the discretionary and convoluted system of execution. It is extremely rare for prisoners to have the kinds of contacts that Tucker had in the ranks of fundamentalists, yet they certainly helped to bring publicity to her case. The often extraordinary solidarity of outsiders with political prisoners demonstrates only that public pressure can effect either a stay or an acceleration of an execution, depending on the circumstances. The solidarity that feminists might feel with a certain prisoner could result in a large-scale movement for amnesty or clemency. However, to my knowledge, there is no feminist case against capital punishment that could possibly unite feminists either on the issue or on particular cases. Nevertheless, political solidarity might alter the strategic field for the condemned.

Finally, and perhaps most powerfully for the relatively powerless, prisoners can tell their stories. Recently, the incredible commodification of biographies and "true stories" has even affected sentencing, which may now explicitly prevent certain prisoners from profiting from book and movie deals. The story of Aileen Wuornos, for example, became a commodity before she was convicted. Indeed, if Wuornos is correct, the selling of her story was a good part of the reason she was convicted. Touted as the first lesbian serial killer, Wuornos saw her story manipulated by everyone she came into contact with. In a court outburst, she vowed to expose the corruption of the police and the courts and their complicity in creating a story that would sell. Nevertheless, on a subcultural level, Wuornos is a heroine for killing men who posed a threat to prostitutes. Similarly, feminists have defended women who kill their batterers by retelling their stories with a feminist twist. Outlaw narratives in films such as Thelma and Louise and Bound suggest the possibility that feminist narratives could be turned to strategic purpose in particular cases.

Indeed, virtually any case could be transformed into a feminist narrative. When women end up on death row, they have committed the ultimate act of their personal liberation from the restrictions of parenting, responsible citizenship, and labor. As Michel Foucault (1977) so famously argued, crime is one way to call the existing order into question. The danger of such retellings is that they fix gender in ways that could be dangerous to the condemned. To tell a story that is always open to contestation and hence always of strategic use is improbable. In order to make sense on one cultural plane—say, Hollywood—it would be necessary to destroy the resonance of a story on another—say, a sexual subculture. Still more improbable is telling the story in a way that sustains the voice of the condemned herself. Tucker found her voice projected by religious fundamentalists, but who knows how that sounded to her ears?

I am not convinced, as Tucker said she was, that one's moral position on capital punishment is the central issue or that appeals to moral conscience might sway the populace to call for an end to capital punishment. Much as I would like to be able to persuade the reader that capital punishment is wrong, any moral or humanist argument I might make about the value of life is pointless in the present context, in which a substantial majority is calling for blood. Capital punishment is not a strategic contest in which morality has no part; it is one in which appeals to morality are themselves a part of the contest.

Note

1. On the struggle for access to law reference materials in prison, see Pens 1998, 231. Mumia Abu-Jamal points out that jailhouse lawyers are singled out for administrative and disciplinary segregation (1998, 191–92).

References

Abu-Jamal, Mumia. 1998. "Campaign of Repression." In *The Celling of America: An Inside Look at the U.S. Prison Industry,* ed. Daniel Burton-Rose, 191–92. Monroe, Maine: Common Courage Press.

Foucault, Michel. 1977. *Discipline and Punish: The Birth of the Prison.* New York: Penguin.

Pens, Dan. 1998. "Hungry for Justice in L.A." In *The Celling of America: An Inside Look at the U.S. Prison Industry,* ed. Daniel Burton-Rose, 231. Monroe, Maine: Common Courage Press.

Verhovek, Sam Howe. 1998. "Dead Women Waiting." *New York Times,* February 8, sec. 4, p. 1.

POSTSCRIPT

Does Gender Affect
Criminal Sentencing?

Cathy Young argues that women receive significantly lighter sentences than men. She offers poignant real-life case vignette to make her point.

> Late one night in August 1997, a Tacoma, Washington, woman named Brenda Lee Working called her estranged husband, Michael, and told him that her car had broken down, stranding her and their two preschool daughters in a wooded area on a military base. When Michael Working came to her aid, it turned out to be an ambush. Brenda shot him several times, hitting him in the arm and the shoulder. Then she beat him in the face with the handgun as he tried to wrench it from her hands and stalked him through the woods for hours after he managed to get away.
>
> Brenda Working's sentence for the attempted murder of her husband: one day in jail.

Any first-year law school student or television viewer of the various off-shoots of "Law and Order" will know that Working's actions are clearly attempted premeditated murder. So why did Working get off with such a lenient sentence? Judicial discretion in the face of Working's depression and fear of her husband. Indeed, as Young tells us, the judge in this case said he would have suspended the five-year sentence for use of a gun in the commission of a crime, but such an offense carries a mandatory minimum under federal law. Worker's sentence was overturned, but as Young points out, this is a classic case of gender-based judicial leniency.

Barbara Cruikshank begins her article with an insightful statement by Karla Faye Tucker, who was put to death under the state-imposed death penalty in Texas. Tucker noted, "If you believe in [capital punishment] for one, you believe in it for everybody. If you don't believe it in, don't believe in it for anybody." Cruikshank goes on to say that Tucker's strategy was to deny the significance of gender because then Governor George W. Bush was denying the relevance of gender and that Tucker wanted to steal his thunder. Cruikshank's view is that Tucker assumed this strategy, rather than appealing on the basis of her gender, because she knew that it might be the only one to avoid the death penalty, since Bush would definitely not retreat from his view that the law had to be uniformly applied. Women on death row present a dilemma for feminists, who would argue for equality and yet are appalled by the state's taking of a woman's life.

For those interested in additional readings on this subject, the following are recommended: Marc Mauer, *Gender and Women Drug Sentencing* and Susan Ehrlich Martin and Nancy C. Jurik, *Doing Gender: Women in Law and Criminal Justice Occupations.*

On the Internet . . .

Gallup Organization

The Gallup Organization provides extensive public opinion research on a wide range of public policy topics.

http://www.gallup.com

Library of Congress

The Library of Congress is the paramount resource for public policy and governmental studies.

http://www.loc.gov

Supreme Court Collection

Supreme Court Collection is crucial for searching key decisions of the Supreme Court.

http://supct.law.cornell.edu/supct/inex.html

People's Movement for Human Rights Education

The People's Movement for Human Rights Education is a Web Site dedicated to human rights learning for social and economic change.

http://www.pdhre.org/index.html

PART 3

Sexual Orientation

*O*ne of the most pressing and controversial of issues facing the United States is that of achieving equality for homosexuals. This issue is one that takes on all the greater fervor because it tends to rally religious groups in opposition.

There is no denying that gay men and lesbians have suffered inordinate discrimination in the past and continue to suffer. Yet the Gay Pride Movement has forced issues of tolerance and equality to the forefront of the political agenda. Once again, a minority is subjected to the dominant culture, which is fiercely heterosexual. Recent years have witnessed the often brutal results of the hostility many Americans feel toward homosexuals. It is not unusual for gays and lesbians to fear for their safety and their lives, and some, like Matthew Sheppard, have been killed because of their sexual orientation. Others face "second-class citizenship" in not being permitted to marry, adopt, or be honest about whom they are. This section addresses some of the public policy, justice, and legal issues of greatest relevance to this minority group. Once again, some of these issues also appropriately apply to other minorities.

- Is Hate Crime Legislation Constitutional?

- Should Same-Sex Marriages Be Permitted?

- Should Gays and Lesbians Be Allowed to Adopt?

ISSUE 10

Is Hate Crime Legislation Constitutional?

YES: Elena Grigera, from "Hate Crimes: State and Federal Response to Bias-Motivated Violence," *Corrections Today* (August 1999)

NO: Andrew Sullivan, from "What's So Bad About Hate: The Illogic and Illiberalism Behind Hate Crime Laws," *The New York Times Magazine* (September 26, 1999)

ISSUE SUMMARY

YES: Elena Grigera argues that since the state has a legitimate interest in implementing harsh penalties for hate crimes, hate crime legislation is constitutional.

NO: Andrew Sullivan agrees that hate crimes are despicable and that government should work toward eliminating violence. But, he argues, a crime is a crime and should not be treated differently depending upon the victim. Sullivan further argues that waging war on beliefs is unconstitutional.

Most thinking people would agree that the First Amendment to the U.S. Constitution allows us to hate. But what if that hatred turns to action? What if, on the basis of what *thinks*, one acts in a manner that is harmful to someone else?

There is a plethora of sub-issues stemming from the larger issue. Is a crime committed out of hatred *worse* than the same crime not based on hate? Should society treat hate crimes differently? Or is a crime a crime, no matter what the motivation? Is it different if a group of whites beat and rob a black man so that they can steal his wallet than if that same group beats and robs the same black man because he is a black man? Some would say, what difference does it make? The black man is still dead, and the group has committed a murder. Others would look to the motivation behind the crime.

Advocates of hate crime legislation argue that harsher penalties should be attached to a hate crime because that crime is a crime against an entire *group* of people. Moreover, if a society seeks to be just, it must work to eradicate hate, even though it cannot prohibit what one thinks. One way of focusing attention on society's intolerance of hate crimes is *by making a statement* through harsher penalties. Indeed, even if the penalties were not harsher, a statement would still be made by *identifying and designating* a particular crime as a hate crime. Attaching the stigma to it would send the message that society recognizes what has taken place and is speaking out against it.

Elena Grigera makes the case that "the intolerance behind [hate] crimes threatens the very fabric of American society." Although it takes no reminding, she vividly depicts the dragging death of James Byrd, Jr. and the beating death of Matthew Shepard merely because the first was black and the second was gay. In these deaths, all blacks and all gays were figuratively attacked. The public attention brought to such actions led to the Hate Crime Sentencing Enhancement Act of 1994, yet the FBI's hate crime statistics report soaring numbers of such actions. No, a just society cannot limit thought, but it must protect all and must make a statement that it will not accept intolerance.

By contrast, Andrew Sullivan, who is himself openly gay, argues that hate-crime laws are "illogical and illiberal." Although he denounces the types of crimes such as those committed against James Byrd, Jr. and Matthew Shepard, and wonders what was going on in the heads of their attackers, Sullivan makes the argument hatred is part of the human condition. It cannot, he argues, be eradicated. He also questions the notion that one violent action is more threatening to society than another.

Sullivan writes a brilliant analysis of the complexities and nuances of hate, and argues that "a free country will always mean a hateful country. . . . [H]ate is only foiled not when the haters are punished but when the hated are immune to the bigot's power." In Sullivan's view, there is "the distinction between toleration and tolerance. Tolerance is the eradication of hate; toleration is co-existence despite it."

Elena Grigera

 **YES**

Hate Crimes: State and Federal Response to Bias-Motivated Violence

Chained to the back of a pickup truck by the ankles and dragged to death—One man's life ended in a heinous murder and the public's conscience awoke to the horrifying headlines describing the mutilated remains of a black man scattered along a road. The slaying . . . of 49-year-old James Byrd Jr. in Jasper, Texas, is a harsh reminder to all Americans that violent crimes motivated by prejudice continue to disrupt our nation's sense of racial harmony. Yet, such brutal attacks do not only occur between blacks and whites but among various groups. The nation was made aware once again of the reality of hate crimes in October 1998 by the fatal beating of Matthew Shepard in Laramie, Wyo. The 21-year-old college student suffered severe head injuries after being beaten and tied to a wooden fence in near-freezing temperatures. While the Byrd murder was motivated by views of white supremacy, the Shepard murder was triggered because of the victim's sexual orientation. These savage attacks, among many others not reported or covered by the media, have prompted nationwide outrage and have renewed the hate crime debate.

Defining the Issue

Due to the mounting public interest in and awareness of hate crimes, as a result of both sensational incidents and general societal concerns, hate crimes have become the subject of highly politicized public debates. While some contend that bias-motivated violence has been a historical part of the American culture and will only change as people become more tolerant of certain groups, others argue that the best way to eradicate such discriminatory behavior is through legal reform. The following focuses on the latter argument by examining hate crime legislation at both the state and federal levels.

A recent and expansive definition of the term "hate crime" can be found in the Hate Crime Sentencing Enhancement Act of 1994, which states, "a crime in which the defendant intentionally selects a victim, or in the case of a

From *Corrections Today*, vol. 61, no. 5, August 1999, pp. 68–72. Copyright © 1999 by American Correctional Association, Lantham, MD. Reprinted by permission.

property crime, the property that is the object of the crime, because of the actual or perceived race, color, religion, national origin, ethnicity, gender, disability or sexual orientation of any person."[1] Thus, hate offenses are directed against members of a particular group simply because of their membership in that group.

According to the FBI's most recent Hate Crimes Statistics Act (HCSA) report for 1997, there were 8,049 hate crimes reported by 11,211 participating law enforcement agencies in 48 states and the District of Columbia (Hawaii and New Hampshire did not participate in 1997 HCSA reporting).[2] The FBI report indicated that about 59 percent of the reported hate crimes were race-based (4,710 incidents); 17 percent were committed against individuals on the basis of their religion (1,385 incidents); 10 percent on the basis of ethnicity 836 incidents); and 14 percent on the basis of sexual orientation (1,102 incidents). This report included, for the first time, crimes directed against disabled individuals. In 1997, there were 12 crimes reported to have occurred due to persons' disabilities.[3]

With a closer look at race-based hate crimes, approximately 39 percent of the reported crimes were anti-black (3,120 incidents); 12 percent were anti-white (993 incidents); 4 percent were anti-Asian (347 incidents); .4 percent were anti-American Indian/Alaskan Native (36 incidents); and 3 percent were anti-multiracial group (214 incidents). Of the incidents motivated by religious bias, 1,087 (about 78 percent) were anti-Semitic in nature. Slightly more than 6 percent were anti-Hispanic (491 incidents) and 4 percent were anti-other ethnicities/national origins (345 incidents).

Although the number of hate crimes may seem small when compared with the incidence of other types of crimes in the United States, it can be argued that hate crimes terrorize not one victim but many and that such assaults threaten the very fabric of the American sense of safety and basic understanding of differences. As a House of Representative report on the proposed HCSA noted, "While each incident [of violence] represents a personal tragedy for the victim, hate crimes are an attempt to intimidate a larger group or class of people."[4] In other words, bias-motivated violence victimizes not only the immediate target but every member of the group represented by that target. In addition, these crimes are typically committed against historically oppressed groups.

According to scholars, the perpetrator of a bias crime acts out of both frustration and the desire to have power and domination over a particular group, viewing his or her victim as deserving of punishment.[5] Bias-motivated crimes are typically committed by individuals or small groups of people rather than organized hate groups, such as the Ku Klux Klan. Often, perpetrators of bias crimes are young males between the ages of 14 and 24 who commit the crimes for excitement, as part of social activities or acts of revenge based upon perceived unfair benefits to the groups to which the victims belong.[5] A violent offense motivated by bigotry can cause a broad rippled of frustration among members of a targeted group, and a violent hate crime can quickly spread feelings of terror through an entire community. Apart from their psychological impact, such bias-motivated crimes continue the oppression of marginalized groups, leaving victims and members of the victims' communities feeling isolated, vulnerable and unprotected by the law.

The Need for Hate Crime Legislation

During the past 30 years, the legislative agenda at both the national and state levels has seen a virtual explosion of political work around the status of minorities. Specifically, in the late 1970s through the 1980s, and continuing into the 1990s, legislation that criminalizes violence and intimidation motivated by bigotry and targeting minority constituencies has been introduced, adopted and invoked for both symbolic and prosecutorial purposes.[6] It is important to keep in mind that, while hate crime legislation is often viewed as a vehicle of protection for such minority groups as blacks and Jews, such laws also protect the white majority from bias-motivated violence.

The primary rationale for hate crime legislation is that harassment and intimidation, assault and property destruction assume a particularly dangerous and socially disruptive character when motivated by prejudice.[7] According to scholars, the passage of these laws was designed mainly to create disincentives for bias incidents (deterrence); at another level, it addresses the problem that many offenders may be indifferent to the legal consequences of their acts (relative absence of fear of legal reprisal).[8] There also exists a symbolic significance to hate crime laws—By recognizing the suffering among members of targeted groups, legislators send the message that perpetrators of bias-motivated crimes present greater harm to society and evidence greater moral culpability. In order to better understand the various forms of hate crime legislation, it is essential to examine such laws at both the state and federal levels.

State Initiatives

There are several types of hate crime legislation distributed throughout the United States. Currently, 41 states and the District of Columbia have enacted legislation that can be invoked to redress bias-motivated violence and intimidation—specifically provisions for enhanced penalties. Of the nine states that have yet to adopt such laws (Arkansas, Georgia, Hawaii, Indiana, Kansas, Kentucky, New Mexico, South Carolina and Wyoming), most have some sort of hate crime statute in place. For instance, with the exception of Wyoming, the states mentioned above have statutes prohibiting institutional vandalism. Arkansas also has a civil action statute providing for victim compensation. In addition to a statute mandating training for law enforcement personnel, Kentucky also has a statute requiring authorities to collect data on bias-motivated crimes. As of this date, the state of Wyoming does not have any form of hate crime legislation.[3]

Although statutes addressing such issues as institutional vandalism, civil action remedies, training for law enforcement and data collection are very important, the current attention on hate crime legislation is directed at laws that punish bias-motivated violence. Convinced that government can do more to deter and remedy bigotry-motivated violence, 41 state legislatures and the

District of Columbia have enacted hate crime statutes that emphasize enhanced penalties for bias-motivated violence. This form of legislation is based on or similar to the model legislation originally drafted by the Anti-Defamation League (ADL) in 1981. The core of the ADL legal approach is a "penalty enhancement" concept. When bigotry prompts an individual to engage in criminal activity, a prosecutor can seek a stiffer sentence. A defendant is subject to an enhanced penalty if he or she "intentionally selects" his or her victim "because of" a given characteristic, such as race or religion.[7] Hate crime statutes increase penalties either by assigning higher sentencing ranges for the offenses or by upgrading the offenses.

While the majority of state legislatures have adopted penalty enhancement provisions, these laws vary among the states in two distinct ways: 1) severity of punishment; and 2) level of coverage offered to minority groups. Since states began passing penalty enhancement statutes in the early 1980s, the provisions have taken many forms as states continue to run the gamut from broad to scant coverage by offering expansive and comparatively restrictive definitions of what level of punishment should be placed against the perpetrator and who counts as a victim of prejudice. Some states, such as California and New Hampshire, have enacted comprehensive statutes that provide both severe punishment against the perpetrator of hate violence and protect the civil rights of a range of constituencies, including victims attacked because of their sexual orientation, gender or disability. In contrast, states such as North Carolina and Utah have adopted more limited legislation by proscribing moderate imprisonment and/or fines and by providing a narrow classification of protected statuses, such as race, religion and national origin.

Scholarly literature seems to attribute the restrictive inclusion of sexual orientation, gender and disability as minority groups deserving of hate violence protection to conservative opposition in state legislatures. These groups remain less embedded in hate crime law, at least in part, because they constitute more heavily contested protected statuses. For instance, of the 41 states that have implemented penalty enhancement provisions, only 20 states have included sexual orientation as a protected category; only 19 have included gender; and only 22 have extended coverage to persons with disabilities. The District of Columbia statute includes all three categories. The lack of comprehensive protection for these three minority groups is a major concern for advocates of federal hate crime legislation.

The diversity of approaches used in the United States reflects each state's struggle to respond effectively to hate-motivated violence. Although 41 states and the District of Columbia have adopted legislation allowing prosecutors to enhance the penalties for in bias-motivated violence, such provisions have faced harsh opposition.

Constitutional Challenges

Critics of statutes aimed at punishing hate violence contend that it would be wrong to say that a crime against one person is more serious than a crime against his or her neighbor. According to some, the law must remain blind to specific motives and should concentrate solely on the acts themselves.[9] Opponents of bias crime legislation often attempt to validate their positions by relying on constitutional challenges to such statutes.

Free Speech.   In *Wisconsin vs. Mitchell,* the U.S. Supreme Court upheld a Wisconsin statute providing for an enhanced sentence in cases in which the defendant intentionally selects the person against whom the crime is committed because of the victim's membership in a social category.[10] The defendant in this particular case incited a young group of African-Americans to assault a young white man. While the defendant argued that Wisconsin's penalty enhancement provision violated the protection granted to him under the First Amendment by punishing offensive thought, the court affirmed that the statute was directed at a defendant's conduct—committing a crime.[3] "The enhanced penalty is appropriate," the court said, "because the conduct is thought to inflict greater individual and societal harm."[10] The court went on to reject the suggestion that the statute would chill free speech by declaring that the bias motivation would have to be connected with a specific act. In other words, these sentence enhancement provisions do not criminalize speech but instead, they simply establish separate punishment for offenders who commit certain criminal acts "because of" prejudice. The statute concerns not the defendant's bigoted speech or thought, but, rather, the act of victim selection, and punishes the discriminatory conduct.[3] Challenges to these statutes on the basis of the First Amendment most likely will continue to be rejected by the judiciary.

Due Process.   Defendants charged with violating hate crime laws often claim that penalty enhancement provisions infringe upon the due process clause of the U.S. Constitution[11] by insufficiently informing them of what conduct on their part will render them liable to its penalties. Litigants contend that the "because of" and "by reason of" language of the statutes are unconstitutionally vague by failing to afford adequate notice of the conduct proscribed. However, because the statutes require the commission of an underlying crime, the state courts have largely rejected these claims.[3]

Equal Protection.   Opponents of penalty enhancement statutes also have argued that such provisions violate the equal protection clause of the U.S. Constitution.[12] According to ADL, "defendants have suggested that either the statutes unconstitutionally benefit minorities, because minorities are more likely to be victims of bias crimes, or that the statutes unconstitutionally burden majority members because majority members are more likely to be prospected."[3] However, state courts have rejected every claim based on this rationale by recognizing that the statutes were designed to be neutral and that the state has a legitimate interest in implementing harsh punishment for hate crimes.

Overall, despite criticism of hate crime statutes, 41 states and the District of Columbia have adopted legislation that enhances penalties for hate-motivated violence and state courts have upheld their constitutionality. . . .

What Is a Hate Crime?

An act of:

- Intimidation
- Harassment
- Physical force or threat of physical force

Against Whom Is it Committed?

Against:

- Person
- Property
- Family
- Supporter

Why Does it Occur?

Motivated in whole or in part by prejudice based on:

- Race
- Color
- Religion
- Ethnicity
- Gender
- Disability
- Sexual orientation
- National origin

Endnotes

1. 28 U.S.C. 994 (1994).
2. Note that the Hate Crimes Statistics Act, 28 U.S.C. 534 (1990), does not require the reporting of gender-based hate crimes.
3. Anti-Defamation League, 1998. 1999 Hate crime laws. New York, 4–21.
4. Wolf, Leslie R. 1991. Violence against women as bias-motivated crime: Defining the issues. Washington, D.C.: Center for Women Policy Studies, 9.
5. Levin, Jack and Jack McDevitt. 1993. Hate crimes: The rising tide of bigotry and bloodshed. New York: Plenum Press, 10.
6. Minkoff, Debra. 1995. Organizing for equality: The evolution of women's and racial-ethnic organizations in America. New Brunswick, N.J.: Rutgers University Press, 5–7.
7. Anti-Defamation League. 1994. Hate crime laws: A comprehensive guide, 1994. New York, 1–2.
8. Pinkney, Alphonso. 1994. White hate crimes. Chicago: Third World Press.
9. Kelly, Robert J. 1993. Bias crime: American law enforcement and legal responses. Chicago: University of Illinois, 30.
10. 508 U.S. 476 (1993).

11. U.S. Constitution, the Fifth Amendment ("No person shall . . . be deprived of life, liberty or property, without due process of the law"); U.S. Constitution, the 14th Amendment, sect. 1 ("nor shall any state deprive any person of life, liberty or property, without due process of law").

12. U.S. Constitution, the 14th Amendment, sect. 1 ("nor shall any state . . . deny any person within its jurisdiction the equal protection of the laws").

NO

Andrew Sullivan

What's So Bad About Hate: The Illogic and Illiberalism Behind Hate-Crime Laws

I.

I wonder what was going on in John William King's head two years ago when he tied James Byrd Jr.'s feet to the back of a pickup truck and dragged him three miles down a road in rural Texas. King and two friends had picked up Byrd, who was black, when he was walking home, half-drunk, from a party. As part of a bonding ritual in their fledgling white supremacist group, the three men took Byrd to a remote part of town, beat him and chained his legs together before attaching them to the truck. Pathologists at King's trial testified that Byrd was probably alive and conscious until his body finally hit a culvert and split in two. When King was offered a chance to say something to Byrd's family at the trial, he smirked and uttered an obscenity.

We know all these details now, many months later. We know quite a large amount about what happened before and after. But I am still drawn, again and again, to the flash of ignition, the moment when fear and loathing became hate, the instant of transformation when King became hunter and Byrd became prey.

What was that? And what was it when Buford Furrow Jr., longtime member of the Aryan Nations, calmly walked up to a Filipino-American mailman he happened to spot, asked him to mail a letter and then shot him at point-blank range? Or when Russell Henderson beat Matthew Shepard, a young gay man, to a pulp, removed his shoes and then, with the help of a friend, tied him to a post, like a dead coyote, to warn off others?

For all our documentation of these crimes and others, our political and moral disgust at them, our morbid fascination with them, our sensitivity to their social meaning, we seem at times to have no better idea now than we ever had of what exactly they were about. About what that moment means when, for some reason or other, one human being asserts absolute, immutable superiority over another. About not the violence, but what the violence expresses. About what—exactly—hate is. And what our own part in it may be.

I find myself wondering what hate actually is in part because we have created an entirely new offense in American criminal law—a "hate crime"— to combat it. And barely a day goes by without someone somewhere declaring war against it. Last month President Clinton called for an expansion of hate-crime laws as "what America needs in our battle against hate." A couple of weeks later, Senator John McCain used a campaign speech to denounce the "hate" he said poisoned the land. New York's Mayor, Rudolph Giuliani, recently tried to stop the Million Youth March in Harlem on the grounds that the event was organized by people "involved in hate marches and hate rhetoric."

The media concurs in its emphasis. In 1985, there were 11 mentions of "hate crimes" in the national media database Nexis. By 1990, there were more than a thousand. In the first six months of 1999, there were 7,000. "Sexy fun is one thing," wrote a New York Times reporter about sexual assaults in Woodstock '99's mosh pit. "But this was an orgy of lewdness tinged with hate." And when Benjamin Smith marked the Fourth of July this year by targeting blacks, Asians and Jews for murder in Indiana and Illinois, the story wasn't merely about a twisted young man who had emerged on the scene. As The Times put it, "Hate arrived in the neighborhoods of Indiana University, in Bloomington, in the early-morning darkness."

But what exactly was this thing that arrived in the early-morning darkness? For all our zeal to attack hate, we still have a remarkably vague idea of what it actually is. A single word, after all, tells us less, not more. For all its emotional punch, "hate" is far less nuanced an idea than prejudice, or bigotry, or bias, or anger, or even mere aversion to others. Is it to stand in for all these varieties of human experience—and everything in between? If so, then the war against it will be so vast as to be quixotic. Or is "hate" to stand for a very specific idea or belief, or set of beliefs, with a very specific object or group of objects? Then waging war against it is almost certainly unconstitutional. Perhaps these kinds of questions are of no concern to those waging war on hate. Perhaps it is enough for them that they share a sentiment that there is too much hate and never enough vigilance in combating it. But sentiment is a poor basis for law, and a dangerous tool in politics. It is better to leave some unwinnable wars unfought.

II.

Hate is everywhere. Human beings generalize all the time, ahead of time, about everyone and everything. A large part of it may even be hard-wired. At some point in our evolution, being able to know beforehand who was friend or foe was not merely a matter of philosophical reflection. It was a matter of survival. And even today it seems impossible to feel a loyalty without also feeling a disloyalty, a sense of belonging without an equal sense of unbelonging. We're social beings. We associate. Therefore we disassociate. And although it would be comforting to think that the one could happen without the other, we know in reality that it doesn't. How many patriots are there who have never felt a twinge of xenophobia?

Of course by hate, we mean something graver and darker than this kind of lazy prejudice. But the closer you look at this distinction, the fuzzier it gets. Much of the time, we harbor little or no malice toward people of other backgrounds or places or ethnicities or ways of life. But then a car cuts you off at an intersection and you find yourself noticing immediately that the driver is a woman, or black, or old, or fat, or white, or male. Or you are walking down a city street at night and hear footsteps quickening behind you. You look around and see that it is a white woman and not a black man, and you are instantly relieved. These impulses are so spontaneous they are almost involuntary. But where did they come from? The mindless need to be mad at someone—anyone—or the unconscious eruption of a darker prejudice festering within?

In 1993, in San Jose, Calif., two neighbors—one heterosexual, one homosexual—were engaged in a protracted squabble over grass clippings. (The full case is recounted in "Hate Crimes," by James B. Jacobs and Kimberly Potter.) The gay man regularly mowed his lawn without a grass catcher, which prompted his neighbor to complain on many occasions that grass clippings spilled over onto his driveway. Tensions grew until one day, the gay man mowed his front yard, spilling clippings onto his neighbor's driveway, prompting the straight man to yell an obscene and common anti-gay insult. The wrangling escalated. At one point, the gay man agreed to collect the clippings from his neighbor's driveway but then later found them dumped on his own porch. A fracas ensued with the gay man spraying the straight man's son with a garden hose, and the son hitting and kicking the gay man several times, yelling anti-gay slurs. The police were called, and the son was eventually convicted of a hate-motivated assault, a felony. But what was the nature of the hate: anti-gay bias, or suburban property-owner madness?

Or take the Labor Day parade last year in Broad Channel, a small island in Jamaica Bay, Queens. Almost everyone there is white, and in recent years a group of local volunteer fire fighters has taken to decorating a pickup truck for the parade in order to win the prize for "funniest float." Their themes have tended toward the outrageously provocative. Beginning in 1995, they won prizes for floats depicting "Hasidic Park," "Gooks of Hazzard" and "Happy Gays." Last year, they called their float "Black to the Future, Broad Channel 2098." They imagined their community a century hence as a largely black enclave, with every stereotype imaginable: watermelons, basketballs and so on. At one point during the parade, one of them mimicked the dragging death of James Byrd. It was caught on videotape, and before long the entire community was depicted as a caldron of hate.

It's an interesting case, because the float was indisputably in bad taste and the improvisation on the Byrd killing was grotesque. But was it hate? The men on the float were local heroes for their volunteer work; they had no record of bigoted activity, and were not members of any racist organizations. In previous years, they had made fun of many other groups and saw themselves more as provocateurs than bigots. When they were described as racists, it came as a shock to them. They apologized for poor taste but refused to confess to bigotry. "The people involved aren't horrible people," protested a local woman. "Was it a racist act? I don't know. Are they racists? I don't think so."

If hate is a self-conscious activity, she has a point. The men were primarily motivated by the desire to shock and to reflect what they thought was their community's culture. Their display was not aimed at any particular black people, or at any blacks who lived in Broad Channel—almost none do. But if hate is primarily an unconscious activity, then the matter is obviously murkier. And by taking the horrific lynching of a black man as a spontaneous object of humor, the men were clearly advocating indifference to it. Was this an aberrant excess? Or the real truth about the men's feelings toward African-Americans? Hate or tastelessness? And how on earth is anyone, even perhaps the fire fighters themselves, going to know for sure?

Or recall H.L. Mencken. He shared in the anti-Semitism of his time with more alacrity than most and was an indefatigable racist. "It is impossible," he wrote in his diary, "to talk anything resembling discretion or judgment into a colored woman. They are all essentially childlike, and even hard experience does not teach them anything." He wrote at another time of the "psychological stigmata" of the "Afro-American race." But it is also true that, during much of his life, day to day, Mencken conducted himself with no regard to race, and supported a politics that was clearly integrationist. As the editor of his diary has pointed out, Mencken published many black authors in his magazine, *The Mercury,* and lobbied on their behalf with his publisher, Alfred A. Knopf. The last thing Mencken ever wrote was a diatribe against racial segregation in Baltimore's public parks. He was good friends with leading black writers and journalists, including James Weldon Johnson, Walter White and George S. Schuyler, and played an under appreciated role in promoting the Harlem Renaissance.

What would our modern view of hate do with Mencken? Probably ignore him, or change the subject. But, with regard to hate, I know lots of people like Mencken. He reminds me of conservative friends who oppose almost every measure for homosexual equality yet genuinely delight in the company of their gay friends. It would be easier for me to think of them as haters, and on paper, perhaps, there is a good case that they are. But in real life, I know they are not. Some of them clearly harbor no real malice toward me or other homosexuals whatsoever.

They are as hard to figure out as those liberal friends who support every gay rights measure they have ever heard of but do anything to avoid going into a gay bar with me. I have to ask myself in the same, frustrating kind of way: are they liberal bigots or bigoted liberals? Or are they neither bigots nor liberals, but merely people?

III.

Hate used to be easier to understand. When Sartre described anti-Semitism in his 1946 essay "Anti-Semite and Jew," he meant a very specific array of firmly held prejudices, with a history, an ideology and even a pseudo science to back them up. He meant a systematic attempt to demonize and eradicate an entire race. If you go to the Web site of the World Church of the Creator, the organization that inspired young Benjamin Smith to murder in Illinois earlier this year, you will find a similarly bizarre, pseudo rational ideology. The kind of literature read by Buford Furrow before he rained terror on a Jewish kindergarten last month and then killed a mailman because of his color is full of the same paranoid loopiness. And when we talk about hate, we often mean this kind of phenomenon.

But this brand of hatred is mercifully rare in the United States. These professional maniacs are to hate what serial killers are to murder. They should certainly not be ignored; but they represent what Harold Meyerson, writing in Salon, called "niche haters": cold blooded, somewhat deranged, often poorly socialized psychopaths. In a free society with relatively easy access to guns, they will always pose a menace.

But their menace is a limited one, and their hatred is hardly typical of anything very widespread. Take Buford Furrow. He famously issued a "wake-up call" to "kill Jews" in Los Angeles, before he peppered a Jewish community center with gunfire. He did this in a state with two Jewish female Senators, in a city with a large, prosperous Jewish population, in a country where out of several million Jewish Americans, a total of 66 were reported by the F.B.I. as the targets of hate-crime assaults in 1997. However despicable Furrow's actions were, it would require a very large stretch to describe them as representative of anything but the deranged fringe of an American subculture.

Most hate is more common and more complicated, with as many varieties as there are varieties of love. Just as there is possessive love and needy love; family love and friendship; romantic love and unrequited love; passion and respect, affection and obsession, so hatred has its shadings. There is hate that fears, and hate that merely feels contempt; there is hate that expresses power, and hate that comes from powerlessness; there is revenge, and there is hate that comes from envy. There is hate that was love, and hate that is a curious expression of love. There is hate of the other, and hate of something that reminds us too much of ourselves. There is the oppressor's hate, and the victim's hate. There is hate that burns slowly, and hate that fades. And there is hate that explodes, and hate that never catches fire.

The modern words that we have created to describe the varieties of hate—sexism," "racism," "anti-Semitism, "homophobia"—tell us very little about any of this. They tell us merely the identities of the victims; they don't reveal the identities of the perpetrators, or what they think, or how they feel. They don't even tell us how the victims feel. And this simplicity is no accident. Coming from the theories of Marxist and post-Marxist academics, these "isms" are far better at alleging structures of power than at delineating the workings of the individual heart or mind. In fact, these "isms" can exist without mentioning individuals at all.

We speak of institutional racism, for example, as if an institution can feel anything. We talk of "hate" as an impersonal noun, with no hater specified. But when these abstractions are actually incarnated, when someone feels something as a result of them, when a hater actually interacts with a victim, the picture changes. We find that hates are often very different phenomena one from another, that they have very different psychological dynamics, that they might even be better understood by not seeing them as varieties of the same thing at all.

There is, for example, the now unfashionable distinction between reasonable hate and unreasonable hate. In recent years, we have become accustomed to talking about hates as if they were all equally indefensible, as if it could never be the case that some hates might be legitimate, even necessary. But when some 800,000 Tutsis are murdered under the auspices of a Hutu regime in Rwanda, and when a few thousand Hutus are killed in revenge, the hates are not commensurate. Genocide is not an event like a hurricane, in which damage is random and universal; it is a planned and often merciless attack of one group upon another. The hate of the perpetrators is a monstrosity. The hate of the victims, and their survivors, is justified. What else, one wonders, were surviving Jews supposed to feel toward Germans after the holocaust? Or, to a different degree, South African blacks after apartheid? If the victims overcome this hate, it is a supreme moral achievement. But if they don't, the victims are not as culpable as the perpetrators. So the hatred of Serbs for Kosovars today can never be equated with the hatred of Kosovars for Serbs.

Hate, like much of human feeling, is not rational, but it usually has its reasons. And it cannot be understood, let alone condemned, without knowing them. Similarly, the hate that comes from knowledge is always different from the hate that comes from ignorance. It is one of the most foolish cliches of our time that prejudice is always rooted in ignorance, and can usually be overcome by familiarity with the objects of our loathing. The racism of many Southern whites under segregation was not appeased by familiarity with Southern blacks; the virulent loathing of Tutsis by many Hutus was not undermined by living next door to them for centuries. Theirs was a hatred that sprang, for whatever reasons, from experience. It cannot easily be compared with, for example, the resilience of anti-Semitism in Japan, or hostility to immigration in areas where immigrants are unknown, or fear of homosexuals by people who have never knowingly met one.

The same familiarity is an integral part of what has become known as "sexism." Sexism isn't, properly speaking, a prejudice at all. Few men live without knowledge or constant awareness of women. Every single sexist man was born of a woman, and is likely to be sexually attracted to women. His hostility is going to be very different than that of, say, a reclusive member of the Aryan Nations toward Jews he has never met.

In her book "The Anatomy of Prejudices," the psychotherapist Elisabeth Young-Bruehl proposes a typology of three distinct kinds of hate: obsessive, hysterical and narcissistic. It's not an exhaustive analysis, but it's a beginning in any serious attempt to understand hate rather than merely declaring war on it. The obsessives, for young-Bruehl, are those, like the Nazis or Hutus, who fantasize a threat from a minority, and obsessively try to rid themselves of it. For them, the very existence of the hated group is threatening. They often describe their loathing in almost physical terms: they experience what Patrick Buchanan, in reference to homosexuals, once described as a "visceral recoil" from the objects of their detestation. They often describe those they hate as diseased or sick, in need of a cure. Or they talk of"cleansing" them, as the Hutus talked of the Tutsis, or call them "cockroaches," as Yitzhak Shamir called the Palestinians. If you read material from the Family Research Council, it is clear that the group regards homosexuals as similar contaminants. A recent posting on its Web site about syphilis among gay men was headlined, "Unclean."

Hysterical haters have a more complicated relationship with the objects of their aversion. In Young-Bruehl's words, hysterical prejudice is a prejudice that "a person uses unconsciously to appoint a group to act out in the world forbidden sexual and sexually aggressive desires that the person has repressed." Certain kinds of racists fit this pattern. White loathing of blacks is, for some people, at least partly about sexual and physical envy. A certain kind of white racist sees in black America all those impulses he wishes most to express himself but cannot. He idealizes in "blackness" a sexual freedom, a physical power, a Dionysian release that he detests but also longs for. His fantasy may not have any basis in reality, but it is powerful nonetheless. It is a form of love-hate, and it is impossible to understand the nuances of racism in, say, the American South, or in British Imperial India, without it.

Unlike the obsessives, the hysterical haters do not want to eradicate the objects of their loathing; rather they want to keep them in some kind of permanent and safe subjugation in order to indulge the attraction of their repulsion. A recent study, for example, found that the men most likely to be opposed to equal rights for homosexuals were those most likely to be aroused by homoerotic imagery. This makes little rational sense, but it has a certain psychological plausibility. If homosexuals were granted equality, then the hysterical gay-hater might panic that his repressed passions would run out of control, overwhelming him and the world he inhabits.

A narcissistic hate, according to Young-Bruehl's definition, is sexism. In its most common form, it is rooted in many men's inability even to imagine what it is to be a woman, a failing rarely challenged by men's control of our most powerful public social institutions. Women are not so much hated by most men as simply ignored in nonsexual contexts, or never conceived of as true equals. The implicit condescension is mixed, in many cases, with repressed and sublimated erotic desire. So the unawareness of women is sometimes commingled with a deep longing or contempt for them.

Each hate, of course, is more complicated than this, and in any one person hate can assume a uniquely configured combination of these types. So there are hysterical sexists who hate women because they need them so much, and narcissistic sexists who hardly notice that women exist, and sexists who oscillate between one of these positions and another. And there are gay-bashers who are threatened by masculine gay men and gay-haters who feel repulsed by effeminate ones. The soldier who beat his fellow soldier Barry Winchell to death with a baseball bat in July had earlier lost a fight to him. It was the image of a macho gay man—and the shame of being bested by him—that the vengeful soldier had to obliterate, even if he needed a gang of accomplices and a weapon to do so. But the murderers of Matthew Shepard seem to have had a different impulse: a visceral disgust at the thought of any sexual contact with an effeminate homosexual. Their anger was mixed with mockery, as the cruel spectacle at the side of the road suggested.

In the same way, the pathological anti-Semitism of Nazi Germany was obsessive, inasmuch as it tried to cleanse the world of Jews; but also, as Daniel

Jonah Goldhagen shows in his book, "Hitler's Willing Executioners," hysterical. The Germans were mysteriously compelled as well as repelled by Jews, devising elaborate ways, like death camps and death marches, to keep them alive even as they killed them. And the early Nazi phobia of interracial sex suggests as well a lingering erotic quality to the relationship, partaking of exactly the kind of sexual panic that persists among some homosexual-haters and anti-miscegenation racists. So the concept of "homophobia," like that of "sexism" and "racism," is often a crude one. All three are essentially cookie-cutter formulas that try to understand human impulses merely through the one-dimensional identity of the victims, rather than through the thoughts and feelings of the haters and hated.

This is deliberate. The theorists behind these "isms" want to ascribe all blame to one group in society—the "oppressors"—and render specific others—the "victims"—completely blameless. And they want to do this in order in part to side unequivocally with the underdog. But it doesn't take a genius to see how this approach, too,can generate its own form of bias. It can justify blanket condemnations of whole groups of people—white straight males for example—purely because of the color of their skin or the nature of their sexual orientation. And it can condescendingly ascribe innocence to whole groups of others. It does exactly what hate does: it hammers the uniqueness of each individual into the anvil of group identity. And it postures morally over the result.

In reality, human beings and human acts are far more complex, which is why these isms and the laws they have fomented are continually coming under strain and challenge. Once again, hate wriggles free of its definers. It knows no monolithic groups of haters and hated. Like a river, it has many eddies, back-waters and rapids. So there are anti-Semites who actually admire what they think of as Jewish power, and there are gay-haters who look up to homosexuals and some who want to sleep with them. And there are black racists, racist Jews, sexist women and anti-Semitic homosexuals. Of course there are.

IV.

Once you start thinking of these phenomena less as the "isms" of sexism, racism and "homophobia," once you think of them as independent psychological responses,it's also possible to see how they can work in a bewildering variety of ways in a bewildering number of people. To take one obvious and sad oddity: people who are demeaned and objectified in society may develop an aversion to their tormentors that is more hateful in its expression than the prejudice they have been subjected to. The F.B.I. statistics on hate crimes throws up an interesting point. In America in the 1990's, blacks were up to three times as likely as whites to commit a hate crime,to express their hate by physically attacking their targets or their property. Just as sexual abusers have often been victims of sexual abuse, and wife-beaters often grew up in violent households, so hate criminals may often be members of hated groups.

Even the Columbine murderers were in some sense victims of hate before they were purveyors of it. Their classmates later admitted that Dylan Klebold and Eric Harris were regularly called "faggots" in the corridors and classrooms of Columbine High and that nothing was done to prevent or stop the harassment. This climate of hostility doesn't excuse the actions of Klebold and Harris, but it does provide a more plausible context. If they had been black, had routinely been called "nigger" in the school and had then exploded into a shooting spree against white students, the response to the matter might well have been different. But the hate would have been the same. In other words, hate-victims are often hate-victimizers as well. This doesn't mean that all hates are equivalent, or that some are not more justified than others. It means merely that hate goes both ways; and if you try to regulate it among some, you will find yourself forced to regulate it among others.

It is no secret, for example, that some of the most vicious anti-Semites in America are black, and that some of the most virulent anti-Catholic bigots in America are gay. At what point, we are increasingly forced to ask, do these phenomena become as indefensible as white racism or religious toleration of anti-gay bigotry? That question becomes all the more difficult when we notice that it is often minorities who commit some of the most hate-filled offenses against what they see as their oppressors. It was the mainly gay AIDS activist group Act Up that perpetrated the hateful act of desecrating Communion hosts at a Mass at St Patrick's Cathedral in New York. And here is the playwright Tony Kushner, who is gay, responding to the Matthew Shepard beating in The Nation magazine: "Pope John Paul II endorses murder. He, too,knows the price of discrimination, having declared anti-Semitism a sin. . . . He knows that discrimination kills. But when the Pope heard the news about Matthew Shepard, he, too, worried about spin. And so, on the subject of gay-bashing, the Pope and his cardinals and his bishops and priests maintain their cynical political silence. . . . To remain silent is to endorse murder." Kushner went on to describe the Pope as a "homicidal liar."

Maybe the passion behind these words is justified. But it seems clear enough to me that Kushner is expressing hate toward the institution of the Catholic Church, and all those who perpetuate its doctrines. How else to interpret the way in which he accuses the Pope of cynicism, lying and murder? And how else either to understand the brutal parody of religious vocations expressed by the Sisters of Perpetual Indulgence, a group of gay men who dress in drag as nuns and engage in sexually explicit performances in public? Or T-shirts with the words "Recovering Catholic" on them, hot items among some gay and lesbian activists? The implication that someone's religious faith is a mental illness is clearly an expression of contempt. If that isn't covered under the definition of hate speech, what is?

Or take the following sentence: "The act male homosexuals commit is ugly and repugnant and afterwards they are disgusted with themselves. They drink and take drugs to palliate this, but they are disgusted with the act and they are always changing partners and cannot be really happy." The thoughts of Pat Robertson or Patrick Buchanan? Actually that sentence was written by Gertrude Stein, one of the century's most notable lesbians. Or take the following, about how beating up "black boys like that made us feel good inside. . . . Every time I drove my foot into his [expletive], I felt better." It was written to describe the brutal assault of an innocent bystander for the sole reason of his race. By the end of the attack, the victim had blood gushing from his mouth as his attackers stomped on his genitals. Are we less appalled when we learn that the actual sentence was how beating up "white boys like that made us feel good inside. . . . Every time I drove my foot into his[expletive], I felt better?" It was written by Nathan McCall, an African-American who later in life became a successful journalist at *The Washington Post* and published his memoir of this "hate crime" to much acclaim.

In fact, one of the stranger aspects of hate is that the prejudice expressed by a group in power may often be milder in expression than the prejudice felt by the marginalized. After all, if you already enjoy privilege, you may not feel the anger that turns bias into hate. You may not need to. For this reason, most white racism maybe more influential in society than most black racism—but also more calmly expressed.

So may other forms of minority loathing—especially hatred within minorities. I'm sure that black conservatives like Clarence Thomas or Thomas Sowell have experienced their fair share of white racism. But I wonder whether it has ever reached the level of intensity of the hatred directed toward them by other blacks? In several years of being an openly gay writer and editor, I have experienced the gamut of responses to my sexual orientation. But I have only directly experienced articulated, passionate hate from other homosexuals. I have been accused over the years by other homosexuals of being a sellout, a hypocrite, a traitor, a sexist, a racist, a narcissist, a snob. I've been called selfish, callous, hateful, self-hating and malevolent. At a reading, a group of lesbian activists portrayed my face on a poster within the crossfires of a gun. Nothing from the religious right has come close to such vehemence.

I am not complaining. No harm has ever come to me or my property, and much of the criticism is rooted in the legitimate expression of political differences. But the visceral tone and style of the gay criticism can only be described as hateful. It is designed to wound personally, and it often does. But its intensity comes in part, one senses, from the pain of being excluded for so long, of anger long restrained bubbling up and directing itself more aggressively toward an alleged traitor than an alleged enemy. It is the hate of the hated. And it can be the most hateful hate of all. For this reason, hate-crime laws may themselves be an oddly biased category—biased against the victims of hate. Racism is everywhere, but the already victimized might be more desperate, more willing to express it violently. And so more prone to come under the suspicious eye of the law.

V.

And why is hate for a group worse than hate for a person? In Laramie, Wyo., the now-famous epicenter of "homophobia," where Matthew Shepard was brutally beaten to death, vicious murders are not unknown. In the previous 12 months, a 15-year-old pregnant girl was found east of the town with 17 stab wounds. Her 38-year-old boyfriend was apparently angry that she had refused an abortion and left her in the Wyoming foothills to bleed to death. In the summer of 1998, an 8-year-old Laramie girl was abducted, raped and murdered by a pedophile, who disposed of her young body in a garbage dump. Neither of these killings was deemed a hate crime, and neither would be designated as such under any existing hate-crime law. Perhaps because of this, one crime is an international legend; the other two are virtually unheard of.

But which crime was more filled with hate? Once you ask the question, you realize how difficult it is to answer. Is it more hateful to kill a stranger or a lover? Is it more hateful to kill a child than an adult? Is it more hateful to kill your own child than another's? Under the law before the invention of hate crimes, these decisions didn't have to be taken. But under the law after hate crimes, a decision is essential. A decade ago, a murder was a murder. Now, in the era when group hate has emerged a sour cardinal social sin, it all depends.

The supporters of laws against hate crimes argue that such crimes should be disproportionately punished because they victimize more than the victim. Such crimes, these advocates argue, spread fear, hatred and panic among whole populations, and therefore merit more concern. But, of course, all crimes victimize more than the victim, and spread alarm in the society at large. Just think of the terrifying church shooting in Texas only two weeks ago. In fact, a purely random murder may be even more terrifying than a targeted one, since the entire community, and not just a part of it, feels threatened. High rates of murder, robbery, assault and burglary victimize everyone, by spreading fear, suspicion and distress everywhere. Which crime was more frightening to more people this summer: the mentally ill Buford Furrow's crazed attacks in Los Angeles, killing one, or Mark Barton's murder of his own family and several random day-traders in Atlanta, killing 12? Almost certainly the latter. But only Furrow was guilty of "hate."

One response to this objection is that certain groups feel fear more intensely than others because of a history of persecution or intimidation. But doesn't this smack of a certain condescension toward minorities? Why, after all, should it be assumed that gay men or black women or Jews, for example, are as a group more easily intimidated than others? Surely in any of these communities there will be a vast range of responses, from panic to concern to complete indifference. The assumption otherwise is the kind of crude generalization the law is supposed to uproot in the first place. And among these groups, there are also likely to be vast differences. To equate a population once subjected to slavery with a population of Mexican immigrants or third-generation Holocaust survivors is to equate the unequatable. In fact, it is to set up a contest of vulnerability in which one group vies with another to establish its particular variety of suffering, a contest that can have no dignified solution.

Rape, for example, is not classified as a "hate crime" under most existing laws, pitting feminists against ethnic groups in a battle for recognition. If, as a solution to this problem, everyone, except the white straight able-bodied male, is regarded as a possible victim of a hate crime, then we have simply created a two-tier system of justice in which racial profiling is reversed, and white straight men are presumed guilty before being proven innocent, and members of minorities are free to hate them as gleefully as they like. But if we include the white straight male in the litany of potential victims, then we have effectively abolished the notion of a hate crime altogether. For if every crime is possibly a hate crime, then it is simply another name for crime. All we will have done is widened the search for possible bigotry, ratcheted up the sentences for everyone and filled the jails up even further.

Hate-crime-law advocates counter that extra penalties should be imposed on hate crimes because our society is experiencing an "epidemic" of such crimes. Mercifully, there is no hard evidence to support this notion. The Federal Government has only been recording the incidence of hate crimes in this decade, and the statistics tell a simple story. In 1992, there were 6,623 hate-crime incidents reported to the F.B.I. by a total of 6,181 agencies, covering 51 percent of the population. In 1996, there were 8,734 incidents reported by 11,355 agencies, covering 84 percent of the population. That number dropped to 8,049 in 1997. These numbers are, of course, hazardous. They probably under report the incidence of such crimes, but they are the only reliable figures we have. Yet even if they are faulty as an absolute number, they do not show an epidemic of "hate crimes" in the 1990's.

Is there evidence that the crimes themselves are becoming more vicious? None. More than 60 percent of recorded hate crimes in America involve no violent, physical assault against another human being at all, and, again, according to the F.B.I., that proportion has not budged much in the 1990's. These impersonal attacks are crimes against property or crimes of "intimidation." Murder, which dominates media coverage of hate crimes, is a tiny proportion of the total. Of the 8,049 hate crimes reported to the F.B.I. in 1997, a total of eight were murders. Eight. The number of hate crimes that were aggravated assaults (generally involving a weapon) in 1997 is less than 15 percent of the total. That's 1,237 assaults too many, of course, but to put it in perspective, compare it with a reported 1,022,492 "equal opportunity" aggravated assaults in America in the same year. The number of hate crimes that were physical assaults is half the total. That's 4,000 assaults too many, of course, but to put it in perspective, it compares with around 3.8 million "equal opportunity" assaults in America annually.

The truth is, the distinction between a crime filled with personal hate and a crime filled with group hate is an essentially arbitrary one. It tells us nothing interesting about the psychological contours of the specific actor or his specific victim. It is a function primarily of politics, of special interest groups carving out particular protections for themselves, rather than a serious response to a serious criminal concern. In such an endeavor, hate-crime-law advocates cram an entire world of human motivations into an immutable, tiny box called hate, and hope to have solved a problem. But nothing has been solved; and some harm may even have been done.

In an attempt to repudiate a past that treated people differently because of the color of their skin, or their sex, or religion or sexual orientation, we may merely create a future that permanently treats people differently because of the color of their skin, or their sex, religion or sexual orientation. This notion of a hate crime, and the concept of hate that lies behind it, takes a psychological mystery and turns it into a facile political artifact. Rather than compounding this error and extending even further, we should seriously consider repealing the concept altogether.

To put it another way: violence can and should be stopped by the government. In a free society, hate can't and shouldn't be. The boundaries between hate and prejudice and between prejudice and opinion and between opinion and truth are so complicated and blurred that any attempt to construct legal and political fire walls is a doomed and illiberal venture. We know by now that hate will never disappear from human consciousness; in fact, it is probably, at some level, definitive of it. We know after decades of education measures that hate is not caused merely by ignorance; and after decades of legislation, that it isn't caused entirely by law.

To be sure, we have made much progress. Anyone who argues that America is as inhospitable to minorities and to women today as it has been in the past has not read much history. And we should, of course, be vigilant that our most powerful institutions, most notably the government, do not actively or formally propagate hatred; and insure that the violent expression of hate is curtailed by the same rules that punish all violent expression.

But after that, in an increasingly diverse culture, it is crazy to expect that hate, in all its variety, can be eradicated. A free country will always mean a hateful country. This may not be fair, or perfect, or admirable, but it is reality, and while we need not endorse it, we should not delude ourselves into thinking we can prevent it. That is surely the distinction between toleration and tolerance. Tolerance is the eradication of hate; toleration is co-existence despite it. We might do better as a culture and as a polity if we concentrated more on achieving the latter rather than the former. We would certainly be less frustrated.

And by aiming lower, we might actually reach higher. In some ways, some expression of prejudice serves a useful social purpose. It lets off steam; it allows natural tensions to express themselves incrementally; it can siphon off conflict through words, rather than actions. Anyone who has lived in the ethnic shouting match that is New York City knows exactly what I mean. If New Yorkers disliked each other less, they wouldn't be able to get on so well. We may not all be able to pull off a Mencken—bigoted in words, egalitarian in action—but we might achieve a lesser form of virtue: a human acceptance of our need for differentiation, without a total capitulation to it.

Do we not owe something more to the victims of hate? Perhaps we do. But it is also true that there is nothing that government can do for the hated that the hated cannot better do for themselves. After all, most bigots are not foiled when they are punished specifically for their beliefs. In fact, many of the worst haters crave such attention and find vindication in such rebukes. Indeed, our media's obsession with "hate," our elevation of it above other social misdemeanors and crimes, may even play into the hands of the pathetic and the evil, may breathe air into the smoldering embers of their paranoid loathing. Sure, we can help create a climate in which such hate is disapproved of—and we should. But there is a danger that if we go too far, if we punish it too much, if we try to abolish it altogether, we may merely increase its mystique, and entrench the very categories of human difference that we are trying to erase.

For hate is only foiled not when the haters are punished but when the hated are immune to the bigot's power. A hater cannot psychologically wound if a victim cannot psychologically be wounded. And that immunity to hurt can never be given; it can merely be achieved. The racial epithet only strikes at someone's core if he lets it, if he allows the bigot's definition of him to be the final description of his life and his person—if somewhere in his heart of hearts, he believes the hateful slur to be true. The only final answer to this form of racism, then, is not majority persecution of it, but minority indifference to it. The only permanent rebuke to homophobia is not the enforcement of tolerance, but gay equanimity in the face of prejudice. The only effective answer to sexism is not a morass of legal proscriptions, but the simple fact of female success. In this, as in so many other things, there is no solution to the problem. There is only a transcendence of it. For all our rhetoric, hate will never be destroyed. Hate, as our predecessors knew better, can merely be overcome.

POSTSCRIPT

Is Hate Crime Legislation Constitutional?

Hate crimes are not new to this society, but the subject of hate crimes has aroused considerable controversy and concern following some very visible and horrific events in the past several years, especially the brutal killing of James Byrd, Jr., a black man killed because of his race, and Matthew Shepard, killed because of his sexual orientation.

What constitutes a "hate crime"? As Grigera notes, the Hate Crime Sentencing Act of 1994 defines a hate crime as "a crime in which the defendant intentionally selects a victim, or in the case of a property crime, the property that is the object of the crime, because of the actual or perceived race, color, religion, national origin, ethnicity, gender, disability or sexual orientation of any person." How must/might a society deal with such crimes? Should society focus on the roots of hatred and deal with underlying causes? Should society more severely punish crimes stemming from hatred? If "hate" is based upon a belief, is it constitutional to punish one for one's beliefs?

Elena Grigera argues that hate crimes, and the intolerance behind them, threaten the very fabric of American society. She argues that although hate crime legislation is often seen as protecting minorities, in reality it protects everyone, for anyone can be the victim of a hate crime. Hate crime legislation is intended to send a message from a society that it will not tolerate such behavior. It is also intended as a deterrent.

Is hate crime legislation constitutional? Grigera points out that the judiciary has thus far made the distinction between punishing "speech" or "beliefs" and acting upon them. Citing the Supreme Court in *Wisconsin v. Mitchell*, Grigera notes that "sentence enhancement provisions do not criminalize speech. . . . [T]hey simply establish separate punishment for offenders who commit certain criminal acts 'because of' prejudice . . . and [punish] the discriminatory conduct." Grigera speculates that the judiciary will continue to see hate crime legislation from this perspective.

Andrew Sullivan also refers to the murders of Byrd and Shepard and others, and questions what was going on in the minds of the perpetrators of such heinous crimes. But Sullivan argues that hatred is part of the human condition and that it stems from beliefs long established. He further disputes whether it is possible to accurately define "hate," and the contemporary terminology—such as "sexism," "racism," "anti-Semitism," "homophobia"—tells us more about the victims than about the perpetrators. Sullivan warns against "-isms" because they may result in "blanket condemnations" of whole groups of people.

It is impossible to legislate against beliefs, or to eradicate hate. Further, he argues, it is unconstitutional to impose penalties for crimes based upon hate—as despicable as they might be—or to impose stiffer penalties. "Why," he questions, "is hate for a group worse than hate for a person?" He argues that "a crime is a crime," regardless of the intent of the perpetrator or the demographics of the victim. Arguing for protecting beliefs, Sullivan says, "A free country will always be a hateful country."

ISSUE 11

Should Same-Sex Marriages Be Permitted?

YES: Lara Schwartz, from "Why Marriage?" *Human Rights Campaign Publication*

NO: Edith M. Humphrey, from "What God Hath Not Joined: Why Marriage Was Designed for Male and Female," *Christianity Today* (September 2004)

ISSUE SUMMARY

YES: Lara Schwartz, Human Rights Campaign senior staff counsel, argues that any other form of same-sex uniform denies equality, financial benefits and security, and social recognition. Settling for anything less than "marriage" would be to abandon the quest for equality.

NO: Edith M. Humphrey argues that same-sex marriages are contrary to biblical teaching. Marriage, she argues, is not a human creation but one enacted by God himself.

In June 1958, Mildred Jeter and Richard Loving of Virginia fell in love. Like so many people who fall in love, Mildred and Richard wanted to marry. The only thing standing in their way was Virginia law, banning interracial marriage. So the couple went to the District of Columbia to have their marriage performed. The story does not end semi-happily here. Upon their return to Virginia, the couple was charged with violating the ban. They pled guilty and received a sentence of a year in prison. The court agreed to suspend the sentence for 25 years if the couple agreed to leave the state. They returned to the District of Columbia and set in motion litigation that eventually reached the Supreme Court.

Some may find this hard to believe, but it was not until 1967 that laws prohibiting interracial marriages were declared unconstitutional by a unanimous vote of the U.S. Supreme Court in the case of *Loving v. Virginia*. The court reversed a lower court finding that had upheld the Virginia law banning interracial marriage. In that case, the trial judge had proclaimed:

> Almighty God created the races white, black, yellow, malay and red, and he placed them on separate continents. And but for the interference with his

arrangement there would be no cause for such marriages. The fact that he separated the races shows that he did not intend for the races to mix.

In stark contrast to the trial judge's views, the U.S. Supreme Court maintained:

> Marriage is one of the "basic civil rights of man," fundamental to our very existence and survival. . . . To deny this fundamental freedom on so unsupportable a basis as the racial classifications embodied in these statutes, classifications so directly subversive of the principle of equality at the heart of the Fourteenth Amendment, is surely to deprive all of the State's citizens of liberty without due process of law. The Fourteenth Amendment requires that the freedom of choice to marry not be restricted by invidious racial discriminations. Under our Constitution, the freedom to marry, or not marry, a person of another race resides with the individual and cannot be infringed by the State.

Social views often lag behind judicial decisions, and in that era many undoubtedly were outraged by the reality that people of different races could marry. Perhaps some people still feel that way. But the world did not end, no matter how unnatural some may have felt interracial marriage was.

Not so coincidentally, this decision came in the midst of the civil rights movement. Can a parallel be made to the efforts of gays and lesbians, in the midst of the gay rights movement? Opponents might argue that race is a characteristic of birth, while sexual orientation is a "choice." Increasingly, data are suggesting that individuals do not "become homosexual," but are born so. If the U.S. Constitution implicitly recognizes the right to marry or not to marry as a fundamental freedom, can government deny this right to gays and lesbians?

The Human Rights Campaign provides a very thorough discussion of the differences between "marriage" and "civil unions," the latter being what some have suggested as a "compromise. It is clear that civil unions are inferior to marriage in all ways and would subject homosexuals to the status of second-class citizenry.

The contrary opinion is expressed by Edith Humphrey, whose views, not so remarkably, could be interchanged with those of the Virginia trial judge's views regarding interracial marriage.

YES

Lara Schwartz

Why Marriage?

We can all agree about the things that matter to us most: freedom from discrimination in the workplace, at home, and under law. Protection from hate crimes. A secure financial future for ourselves, our partners, and our children. It doesn't matter what some people call it: we call it *equality*.

Achieving equality for our families is of the utmost importance. Because same-sex couples may not legally marry in any state except Massachusetts, they cannot—no matter how carefully they plan or how many legal contracts they sign—secure all of the protections that married couples receive with state-sanctioned their civil marriages.

There are other mechanisms for recognizing relationships for limited purposes. Civil unions, which confer state-level benefits for residents of Vermont, and domestic partner registries, some of which are largely symbolic and some of which provide a handful of state-level benefits, are the most familiar.

Current polls show that more Americans support civil unions than full marriage equality. Given the seeming political advantage of civil unions, many proponents of equality for same-sex couples find ourselves asking "why marriage?" Why not something easier to attain? There is not a simple answer, and in fact, any step toward equality should be celebrated. Be it family and medical leave, retirement savings, or the right to visit a partner in her hospital bed, each and every benefit matters in a concrete way, and we cannot brush aside any progress in favor of a symbolic attachment to a *word*. However, as set forth below, it would be a mistake to stop fighting for marriage equality, because no other mechanism has ever provided the complete security that marriage provides, nor is it likely that an "anything but marriage" system could result in true equality in our lifetime.

I. The Things That Only Marriage Can Do

A. Portability

One of the most basic advantages of marriage is portability. When an opposite-sex couple marries in any state or foreign country, the marriage is recognized everywhere in the United States, and for all purposes.[1] Civil unions, on the

From *Human Rights Campaign*. Reprinted by permission.

other hand, are legally recognized only where celebrated. Therefore even couples who travel to Vermont for civil unions do not receive hundreds of state benefits and protections when they return home.[2] Waiting for non-portable civil unions to be enacted would effectively bar same-sex couples in some states from ever achieving equality. Can we afford to leave LGBT Alabamans behind?

B. Federal Benefits

According to a 1997 GAO report, over 1,000 federal rights, privileges, and protections are based upon marital status. These include such critically important protections as the right to take leave from work to care for a family member, the right to sponsor a spouse for immigration purposes, and Social Security survivors benefits that can be worth hundreds of thousands of dollars. Civil unions do not provide access to these federal benefits and protection.

C. State Mechanisms for Enforcing Marriage Rights Would Be Difficult to Replicate

It has been suggested that federal civil unions—which would give same-sex couples access to the 1,049 federal benefits—would be an alternative to marriage. Although this is a good goal, as a policy matter it would be exceptionally challenging because the federal government is not equipped to regulate relationships.

When a couple marries, they subject themselves to an elaborate legal enforcement mechanism for their vows. States can enforce their promises to support one another and their children. When they separate, state laws—both statutory and common law—determine their rights relative to each other. State law determines marital status for the purpose of federal benefits such as Social Security. This means that the federal government does not have to be the arbiter of when, for instance, a couple breaks up, or how their property will be divided when they do.

When same-sex couples achieve full marriage equality in a state, it will be easy and practical as a policy matter to extend federal benefits of all kinds to them.[3] A federal civil union, on the other hand, would not have the benefit of state mechanisms for determining rights under the relationship, nor would it confer the hundreds of state-level rights of marriage.

II. "Everything But Marriage" Is an Untested Legal Fiction

S.J. Res. 1, known as the Marriage Protection Amendment ("MPA") proposes to amend the Constitution of the United States by adding the following language: "Marriage in the United States shall consist only of the union of a man and woman. Neither this Constitution, nor the constitution of any State, shall be construed to require that marriage of the legal incidents thereof be conferred upon any union other than the union of a man and a woman."

A. Marriage as a Man and a Woman—Semantic or Substantive?

Some have argued that the second sentence of the FMA poses the biggest problem, because it could be read to invalidate civil unions and other relationship recognition legislation.[4] Conversely, even allies of GLBT equality have expressed greater comfort with an "Everything But Marriage" approach, creating "marriages" under another name—civil unions. Legally, this approach is problematic because we don't know what excluding gay people from "marriage" will really mean. It is worth noting that there is no other law that prohibits *naming* a certain act a certain way, but otherwise authorizes the act. Try to imagine an environmental regulation that prohibits building a house on the beach . . . unless you call it a shoe. We do not, in fact, regulate names but actions through the law.

It is a basic rule of statutory construction that we do not read statutes in ways that render them meaningless. Sentence one of the FMA—a ban on "marriages" between same-sex couples, is next to meaningless if all it means is that a state must instead call same sex unions "schmarriages." It is therefore not safe to assume that a "mere" ban on marriage leaves the door open to "everything but marriage." The "everything but" that we are fighting for could rightly be called the essence of marriage, and a constitutional ban could exclude same-sex couples from it.

B. Opponents of Equality Oppose "Everything But Marriage," and Will Fight to Interpret Marriage Bans Broadly

The ideas set forth in paragraph A have already been circulating in anti-equality circles. California is a good case study. In March 2000, California voters approved Proposition 22, a ballot measure defining marriage as a union between a man and a woman. California enacted, in 2004, AB 205, a civil union measure that would grant same-sex couples most of the state rights, benefits, and protections given to married couples. Opponents have repeatedly stated that AB 205 violates Proposition 22.

The following quotation from a Campaign for California Families press release illustrates that the "anything but marriage" strategy provides no more political cover than legal clarity: "Like civil unions, AB 205 is gay marriage by another name."[5]

III. Conclusion

It would be comforting to think that by letting go of the word "marriage" we could more easily secure equality for families headed by same-sex couples. However, only marriage provides a system for resolving relationship disputes, determining couples' status and rights relative to each other and the states, provides federal benefits, and is completely portable. Furthermore, we are seeing that at the end of the day, it is relationship recognition itself—not the word "marriage," that energizes opponents. Finally, a constitutional amendment that excludes same-sex couples from marriage could very well exclude them from the same benefits that "Everything but marriage" solutions seek to provide. For all of these reasons, it is important that we continue to resolute in our commitment to marriage equality.

Notes

1. Polygamous marriages, forced marriages, or marriages among very young minors are exceptions.

2. In fact, parties to a Vermont civil union who attempted to secure a divorce in their home state court were unable to do so, because the state would not grant a divorce where it did not recognize a marriage.

3. This would also require repealing or successfully challenging the Defense of Marriage Act.

4. The Legal Department and pro bono counsel have analyzed the language and determined that broad and narrow readings of it are both feasible.

5. http://www.savecalifornia.com/press/newsreleases/release. cfm?nrid=PR030816A. The release also states: "AB 205 awards all the rights of marriage under statute to homosexual partners. The voters aren't stupid. Davis and Bustamante are rejecting the people of California, who voted overwhelmingly three years ago to protect the rights of marriage for a husband and wife, as it should be."

NO

Edith M. Humphrey

What God Hath Not Joined: Why Marriage Was Designed for Male and Female

"Have you not read that the one who made them at the beginning 'made them male and female,' and said, 'For this reason a man shall leave his father and mother be joined to his wife, and the two Shall become one flesh'?" So Jesus declares that in the first marriage and in every marriage since, it is God himself who joins particular members of the opposite sex together in a natural relation unlike any other.

All societies have honored this special union that Christians, Jews, and Muslims tightly recognize to be a gift of the Creator. Even in an atheistic context like Russia during the Communist period, Muscovite couples were married with festal trappings at what passed for a Sacred site, Lenin's tomb.

Our generation has introduced a tear in this universal fabric: Same-sex activists are clamoring for the state to grant homosexual couples marital status. These blows to the definition of marriage are landing not only in the North American civil sphere, but within churches. Theological arguments may not hold much sway in public debate, and there are certainly good social reasons for preserving the definition of marriage. But for the defense of marriage in both civil society and church, Christians must look to—and guard—the deep theological foundations of marriage.

Theological foundations are indeed under attack. On June 3, the General Synod of the Anglican Church of Canada, while deferring the decision to bless same-sex unions in formal ceremonies, declared that longstanding homoerotic relationships were already sanctified. Even while questioning whether this issue touches on core doctrine, the Synod employed a theological term (sanctity) to "support" its gay and lesbian members. Such confusing events lead the faithful to ask: What is the connection between the same-sex debate and doctrine? Can those who desire the "sanctity of marriage" rightly find it for same-sex relationships? Can same-sex unions truly be blessed in the churches?

The cry goes up that the biblical teaching must be surpassed, since "God is doing a new thing." What is the style of God's action in the world? How does the Bible describe God's activity and homoeroticism itself? In Romans 1:18–32,

From *Christianity Today*, vol. 48, issue 9, September 2004, pp. 36–44. Copyright © 2004 by Edith M. Humphrey. Reprinted by permission of the author.

Paul traces the drama of creation, sin, idolatry, and rebellion. Wonderfully, the created order provided a window through which God's glory can be seen. Humanity drew the blinds over this window, however, when it acted willfully, giving neither honor nor thanks to the Creator.

But true atheism is not possible for those made to worship. Human beings simply exchanged loyalties, worshiping creatures rather than God. God's response to this senseless idolatry was to permit the natural consequences. Paul gives a vivid example of this fallout: Human passions are disturbed and the primary created relationship (male and female) is distorted into homoerotic behavior.

Though the emphasis is on bodily disruption, the consequences go beyond the body to the entire self. Thus Romans I understands homoerotic behavior as an example of what happened to humanity in terms of the body and the passions, before it goes on to consider sins that arise within the disordered mind.

Homoerotic activity, then, is symptomatic of the primal rebellion against God—alongside covetousness, murder, strife, gossip, deceit, disloyalty, and pride.

No doubt Paul places it first because this condition shows brokenness in God's creative order and within the ordained union of male and female (Gen. 1:27). Homoeroticism thus represents an exchange (Rom. 1:26) of what is "natural" for what is "against nature," and is a primary breach between the two designed for each other. These relations dramatize human rejection of God's primal purposes.

Some have claimed that, because Paul uses homoeroticism only as an illustration, Romans 1 does not speak regarding sexual ethics. This can hardly be so. Would anyone apply the same reasoning to the other signs of depravity cited here, like murder? Paul assumes that his readers agree with his assessment of homoerotic activity, and helps them to understand it in the context of the scriptural story of origins.

Holiness Narratives

In light of this larger narrative, we go back to the Old Testament. In Genesis 18:16–19:29 (and a similar story in Judges 19), the male inhabitants of a city attempt to rape visitors. Some have argued that Sodom's sin was not sexual but simply a breach of hospitality. This is highly unlikely, since Lot's daughters were offered as a sexual substitute.

The intended sin here is gang rape, though it is true that where other passages mention Sodom (Isa. 1:10ff., Jer. 23:14, Eze. 16:49ff.), they emphasize hypocrisy, falsehood, and arrogance over sexual sin. Yet as Judaism and Christianity encountered later Hellenistic acceptance of homoeroticism, the sexual element in the Genesis story was highlighted: Intertestamental writings cite Sodom as an example of sexual perversion (cf. Jude 7).

We turn from narratives to injunction. Leviticus 18:22 says bluntly: "You shall not lie with a male as with a woman; it is an abomination" (cf. Lev. 20:13). Some within the church argue that such prohibitions concern only cultic practices in ancient Israel and so are no longer binding on Christians.

But some Levitical proscriptions concern immoral behavior, not simply ritual uncleanness. We need to ask, How does the general pattern of the Scriptures direct us to understand this prohibition?

The answer is that homoerotic behavior contradicts God's purpose for all his creatures. It is not in the same category as the cultic or cultural prohibitions regarding nonkosher foods and the twining together of two types of thread. Like the prohibition of incest (Lev. 18:6–18), the prohibition of homoerotic acts addresses every age.

As the New Testament epistles show, the early church did not discard what the Hebrew Bible said about sexual ethics. When Corinthian Christians thought that their spiritual sophistication gave them license to sin, Paul challenged them (1 Cor. 6:9ff.): "Do you not know that evildoers will not inherit God's kingdom?" Then he offered as examples those who steal, get drunk, scorn what is holy, pursue sexual immorality, and practice two modes of male homoerotic behavior.

Some argue that we cannot understand Paul's reference to these two behaviors (malakoi and arsenokoitai, as in 1 Cor. 6 and 1 Tim. 1) in terms of homoeroticism. But arsenokoitai is in fact a compound word derived from the Greek version of Leviticus 20:13 for those men "who lie with a male." Malakoi means literally "soft ones" and in Greek writings frequently identified the passive homoerotic partner. It is a mistake to limit the term's meaning, as do some, to masturbation, or as the NRSV does, to male prostitution.

The Genesis narratives, because they are stories, and the Levitical passages, because they are part of a code given to Israel in particular, must be considered in light of the whole biblical narrative, when we do this, the lists of immoral behavior in 1 Corinthians and 1 Timothy show that the early Christian communities held firm to Old Testament views of sexual immorality—for reasons consistent with Romans 1.

Revising Paul

The moral tradition of the church, from the earliest period into the Reformation and since, has been emphatic: Homoerotic behavior is against the will of God.

Those who reject this tradition take several tacks, for example: "The church has fudged on other controversial issues, and homosexuality is the same." What about female ministry and slavery, critics ask; doesn't the Bible forbid the one and accept the other, yet the church does what it thinks best anyway?

In fact, female ministry and slavery are handled differently from text to text in the Bible (e.g., on female ministry: 1 Cor. 14:33b-35 vs. 1 Cor. 11:4–5; 1 Tim. 2:11 and 1 Tim. 3:11, cf. Rom. 16:1). Without addressing these issues at length, we can see that, at the least, there are internal tensions in Scripture regarding female ministry and slavery. But there is no internal tension among the passages that speak of homoerotic behavior.

Others undermine the biblical teaching by suggesting, "Paul was talking about something else." That is, he forbids homosexual practice to people who are by nature heterosexual; he judges those who are not truly homosexual but who act homoerotically "against [their] nature" (Rom. 1:26). Thus, they say, Paul would not disapprove the practice by those who are by nature homosexual.

The mistake here is to think that in Romans 1, Paul has in mind certain individuals or types. Instead, he is painting on a large canvas, speaking about the problems of Israel in the context of God's dealings with all humanity (Adam and the Gentiles). He is not speaking of individuals, but of humanity in general, and of one sign (homoeroticism) that our original wholeness has been broken. To introduce specific categories, those who act homosexually "according to nature," and those who do so "against nature," is to muddle Paul's point.

Some limit Paul's words by saying that he is decrying those who sell their bodies for gain (so making malakoi or arsenokoitai to mean male prostitution). There is simply no evidence whatever for this, notwithstanding the serpentine arguments of John Boswell's *Christianity, Social Tolerance, and Homosexuality* (1980) and in L. William Countryman's *Dirt, Greed and Sex* (1988). Paul's problem with homoerotic behavior is specifically its same-sex quality, not power-relations or the economics of sexual trade.

But could Paul's disapproval of homoeroticism be limited to those who practiced pederasty, that ancient Hellenistic practice of erotic behavior with young males? In fact, the Graeco-Roman "ideal" of the "love of boys" did not mean children, but teenage males, of the same age that young women would be given in marriage. The exploitation of children is not the issue, as we can see from the parallel judgment upon lesbianism in Romans 1:26.

Still other revisionists sidestep Scripture and tradition in claiming, "It's not immoral; they just thought like that back then." They dismiss the Old Testament as outmoded, then argue similarly that the New Testament material is culturally conditioned. Paul insisted in 1 Corinthians 11 that women cover their heads in worship because it meant something in that culture, but they say it doesn't mean anything now. Similarly, he prohibited same-sex erotic relations because they were not acceptable in his circles at that time, but times have changed.

But Paul's times, in fact, were "gay-positive" or at least "gay-tolerant." Paul and other New Testament writers take a decisive stand against behavior frequently condoned and sometimes idealized in the surrounding cultures. What was wrong then is wrong now.

Sometimes an appeal is made to contemporary opinions about same-sex relations: "Yes, Paul disapproved of such activity, but he had nothing whatsoever to say about homosexuality as we understand it today." The biblical writers, they claim, assumed that homoerotic behavior was an avoidable moral choice, but if Paul had had the benefit of our psychological studies, he would have taken a different position. If people are born gay, how can it be sinful?

In reality, it makes little difference whether nature or nurture inclines us toward any one sexual behavior. Paul was well aware of the compulsive nature of sin. He put forth the gospel as God's means of dealing with the sin that enslaves us, as well as with sins we deliberately choose.

A bold variation on the argument that Paul was scientifically limited is that he was theologically limited. So Eugene Rogers (*Sexuality and the Christian*

Body, 1999) argues that God's grace is wider even than Paul himself suspected, embracing same-sex couples as well as Jew and Gentile.

Paul, Rogers claims, says that God himself acts "against nature" in "grafting" Gentiles into the olive tree, the people of God (Rom. 11). Similarly, Rogers argues, God can act "against nature" in approving same-sex relations. This, however, reads against the sense of both Romans 1 and 11. Romans 1 speaks about what is contrary to nature in the created order. Romans 11 offers a figure of speech to help the Roman Gentile Christians appreciate their inclusion by God.

Rogers strangely clinches his argument: Same-sex couples find in their union "a means of grace," so it must be holy. This appeal to experience that contradicts Scripture is the most common revisionist position today. We know better than Paul and other writers of Scripture, he says, because they just didn't understand the grace that characterizes the loving union of two men or two women. Wasn't Jesus always welcoming outcasts from Israel among his followers? Now God, Rogers says, is doing something similar but new in the church.

A Distorted Image

But what does it mean for the church to give an authentic welcome of people? No one is to be excluded from the church or any aspect of its life by being Jew or Gentile, male or female, slave or free. The revisionists insist that homoerotic orientation (and, they imply, expression) is just as central to a person's identity and equally no bar to inclusion in the church.

But what of Jesus' call to repentance? To a woman caught in another sexual sin, adultery, he says, "Go and sin no more." The revisionists remove homoerotic sin from the lists of sins in the New Testament and treat homoerotic relations as though they fit with Paul's list of Jew or Greek, slave or free, male and female. They obscure the crucial distinction between characteristics over which one may have little or no control (such as same-sex desires), and actions for which one must answer to God. It is true: There is no "gay" or "straight" in the church, but God's purpose in including us all within the household is to heal, not to bless our sinful behaviors (Rom. 6:1–4). Loving those who call themselves gay or lesbian means including them in God's universal call to repentance.

How, then, should Christians view the promotion of the "marriage" or "blessing" of same-sex couples? For 2,000 years Christians have recognized these sexual relations as grievous sin; how could we in a few short years come to call it sanctified? The recklessness of the gay-positive project and the resulting schisms should show even its champions that this change is not from God.

Some would say that this reversal in Christian sexual ethics does not touch the core of the faith and is therefore no grounds for church splits. They are mistaken. This accommodation to a society's declining mores, instead, divides those who embrace it from the church historic.

Is the attempt to bless homoerotic relations truly heretical? It is true that this is not an obvious theological attack on, say, the divinity of Christ or the necessity of the Atonement. But it is indirectly heretical because it upholds a corrupt imitation of marriage, which should properly be a living icon of Christ and the church—a theological picture that mediates God's glory and truth, directing us to the greater reality. Paul calls marriage a "great mystery" that speaks of Christ and the church (Eph. 5:32). So, for example, husbands are to love their wives as Christ loves the church. Indeed, the relations of husband and wife, and of Christ and the church, illuminate each other.

Husband and wife, representing Christ and the church, can only be parodied in same-sex "marriage."

What else do we see in this icon for marriage? For one thing, without Eve, Adam was alone and had no companion fit for him (Gen. 2:20). God gave Eve to Adam and Adam to Eve. The difference in gender of husband and wife, united in marriage, points to the wonder of the Trinity, our ultimate pattern of "other-but-same in relationship." Homoerotic relations reject the gift of sexual otherness and cannot echo the nature of the Trinity.

Furthermore, marriage is not an end in itself but overflows, most obviously to the procreation of children. The original couple is exhorted to "be fruitful and multiply" and thus to take care of creation. By its nature, gay sex cannot bear fruit or fulfill this ecstatic ("going out") role.

God himself enacted the first marriage covenant. A marriage, like the relation of Christ to the church, is not finally a human creation. (Hence the Orthodox insist that a marriage is effected by God himself, and Roman Catholics say the priest is only a witness.) In contrast, God does not join people of the same sex together but calls the behavior they seek to sanctify an abomination. To bless homoerotic relations underscores human willfulness.

If the character of marriage is iconic, what would a same-sex "blessing" or marriage supposedly show us? For one, the church would be giving thanks to God for the sexual union of two men, or two women—declaring that the pair represents God's love and salvation. It would be declaring that couples that exclude one gender represent such love and salvation. It would be claiming that they are taken up together into God's own actions and being. It would be proclaiming that they have a fruitful part in creation, and that they are symbols of the in-breaking rule of God.

"To bless" (Grk., eu-logein) is to "speak a good word" about this alliance, asserting that it brings together the way of the Cross and the way of new life. Such a blessing alleges that the relationship fosters repentance, healing, and glorification for the couple. Precisely here, the church would be saying, you can see the love of God in human form and the glory of humanity. Here would be, in one sense at least, a sacrament—an occasion where God meets us.

A church doing this is replacing God with an idol. It is commending to the family of God, and thus to the world, activities that lead to spiritual death. It is praying against its true nature, indeed, denying its true nature. Finally, the particular body (congregation or communion) is rending itself from the one, holy, catholic, and apostolic church. As Karl Berth has observed, heresy raises the troubling question of the boundaries of the church, while the church may learn from its conflict with heresy, there is no "middle way" here between faithfulness and the revisionist position.

In communions where homoerotic behavior has been accepted, there have been other signs of departure from the faith in the ethical sphere, such as the acceptance of divorce and remarriage on nonbiblical grounds, and of abortion. Promotion in the churches of same-sex blessings or marriages is only the most recent and flamboyant accommodation to declining Northern or Western mores.

This is not the first time the church has had to wrestle with capitulation to the spirit of the age, nor will it be the last.

As serious as things may seem, we hope in the One who said that the gates of hell would not prevail against his church. So we will not lose perspective and begin to treat homoerotic behavior as though it were the worst sin, or as though we did not have to take heed lest we stumble ourselves (see Rom. 2).

Again, we must not assume that those promoting this blessing in the churches cannot change their minds, or that those involved in this lifestyle cannot repent; many have, and many more will. Those wrestling with same-sex desires need support for their healing as persons. Their full inclusion into the life of the church, including the discipline of repentance and the grace of transformation, points to the God who "makes all things new."

POSTSCRIPT

Should Same-Sex Marriages Be Permitted?

It has been said that the 2004 presidential election was decided by three issues, "God, guns, and gays."

Whether that perspective is wholly accurate or not, the United States has been in the throes of controversy regarding gay rights since the Clinton administration and the issue of lifting the ban on gays in the military. That issue, it will be recalled, was "resolved" by the "don't ask, don't tell" "compromise," which most will admit has been a failure. As gay pride and political empowerment continued to expand, the issue was inevitable.

When it seemed as if the Hawaii supreme court might permit gay marriages during the 1990s, Congress raced to enact DOMA (Defense of Marriage Act), which defined "marriage" as being between a man and a woman. As it turned out, the Hawaii supreme court didn't act on behalf of gay citizens after all. Meanwhile, Vermont became the first state in the union to permit "civil unions," a legal arrangement between same-sex individuals.

But then, in 2003, the Massachusetts Supreme Judicial Court, in a controversial 4–3 decision, held that denying homosexuals the right to marry is in violation of the Massachusetts Constitution. This "Goodrich" decision was applauded by gay and lesbian groups across the country, and those opposed to the decision scrambled to have the Massachusetts Constitution amended. Other states, wary of the implications of the Massachusetts' ruling's potential effect on them under the full-faith-and-credit clause of the Constitution (which requires states to recognize civil actions undertaken in states) put referenda opposing same-sex marriage on election ballots. In the 2004 elections, eleven states denied same-sex marriage. Other states are looking at the possibility of "civil unions" as a compromise. At the national level, President George W. Bush proposed an amendment to the U.S. Constitution that would limit marriage to only a man and a woman. This would be the first time in the history of the Constitution that discrimination would be inserted into the document. This amendment is H.J. Res. 56, the Federal Marriage Amendment (FMA).

As far as the Human Rights Campaign (HRC) is concerned, marriage is the only option that would provide equality for gays and lesbians. Only marriage, HRC argues, is "portable"—that is, recognized everywhere. This is not the case for civil unions. Only marriage brings with it federal benefits. Only marriage brings with it the enforcement of marriage rights.

In stark opposition, Edith M. Humphrey, writing for *Christianity Today*, argues the theological opposition to same-sex marriages. She argues that "homoerotic behavior is against the will of God," and that "God himself enacted the first marriage covenant."

The question remains of whether there should be a fundamentalist reading of the scriptures or whether society should recognize its diversity and strive for equality, despite even a fundamentalist reading.

There are numerous works on the controversy of same-sex marriages, including Jonathan Rauch, *Gay Marriage: Why It Is Good for Gays, Good for Straights, and Good for America;* David G. Mayers and L. D. Scanzoni, *What God Has Joined Together? A Christian Case for Gay Marriage;* Evan Wolfson, *Why Marriage Matters: America, Equality, and Gay People's Right to Marry;* and David Moats, *Civil War: A Battle for Gay Marriage.*

ISSUE 12

Should Gays and Lesbians Be Allowed to Adopt?

YES: Ellen C. Perrin, from "Symposium: Adoption by Gay or Lesbian Couples," *Insight on the News* (April 22, 2002)

NO: Timothy J. Dailey, from "Homosexual Parenting: Placing Children at Risk," *Family Research Council* (November 29, 2004)

ISSUE SUMMARY

YES: Citing cases of well-adjusted children of gay/lesbian parents, Ellen C. Perrin argues in favor of adoption rights for homosexual individuals and couples.

NO: Timothy J. Dailey argues that children of gay/lesbian parents are endangered as a result of many factors, including lack of role models, homosexual behavior, and the need for a "traditional" (i.e., mother/father) family structure.

T he controversy regarding foster care or adoption by gay men and lesbians has taken on a life of its own, with most states prohibiting the practice. The arguments on both sides are heated and emotional.

The conventional wisdom in the law is to come down on "the best interests of the child," not just in the case of foster or adoptions, but also across the board in family law. The "gay adoption" issue, particularly from the perspective of the opponents, is that the best interests of the child will not be served if that child lives with a homosexual parent or parents. The advocates of allowing gays and lesbians to adopt is that children are in need of homes and that there is no harm to children of homosexuals, be they biological or adopted children. There are two parts to the problem. The first is that of allowing a gay or lesbian individual to adopt. The second is that of allowing the partner of a gay or lesbian parent (whether biological or adoptive) to co-adopt.

Ellen Perrin provides a diversity of cases involving the lives of gay/lesbian parents and their adopted children. Besides the fact that these stories tug at the heartstrings, Perrin references the American Academy of Pediatrics' (AAP) new policy encouraging the legal recognition of both parents.

Perrin argues that laws "interfere with the rights of certain people to establish a legal relationship with their children." Poignantly, she adds, "And the children suffer as a result."

For gays and lesbians, it is a "catch-22." Unable to marry (except in Massachusetts), "they generally cannot adopt their partner's child" even though they are in actuality co-parenting.

Perrin argues that children of gay/lesbian parents "deserve the same protections that our society provides for other children." In essence, Perrin is arguing the established "best interests of the child" policy.

Timothy J. Dailey repudiates the findings of studies that demonstrate that children being raised in gay or lesbian households are doing just fine. He vehemently argues that the best interests of a child are served by keeping that child away from the homosexual "lifestyle," which Dailey purports to describe in great detail, including promiscuity, violence, mental health problems, substance abuse, reduced life span, and incest. He argues, too, that children of homosexuals suffer "sexual identity confusion."

Dailey continues his opposition to homosexual adoption with the "traditional" argument that children need both a "mom" and a "dad." Of course, this point does not take into consideration the fact that one in two marriages in the United States ends in divorce, and that an ever-increasing number of children are living with one parent. And, in a public policy gone awry—that of welfare—most households are at least nominally "female headed" because the presence of a male in the home would preclude benefits. Dailey makes no mention of prohibiting divorce or of reforming the welfare system to permit two-parent households to receive benefits.

It is up to the reader to determine what the "best interests of the child" are.

Ellen C. Perrin  **YES**

Symposium: Adoption by Gay or Lesbian Couples

NO: Decades of Research Show No Risk to Adopted Children Raised by Gay Parents

Consider the following scenarios that are based on real children's lives:

- Richard adopted Sarah just before her first birthday. Shortly thereafter he met Wesley and, by the time Sarah was 2, she knew the two men as Daddy and Papa. The three were a stable family until Richard's car was hit by a drunk driver when he was bringing Sarah home from school one day. Richard was admitted to the intensive-care unit with serious head and abdominal injuries. Sarah was brought to the emergency room and Wesley was called. The emergency-room nurses said that Wesley could not authorize the emergency surgery Sarah needed to remove glass from her face and right eye because he was not her legal parent.
- Catherine and Vanessa already had been a stable couple for five years when they decided that they wanted to become parents. Vanessa conceived using alternative insemination methods and, nine months later, William was born. Vanessa stayed home full time with her son while Catherine continued to work at her executive position in a financial-consulting firm. They shared equally in household tasks and caring for Will throughout his preschool years. When Will was in the third grade Catherine and Vanessa decided to separate. Their conflicts resulted in disagreements about appropriate visitation and child-support arrangements. Will now is being treated for depression and anxiety because he no longer has an ongoing relationship with Catherine (whom he calls "Momma Kate"), and because Vanessa has had to work very long hours to maintain the family's financial security on her own.
- Samantha is 7 years old and has cerebral palsy. Her parents were addicted to crack cocaine and had several run-ins with the law. When they were convicted of breaking and entering and attempted manslaughter, the Department of Social Services insisted that Samantha, who was then 2 years old, be placed in a foster home. In the five years since then she has been in six different foster homes while she waits

From *Insight*, vol. 18, issue 14, April 22, 2002, pp. 40. Copyright © 2002 by Insight—Washington Times. Reprinted by permission.

for an adoptive home. A lesbian couple wants to adopt Samantha, but their state's laws allow adoption only by people who are heterosexual.

These circumstances and others like them occur every day. They are the result of laws that interfere with the rights of certain people to establish a legal relationship with their children. And the children suffer as a result. Therefore, the American Academy of Pediatrics (AAP) has published a new policy statement that highlights the benefits for children of having both their parents be legally recognized.

Because gay men and lesbians cannot marry, they generally cannot adopt their partner's child, even if they are in every way acting as the child's parents—changing their diapers, taking them to school and church, staying home from work when they are sick and planning their birthday parties. If the biological or adoptive parent becomes disabled or dies, the child's other parent cannot authorize medical care or provide health insurance or Social Security benefits. Another relative can claim custody of the child and thereby cause the child to lose both of his/her parents. If the couple separates, the nonbiologic/adoptive parent has no right to regular visitation and no responsibility to provide child support.

Children whose parents are gay or lesbian deserve the same protections that our society provides for other children. The AAP policy statement says that "Children who are born to or adopted by one member of a same-sex couple deserve the security of two legally recognized parents. Therefore, the American Academy of Pediatrics supports legislative and legal efforts to provide the possibility of adoption of the child by the second parent or coparent in these families."

Paul Cameron of the Family Research Institute and I agree that children fare better with two parents than with only one. Does it not make sense, then, to allow these children to rely on both of their parents for the basic security and protections that our society has guaranteed to all other children?

The critics of the AAP's policy statement have not presented any new evidence to support an alternative position, but have relied instead on challenging the strength of the scientific data on which the policy statement is based. It is far easier to criticize the research that others have done than to conduct original scientific investigations.

In researching this issue for the AAP, I reviewed all the published literature about the well-being of children whose parents were gay or lesbian. My review is published in the technical report that accompanied the publication of the policy statement. It concludes that "a growing body of scientific literature demonstrates that children who grow up with one or two gay and/or lesbian parents fare as well in emotional, cognitive, social and sexual functioning as do children whose parents are heterosexual. Children's optimal development appears to be influenced more by the nature of the relationships and interactions within the family unit than by the particular structural form it takes."

Investigators have concentrated on four areas: the attitudes and behaviors of gay and lesbian parents and the psychosexual development, social experience and emotional status of their children.

With regard to the attitudes and behaviors of gay and lesbian parents, empirical evidence gathered by several researchers during the last two decades (such as F.W. Bozett, R.L. Barrett, J.J. Bigner and J.M. Bailey) reveals that gay fathers have substantial evidence of nurturance and investment in their paternal role. The research shows no differences from heterosexual fathers in providing appropriate recreation, encouraging autonomy, maintaining disciplinary guidelines or dealing with general problems of parenting.

Similarly, few differences have been found when comparing lesbian and heterosexual mothers' self-esteem, psychological adjustment and attitudes toward child rearing. Lesbian mothers demonstrate normal functioning on interviews and psychological assessments, and their scores on standardized measures of self-esteem, anxiety, depression and parenting stress are indistinguishable from those reported by heterosexual mothers. Lesbian mothers strongly endorse child-centered attitudes and commitment to their maternal roles and are typically even more concerned with providing male role models for their children than are divorced heterosexual mothers.

Several studies comparing children who have a lesbian mother to children whose mother is heterosexual (by R.W. Chan, D.K. Flaks, S. Golombok and F. Tasker, among others) have not shown any differences between these groups on personality measures, measures of peer-group relationships, self-esteem, behavioral difficulties, academic success or warmth and quality of family relationships.

The gender identity of children raised by lesbian mothers consistently has been found to be in line with their biological sex. None of the more than 400 children studied to date has shown evidence of gender-identity confusion, wished to be the other sex or consistently engaged in cross-gender behavior. No differences have been found in the toy, game, activity, dress or friendship preferences of boys or girls who had lesbian mothers, compared with those who had heterosexual mothers. Compared with young adults who had heterosexual mothers, men and women who had lesbian mothers were slightly more likely to consider the possibility of having a same-sex partner, but actually very similar proportions of both groups have identified themselves as homosexual.

Critics argue that the small samples on which these studies are based invalidate their findings and, therefore, cannot be generalized to represent what is true for other children and other families. While no one would argue that it would be preferable to be able to enroll larger numbers of children and families for a longer period of time, all research is based on similar compromises.

The scientific approach to answering an important question of large scale is to analyze statistically several smaller studies in what is called a meta-analysis. This technique allows for the prediction of the answer to a particular question as if a large study had been feasible. A meta-analysis was indeed done and published in 1996 (by M. Allen and N. Burrell), addressing the question of whether children's emotional, academic or sexual development had been harmed as a result of being raised in a family in which the two parents were the same sex. The conclusions from this meta-analysis support the weight of evidence gathered during several decades using diverse samples and methodologies—namely, that the data provide no evidence of risk to children based on growing up in a family with one or more gay parents.

Critics argue further that studies investigating the well-being of children whose parents are gay or lesbian have used nonstandardized instruments, inappropriate research designs and inadequate comparison groups. While these critiques are valid for some of the studies done before 1985, they no longer are true. Studies done by Golombok and her colleagues in the last 15 years, for example, are carefully designed, using well-respected measurement and statistical strategies and several appropriately matched comparison groups. What is most impressive is that whatever samples are studied, whatever outcomes are measured and whatever research strategies are employed, the results repeatedly are very similar: No study has demonstrated any risk whatsoever to children as a result of growing up in a family with one or more gay parents.

The research is there showing us what children need: a loving, stable family and assurance of consistency and continuity. Coparent adoption provides legal, financial and emotional security and thus is in the best interests of children. The AAP recommendations simply seek to guarantee children of same-sex parents the same rights and protections that other children have.

Timothy J. Dailey

Homosexual Parenting:
Placing Children at Risk

A number of studies in recent years have purported to show that children raised in gay and lesbian households fare no worse than those reared in traditional families. Yet much of that research fails to meet acceptable standards for psychological research; it is compromised by methodological flaws and driven by political agendas instead of an objective search for truth. In addition, openly lesbian researchers sometimes conduct research with an interest in portraying homosexual parenting in a positive light. The deficiencies of studies on homosexual parenting include reliance upon an inadequate sample size, lack of random sampling, lack of anonymity of research participants, and self-presentation bias.

The presence of methodological defects—a mark of substandard research—would be cause for rejection of research conducted in virtually any other subject area. The overlooking of such deficiencies in research papers on homosexual failures can be attributed to the "politically correct" determination within those in the social science professions to "prove" that homosexual households are no different than traditional families.

However, no amount of scholarly legerdemain contained in an accumulation of flawed studies can obscure the well-established and growing body of evidence showing that both mothers and fathers provide unique and irreplaceable contributions to the raising of children. Children raised in traditional families by a mother and father are happier, healthier, and more successful than children raised in non-traditional environments. . . .

Harmful Aspects of the Homosexual Lifestyle

The evidence demonstrates incontrovertibly that the homosexual lifestyle is inconsistent with the proper raising of children. Homosexual relationships are characteristically unstable and are fundamentally incapable of providing children the security they need.

Homosexual promiscuity   Studies indicate that the average male homosexual has hundreds of sex partners in his lifetime, a lifestyle that—is difficult for

From *Family Research Council*, issue 238, November 29, 2004. Copyright © 2004 by Family Research Council. Reprinted by permission. www.frc.org

even "committed" homosexuals to break free of and which is not conducive to a healthy and wholesome atmosphere for the raising of children.

- A. P. Bell and M. S. Weinberg, in their classic study of male and female homosexuality, found that 43 percent of white male homosexuals had sex with five hundred or more partners, with 28 percent having 1,000 or more sex partners.[1]
- In their study of the sexual profiles of 2,583 older homosexuals published in *Journal of Sex Research,* Paul Van de Ven et al. found that "the modal range for number of sexual partners ever [of homosexuals] was 101–500." In addition, 10.2 percent to 15.7 percent had between 501 and 1000 partners. A further 10.2 percent to 15.7 percent reported having had more than 1000 lifetime sexual partners.[2]
- A survey conducted by the homosexual magazine *Genre* found that 24 percent of the respondents said they had had more than 100 sexual partners in their lifetime. The magazine noted that several respondents suggested including a category of those who had more than 1,000 sexual partners.[3]
- In his study of male homosexuality in *Western Sexuality: Practice and Precept in Past and Present Times,* M. Pollak found that "few homosexual relationships last longer than two years, with many men reporting hundreds of lifetime partners."[4]

Promiscuity among homosexual couples   Even in those homosexual relationships in which the partners consider themselves to be in a committed relationship, the meaning of "committed" typically means something radically different than in heterosexual marriage.

- In *The Male Couple,* authors David P. McWhirter and Andrew M. Mattison report that in a study of 156 males in homosexual relationships lasting from one to thirty-seven years:

Only seven couples have a totally exclusive sexual relationship, and these men all have been together for less than five years. Stated another way, all couples with a relationship lasting more than five years have incorporated some provision for outside sexual activity in their relationships.[5]

Most understood sexual relations outside the relationship to be the norm, and viewed adopting monogamous standards as an act of oppression.

- In *Male and Female Homosexuality,* M. Saghir and E. Robins found that the average male homosexual live-in relationship lasts between two and three years.[6]
- In their *Journal of Sex Research* study of the sexual practices of older homosexual men, Paul Van de Ven et al. found that only 2.7 percent of older homosexuals had only one sexual partner in their lifetime.[7]

Comparison of homosexual 'couples' and heterosexual spouses   Lest anyone suffer the illusion that any equivalency between the sexual practices of homosexual relationships and traditional marriage exists, the statistics regarding sexual fidelity within marriage are revealing:

- In *Sex in America,* called by the *New York Times* "the most important study of American sexual behavior since the Kinsey reports," Robert T. Michael et al. report that 90 percent of wives and 75 percent of husbands claim never to have had extramarital sex.[8]
- A nationally representative survey of 884 men and 1,288 women published in *Journal of Sex Research* found that 77 percent of married men and 88 percent of married women had remained faithful to their marriage vows.[9]
- In *The Social Organization of Sexuality: Sexual Practices in the United States,* E. O. Laumann et al. conducted a national survey that found that 75 percent of husbands and 85 percent of wives never had sexual relations outside of marriage.[10]
- A telephone survey conducted for *Parade* magazine of 1,049 adults selected to represent the demographic characteristics of the United States found that 81 percent of married men and 85 percent of married women reported that they had never violated their marriage vows.[11]

While the rate of fidelity within marriage cited by these studies remains far from ideal, there is a magnum order of difference between the negligible lifetime fidelity rate cited for homosexuals and the 75 to 90 percent cited for married couples. This indicates that even "committed" homosexual relationships display a fundamental incapacity for the faithfulness and commitment that is axiomatic to the institution of marriage.

Unhealthy aspects of 'monogamous' homosexual relationships   Even those homosexual relationships that are loosely termed "monogamous" do not necessarily result in healthier behavior.

- The journal *AIDS* reported that men involved in relationships engaged in anal intercourse and oral-anal intercourse with greater frequency than did those without a steady partner.[12] Anal intercourse has been linked with a host of bacterial and parasitical sexually transmitted diseases, including AIDS.
- The exclusivity of the relationship did not diminish the incidence of unhealthy sexual acts, which are commonplace among homosexuals. An English study published in the same issue of *AIDS* concurred, finding that most "unsafe" sex acts among homosexuals occur in steady relationships.[13]

Of paramount concern are the effects of such a lifestyle upon children. Brad Hayton writes:

> Homosexuals . . . model a poor view of marriage to children. They are taught by example and belief that marital relationships are transitory and mostly sexual in nature. Sexual relationships are primarily for pleasure rather than procreation. And they are taught that monogamy in a marriage is not the norm [and] should be discouraged if one wants a good 'marital' relationship.[14]

Violence in lesbian and homosexual relationships

- A study in the *Journal of Interpersonal Violence* examined conflict and violence in lesbian relationships. The researchers found that 90 percent of the lesbians surveyed had been recipients of one or more acts of verbal aggression from their intimate partners during the year prior to this study, with 31 percent reporting one or more incidents of physical abuse.[15]
- In a survey of 1,099 lesbians, the *Journal of Social Service Research* found that "slightly more than half of the [lesbians] reported that they had been abused by a female lover/partner. The most frequently indicated forms of abuse were verbal/emotional/psychological abuse and combined physical-psychological abuse."[16]
- In their book *Men Who Beat the Men Who Love Them: Battered Gay Men and Domestic Violence*, D. Island and P. Letellier postulate that "the incidence of domestic violence among gay men is nearly double that in the heterosexual population."[17]

Rate of intimate partner violence within marriage   A little-reported fact is that homosexual and lesbian relationships are far more violent than are traditional married households:

- The Bureau of Justice Statistics (U.S. Department of Justice) reports that married women in traditional families experience the lowest rate of violence compared with women in other types of relationships.[18]
- A report by the Medical Institute for Sexual Health concurred:

It should be noted that most studies of family violence do not differentiate between married and unmarried partner status. Studies that do make these distinctions have found that marriage relationships tend to have the least intimate partner violence when compared to cohabiting or dating relationships.[19]

High incidence of mental health problems among homosexuals and lesbians   A national survey of lesbians published in the *Journal of Consulting and Clinical Psychology* found that 75 percent of the nearly two-thousand respondents had pursued psychological counseling of some kind, many for treatment of long-term depression or sadness:

Among the sample as a whole, there was a distressingly high prevalence of life events and behaviors related to mental health problems. Thirty-seven percent had been physically abused and 32 percent had been raped or sexually attacked. Nineteen percent had been involved in incestuous relationships while growing up. Almost one-third used tobacco on a daily basis and about 30 percent drank alcohol more than once a week; 6 percent drank daily. One in five smoked marijuana more than once a month. Twenty-one percent of the sample had thoughts about suicide sometimes or often and 18 percent had actually tried to kill themselves . . . More than half had felt too nervous to accomplish ordinary activities at some time during the past year and over one-third had been depressed.[20]

Substance abuse among lesbians   A study published in *Nursing Research* found that lesbians are three times more likely to abuse alcohol and to suffer from other compulsive behaviors:

> Like most problem drinkers, 32 (91 percent) of the participants had abused other drugs as well as alcohol, and many reported compulsive difficulties with food (34 percent), codependency (29 percent), sex (11 percent), and money (6 percent). Forty-six percent had been heavy drinkers with frequent drunkenness.[21]

Greater risk for suicide

- A study of twins that examined the relationship between homosexuality and suicide, published in the *Archives of General Psychiatry*, found that homosexuals with same-sex partners were at greater risk for overall mental health problems, and were 6.5 times more likely than their twins to have attempted suicide. The higher rate was not attributable to mental health or substance abuse disorders.[22]
- Another study published simultaneously in *Archives of General Psychiatry* followed 1007 individuals from birth. Those classified as gay, lesbian, or bisexual were significantly more likely to have had mental health problems. Significantly, in his comments in the same issue of the journal, D. Bailey cautioned against various speculative explanations of the results, such as the view that "widespread prejudice against homosexual people causes them to be unhappy or worse, mentally ill."[23]

Reduced life span   Another factor contributing to the instability of male homosexual households, which raises the possibility of major disruption for children raised in such households, is the significantly reduced life expectancy of male homosexuals. A study published in the *International Journal of Epidemiology* on the mortality rates of homosexuals concluded:

> In a major Canadian centre, life expectancy at age twenty for gay and bisexual men is eight to twenty years less than for all men. If the same pattern of mortality were to continue, we estimate that nearly half of gay and bisexual men currently aged twenty years will not reach their sixty-fifth birthday. Under even the most liberal assumptions, gay and bisexual men in this urban centre are now experiencing a life expectancy similar to that experienced by all men in Canada in the year 1871.[24]

Concern about children placed in homosexual households who are orphaned because of the destructive homosexual lifestyle is well founded. In 1990, Wayne Tardiff and his partner, Allan Yoder, were the first homosexuals permitted to become adoptive parents in the state of New Jersey. Tardiff died in 1992 at age forty-four; Yoder died a few months later, leaving an orphaned five-year-old.[25]

Sexual identity confusion   The claim that homosexual households do not "recruit" children into the homosexual lifestyle is refuted by the growing evidence that children raised in such households are more likely to engage in sexual experimentation and in homosexual behavior.

- Studies indicate that 0.3 percent of adult females report having practiced homosexual behavior in the past year, 0.4 percent have practiced homosexual behavior in the last five years, and 3 percent have ever practiced homosexual behavior in their lifetime.[26] A study in *Developmental Psychology* found that 12 percent of the children of lesbians became active lesbians themselves, a rate which is at least four times the base rate of lesbianism in the adult female population.[27]

- Numerous studies indicate that while nearly 5 percent of males report having had a homosexual experience sometime in their lives, the number of exclusive homosexuals is considerably less: Between 1 and 2 percent of males report exclusive homosexual behavior over a several-year period.[28] However, J. M. Bailey et al. found that 9 percent of the adult sons of homosexual fathers were homosexual in their adult sexual behavior: "The rate of homosexuality in the sons (9 percent) is several times higher than that suggested by the population-based surveys and is consistent with a degree of father-to-son transmission."[29]

- Even though they attempted to argue otherwise, Golombok and Tasker's study revealed in its results section a clear connection between being raised in a lesbian family and homosexuality: "With respect to actual involvement in same-gender sexual relationships, there was a significant difference between groups. . . . None of the children from heterosexual families had experienced a lesbian or gay relationship." By contrast, five (29 percent) of the seventeen daughters and one (13 percent) of the eight sons in homosexual families reported having at least one same-sex relationship.[30]

- These findings have most recently been confirmed in a study appearing in the *American Sociological Review*. Authors Judith Stacey and Timothy J. Biblarz alluded to the "political incorrectness" of their finding of higher rates of homosexuality among children raised in homosexual households: "We recognize the political dangers of pointing out that recent studies indicate that a higher proportion of children of lesbigay parents are themselves apt to engage in homosexual activity."

- Stacy and Biblarz also reported "some fascinating findings on the number of sexual partners children report," that:

The adolescent and young adult girls raised by lesbian mothers appear to have been more sexually adventurous and less chaste. . . . In other words, once again, children (especially girls) raised by lesbians appear to depart from traditional gender-based norms, while children raised by heterosexual mothers appear to conform to them.[31]

Incest in homosexual parent families   A study in *Adolescence* found:

A disproportionate percentage—29 percent—of the adult children of homosexual parents had been specifically subjected to sexual molestation by that homosexual parent, compared to only 0.6 percent of adult children of heterosexual parents having reported sexual relations with their parent. . . . Having a homosexual parent(s) appears to increase the risk of incest with a parent by a factor of about 50.[32] . . .

Children Need a Mom and a Dad

Attempts to redefine the very nature of the family ignore the accumulated wisdom of cultures and societies from time immemorial, which testifies that the best way for children to be raised is by a mother and father who are married to each other. The importance of the traditional family has been increasingly verified by research showing that children from married two-parent households do better academically, financially, emotionally, and behaviorally. They delay sex longer, have better health, and receive more parental support.[33]

Homosexual or lesbian households are no substitute for a family: Children also need both a mother and a father. Blankenhorn discusses the different but necessary roles that mothers and fathers play in children's lives: "If mothers are likely to devote special attention to their children's present physical and emotional needs, fathers are likely to devote special attention to their character traits necessary for the future, especially qualities such as independence, self-reliance, and the willingness to test limits and take risks." Blankenhorn further explains:

> Compared to a mother's love, a father's love is frequently more expectant, more instrumental, and significantly less conditional. . . . For the child, from the beginning, the mother's love is an unquestioned source of comfort and the foundation of human attachment. But the father's love is almost a bit farther away, more distant and contingent. Compared to the mother's love, the father's must frequently be sought after, deserved, earned through achievement.[34]

Author and sociologist David Popenoe confirms that mothers and fathers fulfill different roles in their children's lives. In *Life without Father* Popenoe notes, 'Through their play, as well as in their other child-rearing activities, fathers tend to stress competition, challenge, initiative, risk taking and independence. Mothers in their care-taking roles, in contrast, stress emotional security and personal safety." Parents also discipline their children differently: "While mothers provide an important flexibility and sympathy in their discipline, fathers provide ultimate predictability and consistency. Both dimensions are critical for an efficient, balanced, and humane child-rearing regime."[35]

The complementary aspects of parenting that mothers and fathers contribute to the rearing of children are rooted in the innate differences of the two sexes, and can no more be arbitrarily substituted than can the very nature of male and female. Accusations of sexism and homophobia notwithstanding, along with attempts to deny the importance of both mothers and fathers in the rearing of children, the oldest family structure of all turns out to be the best.

In his analysis of human cultures, the eminent Harvard sociologist Pitirim Sorokin argued that no society has ceased to honor the institution of marriage and survived. Sorokin considered traditional marriage and parenting as the fulfillment of life's meaning for both individuals and society:

> Enjoying the marital union in its infinite richness, parents freely fulfill many other paramount tasks. They maintain the procreation of the human race. Through their progeny they determine the hereditary and acquired characteristics of future generations. Through marriage they achieve a social

immortality of their own, of their ancestors, and of their particular groups and community. This immortality is secured through the transmission of their name and values, and of their traditions and ways of life to their children, grandchildren, and later generations.[36] . . .

Endnotes

1. A. P. Bell and M. S. Weinberg, *Homosexualities: A Study of Diversity Among Men and Women* (New York: Simon and Schuster, 1978), pp. 308, 309; See also A. P. Bell, M. S. Weinberg, and S. K. Hammersmith, *Sexual Preference* (Bloomington: Indiana University Press, 1981).

2. Paul Van de Ven et al., "A Comparative Demographic and Sexual Profile of Older Homosexually Active Men," *Journal of Sex Research* 34 (1997): 354.

3. "Sex Survey Results," *Genre* (October 1996), quoted in "Survey Finds 40 percent of Gay Men Have Had More Than 40 Sex Partners," *Lambda Report*, January 1998, p. 20.

4. M. Pollak, "Male Homosexuality," in *Western Sexuality: Practice and Precept in Past and Present Times*, ed. P. Aries and A. Bejin, translated by Anthony Forster (New York, NY: B. Blackwell, 1985), pp. 40–61, cited by Joseph Nicolosi in *Reparative Therapy of Male Homosexuality* (Northvale, New Jersey: Jason Aronson Inc., 1991), pp. 124, 125.

5. David P. McWhirter and Andrew M. Mattison, *The Male Couple: How Relationships Develop* (Englewood Cliffs: Prentice-Hall, 1984), pp. 252, 253.

6. M. Saghir and E. Robins, *Male and Female Homosexuality* (Baltimore: Williams and Wilkins, 1973), p. 225; L. A. Peplau and H. Amaro, "Understanding Lesbian Relationships," in *Homosexuality: Social, Psychological, and Biological Issues*, ed. J. Weinrich and W. Paul (Beverly Hills: Sage, 1982).

7. Van de Ven et al., "A Comparative Demographic and Sexual Profile," p. 354.

8. Robert T. Michael et al., *Sex in America: A Definitive Survey* (Boston: Little, Brown and Company, 1994).

9. Michael W. Wiederman, "Extramarital Sex: Prevalence and Correlates in a National Survey," *Journal of Sex Research* 34 (1997): 170.

10. E. O. Laumann et al., *The Social Organization of Sexuality: Sexual Practices in the United States* (Chicago: University of Chicago Press, 1994), p. 217.

11. M. Clements, "Sex in America Today: A New National Survey Reveals How our Attitudes are Changing," *Parade*, August 7, 1994, pp. 4–6.

12. A. P. M. Coxon et al., "Sex Role Separation in Diaries of Homosexual Men," *AIDS* (July 1993): 877–882.

13. G. J. Hart et al., "Risk Behaviour, Anti-HIV and Anti-Hepatitis B Core Prevalence in Clinic and Non-clinic Samples of Gay Men in England, 1991–1992," *AIDS* (July 1993): 863–869, cited in "Homosexual Marriage: The Next Demand," Position Analysis paper by Colorado for Family Values, May 1994.

14. Bradley P. Hayton, "To Marry or Not: The Legalization of Marriage and Adoption of Homosexual Couples," (Newport Beach: The Pacific Policy Institute, 1993), p. 9.

15. Lettie L. Lockhart et al., "Letting out the Secret: Violence in Lesbian Relationships," *Journal of Interpersonal Violence* 9 (1994): 469–492.

16. Gwat Yong Lie and Sabrina Gentlewarrier, "Intimate Violence in Lesbian Relationships: Discussion of Survey Findings and Practice Implications," *Journal of Social Service Research* 15 (1991): 41–59.

17. D. Island and P. Letellier, *Men Who Beat the Men Who Love Them: Battered Gay Men and Domestic Violence* (New York: Haworth Press, 1991), p. 14.

18. "Violence Between Intimates," *Bureau of Justice Statistics Selected Findings*, November 1994, p. 2.

19. *Health Implications Associated With Homosexuality* (Austin: The Medical Institute for Sexual Health, 1999), p. 79.

20. J. Bradford et al., "National Lesbian Health Care Survey: Implications for Mental Health Care," *Journal of Consulting and Clinical Psychology* 62 (1994): 239, cited in *Health Implications Associated with Homosexuality*, p. 81.

21. Joanne Hall, "Lesbians Recovering from Alcoholic Problems: An Ethnographic Study of Health Care Expectations," *Nursing Research* 43 (1994): 238–244.

22. R. Herrell et al., "A Co-twin Study in Adult Men," *Archives of General Psychiatry* 56 (1999): 867–874.

23. D. Fergusson et al., "Is Sexual Orientation Related to Mental Health Problems and Suicidality in Young People?" *Archives of General Psychiatry* 56 (October 1999).

24. Robert S. Hogg et al., "Modeling the Impact of HIV Disease on Mortality in Gay and Bisexual Men," *International Journal of Epidemiology* 26 (1997): 657.

25. Obituaries, *The Washington Blade*, July 16, 1992.

26. A. M. Johnson et al., "Sexual Lifestyles and HIV Risk," *Nature* 360 (1992): 410–412; R. Turner, "Landmark French and British Studies Examine Sexual Behavior, including Multiple Partners, Homosexuality," *Family Planning Perspectives* 25 (1993): 91, 92.

27. F. Tasker and S. Golombok, "Adults Raised as Children in Lesbian Families," p. 213.

28. ACSF Investigators, "AIDS and Sexual Behavior in France," *Nature* 360 (1992): 407–409; J. M. Bailey et al., "Sexual Orientation of Adult Sons of Gay Fathers," *Developmental Psychology* 31 (1995): 124–129; J. O. G. Billy et al., "The Sexual Behavior of Men in the United States," *Family Planning Perspectives* 25 (1993): 52–60; A. M. Johnson et al., "Sexual Lifestyles and HIV Risk," *Nature* 360 (1992): 410–412.

29. J. M. Bailey et al., "Sexual Orientation of Adult Sons of Gay Fathers," pp. 127, 128.

30. Tasker and Golombok, "Do Parents Influence the Sexual Orientation?" p. 7.

31. Judith Stacey and Timothy J. Biblarz, "(How) Does the Sexual Orientation of Parents Matter," *American Sociological Review* 66 (2001): 174, 179.

32. P. Cameron and K. Cameron, "Homosexual Parents," *Adolescence* 31 (1996): 772.

33. See the following: Sara McLanahan and Gary Sandfeur, *Growing Up with a Single Parent: What Hurts, What Helps* (Cambridge: Harvard University Press, 1994), p. 45; Pat Fagan, "How Broken Families Rob Children of Their Chances for Prosperity," Heritage Foundation *Backgrounder* No. 1283, June 11, 1999, p. 13; Dawn Upchurch et al., "Gender and Ethnic Differences in the Timing of First Sexual Intercourse," *Family Planning Perspectives* 30 (1998): 121–127; Jeanne M. Hilton and Esther L. Devall, "Comparison of Parenting and Children's Behavior in Single-Mother, Single-Father, and Intact Families," *Journal of Divorce and Remarriage* 29 (1998): 23–54; Jane Mauldon, "The Effect of Marital Disruption on Children's Health," *Demography* 27 (1990): 431–446; Frank Furstenberg, Jr., and Julien Teitler, "Reconsidering the Effects of Marital Disruption: What Happens to Children of Divorce in Early Adulthood?" *Journal of Family Issues* 15 (June 1994); Elizabeth Thomson et al., "Family Structure and Child Well-Being: Economic Resources vs. Parental Behaviors," *Social Forces* 73 (1994): 221–42.

34. David Blankenhorn, *Fatherless America* (New York: Basic Books, 1995), p. 219.

35. David Popenoe, *Life Without Father* (Cambridge: Harvard University Press, 1996), pp. 144, 146.

36. Pitirim Sorokin, *The American Sex Revolution* (Boston: Porter Sargent Publishers, 1956), pp. 6, 77–105.

POSTSCRIPT

Should Gays and Lesbians Be Allowed to Adopt?

What makes a family?

The "traditional" view is that a family is comprised of a mother, father, and children. But contemporary data defy this stereotype. Divorced parents (and therefore single-parent households) have been on the rise for decades. One in two marriages in the United States ends in divorce. Add to this other single-parent households (typically female-led), and the "traditional" family is the stuff of folklore.

In the midst of these societal changes, and as gays and lesbians have experienced their own sense of self and pride and seen increasingly political, social, and economic recognition, what can be said of adoption by gays and lesbians, be they single or in a relationship?

Ellen C. Perrin's article talks about the lives of real children. Many of these children have been left to flounder in foster care, moving from one location to another, even though there are lesbian or gay individuals or couples eager to adopt. But state law prevails over adoptions, and most states do not permit homosexuals to adopt. Even when one parent in a gay/lesbian relationship is the biological parent of a child, most states deny the non-biological parent to adopt, even though that individual is behaving as a parent in every way. Perrin cites the position of the American Academy of Pediatrics' (AAP) policy statement that argues that the legal recognition of both parents is in a child's best interests.

Perrin disputes the arguments of those opposed to gay adoptions. Opponents argue that children in gay or lesbian households will "become gay," and cites scientific studies supporting her position that this contention is ludicrous.

By contrast, Timothy J. Dailey refers to such studies as "flawed." His article concentrates on the "harmful aspects of the homosexual lifestyle that are detrimental to children." He further argues that children who grow up with same-sex parents suffer sexual identity confusion. Dailey provides a litany of virtually everything that can possibly go wrong in a relationship as being typical of gay and lesbian relationships. Dailey dismisses the findings of researchers who would disagree with his views.

With this controversy being of such importance to so many people, further reading is worthwhile. Some suggestions are Stephen Hicks and Janet MacDonald, eds., *Lesbian and Gay Fostering and Adoption: Extraordinary Yet Ordinary*; Ann Sullivan, *Issues in Gay and Lesbian Adoption*; Steven M. Tannenbaum, *Adoption by Lesbians and Gay Men: An Overview of the Law in 50 States*; and Michael Galluccio, *An American Family*.

Rand

Rand presents research on a wide range of public policy issues.

`http://www.rand.org`

NCPA Idea House

NCPA Idea House provides research material on public policy issues including economics and regulatory policy.

`http://www.ncpa.org/newdpd/index.php`

Federal Web Locator

The Federal Web Locator provides links to governmental agencies and organizations.

`http://www.infoctr.edu/fwl/`

PART 4

Socio-Economics

*I*n *a society whose affluence is almost an embarrassment, is it just that the less well-off suffer from a judicial system that is supposed to be blind? The very nature of the U.S. judicial system is adversarial; the 'truth" is secondary. To discern the truth is expensive. Indeed, to engage in the adversarial process is expensive.*

Prisons in the United States are swollen with inmates, most of whom are minority and indigent. Much of the explosion in the prison population came about in response to the concentrated "war on drugs" of the past several decades, and the stiffer sentences meted out for drug crimes.

Is it that minorities and the poor commit a greater number of crimes? Or is it that they don't have the financial resources to "buy justice"? On the one hand, the judicial system has come to the aid of the indigent by holding that there is a constitutional right to defense for a criminal charge. But the system has yet to address how to achieve a quality defense in a system where the billable hour is the modus operandi of the legal profession and there is lots of money to be made by defending wealthy clients.

Studies tell us that the socioeconomic gap in the United States is ever expanding. So the issues addressed here are urgent. In this section, we discuss several of the public policy, justice, and law issues faced by those of lesser means.

- Can the Poor Receive Adequate Criminal Defense?

- Can "Expert Witness" Testimony in the Courtroom Be Made More Equitable?

- Does the U.S. Income Tax System Favor the Rich?

ISSUE 13

Can the Poor Receive Adequate Criminal Defense?

YES: Virginia E. Sloan, Cait Clarke, and Daniel Engelberg,
from "Gideon's Unfulfilled Mandate: Time for a New Consensus,"
Human Rights (Winter 2004)

NO: *The Economist* Staff Writer, from "Too Poor to Be
Defended," *The Economist* (April 11, 1998)

ISSUE SUMMARY

YES: Sloan, Clarke and Engelberg argue that while the 1963
Supreme Court decision in *Gideon v. Wainwright* held that everyone is entitled to a defense attorney in criminal cases, the reality is
that defense of the indigent is woefully inadequate.

NO: *The Economist* presents an argument that the poor cannot be
adequately defended because funding for public defenders has
dropped dramatically. Public defenders are not able to match better-
funded and prepared prosecutors.

James Baldwin once noted, "Anyone who has ever struggled with poverty knows how extremely expensive it is to be poor."

We have also often heard that "the poor pay more" in a literal sense. It is
not apocryphal that prices are higher in neighborhoods where people can least
afford to pay them, that obtaining credit is typically at a higher percentage and
often for inferior products, that living conditions are typically sub-human.

What greater expense can there be than to have to forfeit one's freedom
without warrant? And yet, the system of jurisprudence in the United States
every day finds individuals forfeiting their freedom because they do not have
the financial means by which to hire adequate legal assistance, or as we saw in
Issue 3, because they have entered into plea bargains out of fear?

So it is appropriate to ask the question, Can the poor receive adequate
criminal defense? In an effort to create a more just society, what can we do to
move away from "warehousing" disproportionately poor prisoners?

Virginia E. Sloan, Cait Clarke, and Daniel Engelberg re-visit *Gideon v.
Wainwright,* in which the U.S. Supreme Court broke major ground by ruling

that the U.S. Constitution requires the right to counsel and that indigent defendants in criminal trials must be afforded counsel at public expense. As Sloan, Clarke, and Engelberg note, however, there is a gap between the ruling and the fulfillment of it. Being afforded counsel does not necessarily mean that competent counsel will be assigned, or that counsel will spend very much time on an indigent client.

Sloan, Clarke, and Engelberg argue that it is not the law alone that is at fault, but the governmental authorities responsible for the public policy that has created an inadequate system to meet the spirit of *Gideon*. The authors point out that *Gideon* did not provide guidelines to the states and did not tell us what constitutes an adequate defense system. Beyond this, there is a rather consistent use of underfunded indigent defense programs. As a result, "the odds are stacked against an indigent person."

Sloan, Clarke, and Engelberg are hopeful that we can become a more just society.

They astutely point out the lack of structure for the indigent defense system. Beyond this, not even the best structured system will work well without "competent, vigorous legal representation" and that without this the results of the criminal justice are illegitimate.

A solution rests not only in national standards for public law, but in the sufficient and equitable funding that will attract competent criminal defense attorneys. They argue that the approach to realizing the spirit of *Gideon* must be a bipartisan one and must carry with it a nationwide consensus for "reform of a system that is, in many places, broken."

As a society, can we afford not to make systemic changes that would "reinvent" poverty law? The poor are losing ground, not gaining. In the face of an economic system in which the middle class and the poor are increasingly economically separated from the wealthy, the criminal justices are in serious need of recognizing that something must be done. None of this is "our fault." But it becomes our fault if we fail to change tactics in the face of an altered reality.

So, we are reminded of the protagonist in "The Year of Living Dangerously," who asks "What then must we do?"

The Economist is pessimistic. They depict an America in which money buys "justice" or at least an outcome, be it just or unjust. The system, they argue, has moved steadily to a pejorative view of the poor and their needs, especially the poor who commit crimes. They term the interaction between the indigent accused and his/her court-appointed attorney a "meet 'em and plead 'em" defense, where the client is advised to plead guilty, and if and when a trial occurs it is heavily financially weighted against the defendant. A society would have to make a serious commitment to systemic changes to bring justice to the poor. So we come full circle to Sloan, Clarke, and Engelberg's optimism that with the proper identification of the problem, we can achieve an equitable system of criminal defense in the United States.

Virginia E. Sloan, Cait Clarke, and
Daniel Engelberg

 **YES**

Gideon's Unfulfilled Mandate: Time for a New Consensus

Gideon's Unfulfilled Mandate: Time for a New Consensus

Forty years after *Gideon v. Wainwright,* 372 U.S. 335 (1963), the landmark Supreme Court case establishing the right of counsel for indigent defendants in criminal trials, the public occasionally glimpses the gap between Gideon's mandate and reality. There are still places in this country, for example, where indigent defendants sit in jail for months without seeing a lawyer. In Mississippi, Waller Williams was not appointed a public defender until the day of his arraignment—more than eight months after his arrest and incarceration. Still others are not even given access to an attorney at all. In some parts of Georgia, defendants are told to speak first with prosecutors and urged to plead guilty before being allowed to talk to a defense lawyer.

In other parts of the country, the problem for poor defendants is not the lack of a lawyer but the lack of a competent lawyer. Some defendants, like George McFarland, whose publicly funded lawyer slept through much of his capital murder trial, have attorneys who blatantly damage [their] cases. Others, like several Illinois inmates whose death sentences were commuted to life by Governor George Ryan's commutations in 2000, are represented at trial by inept attorneys who are subsequently disbarred or suspended.

Of course, the responsibility for shortchanging the indigent client is never the lawyer's alone. The buck stops [with] the government authorities responsible for designing and funding our indigent defense system, whose job ostensibly is to ensure that lawyers are assigned indigent cases and have the time, tools, and training necessary to deliver quality representation.

Recreating the Bipartisan Spirit

There is a strong consensus across political lines that, as U.S. Supreme Court Justice Hugo Black wrote in 1956, "there can [be] no equal justice where the kind of trial a man gets depends on the amount of money he has." In 1963 twenty-two

From *Human Rights,* vol. 31, issue 3, Winter 2004, pp. 3–5. Copyright © 2004 by American Bar Association. Reprinted by permission.

state attorneys general were asked by the State of Florida to join in opposing Clarence Earl Gideon's right to counsel before the Supreme Court. However, led by then-Minnesota Attorney General (and later senator and vice president) Walter Mondale, they decided instead that the only decent course was to file a brief supporting Gideon. Their willingness to support Gideon's petition was central to the Court's unanimous judgment in favor of Gideon, and to the overwhelming national [acceptance] of the right to counsel—at a multibillion dollar cost to taxpayers—in the years immediately following. The unmistakable impression around the country was that ensuring a fair day in court for poor people accused of crimes was not solely in the interests of the defendants but essential for everyone—including the officials whose job is to punish lawbreakers—because it ultimately represents the quality of our justice system and our democracy.

In response to a growing recognition of Gideon's uncompleted mandate, the Constitution Project and the National Legal Aid and Defender Association (NLADAs), both national nonprofit organisations, have created a new initiative to review the status of indigent defense systems throughout the nation and consider what types of improvements may be necessary. This initiative will build on the same bipartisan spirit that laid the foundation for Gideon and, through a coming together of powerful, diverse voices, including Walter Mondale as a co-chair, will seek a consensus for reform. There will be two [basic] stages of the project: first, an examination of the precise nature and scope of the problems confronting indigent defense in the United States, and second, the development, by a group of distinguished citizens, of polices and strategies [for] remedying the identified deficiencies.

What Gideon Left Out

During a March 2003 symposium to mark Gideon's fortieth anniversary, Abe Krash, one of Gideon's lawyers, noted that in 1963 even the most dedicated reformers did not appreciate how much the Supreme Court's decision neglected to say. Gideon did not deal with several crucial issues: what constitutes adequate funding for indigent defense; what effective indigent defense systems should look like; and what standards of quality should be required of a publicly funded lawyer.

Gideon gave states no guidance about how to manage their indigent defense systems. As a result, the nation has a patchwork of systems that lack centralization, uniformity, and clear standards of quality. In many courtrooms throughout the country, defendants are given underpaid [defense] attorneys who have neither time nor resources to devote to their cases. Many of the lawyers have no interest in or dedication to criminal defense. As a Department of Justice (DOJ) report stated in 2000, because of the combined forces of severe underfunding and weak organizational structures, "Indigent defense in the United States today is in a chronic state of crisis."

A Crisis of Funding

Nationwide, most state indigent defense programs, with a few notable exceptions, are woefully underfunded. The odds are stacked against an indigent person accused of a crime—largely as a result of extreme disparities in funding for prosecutors and publicly funded defenders. A 1990 DOJ report found that nationally, three times as much was spent on prosecution as on indigent defense—a continuing pattern, according to recent figures from states such as Delaware and Kentucky.

In states where the money for indigent defense funding comes mostly from county coffers, the funding discrepancies for the two sides are especially extreme. The chancery clerk of Quitman County, Mississippi, told USA Today, "In every criminal case, it's like fielding a high school team to play the Green Bay Packers." (Kevin Johnson, How Good a Defense Should a Suspect Get? USA TODAY, Apr. 29, 2003, at 1A.)

In 1999 Quitman County sued the state to help with indigent defense funding, and a trial judge recently urged the legislature to fix the funding problems. The problems in Quitman County are symbolic of those in poor jurisdictions nationwide. As a result of chronic underfunding, lawyers for the poor in many parts of the country have few resources for essential parts of a criminal defense. Without necessary resources, cases cannot be investigated, experts cannot be hired, and critical motions cannot be filed. Overworked and understaffed attorneys lack either the time or the energy necessary for an adequate defense. The result can be that little or no defense is offered in a "meet 'em and plead "em" system. In California, one contract defense lawyer said in a deposition that he was proud of the fact that he pleads 70 percent of his clients guilty at the first court appearance, after having spent only thirty seconds explaining the prosecution's "offer." (NO EXCEPTIONS: A CAMPAIGN TO GUARANTEE A FAIR JUSTICE SYSTEM FOR ALL, VOLUME 3: THE NEED FOR INDPENDENT PUBLIC DEFENSE SYSTEMS (July/Aug.), available at http:// www.noexceptions.org/pdf/july%5fpub.pdf).

A Crisis of Structure

Many of the same problems also result from the structure—or lack thereof—of indigent defense systems. States generally deliver publicly funded services in three basic ways. Some jurisdictions have a staffed public defender office with employees on salary. More than half of the nation's counties appoint private attorneys, often through an unstructured ad hoc process. Other locales use a contract system in which individual attorneys of firms bid to provide some or all of the public defense services.

Any system, whether public defender, contract, or assigned counsel, can deliver quality representation if properly run according to national standards. But these arrangements can be horribly abused—most commonly by underfunding. Contract systems in which public defenders are paid a flat fee for each case may create an incentive to dispose of cases quickly without investigation or filing needed motions. Time, resources, and motivation can also be lacking for appointed lawyers in jurisdictions with low hourly rates, arbitrary fee caps, or judges with untrammeled discretion to cut or reduce pay for arbitrary reasons (such as the lawyer's failure to move cases fast enough). Recent budget cuts in Minnesota doubled the workload of a public defender who had planned to spend the rest of his career in his job. Citing the stress and burdens

on his family, he took a new job—as a prosecutor. (NO EXCEPTIONS: A CAM-
PAIGN TO GUARANTEE A FAIR JUSTICE SYSTEM FOR ALL VOLUME 4:
UNIQUE RESOURCES RESULT IN UNEQUAL JUSTICE (Sept.), available at
`http://www.noexceptions.org/pdf/sept.pub.pdf`).

Tackling the Crisis

Ultimately, the lack of competent, vigorous legal representation for indigent
[defendants] calls into question the legitimacy of criminal [convictions] and the
integrity and [efficiency] of the criminal justice system as a whole. Judges, prosecutors, and defense lawyers alike understand that without sufficient resources
and restructuring of indigent defense systems, the Sixth Amendment rights on
which Gideon rests may be significantly undermined.

Trying to reform the quality of indigent defense systems through the
courts has been difficult. The 1984 Supreme Court decision in *Strickland v.
Washington*, 467 U.S. 1267 set the bar for competence of counsel so low that
individual "ineffective assistance of counsel" claims mostly fail. In the state
courts, attempts at system-wide reform in Arizona, Louisiana, Oklahoma,
Minnesota, and New Jersey have met with limited or no success.

Change also has been slow in coming from state legislatures. Although
public opinion research shows very strong public support for indigent defense
and the principle of parity with prosecution resources, political consensus for
change is often lacking. Some states recognize the need for reform but
already-slashed budgets render funding elusive. Mississippi's state legislature
passed a sweeping reform act to create a [statewide] indigent defense system in
1998 but [eventually] repealed it after funding never materialized. The Georgia
legislature early in 2003 passed a similar law to create an integrated statewide
system with full-time public defender offices in each of the state's forty-nine
judicial circuits—although funding remains an [enormous] challenge.

Throughout the country, grassroots efforts are being made in many states
to point out the injustices and inefficiencies in public defender systems. Small
gains are being won. After years of deliberation, North Carolina's general assembly
enacted the indigent Defense Services Act of 2000, which led to statewide reform.
After eight years of attempts, Texas passed the Fair Defense Act in 2001 to improve
local procedures for appointing counsel. But much work remains to be done.

Where Do We Go from Here?

The Gideon Initiative

To tackle the systemwide need for reform, solutions must start in state capitols.
The bipartisan Gideon initiative undertaken by the Constitution Project and
NLADA hopes to [facilitate] high-level political consensus in support of quality
indigent defense systems. The Gideon initiative will make the case that our
country's system of justice demands that the rights established in Gideon be
fully and effectively implemented and will develop recommendations for how
the states can do so.

Given the issue's ongoing crisis status and common misconceptions about criminal defense and the need for reform, this [initiative] could not have come at a more opportune time. It has been twenty-seven years since the last comprehensive review of indigent defense by a national commission. NIADA convened the National Study Commission on Defense Service in 1976, which issued a 560-page final report that examined the country's problems with indigent defense and recommended a comprehensive set of standards, [Guidelines] for Legal Defense Systems in the United States.

The Guidelines essentially elaborated upon and expanded the results of a 1973 commission, the National Advisory Commission on Criminal Justice Standards and Goals (NAC). Established to carry out the recommendation of the 1967 President's Commission on the Challenge of Crime in a Free Society, the NAC's mission was to develop the standards that would bring uniformity and professionalism to each of the components of the nation's criminal justice systems. The NAC's recommendations, drafted by prominent leaders from across the political spectrum including two governors, a big-city mayor, chief prosecutors, and others, have formed the foundation of each subsequent initiative dealing with standards and accreditation.

The bipartisan spirit evident in Gideon and in the work of the above commissions will continue in the Constitution Project/NLADA initiative, which will bring together experts and other interested citizens to create consensus recommendations for reforms. The committee will include individuals with a diversity of viewpoints and experiences, such as state and federal judges, prosecutors, law enforcement leaders, policymakers, defenders, corporate and civic leaders, and clients, such as exonerated individuals.

The bipartisan committee's work will be informer by nationwide research conducted by scholars with expertise in social sciences and criminal justice, and by previous research from academia and organizations such as the ABA, the NLADA, and the Spangenberg Group. The committee will [identify] the common obstacles to the realization of Gideon's promise; describe "best practices" indigent defense adaptable to different types of systems; prepare a checklist for reform that any jurisdiction may use; and create consensus recommendations for reform, including model federal and state legislation.

Many of the ingredients for reform are already present. Well-settled standards for quality, resources, and independence have long been available; but systemic changes will not be easy. The mission of the initiative by the Constitution Project and NLADA is to create a nationwide consensus for . . . a system that is, in many plates, badly broken. We have too long ignored Justice Black's warning linking justice to money. It is time for the system to change once again.

It has been twenty-seven years since the last comprehensive review of indigent defense.

NO  *The Economist* Staff Writer

Too Poor to Be Defended

IN AMERICA'S fiercely adversarial legal system, a good lawyer is essential. Ask O.J. Simpson. In a landmark case 35 years ago, *Gideon v Wainwright,* a unanimous Supreme Court ruled that indigent defendants must be provided with a lawyer at state expense because there could be no fair trial in a serious criminal case without one. "This seems to us to be an obvious truth," wrote Justice Hugo Black in his opinion. At the time, the decision was hailed as a triumph for justice, an example of America's commitment to the ideal of equality before the law.

This is the image most Americans still have of their criminal-justice system-the fairest in the world, in which any defendant, no matter how poor, gets a smart-aleck lawyer who, too often, manages to get the culprit off on a technicality. Nothing could be further from the truth. About 80% of people accused of a felony have to depend on a publicly-provided lawyer; but over the past two decades the eagerness of politicians to look harsh on crime, their reluctance to pay for public defenders, and a series of Supreme Court judgments restricting the grounds for appeal have made a mockery of Gideon. Today many indigent defendants, including those facing long terms of imprisonment or even death, are treated to a "meet 'em and plead 'em" defence—a brief consultation in which a harried or incompetent lawyer encourages them to plead guilty or, if that fails, struggles through a short trial in which the defence is massively outgunned by a more experienced, better-paid and better-prepared prosecutor.

"We have a wealth-based system of justice," says Stephen Bright, the director of the Atlanta-based Southern Centre for Human Rights, a legal-aid and advocacy group. "For the wealthy, it's gold-plated. For the average poor person, it's like being herded to the slaughterhouse. In many places the adversary system barely exists for the poor."

Many lawyers, of course, have made heroic efforts for particular defendants for little or no pay, but the charity of lawyers can be relied on to handle only a tiny fraction of cases. As spending on police, prosecutors and prisons has steadily climbed in the past decade, increasing the number of people charged and imprisoned, spending on indigent defence has not kept pace, overwhelming an already hard-pressed system.

From *The Economist,* vol. 346, no. 8063, April 11, 1998, pp. 21–22. Copyright © 1998 by Economist.

A rise in the hourly rate paid to defence lawyers preparing a case in the federal courts, approved by Congress in 1986, has still not been implemented in 77 of the country's 94 federal districts because Congress itself refuses to appropriate any additional money. At $45 an hour, many defence lawyers practising in the federal courts are not paid enough to cover their hourly overhead costs for maintaining a law office, according to the federal government's own calculations. Even in those districts where the rise has been implemented, the maximum $75-an-hour fee allowed is less than half the $150–$200 an hour the average private lawyer would receive.

At state level, where the vast majority of criminal trials are held, the situation is often far worse. In Louisville, Kentucky, salaried lawyers in the public defender's office handle a staggering 750 cases a year. In Virginia, private lawyers are paid a maximum fee of $265 for felony cases that carry a sentence of up to 20 years and $575 if the potential penalty is more than 20 years. Alabama pays defence lawyers a mere $20 an hour, up to a maximum of $1,000, to prepare for a death-penalty case. Mississippi pays a maximum of $1,000, above overhead expenses, for work in the courtroom during a death-penalty trial. Other states pay more, but few approach the fees that would be paid by individuals with the means to hire their own lawyers. The amounts public defenders are allowed to spend on investigation or expert witnesses—widely available to prosecutors—are often severely restricted and sometimes not allowed at all.

In addition to the sheer lack of money, the methods of appointing and paying defence lawyers are also open to abuse. This varies from state to state and even from county to county within some states. In many state jurisdictions, trial judges appoint defence lawyers on a case-by-case basis and set the level of their fees. These fees can sometimes be so low that no lawyers can be found to accept the job. In that event, judges can force lawyers practising in the area to take turns defending indigent clients, whether or not the lawyers have any criminal-law experience. "This is like forcing a podiatrist to do brain surgery," observes Paul Petterson, indigent-defence coordinator for the National Association of Criminal Defence Lawyers (NACDL).

Even when there are lawyers willing to take on indigent cases, judges often appoint cronies, or those they know will not vigorously contest a case. Most state judges are elected or subject to recall votes. Faced with crowded lists, they have little incentive to bend over backwards to ensure that the hundreds of impoverished defendants who pass through their courts, many accused of heinous crimes, are represented by well-paid or zealous lawyers. Judges in Houston, Texas, have repeatedly appointed one local lawyer who is famous for hurrying through trials like "greased lightning" to represent indigent defendants. Ten of his clients have been sentenced to death. During one death-penalty case, he fell asleep on several occasions. Nevertheless, the death sentence was upheld on appeal and the defendant has since been executed.

A second approach is to contract out to a single lawyer or group of lawyers all a county's defence work. Too often this means the contract goes to the lowest bidder. In 1993 one Georgia county cut the cost of its indigent-defence budget by awarding the contract to a lawyer who, at $25,000 a year, bid almost $20,000 less than the other two bidders. In the next three years the contracted defender tried only one felony case in front of a jury, while entering guilty pleas in 213 other cases.

The most reliable method used to provide lawyers for poor defendants is to appoint salaried public defenders. But public-defender offices are often grossly underfunded. Training programmes for defenders are scarce. Inexperienced lawyers fresh out of law school are often buried under a gigantic caseload, as in Louisville. The amount spent on defender offices is typically one-third or less that spent on the teams of prosecutors they face.

It is hardly surprising that many poor defendants receive less than sterling representation. Mr. Bright's files are stuffed with examples of people whose public defenders were either grossly negligent or ignorant. This can be a disaster for any defendant. The innocent face wrongful conviction. However, even the guilty may suffer because their lawyer failed to raise mitigating factors which, by law, entitle them to a milder sentence. Once, wrongful convictions because of lawyer error stood a good chance of being overturned on appeal, especially in death-penalty cases. But Congress and the Supreme Court have recently made appeals far more difficult.

In 1996 Congress eliminated all federal funding for death-penalty resource centres, which had handled or advised on most death-penalty appeals. Most of these centers have since closed. The same year Congress also passed an anti-terrorism law which included strict new procedural rules that make it much more difficult to mount an appeal in a death-penalty case, even when new evidence is found.

The Supreme Court has ruled that appeals based on lawyer error must prove not only that a defence lawyer was incompetent, but that his incompetence changed the outcome of the trial. Proving such a negative is often impossible. Lower courts have used this ruling to uphold convictions, even in death-penalty cases, in which the defence lawyer was drunk, asleep during the trial or completely ignorant of the relevant law. As a result, most wrongly convicted poor defendants now face a catch-22: to prove their original lawyer incompetent, they must find a highly competent lawyer to navigate the bigger appeal hurdles recently erected, although behind bars they are in an even worse position to do that.

Providing poor defendants with proper legal representation would cost money, but it is affordable. The estimated spending on indigent defence is less than 2% of total national spending on law enforcement, and only about 10% of spending on all judicial and legal services. Some states, such as Minnesota and Colorado, have found the money for a reasonably financed public-defender programme. Criminal legal aid is also starved of support in many other countries, but some, such as Britain and the Scandinavian countries, can find the money to do the job well.

POSTSCRIPT

Can the Poor Receive Adequate Criminal Defense?

Case law in the United States guarantees legal representation in criminal cases for those who are unable to provide counsel for themselves (*Gideon v. Wainwright*). On the face of things, this seems fair and equitable. But, as *The Economist* staff points out, the indigent defendant is not receiving adequate, let alone equal, legal protection. The American people see the justice system as the fairest in the world, but the reality is that the system is wealth-based.

The problem, argues *The Economist*, is that of inadequate, ever-decreasing funding for public defenders. A full 80 percent of those accused of a felony need public defense. But they are not getting the kind of defense an affluent defendant would be able to purchase. *The Economist* argues that a changed political climate—one that sees crimes and criminals stereotypically—has resulted in politicians' reluctance to provide sufficient funding to make the public defense system work equitably and satisfy the mandate of the Constitution. Perhaps the phrase the best captures the picture drawn by *The Economist* is that the poor have a "meet 'em and plead 'em" defense.

And it gets worse. Once convicted, mounting an appeal based on attorney error requires proving that "but for" the attorney's malfeasance, the outcome of the trial would have been different. As *The Economist* notes, to prove this, the indigent defendant/now prisoner has to hire a very competent lawyer, which usually translates into big dollars. *The Economist*'s picture is a dismal one for the indigent.

By contrast, Virginia Sloan, Cait Clarke, and Daniel Engelberg are optimistic that "Gideon's Mandate" can be fulfilled. As with flaws in any public policy, the key is in understanding what went wrong to begin with and in adopting changes that will bring us to where *Gideon* should have brought us in 1963. For all intents and purposes, Sloan, Clarke, and Engelberg are talking about reinventing poverty law.

If the court in *Gideon* had been clearer in its mandate, poverty law in the United States might have been more equitable for over the past 40-plus years. So we need to address the lack of equity across the nation, with most states struggling under a heavy financial burden. Although the authors do not refer to Martin Luther King's view of justice, we can argue that King's statement "Justice too long delayed is justice denied" is applicable to this public policy problem and the myriad of people it affects. The solution lies in clearer-cut guidelines regarding what constitutes an "adequate" defense and in providing the funding for it.

Additional worthwhile readings include Robert Hermann, *Counsel for the Poor: Criminal Defense in Urban America*; Lee Silverstein, *Defense of the Poor in Criminal Cases in American State Courts*; and Tara Herival and Paul Wright, eds., *Prison Nation: The Warehousing of America's Poor*.

ISSUE 14

Can "Expert Witness" Testimony in the Courtroom Be Made More Equitable?

YES: Anna Maria Gillis, from "Science in the Courtroom," *BioScience* (January 1992)

NO: Preston Lerner, from "A New Breed of Hired Gun: In Today's Legal System, You Not Only Need the Best Lawyers Money Can Buy—But Also the Best Expert Witnesses," *Washington Monthly* (April 1977)

ISSUE SUMMARY

YES: Anna Maria Gillis argues the need for expert witnesses in the courtroom, given the increasing complexity of many issues before judge and jury. She believes fairness can be achieved with closer judicial scrutiny of "experts'" credentials and with court-appointment expert witnesses.

NO: Preston Lerner argues that money will always prevail in a judicial proceeding, and that finding the best "expert witnesses" is no different than hiring the best attorney.

The observations of the poet Robert Frost and the writer/actor Woody Allen set the scene for this issue. Said Allen, "Money is better than poverty, if only for financial reasons." And Frost commented that "A jury consists of twelve persons to decide who has the better lawyer." Extrapolating from Frost, we might add "and can obtain the best expert witnesses."

Although relatively few cases reach trial, either on the criminal or civil side, those that do have been increasingly more complex. That complexity has brought with it the "expert witness" who can seemingly provide solid information about everything, including the number of angels that can fit on the head of a pin. The judicial community has welcomed expert witnesses with open arms. Some "experts" make their living by being witnesses.

At the risk of including too many quips, let's just add one more, since it is so a propos. Anatole France observed, "The law, in its majestic equality, forbids the rich as well as the poor, to sleep under bridges, to beg in the streets, and to steal bread." Anyone can have expert witnesses, in theory. But when the reality of paying for these witnesses sets in, there is a clear disadvantageous not only to the poor, but also to the middle class.

So, does the use of expert witnesses in the courtroom give the wealthy an unfair advantage? Relatedly, does it also give the prosecution an unfair advantage when dealing with indigent defendants?

Preston Lerner argues, "In today's legal system, you not only need the best lawyers money can buy, but also the best expert witnesses." Lerner cites case after case in which victory was achieved because of the presence of an "expert" witness. So juries are won over by these experts. But, as Lerner points out, what are their credentials? Many are not experts at all, but that doesn't seem to matter. If jurors believe someone to be an expert, that person is an expert. So Lerner decries not only the ever-expanding use of expert witnesses in the courtroom, but also "the absence of clear-cut standards regarding their expertise."

Anna Maria Gillis places value on expert witnesses' testimony. She points out that "many cases hinge on the ability of judges, lawyers, and juries to understand fine points of epidemiology, toxicology, ecology, nutrition, animal husbandry, psychology, or statistics." The problem is that "experts hold so much sway over juries that they have, in effect, become thirteenth jurors."

So how can the usefulness of expert witnesses be balanced against their perhaps excessive persuasiveness? And how can the system achieve equity in the face of the costs of expert witnesses? How can the system avoid what has been termed "the battle of the experts"?

Gillis looks to the judicial system to mend itself. She argues the need for court-appointment experts as well as for greater scrutiny of witnesses' credentials. Gillis points to a report entitled "Enhancing the Reliable and Impartial Scientific and Technical Expertise to the Federal Court" prepared for the Carnegie Commission's review as it seeks to improve the role of expert witnesses in the courtroom and to make the system more just.

YES

Anna Maria Gillis

Science in the Courtroom

Efforts Afoot to Improve the Quality of Expert Testimony

Last summer, the *The New York Times* ran an ad with a picture of a good-sized porker sporting a pair of wings. The ad said, "In a courtroom, anything will fly if a scientist testifies to it."

The ad was placed by *Forbes* magazine to promote a hard-hitting story (8 July 1991) on the use of expert testimony in the courtroom. The article said, "Carrying the traditional American adversary system to absurd extremes, judges are allowing crackpot scientists to pollute the legal process, at a cost to consumers and business in the billions." Peter Huber, the author of the article and of the book *Galileo's Revenge: Junk Science in the Courtroom* (Basic Books, New York, 1991), wrote that there "is a need to bring scientific order to the courtroom."

Many in legal circles agree with Huber's demand for improved expert testimony. But they view as extreme Huber's claim that the use of "junk science" is rampant. "The purveyors of the view that there is a lot of junk science in civil court keep wheeling out the same sorts of cases. You don't condemn the whole [expert testimony] system based on a few outrageous cases," says Cornell University's Sheila Jasanoff, a lawyer member of an American Association for the Advancement of Science-American Bar Association (AAAS-ABA) task force. Focusing on junk science avoids the real problem—that courts do not know how to interpret scientific information, says Jasanoff.

The Court's Problem

"Courts are seriously hampered in scientific and technical controversies by their inability to understand the true implications of the evidence before them," wrote Donald Elliott, a Yale law professor and former general counsel for the Environmental Protection Agency, in a 1989 report for the Carnegie Commission on Science, Technology, and Government. In the course of doing business, he estimated that courts encounter scientific and technical issues in as many as 20 to 30% of all cases.

Many cases hinge on the ability of judges, lawyers, and juries to understand fine points of epidemiology, toxicology, ecology, nutrition, animal husbandry, psychology, o statistics. Historically, courts have relied on expert witnesses to explain scientific and technical matters so that judges could decide whether a case should go to trial. In theory, once in court, the expert's role is to help the judge or jury understand an issue well enough to make a reasoned decision. However, in American University law professor Paul Rice's opinion, experts hold so much sway over juries that they have, in effect, become thirteenth jurors.

There is a general sense among lawyers and judges that since the 1970s there has been an increased use of expert witnesses and a decline in their calibre. They attribute problems with experts to Congress's 1975 codification of the Federal Rules of Evidence, which govern the use of experts in federal courts. The rules loosened the previous standards for experts that had developed under common law; it lowered qualifications for experts and broadened the areas of acceptable expertise. What developed was a "let it [any kind of evidence] all in" attitude, says Steven Gallagher, a senior legal associate with the Carnegie Commission on Science, Technology, and Govern meet.

Courts complain that overuse of experts boosts the cost and time of litigation, and many judges see some experts as "hired guns" who willingly distort their discipline's knowledge on the witness stand. At the same time, courts recognize that most experts are uncomfortable as advocates and do not want the role.

"It is a credit to the scientific community that there are not that many lousy experts, but the bad ones seem to testify with depressing frequency," says Atlanta-based defense attorney Bert Black. He says most experts want to present data in an unbiased and thorough way, but they are frustrated by the traditional adversarial process that often prohibits them from doing so. "No lawyer wants his witness to divulge something damaging to his case," says Black.

The adversarial tradition so sacred to lawyers will not be tossed away in the interest of better courtroom science. But the legal community is looking for ways to vet expert witnesses and improve the court's understanding of science, possibly through the appointment of impartial witnesses. Proposals to change the federal rules governing expert witnesses are moving through the judiciary, and a study on the use of court-appointed witnesses by federal judges was completed last fall by the Federal Judicial Center. The center also has begun a survey of federal judges to determine what type of experts are used in court, the issues on which they testify, and problems that arise from their use. In September, an AAAS-ABA task force on science in the courts submitted a study to the Carnegie Commission that dealt with ways scientific and engineering professional societies could help the courts find impartial experts and ease judges' difficulties in assessing science materials.

Federal Rules of Evidence

"There is a crisis," says Paul F. Rothstein, a Georgetown University law professor who specializes in evidence. "The federal rules opened the door wide to experts."

One federal rule liberalized the definition of an expert, says Rothstein. An expert can be anyone with scientific, technical, or specialized knowledge who can help a jury understand the evidence. Previously, experts had to be professionals, such as scientists or other persons with specialized university degrees. Experts can now include anyone with skills and knowledge in a particular area that are only incrementally greater than those of the jury. If their tiny bit more of knowledge will help a jury even by a tiny degree, they might be let in as a witness, says Rothstein. Judges, who have the job of deciding which expert witnesses can appear in court, have no good way to sort out reputable witnesses from frauds, he says.

Another of the rules says that, if the information on which an opinion is based is the sort used by persons in the expert's field, the background material does not have to be "admissible in evidence." This rule allows the expert to testify using documents and hearsay that might not otherwise be allowed in court. Rothstein says experts can now base their testimony on unpublished data that may not stand up to peer review, and they can come to conclusions based on evidence the jury never hears.

Under the common law tradition, ordinary witnesses are only allowed to testify about things of which they have first-hand knowledge, for example, something they have seen or done. They cannot give opinions or make conclusions. However, the 1975 rules permit expert witnesses to give opinions and make inferences without disclosing the facts or data on which they are based, unless asked on cross-examination. They also allow experts to make statements that "embrace an ultimate issue to be decided by the trier of fact." For example, an expert could opine that "substance x caused Mr. Y's death," a conclusion that previously would have been left strictly in the jury's domain. (Many state courts still prohibit expert witnesses from making ultimate issue statements.)

The loosening of standards has allowed groups like the clinical ecologists to get a toehold in court, says Black. Clinical ecologists have blamed a wide variety of illnesses on trace chemicals in the environment. Black says the field, considered on the fringe by most scientists, "is of great concern because it allows plaintiffs to argue that virtually anything causes virtually anything. Marginal fields should not be allowed in the courtroom."

Judicial Reform

Last August, a rules committee of the Judicial Conference of the United States, the federal judiciary's policy-making arm, circulated to the bench and bar proposed changes to the Federal Rules of Evidence. The changes would require that expert testimony be based on information that is "reasonably reliable" and will "substantially assist" the jury. Another proposed change would require that the factual basis of testimony be divulged when experts give opinions. After the bench and bar comment on the proposed changes, the changes go back to the rules committee and the full Judicial Conference, then to the U.S. Supreme Court, and ultimately Congress. Even if approved expeditiously, the changes would not go into effect before 1993.

Around the time the proposed changes were released, the President's Council on Competitiveness released its report Agenda for Civil Justice Reform in America, which stated, "An area of the law particularly ripe for reform is expert witness practice." The council suggested banning contingency fees (compensation based on a successful outcome) for experts. Abolishing contingency fees would "keep experts from becoming mercenaries or advocates, instead of remaining impartial and objective," the report said.

One of the council's principal recommendations is to require that expert testimony be based on "widely accepted" theories. Lawyers would have to demonstrate that their experts' opinions were based on an established theory supported by a significant portion of experts in the relevant field. "This revision is designed to eliminate testimony that is far afield from mainstream professional practice or current scientific knowledge. . . . [It] would allow testimony based on respected minority or majority theories while excluding fringe theories," the report said. In October, President Bush signed an executive order that requires government lawyers to implement the expert witness reform measures proposed in the Council on Competitiveness report. The order went into effect January 1992 and covers all civil cases involving the US government.

The council's proposal is a modified, less stringent version of a requirement known as the Frye standard, Rothstein says, which until 1975 largely governed scientific testimony in state and federal courts. It still holds sway in many state courts. The Frye, or "general acceptance," test was developed in 1923 in a case that involved the admissibility of polygraph test results. Judge Van Orsdel wrote: "Just when a scientific principle or discovery crosses the line between the experimental and demonstrable stages is difficult to define. Somewhere in this twilight zone the evidential force of the principle must be recognized, and while courts will go a long way in admitting expert testimony deduced from a well-recognized scientific principle or discovery, the thing from which the deduction is made must be sufficiently established to have gained general acceptance in the particular field in which it belongs."

The major similarity between the proposals is that they tighten standards for and exert greater control over expert witnesses. According to Rothstein, the council's proposal tightens standards more than the Judicial Conference's. How proposed changes will be received by the bar cannot be easily predicted, says Gallagher. "The plaintiff's bar would want looser science standards because they have the burden of proof. The defendant's bar prefers strict standards."

Black says that neither the proposed changes in the rules of evidence nor the old Frye standard are sophisticated enough to deal with today's science-based cases. The problems are more subtle than the pitting of experts against each other or the integrity and credentials of experts.

The general acceptance standard is vague and causes problems because it leaves too many questions unanswered, says Black. How does a judge know what is generally accepted? How does a judge identify good representatives of a field? When does a theory become generally accepted? What should the court do when a particular expert's field is not recognized by the rest of the scientific community as a legitimate field? If experts from several fields are called, what weight should judges give the various fields?

As an example of disciplines colliding in court, Jasanoff and Black, in an unpublished paper for the Carnegie Commission, point to controversies over low-level electromagnetic field effects. Some epidemiologists say cancer and other health problems have been associated with electromagnetic-field exposure, whereas physicists have been skeptical of the claims. Black asks, Who do you believe?

"If courts are to rule intelligently on the admissibility or sufficiency of scientific testimony, or provide meaningful instructions to juries on how to decide cases involving scientific disputes, judges must develop a better sense and understanding of the nature of scientific inquiry. . . . Courts must recognize that while some scientific conclusions are far more certain and reliable than others, no area of science produces absolute truth or certainty. Courts must also understand that different kinds of scientific disputes may require different approaches to evaluating expert testimony," Jasanoff and Black wrote.

Black says courts must overcome "the false notion that there is one scientific truth and that scientists see absolutes." He says that when judges see lack of consensus, some interpret that to mean the scientific evidence is useless. They then toss out this evidence and rely on other evidence. The result, he says, can be decisions completely at odds with scientific reality.

Courts Frustrated

Faced with experts who polarize a case and with complicated or irrelevant science that might confuse juries, judges may become more willing to inquire into the foundations of expert testimony and exclude questionable witnesses, says Joe Cecil, project director at the Federal Judicial Center. Where there is no adequate basis for expert testimony supporting one side, the judge may enter summary judgement, thereby deciding the case without sending it to a jury. No witnesses, no case, says Cecil.

A classic summary judgement involved a 1985 Agent Orange case. The plaintiff had to show that her husband's illness and death were caused by exposure to the herbicide. Although the plaintiff had an expert witness willing to testify, Judge Jack Weinstein disqualified the witness. He noted in his summary judgment that the witness ignored epidemiological studies important to the case and resorted to inappropriate studies of animals and workers exposed to the compound. More recently, several judges have made summary judgements in cases involving the morning-sickness drug Bendectin, which plaintiffs have claimed caused birth defects. Instead of allowing testimony from experts who said the compound caused defects, judges relied on the available epidemiological studies that do not support the claim, says Black.

Cecil says that if judges knew more science they could tell when testimony is based on unfounded methodologies, but there is a risk that judges may overstep their interpretative role. According to Cecil, "With complicated expert testimony, there is a risk that judges may exclude appropriate testimony and deprive the jury of an opportunity to consider a valid position held by a minority of scientists."

Cecil notes that, even if the federal rules do not change, more judges may tighten the standards for experts in their courts in response to recent appellate court opinions. In August 1991, for example, the US Court of Appeals for the Fifth Circuit, which covers Texas, Louisiana, and Mississippi, set an especially high standard for expert testimony in toxic tort litigation. By a vote of 9 to 4, the appellate court judges upheld a lower court's decision to exclude an expert's testimony because it was unreliable. In the case of *Christophersen v. Allied-Signal Corp.*, the plaintiff, Rosemarie Christophersen, claimed that workplace exposure to fumes containing nickel and cadmium were responsible for her husband's colon cancer and eventual death. The excluded expert based many of his conclusions on the affidavit of a plant employee who described the fumes at the plant.

The appellate court stressed the importance of inquiring into the methodology used by the expert in reaching his decision and endorsed the Frye test in requiring that the methodology be "generally accepted within the relevant scientific community." This standard exceeds the standards set by other courts of appeals and presents a conflict that the US Supreme Court may be asked to resolve, says Cecil. "The majority and dissenting opinions in the Christophersen case reflect the frustration of many judges in dealing with scientific evidence."

Court-Appointed Witnesses

Polarization, concerns about impartiality, and confusion of jurors might be minimized in cases involving expert testimony if court-appointed witnesses were used more often, says Gallagher of the Carnegie Commission, which is looking at ways to make reliable and impartial expertise available to the courts.

The Federal Rules of Evidence allow judges to appoint experts, but judges tend to be reluctant to do so. Legal sources cite several reasons for this hesitance. Some judges fear that by picking witnesses, they will be putting a thumb on the judicial scales, possibly directing the outcome of a case through their choice. There is also the possibility that juries would be more easily swayed by witnesses of the court's choosing. Money is also an issue. The rules allow the court to direct the parties in a case to pay for court-appointed witnesses, but judges are uncomfortable with requiring parties to pay for testimony that might harm their cases.

Maybe even more important is an entrenched idea that US judges have of their role. Judges mostly see themselves as umpires, refereeing while the adversaries duke it out in front of the jury. Many judges believe that it is the responsibility of the adversaries to bring in the witnesses, and they do not want to interfere with the lawyers' jobs, says Rothstein.

Even if judges were enthusiastic about using their own witnesses, the witnesses and lawyers pose problems. "A court-appointed witness is like a horse without a rider. Trial lawyers hate court-appointed witnesses because they are out of their control and unpredictable," says Sam Gross, a University of Michigan law professor.

In the American system, testimony in court assumes preparation. Experts particularly need to prepare. But the court has no structure to coach court-appointed witnesses, says Gross. Judges are reluctant to prepare them, and the lawyers in the case do not want to do it. The court-appointed witness shows up in court and somehow is expected to be ready for vigorous cross-examination from plaintiff and defense lawyers.

A Federal Judicial Center study completed last fall seems to bear out Gross's belief that "court-appointed witnesses are as common as hen's teeth." The survey of 428 federal judges indicated that 86 judges had appointed witnesses. Half of those who appointed witnesses had only used the option once. Only four judges had appointed witnesses in more than 10 cases, says Cecil. At the same time, 87% of the judges said the court-appointed witnesses would probably be helpful.

"We found that judges who appointed experts reserved the procedure for unusual cases with particularly technically demanding evidence," says Cecil. Also, judges were most likely to appoint experts in cases where there were two credible experts but the competing claims could not be sorted out by the jury or in cases where one side had an expert who lacked credibility and the indigent opposition had no expert. The judges in the federal study also said the juries' decisions were positively influenced by the testimony of the court-appointed witness.

In a small empirical study, Judge Carl B. Rubin of the federal circuit in Cincinnati, Ohio, also found that jurors tended to give great weight to the testimony of court-appointed witnesses. Rubin looked at 16 cases tried between September 1987 and September 1990 where plaintiffs claimed that asbestos was responsible for asbestosis and pleural plaque. The court-appointed experts examined the plaintiffs to determine whether they had either asbestos-related condition. Approximately 80% of the jury decisions were in agreement with the experts' findings. "The conclusion is inescapable: A court's expert will be a persuasive witness and will have a significant effect upon a jury," Rubin wrote in September 1991 in Federal Rules Decisions.

"It concerns me that by merely selecting a witness I could be determining the outcome of a case, but I don't know of any other solution," says Rubin. "You have juries with high school educations listening to the plaintiff's expert saying white is black and the defendant's expert saying black is white. Who do you believe? If there is the potential for confusion, the only thing I can do is appoint my own expert. As long as I have the rule at my disposal, I'll use it."

A Stable of Experts

Even if more judges chose to use court-appointed witnesses, they do not have an impartial stable available when the need for one arises. Judges surveyed in the Federal Judicial Center study said they were happy with the services of the court-appointed witnesses, but they had problems finding them. "We found judges tended to use experts they knew. While this ensured impartiality, it doesn't mean they always got the most knowledgeable expert," says Cecil. Cecil believes that cooperation between the judiciary and professional scientific and engineering societies might help the courts find neutral experts who are also in the upper ranks of their fields.

But increasing the use of court-appointed witnesses requires leaping over two hurdles: the inertia of the judiciary in using available scientific resources and the reluctance of many academics to appear in court, says Gallagher. He notes that a recent AAASABA project conducted for the Carnegie Commission points out that the judiciary does not want to tamper with the traditional adversarial process and scientists generally see no point in being an expert because it provides no honor in academia and and is often viewed unfavorably by peers.

The report, called Enhancing the Reliable and Impartial Scientific and Technical Expertise to the Federal Courts is under review by the Carnegie Commission. Among the report's recommendations:

> The Carnegie Commission should determine the extent to which judges are willing to use court-appointed experts and whether they are receptive to the use of scientific and engineering communities as sources of expertise.
>
> Professional societies should begin programs that would encourage members to respond to court requests for assistance. The committee suggested that professional societies consider court activity as public and professional service. It also said societies could train their members for the courtroom and the challenges of cross-examination.
>
> Professional societies should develop guidelines for experts who testify as experts and criteria and procedures for identifying and screening potential witnesses.

Jasanoff, a member of the task force that prepared the report, says that although the scientific-society executives contacted for the report were enthusiastic about helping the courts, they did not have the mechanisms in their organizations to make assistance immediately feasible. They would have to develop codes of professional responsibility, training programs, and sanctions for ethical violations, she says. "I am skeptical that more judges would use experts from societies, even if they were available. The trial bar is opposed to court-appointed witnesses. By adding the court-appointed witness, you're adding another voice to the adversarial process."

Proposed changes to the rules of evidence are more likely to change lawyers' courtroom practices than scientists' attitudes about testifying, says Jasanoff. "Academics will only become more willing to testify," she concludes, "if they see that courts are willing to let them testify in a way that allows them to explain science based problems completely."

NO

Preston Lerner

A New Breed of Hired Gun: In Today's Legal System, You Not Only Need the Best Lawyers Money Can Buy—But Also the Best Expert Witnesses

In today's legal system, you not only need the best lawyers money can buy— but also the best expert witnesses

Carmen Mistich was tootling down St. Bernard Highway just outside New Orleans when a full-size pickup truck traveling at least 40 mph faster than her Volkswagen plowed into the back of her car. Mistich wasn't wearing a seat belt, and as the VW rolled over, she was hurled through the rear window. Two months later, she died as a result of her injuries.

The accident could have happened anywhere, anytime. But this being America, the most litigious nation on the planet, Mistich's heirs hit Volkswagen with a product liability lawsuit. And this being the '90s, they were able to find not one, not two, but three experts willing to testify that Mistich died because the design of her car's seat anchorage system was flawed.

Never mind that she wasn't wearing a seat belt; that the Volkswagen performed better than most cars in its class in a federal study of seat anchorage systems; that the accident, on its face, had all the makings of a textbook fatality: massive, fast-moving truck smashes into a tiny, nearly stationary car. A no-brainer, right? Hardly. As one cynical attorney puts it, "You can hire an expert to say just about anything."

The star witness in the case against Volkswagen was a self-proclaimed automobile design expert named Byron Bloch, who testified that the Volkswagen seat was "a unique aberration in design . . . the weakest, minimalist seat anchorage ever put in a production car . . . the worst seat anchorage system ever."

And who exactly was Byron Bloch, and why was he qualified to say these terrible things about Volkswagen?

According to court records, he'd been dismissed from one collegiate engineering program, was placed on academic probation by the electrical engineering and industrial design departments at a second college, then ended up getting a B.A. from a third school. He was laid off from his first job after three months, fired from his second after six months, fired from his third after less than a year and released from his fourth after two years. When he embarked on a career as a consultant/expert, often testifying against Volkswagen, he hadn't worked on a single job involving automobiles, much less engineering.

Despite the defense's strenuous objections, Bloch was permitted to testify as an expert witness. "He has been qualified by courts across the land," the judge ruled, "and I do not presume that all of them were incorrect." Partly on the strength of Bloch's damning testimony, the Mistich family won its suit against Volkswagen and was awarded damages in excess of $2 million. Justice is blind all right. And sometimes, it would seem, deaf and dumb.

The Mistich case highlights one of the most vexing currents in the American legal system: the growing reliance on expert witnesses, and the absence of clear-cut standards regarding their expertise. "When you've got $3 billion product liability lawsuits being decided on the strength of junk science that's just wildly out of whack with objective reality, and when you've got people being sent to Death Row because some lunatic shrink says he can predict "future dangerousness" on the basis of some criteria known only to him, then, yeah, you've got a problem," says Peter W. Huber, author of the psychological impact reformers had hoped to see. Fewer people are including reliance on welfare in their plans for the future.

There is also good news from some states that are acting to soften the law's horrible features. For example, New York and 39 other states have asked for at least partial waivers of the requirement that food stamps for the unemployed be limited to 90 days.

The bad news is that way too little is being done about providing health care for the working poor, including those who leave welfare and then lose their Medicaid when they get jobs as we urge them to do.

At least Bill Clinton has proposed health insurance for the 5 million children of the working poor. But Republicans are opposing even this modest program. Their position seems to be, in the words of my friend Matthew Miller, "that insuring kids is just the camel's nose under the tent, the beginning of the slippery decline into socialism. Why, if we insure poor kids today, they argue, look out: Before long, every American may have decent healthcare coverage!"

The problem is not going to go away. Indeed, according to a recent study reported by Elisabeth Rosenthal in *The New York Times,* the problem is growing: "One quarter of New York City residents under 65 now have no health insurance at all: the exact figure is 24.8 percent, up from 20.9 percent five years ago. . . . The number of children without insurance has gone up twice as fast as the number of adults."

One state, Massachusetts, has done something about the problem. It has enacted the Massachusetts Children's Medical Security Plan, which insures children whose parents earn too much to qualify for Medicaid but too little to pay for private health insurance. The program, financed by a 25-cent-a-pack increase in the cigarette tax, was enacted over the veto of the state's Republican governor, William Weld.

Some tapes of Lyndon Johnson's phone conversations were recently made public by the LBJ Presidential Library. Two of them, recorded on the same day in 1964, will make you weep. In one, Johnson is talking to one of the most powerful hawks in the Senate, Richard Russell, then the chairman of the Armed Services Committee.

Johnson mentions a sergeant he knows who he realizes might have to serve in Vietnam: "Thinking about sending that father of those six kids in there . . . and what the hell we're going to get out of his doing it? It just makes the chills run up my back."

Russell: "It does me, too. We're in the quicksands up to our neck, and I just don't know what the hell to do about it."

How then, could LBJ, with Russell's support, proceed to send more than 58,000 men to die in Vietnam? A clue may be found in something Johnson said to his national security advisor, McGeorge Bundy, that same day: "They'd impeach a president, though, that would run out, wouldn't they?"

A measure to allow casino gambling in New York state was defeated in late January. As you might expect, a coalition of religious groups played a major role. But some of their allies could not exactly be described as selfless. Prominent among them was that great moralist, Donald J. Trump, who it is suspected was not enthusiastic about having competition for his own casinos in New Jersey.

Have you heard about the danger you're in from those drivers with one hand on the steering wheel and the other holding a cellular telephone? As they hear their boss tell them they're fired or a lover advising them to buzz off, the risk of an accident increases fourfold, according to a study published by The New England Journal of Medicine. I have a solution. No talkee while car movee. If you want to use the phone, pull the car off the road and make your call.

Galileo's Revenge: Junk Science in the Courtroom

A scathing indictment of expert witnesses, Huber's book is admittedly more polemic than even-handed policy prescription. Less partisan observers say expert witnesses are an integral cog in the American judicial machine, and the vast majority of them, testifying in prosaic cases that generate no media buzz, are competent. They allow that, naturally, there are exceptions, but that these problems are often self-correcting. For example, after being stung by a series of particularly ugly misconduct cases, forensic scientists voluntarily raised their expert witness standards. Equally, if not more important, a landmark product liability case decided by the U.S. Supreme Court in 1993 gives judges more latitude to exclude dubious testimony from experts peddling not-ready-for-prime-time theories about everything from handwriting analysis to repressed memories of childhood sexual abuse.

At least that's the theory. In practice, though, the situation is more complicated. First of all, a researcher publishing in Scientific American must meet a much higher standard of proof than an expert witness testifying in court. Second, our adversarial system of jurisprudence seems—at least to lay people—designed to elicit a legalistic notion of truth rather than objective truth. When in doubt, judges tend to err on the side of admitting too much testimony rather than too little, then letting the jury decide whether it makes sense. If, during cross-examination, an attorney can demolish an "expert" who claims that fill-in-the-blank (cellular telephones, photocopy machines, power lines) causes cancer, so be it. If not, well, them's the breaks.

"A lot of cases come down to a battle of the experts," says William T. Pizzi, a law professor at the University of Colorado at Boulder. "You get your expert at one extreme, and I get my expert at the other. The first one says, 'Yes, it definitely happened this way.' The second says, 'No, it couldn't possibly have happened that way.' What's the jury supposed to do?"

Experts, by definition, are the only witnesses permitted to testify about their opinions, and their opinions carry substantial weight. According to a study conducted by *The National Law Journal* and Lexis-Nexis, 71 percent of jurors polled said that experts influenced their verdicts. Nearly 90 percent said they found experts credible.

Funny, because legal critics have been complaining about expert witnesses—about their unreliability and their willingness to say whatever they were paid to say—ever since these pointy-headed hired guns started testifying. By 1923, the grumbling was loud enough to compel the U.S. Supreme Court to adopt what's known as the Frye standard, which established a general-acceptance test for admitting expert testimony. In other words, only evidence that was generally accepted by the scientific community could be admitted in court.

Frye worked reasonably well for several decades, largely because scientific evidence figured so rarely in court cases. As recently as 30 years ago, the typical tort action involved a fender-bender at Fifth and Main, and the typical expert witness was a physician testifying in a medical malpractice suit. But the Agent Orange and Love Canal cases of the '70s spawned a deluge of toxic tort litigation. Around the same time, a new breed of "soft" scientists appeared with novel and often untestable theories about human behavior and the causes of disease.

Judges generally responded by adopting a more relaxed standard toward the admission of expert testimony. This liberalized attitude was codified in the Federal Rules of Evidence adopted in 1975. In place of Frye's general-acceptance test, Rule 702 said a witness could be "qualified as an expert by knowledge, skill, experience, training, or education," which pretty much made everybody from Linus Pauling to Doctor Mom an expert on the common cold.

The result? Even as our culture is being dumbed-down, the number of experts is skyrocketing: The nation's largest referral service, Technical Advisory Service for Attorneys, now has 24,000 experts on its rolls, up from 10,000 in 1987. Within the 758 pages of California's *The Legal Expert Pages*, browsers can find experts on everything from cemeteries and garage doors to theater and termites, not to mention William M. Jones, who bills himself as "Mr. Truck." "There's an expert testifying in every field you can possibly imagine," says Steven Babitsky, editor of The Expert Witness Journal. "I remember one case in which a prison inmate who claimed he was no longer using drugs tried to get another prison inmate who was a drug addict qualified as an expert on drug addiction."

To a certain degree, this growing reliance on experts reflects the growing complexity of modern life. By their very nature, product liability suits turn on complicated questions of causation that can't be resolved simply by resorting to common sense. But more than ever, we're seeing expert testimony on subjects that never before required it. For centuries, for example, the time-honored method of impeaching eyewitnesses was to question their credibility under cross-examination: You wear glasses, don't you, Mr. Jones? Now, experts are being hired to discuss the unreliability of eyewitness testimony.

Finding the right expert witness is a how-to staple of bar journals and other trade magazines, and why not? Though it may sound unseemly, witness-shopping is a key to success in many cases, especially civil suits. While it's unethical, if not strictly illegal, for an attorney to tell an expert witness what to say in court or during a deposition, it would be unprofessional, if not downright stupid, for him to hire somebody whose testimony wouldn't help his case. Expert witnesses understand how the game is played. When an attorney representing a family killed in an airplane crash calls up an engineer who specializes in metal fatigue, the dialogue pretty much writes itself. "You don't have to be a rocket scientist to know what the attorney is looking for," lawyer Michael Kranitz says.

The fact that there aren't many full-time expert witnesses out there is less a function of propriety than the realization that holding down a day job makes their resume look more credible. Certainly, with fees that reach as high as $1,000 an hour, there's more than enough money around to keep expert witnesses in a top tax bracket. According to one study, physicians' insurance companies paid $18 million for medical experts to defend malpractice cases in 1992. And then there's the economist who testified in 154 Los Angeles-area cases from 1990 to 1994. Who knows how many others he consulted on?

This isn't to suggest that most, or even many, experts lie on the witness stand. But while they're required to tell the truth and nothing but the truth, they're also being paid by one of the interested parties, and it would be naive to think that this has no effect whatsoever on their testimony.

Consider this togue's gallery of prosecutors' dreams:

Dallas psychiatrist James Grigson, dubbed Dr. Death because he so rarely met a murderer he didn't think ought to be executed. By 1989, he had testified about the "future dangerousness" of one-third of the inmates on Texas's death row. Twice reprimanded by the American Psychiatric Association, he's since been expelled from the organization.

Serologist Fred Zain, a West Virginia state trooper and later chief serologist in the Bexar County (Texas) Medical Examiner's office, indicted for perjury for falsifying results used to convict several wrongly imprisoned defendants.

The late Louise Robbins, a college anthropology professor whose now-thoroughly-debunked footprint "expertise" was a featured element in 20 criminal cases in 11 states and Canada.

Michael H. West, a forensic dentist with an unprecedented, even preternatural, ability to match wounds with teeth, weapons, fingernails, whatever. A key witness in nearly 20 capital cases, he uses a controversial blue light to examine wounds invisible to the naked eye—and, apparently, all other forensics experts. West remains a prosecutor's favorite even though he resigned from the American Academy of Forensic Sciences after the ethics committee recommended his expulsion.

Disturbingly enough, most observers agree that the evidentiary standards for expert witnesses tend to be higher in criminal cases than civil suits, which keeps a lot of junk science out of court. Also, since the monetary stakes are usually lower on the criminal side, very few cases degenerate into trial by highly paid expert.

Things get murkier on the civil side, where the line between expert and advocate is often blurred. "The question of causation in a tort case isn't purely a scientific issue. It's a political and social issue as well," says Christopher Mueller, a law professor at the University of Colorado at Boulder. "Scientists think of causation in different terms than judges do."

A scientist demands what Mueller calls Rube Goldberg-style linear causation: A marble rolls into a lever, which strikes a match, which lights a cherry bomb, which then explodes. Cause and effect are clear-cut. In some courts, by way of contrast, a statistical correlation between a product and a disease may be enough to justify a finding of causation even if nobody understands the mechanism by which the disease develops. Because who knows? Maybe fax machines will turn out to cause cancer.

The classic illustration of the chasm between the legal and scientific definitions of causation came in the celebrated paternity suit against Charlie Chaplin, who was found to have fathered a child even though blood samples conclusively proved that he couldn't have been the father. More recently, a federal judge ruled that a spermicide caused birth defects despite a mountain of unrefuted evidence to the contrary. Later, the study whose "tentative" findings were the principal evidence against the spermicide was repudiated by two of its authors. Even so, an appellate court affirmed the $5.1 million award, arguing that "it does not matter in terms of deciding the case that the medical community might require more research and evidence before conclusively resolving the question."

In recent years, courts have found that seemingly harmless PCBs caused cancer, that an acne medication caused brain damage and that an over-the-counter painkiller led to a liver transplant. Other experts have argued unsuccessfully that Retin-A and Primatene Mist cause, respectively, "reactive airway dysfunction syndrome" and "multiple chemical sensitivity disorder" On the product-liability front, Beech Aircraft analyzed lawsuits arising from 203 airplane crashes. Although all of the accidents were attributed by federal investigators to weather, poor maintenance or pilot error, each of the plaintiffs blamed the manufacturer for the crashes. The lawsuits cost Beech, on average, $530,000 per case.

And perhaps most notably, the O.J. Simpson civil trial featured no shortage of expert testimony, including much-publicized debate over whether a photo of Simpson wearing the notorious Bruno Magli shoes had been doctored.

Inevitably, there's been a backlash. At the federal level, the rules of the game were comprehensively rewritten by the U.S. Supreme Court in the Daubert case, one of several suits alleging that the morning-sickness medication

Bendectin caused birth defects. In principle, at least, the Daubert decision dramatically raised the standard of admissibility for scientific evidence by requiring judges to look beyond the credentials of an expert witness and to delve into the methodology behind his findings, not to mention determining whether his research has been published and peer-reviewed. "In my mind, the new standard is superior to the old one," says Joseph L. Peterson, professor of criminal justice at the University of Illinois in Chicago. "Daubert gives us a road map for what should be admitted and what should be excluded."

While a step in the right direction, Daubert will no more end expert witness abuse than a balanced-budget amendment will make the deficit disappear. First of all, the decision applies only to federal courts, and to date, it's been adopted by fewer than half the states in the Union. Second, even in courts where it has been adopted, most judges have interpreted it as applying only to "hard" scientists, which means that it will have no effect on the vast majority of the experts who testify. Third, the dozens of law review articles published about Daubert spotlight the widespread disagreement about the ramifications of the decision. Among the most disturbing predictions is that Daubert will open the door to even more goofball science since it no longer requires a general consensus of the scientific community.

Last but not least, there are those who question the ability of judges to make any more sense of esoteric scientific testimony than juries. As a result, several programs have been created to turn jurists into quasi-Mr. Wizards. Meanwhile, in complicated cases, judges themselves have begun appointing independent experts of their own to slog through the morass of competing testimony. There has even been talk, though no action, of establishing so-called science courts with panels of judges drawn from the ranks of eminent scientists.

Still, for these efforts to have any significant impact, Daubert will need to be expanded in jurisdiction as well as interpretation. State systems should be pressured to adopt tougher expert witness standards, and "soft" science should be held to standards at least as exacting as the more traditional disciplines. Of course, if all else fails, there's always the threat of malpractice to keep experts in line. As Carol Henderson, a former federal prosecutor now teaching law at Nova Southeastern University, puts it: "If experts are professionals, they ought to be held accountable just like any other professionals" Although expert witnesses generally can't be sued by the people they testify against, there's nothing stopping their own employers from taking them to court. Malpractice suits of this sort are on the rise, with a recent $42 million judgment against an accounting firm sending fear and trembling through the world of hired guns. "Expert witnesses are worried," Babitsky says. "One of the questions we hear at our seminars is, 'Where can I get liability insurance?'"

Soon, no doubt, court dockets will be full of cases in which expert witnesses are testifying against expert witnesses. This somehow seems fitting: What goes around, comes around.

POSTSCRIPT

Can "Expert Witness" Testimony in the Courtroom Be Made More Equitable?

At the heart of the use of "expert witnesses" is a controversy that pervades the U.S. judicial system: Is the goal to discern the "truth," or is it to resolve conflicts? This is a similar dilemma as presented in Issue 3 regarding plea-bargaining. And it is important to keep in mind that so much of the U.S. jurisprudential system revolves around this dilemma.

Certainly, expert witnesses can help us to discern the truth as Anna Maria Gillis points out Indeed, Federal Rules of Civil Procedure and Rules of Evidence encourage the use of experts. This is especially and increasingly true as science has become an integral part of the courtroom. But what if there is an unequal use of expert witnesses, be the inequity in favor of the defense or the prosecution? Given the monetary consideration attached to expert witnesses, can there be complete equity?

Anna Maria Gillis begins her article by citing a *Forbes* magazine story blasting expert witnesses in the courtroom. "Carrying the traditional American adversary system to absurd extremes, judges are allowing crackpot scientists to pollute the legal process, at a cost to consumers and business in the billions. . . . [There] is a need to bring scientific order to the courtroom."

Gillis argues that with science of ever-increasing importance in the judicial system, judges, lawyers and juries need the help of expert witnesses. Gillis provides an excellent overview of the arguments against the use of expert witnesses, but argues that the solution to equity is not to eliminate expert witnesses, but for court-appointed witnesses.

Preston Lerner argues that in our jurisprudential system, which is adversarial, the truth is not the paramount goal and that money is the key to success. Lerner blasts the "skyrocketing" number of experts and questions how unbiased valid their testimony can be when they are "hired guns." He points out that as judicial issues have become more complex, "judges generally responded by adopting a more relaxed standard toward the admission of expert testimony. This liberalized attitude was codified in the Federal Rules of Evidence in 1975." Expert witnesses, he points out, are the only witnesses permitted to give their opinion in court. Lerner believes tougher standards should be adopted before an individual is deemed qualified as an "expert."

Lerner uses a number of cases to make his point He cites specific "experts" in real-life cases and the effect of their testimony.

Further readings on this subject include Elizabeth Loftus and Katherine Ketcham, *Witness for the Defense: The Accused, the Executive and the Expert Who Puts Memory on Trial;* F. Rossi, *Expert Witnesses;* Catherine Bond, et al., *The Expert Witness in Court;* and Theodore H. Blau, *The Psychologist as Expert Witness.*

ISSUE 15

Does the U.S. Income Tax System Favor the Rich?

YES: David Cay Johnston, from "Stroke the Rich: IRS Has Become a Subsidy System for Super-Wealthy Americans," *San Francisco Chronicle* (April 11, 2004)

NO: Jim Nintzel, from "The Tax Bite's Not As Bad As You Think, But It Could Get a Lot Worse," *Tucson Weekly* (April 17, 2000)

ISSUE SUMMARY

YES: David Cay Johnston of the *San Francisco Chronicle* argues that tax laws favor the top 1/100th of 1 percent of Americans.

NO: Jim Nintzel argues that the wealthy actually pay significantly more income tax dollars than the overwhelming majority of Americans.

How many times have you heard, "The rich get richer and the poor get poorer? or "In order to make money, you have to have money"? In the midst of an affluent society, why is it so difficult to move out of one's socioeconomic class (in either direction)?

Does the income tax system help the wealthy to not only remain wealthy, but also become even wealthier?

The U.S. income tax system is supposedly progressive (i.e., the more one earns, the more one pays). That sounds simple enough. However, features of the system permit significantly reducing one's "taxable income." So, for example, interest on a mortgage is tax-deductible. Since most students may be unfamiliar with how this works, here is a hypothetical.

Mr. Smith earns $100,000 a year. He purchases a house at the price of $400,000. Let's say he puts down a 20 percent down payment ($80,000) and takes out a mortgage for the remaining $320,000. Let's also say, to keep the math simple, that the rate of interest on the mortgage is 5 percent. Roughly, then, Mr. Smith is paying approximately $16,000 a year in mortgage interest. That $16,000 is subtracted from his $100,000 income, which means his taxable income is now $84,000. Let's continue the hypothetical.

Five years later, Mr. Smith's house is worth, say $600,000 (there has been a keen interest in housing in the town in which Mr. Smith lives). The difference between what Mr. Smith owes on the house ($320,000 mortgage) and the current value of the house ($600,000) is equity (in this case, $280,000). Most banks will permit Mr. Smith to borrow up to 75 or 80 percent of that equity. So, Mr. Smith could borrow $210,000 and buy another piece of property for, say, $500,000. If he used all of the equity ($210,000), he needs a mortgage on the second home for $290,000. At 5 percent interest, Mr. Smith pays $14,500 on that second house. If we add together the interest paid on both houses, we come to $30,500 that Mr. Smith can deduct from his taxable income. Let's say Mr. Smith is now earning $110,000. His taxable income is not $110,000, but $79,500.

Continuing the hypothetical, let's say that Mr. Smith's profession requires him to travel a great deal, and he is not reimbursed for his expenses. All of these are tax deductible. The bottom line is that tax deductions significantly reduce the amount of income people with sufficient income to purchase a house(s). If Mr. Jones earned, say $30,000 a year, he is unlikely to be able to purchase a house, and if he has no other dedications he will pay income taxes on his full income. Meanwhile, Mr. Jones is paying rent, and Mr. Smith's houses are appreciating in value.

The argument over whether the income tax system favors the wealthy (and, by the way, Mr. Smith's $100,000 is nothing in comparison to the very wealthy in the United States) is here debated by David Cay Johnston, who argues that the system benefits the top 1/100th percent of Americans. "People making $60,000 paid a larger share of their 2001 income in federal income, Social Security and Medicare taxes than a family making $25 million," notes Johnston, and then there are the benefits to corporations.

While the wealthy and corporations receive hefty tax relief, the tax burden has shifted to the middle class.

Jim Nintzel argues that while it is true that the U.S. income tax system provides significant tax deductions for the wealthy, nonetheless the *actual dollars* paid by the wealthy, with the top 50 percent paying 95.7 percent of all the tax revenue collected by the federal government.

So, does it all depend upon how one looks at the numbers? As Albert Einstein purportedly said, "The hardest thing in the world to understand is the income tax."

YES

David Cay Johnston

Stroke the Rich: IRS Has Become a Subsidy System for Super-Wealthy Americans

The federal tax system that millions of Americans are forced to deal with before April 15 is not at all what you think it is. Congress has changed it in recent decades from a progressive system in which the more one earns the more one pays in income taxes. It has become a subsidy system for the super rich.

Through explicit policies, as well as tax laws never reported in the news, Congress now literally takes money from those making $30,000 to $500,000 per year and funnels it in subtle ways to the super rich—the top 1/100th of 1 percent of Americans.

People making $60,000 paid a larger share of their 2001 income in federal income, Social Security and Medicare taxes than a family making $25 million, the latest Internal Revenue Service data show. And in income taxes alone, people making $400,000 paid a larger share of their incomes than the 7,000 households who made $10 million or more.

While millions of Americans in the last quarter-century debated about who shot J.R. and scurried for news about who would be Jennifer Lopez's next lover, Congress quietly passed tax laws that shift the tax burden from the 28,000 Americans in households with incomes of $8 million per year or more.

One 1985 law, promoted in the Senate as relieving middle class Americans, gave a huge tax break to corporate executives who make personal use of company jets. CEOs may now fly to vacations or Saturday golf outings in luxury for a penny a mile. Congress shifted the real cost of about $6 per mile to shareholders, who pay two-thirds, and to taxpayers who suffer the rest of the cost lost as a result of reduced corporate income taxes.

Since 1988, Congress has also cut in half the Internal Revenue Service's capacity to enforce tax laws, replacing it with extra effort to reduce audits of corporations and the rich.

On March 30, Congress was told that 78 percent of known tax cheats in investment partnerships are not even asked to pay because there are not enough tax collectors to go after them. Congress and the Bush administration rejected the request by the IRS Oversight Board, a citizen panel Congress created, for extra money to pursue some of these tax cheats and stop about 1 percent of the $311 billion in estimated annual tax cheating.

In the late '90s, a crooked banker gave the IRS records on 1,600 criminal tax cheats who used his Cayman Islands bank. The Justice Department prosecuted 49 of them, but the other 1,551 were not even asked to pay, lawyers for some of them say.

Two billionaires in New York, the art dealer Alec Wildenstein and his former wife, Jocelyn, testified under oath in their divorce that for 30 years they never filed a tax return. They have not been prosecuted.

There are now seminars that show business owners how to drop out of the tax system with virtually no risk of detection by the IRS, which relies on a computer system installed when John F. Kennedy was president.

As tax law enforcement has declined, illegal tax evasion has risen, especially among the rich and more recently among the young.

All of these actions reward cheats at the expense of honest taxpayers, but because "tax" is a four letter word in Washington, nothing is done. Those who support tax law enforcement are denounced on the campaign trail as advocates of higher taxes.

While letting rich tax cheats run wild, Congress did finance a crackdown on the poor. The working poor, most of whom make less than $16,000, are eight times more likely to be audited than millionaire investors in partnerships.

The audits of low-income taxpayers found little cheating. Two-thirds of the poor get either their full refund or more than they sought.

These and other unseen changes in the tax system are major factors in profound economic changes that have caused so many in America to lurch from job to job, a fourth of which pay less than $8 an hour, while helping a very few grow very rich.

Because the news media focus on what politicians say about the tax system, rather than how it actually operates, few Americans realize that:

- Corporate income tax laws reward companies that move jobs offshore, allowing them to earn untaxed profits as long as the money stays offshore.
- Widespread cuts in health insurance and pensions for the rank-and-file are driven by a special law that lets top executives defer paying taxes for years, in a way that adds 35 percent to the cost of their bloated pay.
- The 2001 Bush tax cuts included a stealth tax increase on the middle class and upper-middle class that will cost them a half trillion dollars in the first 10 years and, for 35 million families, wiping out part or all of their Bush tax cuts.
- The stealth tax boost on people making $30,000 to $500,000 was explicitly used to make sure that the super rich would get their entire Bush tax cuts.
- A California couple who make $75,000 to $100,000 and have two children face a 97 percent chance of losing part of their Bush tax cuts to this stealth tax increase and overall will lose 42 percent of their Bush tax cuts by next year.
- If your child becomes seriously ill, Congress, under this same law, will raise your income taxes if you spend more than 7.5 percent of your income trying to keep your child alive.

- Since 1983, under a plan devised by Alan Greenspan, Americans have paid $1.8 trillion more in Social Security taxes than have been paid out in benefits, money that is used to finance tax cuts for the super rich while robbing the middle class of their capacity to save.
- A family earning $50,000 this year will have about $1,500 of its money funneled to the super rich because of the Greenspan plan.
- Since 1993, the income tax burden on the 400 highest-income Americans has been cut 40 percent when measured the way that President Bush prefers, which is by counting how many pennies out of each dollar go to income taxes. In 1993 the top 400 paid 30 cents out of each dollar in federal income taxes. By the end of the Clinton administration in 2000 they were down to 22 cents. Under Bush, their burden is less than 18 cents. Everyone else felt their tax bite rise to 15 cents on the dollar from an average of 13 cents.

Over time, the impact of tax relief for the super rich and more taxes for everyone else is profound. The rich can save and invest more and more, increasing their incomes and political power over time through the magic of compound interest, while everyone else has less of their money to spend or save and millions of people are mired in debt.

While wage earners have every dollar of income reported to the government, the super rich control what the IRS knows about their incomes. But the rich are rarely audited anymore. Congress also gives them many perfectly legal devices to defer reporting income for years or decades. That means that the real incomes of the super rich are much larger than the IRS data show and their tax burden is even lighter.

IRS data, adjusted for inflation, show that the poor are really getting poorer and the super rich are getting fabulously richer, a trend enhanced by their falling tax burden. In 1970, the poorest third of Americans had more than 10 times as much income as the super rich, the top 1/100th of one percent. Back then the poor had more than 10 percent of all income and the super rich had one percent.

By 2000 the two groups were equal—the 28,000 Americans at the top had as much income as the 96 million at the bottom. The poor's share of income fell by half while the super rich's share rose to more than 5 percent of all income.

Not only did the poorest third's share of income shrink, they actually had less money. The average 25-year-old man in 1970 made $2 per hour more, adjusted for inflation, than in 2000.

Over those three decades the bottom 99 percent of Americans had an average increase in total income of $2,710. That is an annual raise of less than $100 per year, the equivalent of a nickel an hour raise each year for 30 years. The super rich did fabulously better, their average incomes rising $20. 3 million to an average of $24 million each.

Plot these figures on a chart and the results astound. If the increase for 99 percent of Americans is a bar 1-inch high, the bar for the super rich soars heavenward 625 feet.

All of this is having a devastating impact on America, which the preamble to our Constitution says was created to "promote the general welfare." Until Americans decide to take back their democracy and become actively engaged in politics, the super rich will continue to rig the tax system for their benefit only.

Jim Nintzel

The Tax Bite's Not As Bad As You Think; But It Could Get a Lot Worse

If you're like most people, April 15 isn't your favorite day of the year. Sometime in the last couple of months you've been bewildered by IRS forms, baffled by arcane formulas and convinced that everybody else is paying a lot less in taxes than you are.

Cheer up!

The federal income tax system really does soak the rich. In 1997, as pundit Tony Snow recently observed, the top 1 percent of earners paid 27 percent of income taxes; the top 10 percent paid 63 percent; the top 20 percent paid 77 percent; and the top 50 percent paid about 95.7 percent. That means the bottom half pays very little income tax (although those taxpayers do pay Social Security taxes, a regressive tax that is only paid on the first $68,400 earned).

Given the tendency of congressmen to serve their contributors, many of us naturally assume the wealthiest Americans use loopholes to escape their tax burden—but there's no getting around the fact that they do pay the most in taxes.

"They perhaps don't pay at the nominal rate, but the data is indisputable," says Michael Ettinger of Citizens for Tax Justice, a Washington, D.C., watchdog outfit that advocates relief for middle- and low-income taxpayers. "They pay a lot more in income taxes than they do in other taxes."

It's a similar situation in Arizona, although the state income tax isn't nearly as progressive as the federal tax. According to figures from the Joint Legislative Budget Committee, in 1997 the top 1.4 percent of filers (those with more than $200,000 in federal adjusted gross income) paid 17.3 percent of all state income taxes; the top 5.7 percent (income of more than $100,000) paid 31.2 percent of all state income taxes; and the top 11.2 percent (income of more than $75,000) paid 42.7 percent.

None of which means there isn't plenty of waste, fraud and abuse in government, both national and local. (More on that later.) Nor does it mean that the current tax system is so perfect it couldn't benefit from reform. It just means that, despite popular perception, wealthy Americans do shoulder much of the federal income-tax burden—and to a lesser extent, the state income-tax burden.

Now, if you happen to be in the top 1 percent of incomes, you probably don't find much of the above to be happy news. But there's probably not much reason for you to be glum either, because the last decade has likely been very, very good for you; in 1997, after taxes, the top 1 percent had an average $515,600 left to play with, according to the Center on Budget and Policy Priorities, another D.C.-based non-profit dedicated to advocating for low-income families. In a report released last year, the organization reported an evergrowing gap between rich and poor, to the point where the top-earning 2.7 million Americans—that cream of the crop in the top 1 percent of income—have as many after-tax dollars as the bottom 100 million.

Bottom line: If you're earning that much, you can probably afford to shell out a little more than the Average Joe. Besides, Congress continues to create more and more of those blessed loopholes, even as many elected officials are complaining the tax code is too complex and needs to be scrapped altogether.

The ultimate result of most of these schemes to replace the much-despised Infernal Revenue Service—with simplified flat taxes or a national sales tax—will mean lower taxes for the wealthiest Americans, who likely don't need a break. And if we're going to make up the difference, that means a tax hike for the rest of us, who probably can't afford it.

Take, for example, the Taxpayer Protection Alliance, which is currently collecting the 152,643 signatures they'll need by July 6 to put the Taxpayer Protection Act of 2000 on the ballot in November. The initiative would phase out the state income tax over four years. To replace the revenue generated by income taxes, lawmakers would have to get public approval at the ballot box for any new tax.

Lori Klein, executive director for the Arizona Taxpayer Alliance, says the group has collected more than 100,000 signatures. She reports the group has raised about $150,000 and is paying petition gatherers $2 per signature.

The Arizona Taxpayer Alliance is chaired by Dick Mahoney, a Democrat who served as Arizona secretary of state from 1990 to 1994, when he stepped down to make an unsuccessful bid for the U.S. Senate. (Mahoney was unavailable for comment, Klein said, because he was building orphanages in Latin America.) Other notable supporters include Arizona Congressman Matt Salmon, former Arizona attorney general Grant Woods, and Dr. Jeffrey Singer, a Phoenix physician who has also been active in the state's medical marijuana initiative battles.

Although Klein argues that wealthy taxpayers escape paying taxes through loopholes, she concedes that the numbers show that most income-tax revenue comes from the highest brackets. "The wealthy in this country don't have problems with the income tax, but the little small guys often take a big hit," says Klein, who describes "little, small guys" as "small entrepreneurs making between $100,000 to $1 million a year"—which accounted for approximately 5.6 percent of the filers in Arizona in 1997.

Singer argues that cuts in the income tax over the last decade have resulted in a corresponding rise in job creation, and that states without income taxes have attracted many high-tech jobs. So eliminating our state income tax would give everybody more money to spend, lure New Economy corporations to Arizona and spur a massive economic boom. "Eliminating the Arizona personal and corporate income taxes is the most effective and efficient social welfare program our state can ever put into place," Singer says.

Elizabeth Hudgins, a staffer with the Children's Action Alliance, has a different spin. "As I understand the initiative, it eliminates half of our state budget and makes it incredibly difficult to replace," Hudgins says. "It gets rid of our most progressive tax feature, which is the income tax, and if it is replaced with anything, it's going to have to be something more regressive, so eliminating half the state budget without a good way to replace it isn't the best possible thing you can do for Arizona."

Hudgins points to a recent study by the Center on Budget and Policy Priorities, which reported that Arizona's income tax was among the best in the nation for low-income families, who can earn up to $23,600 before they owe any income tax.

She also notes that a Joint Legislative Budget Committee reported that a typical household that earns $35,000 paid about $515 (or 15 percent of its annual state tax bill) in income tax, while shelling out about $1,440 in sales taxes (or 42 percent of the annual bite). The JLBC estimated that households with annual income of less than $500,000—that's about 99.7 percent of the state's population—paid more in sales taxes than in income taxes.

"It's not as if the money goes into some black hole," Hudgins says. "It builds roads and schools and libraries and provides services for abused children and a whole host of things that people value from those dollars."

Ettinger, of Citizens for Tax Justice, predicts the effect of eliminating the state income tax would be to increase taxes on the average Arizonan. "It would shift the relative tax burden off higher-income people and onto lower-income people, because relatively speaking, the state would be getting more money from sales taxes and other consumption taxes, and property taxes, and less from progressive income taxes. If you don't replace the revenue, then the middle- and low-income people wouldn't see their taxes go up, but they'd see government services decline to a much greater degree than their taxes would go down, because so much of the tax benefit would go to the wealthy."

Marshall Vest, the UA economics professor who frequently serves as the voice of conventional wisdom in these sorts of policy matters, notes that flushing the income tax will place the entire burden of financing government on the sales tax, give or take the occasional fee. "That would be a very, very different tax system than what we're used to," Vest says. "If we were to eliminate the state income tax, it would mean one of two things: Either you'd have to raise the sales tax, which now is 5 percent, and it would probably have to go to 9 or 10 cents on the dollar; or you would have to shrink government by a third, or about 40 percent. The question is: if you're going to do that, what is it you're going to eliminate?"

That's a question advocates of the Taxpayer Protection Act don't tackle. Although the group's Web page notes that "there certainly must be one or two areas where savings can be realized," potential trims are not forthcoming. The Web page sidesteps the issue of replacing the revenue stream with this dodge: "The important thing to remember is the Taxpayer Protection Act only deals with the WAY in which revenues are collected—not the way in which they are next distributed or allocated. To link the two issues is to mix apples with oranges."

"It's comparing apples to apples," Ettinger argues. "You're losing this revenue and you have to make it up somehow. It's unclear to me how voters are supposed to make an intelligent decision on the consequences of eliminating the income tax if they don't know (a) if it's going to be replaced and (b) if it is replaced, how it's going to be replaced."

Singer argues that it might not have to be replaced at all. He projects that at the current rate of growth, the Arizona economy will reach a point by the year 2006 where sales taxes alone bring in as much money as sales and income taxes do today. Thus, the income tax could be trimmed significantly each year, as long as the state budget remained frozen at $6.5 billion a year for the next seven years. Given that the state budget has grown from just under $4 billion seven years ago to roughly $6 billion this year—an increase of 50 percent—it seems unlikely, with a steadily growing population demanding more services, that a seven-year budget freeze is politically viable.

In his best-case scenario, Singer suggests the elimination of both personal and corporate income taxes would result in an economic boom that will trigger a rapid rise in sales-tax revenue.

Vest is "more than a little skeptical" of that claim. "It just doesn't work that way. . . . That's the supply-side argument. Not too many people understand what the supply-side argument is all about. What they're contending there is that the economy would grow so much that the revenues would more than replace the amount of revenues lost through the elimination of the income tax. That means the economy would almost have to double in order to do that."

That's unlikely enough, but if it were to happen, it would raise another question, says Vest: "If the economy does double, doesn't the demand for public services go up? And how do you pay for that? If you have twice the number of businesses and twice the people, doesn't welfare double, the cost of educating children double, right on down the line?"

Singer admits that things might be tough for seven or eight years with his plan, but says government needs to tighten its belt, although he's vague when it comes details. He doesn't see any area of government that needs any more money—not even Arizona's chronically underfunded education system, which is potentially facing a billion-dollar bill just to build new schools and bring old classrooms up to a reasonable standard.

Klein is more generous—she says she supports Gov. Jane Dee Hull's recent proposal to ask voters to approve a .6 percent sales-tax increase, because that's a tax increase that has to pass at the ballot box.

Analyses by Citizens for Tax Justice show that states without income taxes tend to collect a greater share of taxes from lower- and middle-income taxpayers than states with income taxes. Ettinger has no doubt that "if you replaced (the income tax) dollar-for-dollar with consumption taxes, including a sales tax, you would end up with a system where middle- and low-income people pay more and upper-income people pay less. Low-income people have to spend all their money to survive, basically. Middle-income people, to have a decent lifestyle, spend most of their money. Wealthy people spend a relatively small percentage of their money, so by definition a tax that taxes what people spend is going to hit middle- to low-income people much harder than wealthy people."

Increasing the sales tax could have another detrimental effect on the business community: since there's no sales tax on Internet commerce, a steeper sales tax—particularly in the 10 percent range—would increase the incentive to shop online, which further hurts local business owners. Not only would the brick-and-mortars lose sales and see their profit margin shrink, but the tax burden would further shift onto taxpayers who don't shop online.

For the taxpayer Protection Alliance, the elimination of the state income tax is just the first step in the elimination of the federal income tax. As the Web site proclaims: "We can start the second American revolution right here in Arizona!" Singer points out that no other state has ever voted to dismantle an income tax. If Arizona were to do so, he reasons, other states would soon follow suit, and the federal government would soon be forced to follow suit and shut down the IRS.

While they shy away from backing any specific federal tax-reform plan, Singer and Klein both have kind words for the proposed "FairTax," which was scheduled for a hearing this week in Washington, D.C.

The FairTax is the brainchild of Houston multi-millionaire construction magnate Leo Linbeck Jr., and a few of his close associates, who as of 1998 had contributed the lion's share of the $15 million the group raised to fund economic studies at prestigious universities, a large-scale polling project and an advertising blitz.

The FairTax would replace the income tax, corporate taxes, estate taxes and Social Security payments with a national sales tax of 30 percent. To address the regressive nature of such a tax, every American would also get rebate checks from the government each month to cover the cost of the tax on necessities like groceries and housing.

Fair Tax supporters don't actually say their proposal would require a 30-percent tax, however. They call it a 23-percent "tax-inclusive" rate. In other words, they've arrived at their 23 percent number by figuring that $30 is 23 percent of $130—the $100 price tag on an item, plus the 30 percent tax—"which isn't the way anyone thinks about a sales tax," says Ettinger.

The tax-inclusive rate seems to confuse even the FairTax's supporters. Singer and Klein, for example, were convinced that under the proposal, the tax would be $23 on a $100 purchase. Klein's misunderstanding is particularly surprising, given that she was working with the Arizona chapter of the FairTax's organization.

After Klein was faxed information about the math trick, she told *The Weekly*, "That was the first I had ever heard anything like that and I need to investigate that further before I even want to comment on that." Asked her opinion of a 30-percent national sales tax, she said, "I personally think it's way too high. . . . But then again, if they're going to truly rebate everybody up to subsistence or poverty level, then I think it is worth it."

Ettinger says the group's numbers are flawed beyond the funny percentages. "A third of their revenue comes from taxing government, as if taxing government purchases raises any money," Ettinger says. "Yeah, on paper you could say we're going to raise a ton of money by taxing government, but everything the government buys now costs 30 percent more. So you have to raise taxes more if you're going to do that. If this worked, we could just leave us people out of it and just have government continually taxing itself to pay for everything. It's ridiculous. If you take that out, you're up to about a 40- to 42-percent rate."

And that's before you figure in state and local sales taxes, which could drive the rate higher than 50 percent.

Supporters of the FairTax say the increase in prices wouldn't necessarily be that high, because eliminating corporate taxes would allow businesses to drop the price on goods.

But even so, a sales tax nearing 50 percent will create a huge incentive to evade the tax by shopping across the border, at off-shore Internet shops or at second-hand shops.

"Look, when you start getting up around a 50 percent sales-tax rate, the efforts people will make to evade it would be incredible," Ettinger says. "And it wouldn't be that hard. To evade the income tax takes some pretty fancy footwork and collusion among the (political) parties. Evading the sales tax would be much easier. All of a sudden I think Nogales would have a lot of shopping malls. I don't think Tucson would have many left."

As mentioned above, there's no question that government at every level squanders several tax dollars. Just last week, Citizens Against Government Waste released its annual Congressional Pig Book Summary, exposing pork-barrel spending in Washington. Thomas A. Schatz, president of the group, charged that Congress broke all previous records for pork with a staggering $17.7 billion in worthless spending. (For details, check out the group's website at www.cagw.org.)

The income-tax system, particularly at the federal level, would benefit from reform as well. For example, Congress could trim some of the loopholes that allow wealthy taxpayers to escape paying some of their taxes. Congress did just that in 1986, but persistent lobbying has allowed many of the barnacles to grow back. Ettinger estimates, for example, that last year's bill increasing the minimum wage by a dollar had $11 of tax relief for wealthy Americans for every buck in increased wages for the lowest-paid workers. "It was a joke to call it a minimum wage bill," says Ettinger.

Ask Marshall Vest what the best overall tax policy is, and he doesn't equivocate. "Absolutely the best policy is to keep a broad tax base and keep rates low. If you keep rates low, you don't mess up the decision-making of economic agents. And that's what you want. You don't want behavior to change because taxes are so high that people spend a lot of time and effort to avoid the tax. If you keep the rates low and the gain small for engaging in those sorts of activities, then you won't affect economic activity.

"That's the best designed system and it's been in the textboks for years and years and years. In the last decade or two that teaching has fallen by the wayside," Vest adds. "People have either not learned that or they've forgotten it."

POSTSCRIPT

Does the U.S. Income Tax System Favor the Rich?

The public policy process, regardless of the issue, is one of burdening and benefiting. Perhaps nowhere is this more controversial than when it comes to the larger policy issue of raising revenues to pay for policies, be they domestic or foreign. Who should pay? How? How much?

The United States ostensibly has a progressive income tax system (i.e., the more one earns, and the more taxes one pays by virtue of being in a higher tax bracket). But the income tax system in the United States permits many "deductible" items, and taxpayers are taxed not on the full amount of earned income, but on *adjusted* gross income. Adjustments come about as a result of deductions. Some examples of eligible deductions are dependent children or interest paid on a mortgage. So, is the income tax system truly progressive?

David Cay Johnston, staff writer for the *San Francisco Chronicle*, argues that the income tax system in the United States actually *subsidizes* the very wealthy, especially the top 1/100th of 1 percent of Americans. Johnston further argues not only does the average American pay more in taxes because of what it not paid by the super-rich, the "merely" "well-to-do" are also subsidizing the "super-rich."

Corporate executives, too, are benefiting from existing tax laws; one example used by Johnston is that "CEOs may now fly to vacations or Saturday golf outings in luxury for a penny a mile," while shareholders are paying the real cost (approximately $6 per mile). Meanwhile, the average American taxpayers lose because reduced corporate taxes mean either higher taxes for remaining taxpayers or cuts in public programs.

Jim Nintzel's argument is the polar opposite. Nitnzel argues that instead of the rich unjustly benefiting from the U.S. income tax system, the tax system "really does soak the rich." Citing data from Washington, D.C.–based Citizens for Tax Justice, Nintzel points out the rich pay more in actual dollars, even if the percentage of their taxes is lower.

Nintzel reports that the top 1 percent of taxpayers paid a whopping 27 percent of income taxes to the federal treasury; the top 10 percent paid 63 percent; the top 20 percent paid 77 percent; the top 50 percent paid 95.7 percent! He admits that the wealthy are still doing fine, and that a gap between the rich and the poor continues to grow, as reported by the Washington-based Center on Budget and Policy Priorities, despite the tax loopholes that remain for the rich. Indeed, "the top-earning 2.7 million Americans—that cream of the crop in the top 1 percent of income—have as many after-tax dollars as the bottom 100 million."

Nintzel uses Arizona's policies to discuss state tax issues, and argues that all governmental levels could cut wasteful spending, and that income tax reform, while necessary to all levels of government, is particularly needed at the federal level.

Further readings on the U.S. income tax system include Jim Saxton, *The Economic Problems of the Income Tax system: Congressional Hearing;* William E. Simon, *Reforming The Income Tax System;* and Edward J. McCaffrey, *Fair Not Flat: How to Make the Tax System Better and Simpler.*

Gallup Organization

The Gallup Organization provides extensive public opinion research on a wide range of public policy topics.

http://www.gallup.com

United States Senate

The United States Senate provides a useful link to such key resources as committee activity and public policy and legislative issues.

http://www.senate.gov

U.S. House of Representatives

The U.S. House of Representatives provides a useful link to such key resources as committee activity and public policy and legislative issues.

http://www.house.gov

Education Index

The Education Index is an annotated guide to the best education-related sites on the Web.

http://www.educationindex.com/

PART 5

Education

*E*ducation has always been viewed as a route to success. But, once again, in a land of great affluence, have we made it possible for every child to make maximum use of society's resources? Study after study demonstrates the inferiority of the U.S. educational system as compared to other industrialized nations. Yet this is not a completely accurate view. There are many, many students who are doing quite well. We face a circular conundrum. Education is the route to success, to a good job. But a good job (and supposedly, a good income) is a route to a good neighborhood. And a good neighborhood usually translates into a school system that is much superior to those in less affluent neighborhoods.

Once again the stereotypes take hold, assumptions are made, and children's futures are dismissed as pre-ordained. This section addresses the public policy, justice, and law issues related to this country's failure to provide equal educational opportunity and equal education achievement.

- Do the States Provide Educational Equality?

- Should Standardized Tests Be Relied Upon to Determine Student Potential?

- Should There Be Federal Education Standards?

- Can No Child Left Behind Provide Equitable Education?

ISSUE 16

Do the States Provide Educational Equality?

YES: Michele Moser and Ross Rubenstein, from "The Equality of Public School District Funding in the United States: A National Status Report," *Public Administration Review* (January/February 2002)

NO: Susan E. Mayer, from "How Did the Increase in Economic Inequality Between 1970 and 1990 Affect Children's Educational Attainment?" *The American Journal of Sociology* (July 2001)

ISSUE SUMMARY

YES: Michele Moser and Ross Rubenstein discuss the strides the states have made in closing intrastate gaps for students.

NO: Susan E. Mayer argues that growing economic inequality, which results in greater neighborhood differential, has increased educational inequality.

In the aftermath of the American Revolution and the establishment of a new and independent nation, the former colonies, now states, were very protective of their individual rights. At first, they aligned in a confederation, which proved to be unsuccessful. With the recognition that a stronger central government was necessary, the states nonetheless held onto as much individualism and power as they could. Under this new system of federalism, the layering of governmental levels—national and states—also includes a distribution of powers.

Education is a crucial policy-making area retained by the states, and this policy making is further decentralized to the local community. Thus, localism is the norm in education. On the positive side, communities can determine what their children need. But this can work to students' detriment, and the question remains whether there is educational equality among the states when local school districts determine the curriculum, teacher salaries, student-teacher ratios, extracurricular programs, etc.

Michele Moser and Ross Rubenstein discuss this issue from the perspective of school finance equity. As they point out, this is a difficult issue area to explore, since funding comes from both the state and local communities.

How much funding each level gives depends upon the state. The states' problem is that of attempting to equalize what the local communities intrastate provide their students. As Moser and Rubenstein point out, "public education is the largest area of state and local government spending in the United States," and not surprisingly, "states with fewer school districts relative to students [tend] to have a more equal distribution of education dollars than states with more districts." Moser and Rubenstein's longitudinal study reports a slow, but steady increase in intrastate funding equality.

By contrast, Susan E. Mayer argues that significant changes in economic inequality have negatively affect children's education achievement. Mayer notes, "Disparities in hourly wages, annual earnings, and household income have all increased over the past generation in the United States." Mayer points out that while a great deal of research has focused on the "whys" of growing economic inequality, little research has focused on the effects of increasing economic inequality. The growing socioeconomic gap, Mayer says, have had several effects: "changes in subjective feelings of relative deprivation or gratification, changes in the political processes that shape educational opportunities and costs, and changes in economic segregation." Moser's analysis is centered on the types of changes in the dispersion of household incomes.

Income inequality dramatically affects the local tax base as well as voters' willingness to pay school taxes. In addition, Mayer points out, parental choice of housing is affected by the quality of schools in a neighborhood, and the cycle is a vicious one. The states generally fill in where the local communities fall short. Following the typical path of a child from elementary through high school, Mayer points out that while "between the early 1980s and 1992 the proportion of children in the poorest income quartile who went on to some postsecondary schooling increased from 57% to 60%. But the proportion of children in the top income quartile getting some postsecondary schooling increased from 81% to 90%. Thus the increase in college entrance rates was greater among affluent than among low-income children, suggesting that the growth in inequality may have had different effects on children from different family backgrounds." Thus, Mayer would conclude, while strides have been made, educational inequality remains.

Michele Moser and
Ross Rubenstein

 YES

The Equality of Public School District Funding in the United States: A National Status Report

Public education is the largest area of state and local government spending in the United States, accounting for almost one-fifth of direct state and local government expenditures in 1996. Given the enormous resources involved and—more importantly—the critical private and societal benefits that education produces, the distribution of educational opportunities across communities has generated considerable interest among policy makers, the public, and the courts. This article takes advantage of national data sets to examine the equality of education funding across school districts in 49 states for fiscal years 1992 and 1995. It presents rankings of each state's funding equality and explores factors that may be related to the level of equality within states and to changes across years.

The focus of this article is the equality of revenues that are available to school districts within states, one of a number of broad goals of education financing systems. In recent years, policy initiatives and court cases in many states have focused on other goals, such as eliminating the relationship between local property wealth and education spending or achieving an adequate level of funding for all students. Still, ensuring equality of resources across school districts (often referred to as "horizontal equity") remains a fundamental benchmark in evaluating state education funding systems, and it continues to be an important concern of the public and the broad education community.

Comparing the national averages of a number of intrastate equity measures, our results show that the equality of the distribution of education revenues improved slightly between 1992 and 1995. Relative equity rankings for most states changed little between 1992 and 1995, however. . . .

The Role of Equity in School Finance

Concerns over the equality of educational opportunity date back well over 40 years. In 1954, the U.S. Supreme Court's decision in *Brown v. Board of Education* (347 U.S. 483 [1954]) overturned the long-standing system of separate educational institutions for whites and African Americans, ruling

From *Public Administration Review*, vol. 62, issue 1, January–February 2002, pp. 63–66. Copyright © 2002 by Blackwell Publishing, Ltd. Reprinted by permission. References and notes omitted.

that "separate but equal" schools are inherently unequal. The country's awakening to the perils of unequal access to employment and education helped bring about the enactment of three important pieces of federal legislation related to education: the Civil Rights Act of 1964, the Economic Opportunity Act of 1964, and the Elementary and Secondary Education Act of 1965. The latter act created new federal funding (Title 1) for "at-risk" pupils, while the Civil Rights and Economic Opportunity acts more broadly addressed poverty and discrimination in society. The Civil Rights Act, in particular, is important for proponents of educational equity because it required a study of the factors leading to unequal educational opportunity. A team of researchers led by James Coleman conducted the study, which produced a long line of quantitative research examining the factors, including dollars and the resources they buy, that might affect student achievement.

While the debate about whether (and how) money matters to educational achievement continues among researchers, courts in virtually every state have addressed the constitutionality of funding disparities across districts within states. Beginning with California's 1971 *Serrano v. Priest* (5 Cal. 3d 584, 487 P.2d1241, 69 Cal. Rptr. 601 [1971]) case, in which that state's highest court ruled that a child's education could not depend on the wealth of the child's parents or neighbors, state supreme courts in 19 states have invalidated state systems of funding public education. While the U.S. Supreme Court ruled five to four in *San Antonio School District v. Rodriguez* (411, U.S. 1 [1973]) that the Texas school-finance system did not violate the Fourteenth Amendment of the U.S. Constitution, plaintiffs continued to use the equal opportunity clauses in state constitutions, along with other education clauses that focus on efficiency and adequacy, to support their claims in state courts.

School-finance equity has been a particularly intractable issue in many states because of the traditional reliance in the United States on a combination of state and local funding, with the relative share of total funding provided by each level of government varying considerably across states. With the majority of local revenues raised through property taxes, vast differences in property wealth across localities typically result in large disparities in education spending. In many cases, these differences may be unrelated to any differences in local "taste" for education. Responsibility for equalizing these disparities has rested with state governments, which have developed a variety of intergovernmental grant schemes intended to promote equity in education spending. State government defendants in school-finance suits often argue that spending differences are related to local taxing and spending decisions, or that these differences are irrelevant because there is no convincing evidence linking higher spending to improved student achievement. Courts have typically rejected these arguments, though, and have often ordered tight limits on spending differences across districts. The Supreme Court's Rodriguez decision returned school-finance litigation to state courts, resulting in state-by-state analyses of equity and the constitutionality of state funding systems. Studies of more recent court cases and legislative initiatives in states such as Georgia, Kansas, and Michigan, suggest that slight improvements in funding equality have occurred in selected states.

While these and numerous other studies have focused on funding changes and the distribution of resources in individual states, relatively little work has been done to examine equity from a national perspective and to compare within-state disparities across the country. There are several notable exceptions: Schwartz and Moskowitz and Wyckoff, for instance, examine changes in intrastate equity in 1977–85 and 1980–87, respectively. Wyckoff found that equity gains were greatest in states with large increases in expenditures over the period. Similarly, Evans, Murray, and Schwab study the impact of judicial and legislative activity on within-state equity over a 20-year period and find that states where the funding system was found unconstitutional had larger increases in state spending and greater improvements in equity than did states with purely legislative efforts. Other recent work using National Center for Education Statistics (NCES) data for 1992 indicates that, although state and federal revenues help to improve the equity of funding across districts, persistent inequalities remain; most often, these inequalities are related to differences in property wealth and income. Odden and Clune point out, however, that recent state court decisions have shifted the focus of litigation from the relationship between spending and property wealth to a more stringent emphasis on reducing per-pupil spending disparities. . . .

Equity Results and Trends

Equity is a relative rather than an absolute concept, and it can be defined and measured in a variety of ways. Berne and Stiefel, in their groundbreaking work on school-finance equity, set out a three-part framework for defining equity: horizontal equity, vertical equity, and equal opportunity. In this study, we focus on the first of these concepts, horizontal equity. Defined as the equal treatment of equals, horizontal equity examines the dispersion of per-pupil resources across districts or schools. Greater equality of per-pupil funding indicates higher levels of horizontal equity.

Comparing the national averages of the dispersion measures, the data indicate that funding equality improved slightly between 1992 and 1995. . . . All measures show a slightly more equitable distribution of revenues in 1995. . . .

Horizontal Equity by Number of Districts

One factor within the control of state and local policy makers is the number of school districts in a state. One might expect that as the number of districts increases—particularly if the average size of districts also declines—greater differences may arise across localities as people sort themselves among communities. These interdistrict differences are likely to affect districts' abilities to raise revenues for education, as some communities will have smaller tax bases or citizens who desire a lower level of education spending. Conversely, fewer larger districts within a state may discourage sorting, resulting in fewer revenue disparities. . . .

Horizontal Equity by State's Share of Revenue

A number of states have responded to equity concerns by increasing state revenues for education in combination with stable or decreasing local revenues. A state government's ability to redistribute resources across districts seems to make this a reasonable approach. Therefore, it is important to examine whether, in practice, a higher state share of education funding is closely linked to greater equality.

Nationally, states' average contributions to public education remained relatively stable from 1992 to 1995 at approximately 47 percent. New Hampshire contributed the smallest percentage of revenues in both years, while New Mexico contributed the largest. While the national average share of revenues remained stable, the data strongly suggest that as a state's share of revenues for education increases, horizontal equity improves. In 1995, the equity measures for the bottom quartile of state share (less than 40 percent state funding) showed considerably more inequality than those for the highest quartile (greater than 58 percent state funding), with an even larger spread between the lowest and third quartiles. The 1992 data show an even more dramatic difference between states at the lowest level of state assistance and those at the upper levels.

One example of how the relative share of state funding may affect horizontal equity is the state of Michigan, which has significantly altered its revenue sources for education since 1993. In 1992, the state contributed 26.6 percent of education revenues; by 1995, that share had increased dramatically to 67.3 percent. Michigan shifted from a funding system that relied heavily on property taxes to a more complex system of tax reform that includes a two-cent sales tax increase, a 50-cent-per-pack tax increase on cigarettes, a reduction in the state income tax rate, and a standard statewide property tax millage rate. Comparing the horizontal-equity measures for Michigan in 1992 and 1995, revenue distribution appears to be more equitable following this effort, which reduced reliance on local wealth and distributed state funding for education more evenly. . . .

Conclusions

This article presents a longitudinal "status report" on intrastate school-finance equity in the United States. Using national data on school district revenues and on differences in the cost of education across localities, the study provides a method for combining numerous measures to more readily compare equity across states. Results of the analyses suggest the following:

- When comparing the national averages of the equity measures, overall intrastate funding equality improved slightly between 1992 and 1995.
- The relative rankings for most states changed little between 1992 and 1995.
- States with fewer school districts tended to have a more equal distribution of education dollars than states with more districts. States with a higher number of districts made larger equity gains than states with

fewer districts, but the disparities still tended to be larger in states with more districts.

- States with higher proportions of revenues provided by state governments generally showed a more equal distribution of resources than states that were more dependent on local revenue sources.
- While these patterns suggest that increasing state responsibility for funding education or consolidating school districts might improve horizontal equity, they should not be taken as an easy prescription to remedy this systemic problem. As with most complex public policy issues, there are multiple causes of school-finance inequities, as well as institutional barriers to implementing reforms. However, the availability of national benchmarks can help policy makers to identify similar states with more equitable funding systems and to use them as models to develop reform alternatives for their own states. Additionally, case studies and analyses of individual states can help to determine the factors that may help such reforms to succeed or fail. In an area as complex and politically contentious as school-finance reform, data and analysis alone cannot resolve debates about the best way to provide equitable educational opportunities to all children. But the availability of national analyses and state-by-state information can provide an important resource as states move ahead on the path to reform. . . .

NO

Susan E. Mayer

How Did the Increase in Economic Inequality Between 1970 and 1990 Affect Children's Educational Attainment?

Disparities in hourly wages, annual earnings, and household income have all increased over the past generation in the United States. A considerable amount of research has tried to determine why income inequality grew over this period. Much less research has been done on the consequences of inequality than on its causes. This article estimates the effect of changes in income inequality on mean educational attainment and on the disparity in educational attainment between rich and poor children. I also separate the effect of income inequality that is due to the nonlinear effect of a family's own income from other effects of inequality. If growing income inequality contributes to inequality in educational attainment between children from rich and poor families, inequality in one generation will be perpetuated in the next generation.

This article focuses entirely on changes in the overall dispersion of household income. Inequality of household income increased between 1970 and 1980 and increased even more between 1980 and 1990. Inequality among families with children also grew. Changes in inequality between groups, such as blacks and whites or men and women may or may not parallel changes in the level of overall economic inequality, and their effect on educational attainment may differ from the effect of overall economic inequality.

The proportion of 25–29 year olds who had graduated high school or earned a GED increased from 75.4% in 1970 to 85.4% in 1980, then did not change between 1980 and 1990, when inequality increased. The percentage of 25–29 year olds who had enrolled in college declined from 44% in 1970 to 52% in 1980, and the percentage who had graduated college increased from 16.4% in 1970 to 22.5% in 1980. Neither college enrollment nor college graduation increased between 1980 and 1990.

Ellwood and Kane show that between the early 1980s and 1992 the proportion of children in the poorest income quartile who went on to some postsecondary schooling increased from 57% to 60%. But the proportion of

From *American Journal of Sociology*, vol. 107, issue 1, July 2001. Copyright © 2001 by University of Chicago Press. Reprinted by permission. References and notes omitted.

children in the top income quartile getting some postsecondary schooling increased from 81% to 90%. Thus the increase in college entrance rates was greater among affluent than among low-income children, suggesting that the growth in inequality may have had different effects on children from different family backgrounds.

Hypotheses About the Effect of Inequality

Income inequality can affect educational attainment in several ways. The first is through the incentives provided by higher returns to schooling. The second is through the declining utility of family income. Income inequality can also affect educational attainment through processes that are independent of a family's own income. Social scientists have identified at least three such processes. They involve changes in subjective feelings of relative deprivation or gratification, changes in the political processes that shape educational opportunities and costs, and changes in economic segregation.

Change in Incentives

Part of the growth in inequality in the United States was due to increased returns to schooling. Because higher returns increase the incentive for children to stay in school, we would expect educational attainment to increase when economic inequality increases.

The Declining Utility of Family Income

If the relationship between educational attainment and parental income is linear, then when the rich gain a dollar and the poor lose a dollar, the educational attainment of the rich will increase by exactly as much as the educational attainment of the poor decreases, leaving the mean unchanged. However, suppose that a 1% increase in income generates the same absolute increment in educational attainment, regardless of whether income is initially high or low. If the relationship between parental income and children's schooling takes this semilogarithmic form, and all else is equal, a costless redistribution of income from richer to poorer households will increase children's mean educational attainment, because shifting a dollar from the rich to the poor increases the education of poor children by a larger percentage than it decreases the education of rich children.

Relative Deprivation and Gratification

Social comparison theory assumes that individuals evaluate themselves relative to others. Relative deprivation theory holds that people compare themselves to others who are more advantaged than themselves. Imagine two families with the same income. Family A lives in a wealthy area, while family B lives in a poor area. Assuming their choice of where to live is entirely exogenous and that other families in the same area are their only reference group, relative deprivation theory predicts that members of family A will feel more deprived than members of family B. Feelings of relative deprivation can lead to isolation and alienation from the norms and values of the majority. If children feel relatively deprived, they may be less inclined to study or stay in school. Relative deprivation can also make parents feel stressed and alienated, lowering their expectations for their children or reducing the quality of their parenting.

Relative deprivation theories assume that children or parents compare themselves to others who are better off, while largely ignoring those who are worse off. If parents all compare themselves to the richest people in society, for example, they will feel poorer whenever the rich get richer. Of course, people also compare themselves to others who are worse off. Sociologists refer to this as "relative gratification." If either children or their parents mostly compare themselves to the poorest people in society rather than to the richest, increases in inequality will make most people feel richer because the distance between them and the people at the bottom of the distribution will grow. If people mostly compare themselves to some real or imagined national average, increases in inequality will make the rich feel richer and the poor feel poorer. How this will affect either educational attainment or other outcomes is unpredictable.

Relative deprivation usually cannot be directly observed, so it is often inferred from its behavioral manifestations. A large social-psychological research literature uses experimental evidence to document the importance of interpersonal comparisons, in general, and relative deprivation, in particular. Most of the sociological research on the importance of interpersonal comparisons to educational outcomes has been done in the context of neighborhood and school effects. In one of the earliest of such efforts, Davis argued that reference groups have both a comparison function and a normative function (as "sources and reinforcers of standards"). Although the latter could make living in an affluent area an advantage for low-income children, the former could make it a disadvantage because it fosters academic competition and relative deprivation. Davis showed that the more academically selective a college was, the lower any given student could expect his grades to be. As a result, students who chose selective colleges were less likely to choose careers that required graduate training. Other studies find that attending high school with high-achieving classmates reduces educational attainment, while attending school with high-SES classmates increases it. Because SES and achievement are correlated, attending a high-SES school has little net effect on educational attainment. These studies do not prove that children feel relatively deprived when they must compete with higher achieving students, but they demonstrate that more advantaged classmates or neighbors can be both an advantage and a disadvantage. When a child's own family income stays the same but inequality increases, the child will be exposed both to more advantaged and more disadvantaged children. This could have either positive or negative effects on the child's educational attainment.

Changes in Political Behavior

Changes in inequality can affect political behavior. Some research suggests that increases in economic inequality may decrease voters' willingness to support redistributive policies at the national level. This could also happen at the state or local level. For example, high levels of inequality could encourage the rich to enroll their children in private schools, making them less interested in supporting public schools. But high levels of inequality could also increase voters' willingness to support redistributive policies if they fear political instability or think that poverty contributes to crime. Other research suggests that redistributive spending reduces economic inequality at the national level. Redistributive policies can thus be both a cause and an effect of economic inequality. Disentangling cause from effect using cross-national data (as these studies do) is difficult, because samples are generally very small, lag structures are uncertain, and exogenous shocks that constitute national experiments are rare. Still it is clear that changes in economic inequality can in principle affect political support for redistributive policies, which can thereby affect spending on schools.

Nationwide, per pupil expenditures for elementary and secondary schooling have increased since 1970, and spending has become more equal across school districts in many states. Research on the effect of per pupil school expenditures on children's school performance is equivocal, but most evidence suggests that higher expenditures improve children's test scores by at least a little, which could in turn increase their educational attainment.

Research also shows that higher college tuition reduces enrollment and graduation. Although real tuition rates at state four-year colleges and universities have increased since 1980, so has both state and federal financial aid for college students. The number of two-year community colleges, which have low tuition, has also increased. However, the extent to which state differences in economic inequality affect the cost of attending a public college in the state is unknown.

Economic Segregation

The effect of economic inequality depends to some extent on the geographical proximity of the rich to the poor. This assumption is built into conventional measures of inequality, which describe the dispersion of income among all households in some geographic area, such as a nation, state, or neighborhood. Durlauf argues that as inequality increases, the rich and poor have less in common and therefore segregate more geographically. According to this argument, the degree of economic inequality at, say, the city level may affect the degree of economic segregation within the city. This will in turn affect the degree of economic inequality within neighborhoods. Wilson argues that economic segregation causes economic inequality, rather than the other way around. This happens because economic and racial segregation reduce the quality of inner-city schools and other institutions and leads to a spatial mismatch between jobs and low-skilled workers. Both Durlauf and Wilson argue that economic segregation hurts children's life chances.

A pernicious potential consequence of economic inequality is to recreate economic inequality in the next generation. This could happen if inequality benefits advantaged children and hurts disadvantaged children. For example, if economic inequality is associated with increased economic segregation, this could hurt low-income children's educational attainment while increasing high-income children's educational attainment. Because educational attainment is associated with future earnings, this could exacerbate inequality in the next generation. . . .

[School] districts . . . share in funding decisions and make significant decisions about policies that affect educational outcomes. Income inequality within school districts might affect both voters' inclination to pay taxes for schools and other school policies. However, parents often choose their school district partly on the basis of who lives there. If the same parental characteristics that cause parents to choose one district over another also affect their children's educational outcomes, and if these parental characteristics are not measured accurately, the estimated effect of school district inequality on educational attainment could be biased. This form of selection bias should be less important for estimating the effect of state-level characteristics on educational attainment because parents are less likely to move to a different state than to move to a different school district in order to improve their children's educational prospects.

Theories about the effect of income inequality that involve interpersonal comparisons are ambiguous about what is the most relevant geographic unit because it is not clear how individuals select the people to whom they compare themselves. If children compare themselves to the people they see on television, the nation as a whole is probably the relevant comparison group. If the nation is the relevant comparison group, the only way to study the impact of inequality would be to make cross-national comparisons or comparisons across time. If children compare themselves mainly to their neighbors and classmates, inequality in a relatively small geographic area, such as a neighborhood or school attendance area, may be more relevant than inequality in a larger unit. But, as I have noted, selection problems are likely to be more serious at the level of the neighborhood or school district. . . .

Conclusions

My results suggest five conclusions. First, the growth in inequality since 1970 probably did not have much affect on high school graduation.

Second, the growth in inequality since 1970 increased overall years of schooling mainly by increasing college entrance rates. Model 3 . . . suggests that a one standard deviation increase in the Gini coefficient results in a 0.058 increase in a student's probability of going to college (13.4% of the mean) and an additional 0.173 years of schooling.

Third, the growth in income inequality contributed to an increase in inequality in educational attainment between rich and poor children. . . .

Fourth, the effect of inequality is only partly due to the nonlinear relationship between parental income and children's outcomes and the incentive provided by increasing returns to schooling. Fifth, an increase in per pupil expenditures at the elementary and secondary level and lower college costs are positively associated with state inequality, and both raise educational attainment. Greater inequality is also associated with greater economic segregation, but this does not appear to affect children's educational attainment.

The results in this article present a problem. Growing income inequality raised mean educational attainment but also exacerbated disparities in educational attainment between rich and poor children. This is likely to contribute to economic inequality in the next generation. These findings suggest that it is important to find ways to reduce the potentially harmful effects of inequality on low-income children. The results in this article suggest that higher spending on elementary and secondary schooling and lower college tuition increase the educational attainment of low-income children and by doing so reduce the gap in schooling between high- and low-income children. But these efforts were not enough to prevent inequality from hurting low-income children's educational attainment. . . .

POSTSCRIPT

Do the States Provide
Educational Equality?

The system of federalism—with several layers of government constitutionally established and empowered—exacerbates the problems faced by the educational community. Education in the United States is decentralized, with individual states and localities in control of and responsible for the content and quality of their systems. This decentralization also places upon states the burden of funding education, with one-fifth of state and local government expenditures going to education, according to authors Michele Moser and Ross Rubenstein. Of course, it takes no great insight to realize that one-fifth of poorer states' revenues are grossly lower than one-fifth of wealthier states. Absent major increases in federal funding for education, it is unlikely that the education gap from one state to another can be leveled.

Moser and Rubinstein point out, however, that on the whole, states have been doing an incremental job of achieving intrastate "horizontal equity"—that is, a more even distribution of state revenues to districts within a state. They argue that horizontal equity is a "fundamental benchmark in evaluating state education funding systems," and their research presents a longitudinal "status report" on how the states are performing. Of course, a major problem the states face is that most state and local revenue comes from property taxes that vary widely intrastate. A broad philosophical as well as practical question is whether and how these revenues can be more equitably distributed. The authors argue that equality of public school district fund in the United States *can* be achieved once the states—as have many—face these tough and political unpopular questions.

On a more pervasive level, Moser and Rubinstein provide a useful overview of the issue of equality of educational opportunity beginning with the U.S. Supreme Court's landmark 1954 *Brown v. Board of Education* decision that overturned the "separate but equal" doctrine, proclaiming such a doctrine and its effects as "inherently unequal." They bring this review into the twenty-first century.

Susan E. Meyer argues that a great disparity exists intrastate between high-income and low-income children. Meyer provides an excellent and thorough analysis of the demographics and their implications.

Meyer argues that inequality can be remedied independent of family income. She argues for changes in incentives in keeping children in school, addressing relative deprivation and relative gratification (i.e., individuals comparing themselves to those better off and worse off, respectively), changes in political behavior, and economic segregation. As Meyers points out, relative deprivation, because it cannot be directly observed, is often viewed through "behavioral manifestations," and provides a brief literature review on that subject.

With regard to political behavior, Meyers notes a potentially circular set of dynamics. Increases in economic inequality may result in the wealthy putting their children into private schools and therefore being less willing to redistribute resources to public schools. At the same time, she argues, high levels of inequality might lead to voters' willingness to support redistributive policies for fear of political instability.

There are studies available on every state's educational system; these would be too numerous to list here as further readings, but the interested reader can search for these on-line. Among the works that are all-inclusive are *The Educational System in the United States Case Study Findings* (U.S. Department of Education) and William W. Brickman, *Educational Systems in the United States*.

ISSUE 17

Should Standard Tests Be Relied Upon to Determine Student Potential?

YES: Donna Y. Ford and Deborah A. Harmon, from "Equity and Excellence: Providing Access to Gifted Education for Culturally Diverse Students," *Journal of Secondary Gifted Education* (Spring 2001)

NO: Annie Nakao, from "How Race Colors Learning," *The Examiner* (June 7, 1998)

ISSUE SUMMARY

YES: Authors Ford and Harmon argue that students who are different from the "dominant culture" often go unrecognized, especially in programs for the gifted.

NO: *The Examiner* staff writer Annie Nakao argues that a diversity of factors—not bias—accounts for lower standardized test scores for minorities.

William Wordsworth wrote, "The child is father to the man," meaning that what we are as children determines the adults we will become. So what happens to children whose educational achievement potential is labeled early on?

The controversy over the use of standardized tests to predict a child's future performance has been raging for decades. Is it "fair" to set up self-fulfilling environments for children, knowing that the early labeling will follow them throughout life?

Donna Y. Ford and Deborah A. Harmon argue that it is not so much the standardized tests that are at fault; rather, it is both the *emphasis* placed upon them and the *misunderstanding of test results*, especially in relationship to particular groups in society.

Ford and Harmon express great concern over the loss of talent, especially within minority groups. Why are culturally diverse students increasingly underrepresented in programs for gifted students, ask Ford and Harmon? Again, Ford and Harmon argue that it is not the fault of standardized tests. Rather, it is the failure of educators to use "more than one test to make educational and placement decisions about gifted students and to seek equity in their identification and assessment instruments, policies and procedures." Rather than eliminate useful standardized tests, they argue, it is imperative that educators make greater efforts towards identifying multicultural competence, to encourage family involvement in student achievement—indeed, to "build partnerships" with families and to focus on "family education."

By contrast, Annie Nakao argues that although many minorities do well in academe, the great majority "lag behind their peers in every school at every socioeconomic level and by every traditional measure of academic achievement, from standards tests to college graduation rates." Nakao points out an interesting phenomenon: it is not only lower socioeconomic minorities who are lagging behind. Increasingly, it is the middle class African American student who does poor on standardized tests.

Nakao cites the findings of a *San Francisco Examiner* study regarding this phenomenon. The study suggests a number of forces working against student achievement on standardized tests, including "historical racism and its impact on school practices; teacher expectations; student attitudes and peer pressures; educational levels achieved not only by parents, but by preceding generations; black/white differences in parenting styles."

Although there are multiple factors working against minority student achievement, Nakao argues that standardized tests are faulty indicators of student potential. These tests just continue the stereotyping and tracking students have experience throughout their lives.

YES

**Donna Y. Ford and
Deborah A. Harmon**

Equity and Excellence: Providing Access to Gifted Education for Culturally Diverse Students

. . . Why do culturally diverse students persist in being underrepresented in gifted education? While a majority of publications point to testing and assessment issues, our experiences suggest that the primary barrier is the pervasive deficit orientation that prevails in society and our schools. After examining this orientation, we discuss symptoms of this orientation, such as the low referral rates of diverse students for gifted education services and the heavy reliance (sometimes exclusive reliance) on tests that inadequately capture the strengths and cultural orientations of diverse students.

Deficit Ideologies: Limiting Access and Opportunity

Perceptions about differences among students manifest themselves in various ways, and they exert a powerful influence in educational settings. A common saying among African Americans is "The less we know about each other, the more we make up." For instance, if a teacher does not understand how some cultural groups value cooperation or communalism over competition, that teacher may perceive the diverse child as being "too social." Communalism is a commitment to social relationships and social learning (e.g., working in groups, helping others). It is a "we, us, our" philosophical orientation. Likewise, if teachers do not understand that some cultures come from an oral tradition, they may neither recognize nor appreciate the strengths of students who prefer speaking more than writing and reading. They may not recognize that students who speak nonstandard English can still have strong verbal skills. Thus, teachers may not refer culturally and linguistically diverse students for gifted education services if they equate giftedness with verbal, reading, and/or writing proficiency.

Essentially, ideas about cultural diversity influence definitions, policies, and practices. Too often, differences are equated with deficits. Most recently,

From *Journal of Secondary Gifted Education,* vol. 12, no. 3, Spring 2001. Copyright © 2001 by Prufrock Press. Reprinted by permission. References and notes omitted.

the publication of *The Bell Curve* has revived the deficit orientation. Among other grievous errors (e.g., equating IQ with actual intelligence, viewing intelligence as static and almost totally inherited, misinterpreting correlation as causation, etc.), the authors over-interpreted and misinterpreted results of studies on the intelligence of African American children. They ultimately drew the fatal conclusion that African Americans are intellectually and culturally inferior to other cultural and ethnic groups. To state the obvious, this premise is harmful and unsound.

Menchaca traced the evolution of deficit thinking and demonstrated how it influenced segregation in schools and resistance to desegregation during the Civil Rights era and today. To what extent have educators resisted desegregation and used tracking and ability grouping to resegregate students racially? Below, we discuss how deficit orientations influence a myriad of gifted education practices and, thereby, limit diverse students' access to gifted education.

Testing and Assessment Issues

Extensive reliance on tests. Test scores play a dominant role in identification and placement decisions. More than 90% of school districts use intelligence or achievement test scores for decision making. This near-exclusive reliance on test scores for placement decisions keeps the demographics of gifted programs primarily White and middle class. Traditional tests have been less effective with diverse and economically disadvantaged students, which raises the question, "Why do we continue to use these tests so exclusively and extensively?" There are at least three explanations offered for the ineffectiveness of standardized tests: (1) the fault rests with the test (e.g., test bias); (2) the fault rests with the educational environment (e.g., poor instruction and lack of access to high-quality education contributes to poor test scores); or (3) the fault rests with (or within) the student (e.g., he or she is cognitively inferior or "culturally deprived").

The first two viewpoints consider the influence of the environmental or external forces on test performance. Therefore, if the test is being questioned, alternative tests and assessment tools will be considered and adopted. Further, if the quality of the instruction and resources are poor, then educators recognize that test scores are likely to be low. Poor quality curriculum and instruction beget poor test scores.

Conversely, the last explanation rests in deficit thinking; it points to shortcomings within the students and, thus, it blames the victim. Educators who support this view abdicate any responsibility for minority students' lower test scores because of the belief that genetics exclusively or primarily determine intelligence and that intelligence is static—that genes are destiny. Such advocates are also likely to believe that the environment (e.g., families) in which culturally diverse students are reared is inferior to those of other groups. Both views are indicative of a deficit-oriented philosophy that hinders educators from seeing the potential of diverse students and prohibits them from working effectively with such students.

IQ-based definitions and theories. Educators continue to define gifted-ness unidimensionally—as a function of high IQ scores. Thus, definitions and theories are based extensively on the results of intelligence tests. Essentially, giftedness is defined as an IQ of 130 or higher or a score that is two standard deviations above the mean on an intelligence test. IQ- or test-driven defini-tions often ignore the strengths of those who are culturally diverse, who are linguistically diverse, who live in poverty, or who are poor test takers. These students may very well be capable, but lack experiences deemed necessary for school success, as explained earlier.

Achievement-based definitions and theories. Along with high intelli-gence test scores, giftedness is often defined in terms of high achievement, as measured by achievement tests and grades. Gifted students are expected to demonstrate their ability in above-average school performance. Such defini-tions arid theories, of course, ignore the reality that gifted students can and do underachieve. Gifted underachievers may be teachers' greatest "nightmare" because the students have the ability and potential to excel, but they do not. When we equate giftedness with achievement, we ignore an important real-ity: Gifted children may lack motivation, may have a conflict between the need for achievement and the need for affiliation, and may have personal problems that hinder their productivity and interest in school. Compounding these realities is another reality: Diverse students face social injustices (e.g., dis-crimination, stereotypes, negative peer pressures, etc.) that can contribute to underachievement.

Inadequate policies and practices. Procedural and policy issues also con-tribute to the under-representation of diverse students in gifted education. Specifically, teachers (including culturally diverse teachers) under-refer diverse students for gifted education services. Ford found many Black students, for example, with high test scores who are under-represented in gifted education because teachers did not refer them for screening. Thus, when teacher referral is the first (or only) recruitment step, diverse students are likely to be under-represented in gifted education.

Equity versus Excellence Debate

The aforementioned barriers are empowered by debates over excellence versus equity, as if the two cannot coexist. This debate begs the question, "If we address issues of diversity (i.e., equity), will the quality of programs suffer (i.e., excellence)?" We are often asked by teachers and administrators, "If under-achieving gifted students are identified and served, will this 'water down' the gifted education class?" We are convinced that beliefs—conscious or unconscious—about inferiority lie at the heart of this question.

Into the Future: Recommendations for Change

Schools must eliminate barriers to the participation of economically disadvan-taged and minority students in services for students with outstanding talents . . . and must develop strategies to serve students from underrepresented groups.

To effectively recruit and retain diverse students in gifted education, educators must shed deficit thinking. As Einstein once said, "The world we have created is a product of our thinking. We cannot change things until we change our thinking." What follows are some suggestions for moving the field of gifted education into the next millennium in proactive, student-centered ways.

Adopt Contemporary Theories and Definitions

A number of theories of intelligence and giftedness exist, but two appear to capture the strengths, abilities, and promise of gifted diverse learners: Sternberg's Triarchic Theory of Intelligence and Gardner's Theory of Multiple Intelligences. These two comprehensive, flexible, and inclusive theories contend that giftedness is a social construct that manifests itself in many ways and means different things to different cultural groups. The theorists acknowledge the multifaceted, complex nature of intelligence and how current tests (which are too simplistic and static) fail to do justice to this construct. In addition, the USDE's most recent definition broadens notions of giftedness with its attention to potential and talent development. It recognizes that giftedness also exists among children living in ghettos, barrios, and hollows. Unfortunately, as with other definitions and theories, practical, valid, and reliable instruments have yet to be developed to assess these proactive and contemporary theories of intelligence. Our hope is that this will be rectified in the near future.

Adopt Culturally Sensitive Instruments

To date, the most promising instruments for assessing the strengths of culturally diverse students are nonverbal tests of intelligence such as the Naglieri Non-Verbal Abilities Test and Raven's Matrix Analogies Tests, which are considered less culturally loaded than traditional tests. Accordingly, these are likelier to capture the cognitive strengths of culturally diverse students. Saccuzzo et al., identified substantively more Black and Hispanic students using the Raven's than using a traditional test, and reported that "50% of the non-White children who had failed to qualify based on a WISC-R qualified with the Raven." They went on to state that "the Raven is a far better measure of pure potential than tests such as the WISC-R, whose scores depend heavily on acquired knowledge."

Educators should understand that nonverbal tests assess intelligence nonverbally. This is not to say that students are nonverbal (e.g., cannot talk); rather, the tests give students opportunities to demonstrate their intelligence without the confounding influence of language, vocabulary, and academic exposure. Gardner, Sternberg, and others contend that some gifted individuals do not have strong verbal or linguistic skills, as may be the case with musically gifted students, creatively gifted students, spatially gifted students, and those having a great deal of practical or social intelligence. Thus, we must find ways to assess the strengths, the gifts, of these capable students. At this time, nonverbal tests hold much promise for identifying such students—one test and one type of test cannot possibly measure the many types of intelligences that exist.

Identify and Serve Underachievers and Low Socioeconomic-Status Students

Underachievement is learned. Children are not born underachieving. Yet, when one equates giftedness with high achievement, gifted underachievers will be under-referred for gifted education. Considering the reality that a disproportionate percentage of diverse students live in poverty, they are likely to be underachievers—not due to lack of intelligence, but due to lack of opportunity. Thus, educators must be mindful of why students underachieve and recognize that poverty is predominant among these reasons. Few articles have focused on gifted students who live in poverty. Therefore, it is essential that we adopt definitions and programs that center on potential and talent development so that we can change the demographics of gifted education and open doors that have historically been closed. Further, more research is needed that focuses on the characteristics and needs of gifted students who live in poverty—a disproportionate percentage of whom are culturally diverse students.

Provide Multicultural Preparation for Educators

With forecasts projecting a growing minority student population, teachers will have to bear a greater responsibility for demonstrating multicultural competence. Multicultural education preparation among all school personnel may increase the recruitment and retention of diverse students in gifted education. To become more culturally competent, educators must, at minimum: (1) engage in critical self-examination that explores their attitudes and perceptions concerning cultural diversity and the influence of these attitudes and perceptions on diverse students' achievement and educational opportunities; (2) acquire and use accurate information about culturally diverse groups (e.g., histories, cultural styles, norms, values, traditions, customs) to inform teaching and learning; (3) learn how to infuse multicultural perspectives and materials into curriculum and instruction so as to maximize the academic, cognitive, social-emotional, and cultural development of all students; and (4) build partnerships with diverse families, communities, and organizations. In teacher education programs and staff development initiatives, we must prepare future and current teachers to work with culturally diverse students. Theories, models, and strategies proposed by Banks, Ford and Harris, Shade et al., and others should be shared with school personnel so they can create multicultural learning environments—classrooms and schools that are culturally responsive.

Provide a Multicultural Education for Gifted Students

Many scholars emphasize the need for all students to have a multicultural education. What resources accurately and effectively teach about slavery? What materials and resources offer multiple perspectives on the Trail of Tears?

How can we ensure that all subject areas (including math and science) have a multicultural focus?

Students have the right to see themselves reflected (and affirmed) in the curriculum. Minimally, this means that teachers must expose students to high-quality multicultural books and materials, create lesson plans that focus on multicultural themes and concepts, and expose students to culturally diverse role models (e.g., using biographies and having speakers visit classrooms).

. . . Banks has proposed that there are four approaches to infusing multicultural content into the curriculum: contributions approach, additive approach, transformation approach, and social action approach. Teachers must try to teach at the highest levels so that students have a substantive understanding and appreciation of diverse populations.

Develop Home-School Partnerships

In theory, school districts consider family involvement central to student achievement. In practice, few schools consistently and aggressively build partnerships with diverse families. During the first week of school and constantly thereafter, teachers and administrators must make sure that diverse families know that the school district offers gifted education services, understand referral and screening measures and procedures, and know how placement decisions are made. Just as important, diverse families must understand the purpose and benefits of gifted education. Efforts by schools must be aggressive and proactive; school personnel will need to go into diverse communities (e.g., visit homes), attend minority-sponsored events, and seek the support of minority churches and corporations in order to build home-school partnerships.

Equally important, efforts should focus on family education—holding workshops and meetings designed to educate diverse parents about how to meet the needs of, and advocate for, their gifted children. As I have noted elsewhere, diverse parents need strategies for helping their children cope with peer pressures and social injustices, for maintaining achievement, and for staying motivated and goal-oriented in the face of social injustices.

On-Going Evaluation

There are no easy or quick fixes to increase opportunities for diverse students to have access to gifted education services. Educators at all levels (e.g., teachers, administrators) and in all positions (e.g., counselors, psychologists) must constantly evaluate and re-evaluate their efforts to recruit and retain diverse students in gifted education. This examination must focus on instruments, definitions, policies and procedures, curriculum and instruction, and staff development. Armed with such information and data, schools can be proactive in opening doors that have been historically closed to diverse students.

The success schools achieve at diversifying or "desegregating" gifted education depends heavily on critical self-examination and on a willingness to move the equity versus excellence debate beyond deficit thinking. As Borland suggested, gifted education must begin to question and examine its fundamental premises and practices to see if they remain (or ever were) valid. Students in the gifted program should closely represent the community's demographics. The reasons for the disparities must be evaluated and decreased.

A Final Thought

"There is a wealth of talent and intelligence in this field [of gifted education], but I worry that we are using it to defend yesterday, not to imagine and build tomorrow." Clearly, controversy exists regarding why diverse students are under-represented in gifted education. The controversy focuses on whether the causes include deficiencies in the children and their families or discriminatory practices of schools and society that restrict the search for, and discovery of, minority talent. Giftedness is a social construct; therefore, inclusiveness is the philosophy of choice for increasing the power of those predictions. For the sake of children, we must err on the side of inclusion rather than exclusion.

The persistent and pervasive under-representation of diverse students in gifted education is likely to have devastating, long-lasting effects. We can attribute much of this difficulty to deficit thinking, which limits access and opportunity. Likewise, doing what is in the best interest of diverse students has been hampered by debates between equity and excellence. How many more diverse children must suffer while we debate this issue? What changes are we willing to make in the new millennium?

Annie Nakao  **NO**

How Race Colors Learning

It's a fact of education that few feel comfortable discussing: race matters when it comes to academic achievement.

Studies show that the most well-off African American youngsters—children of middle- and upper-income families that have come the farthest since the civil rights movement—generally perform worse than Asian and white children from lower-income families.

True, many African Americans are academic superstars, wooed by the nation's most prestigious universities and who later enjoy brilliant careers.

But many more lag behind their peers in school at every socioeconomic level and by every traditional measure of academic achievement, from standardized tests to college graduation rates.

Disparities in the academic performance of blacks and, to a lesser degree, Latinos and Native Americans helped fuel the affirmative action debate that led UC regents to ban the use of race in admissions.

The result: a 51 percent drop in African Americans, Latinos and Native Americans from the 1997–98 freshman class at the system's premier campus, UC-Berkeley, to this fall's, and a 2 percent overall drop at the university's eight undergraduate campuses.

And, to the chagrin of educators, the gaps are largest among the most educated middle class.

"I don't know if anyone has an entirely persuasive explanation . . . cultural or otherwise," said conservative African American political economist Glenn C. Loury of Boston University. "It's hard to talk about this without seeming to be pejorative, without judging. It confirms too many stereotypes. But it's alarming and it cries out for concern."

Jared Boyd entered Oakland's Skyline High School with an A-minus average from junior high and a recommendation that he be placed in honors classes. He got none.

After his parents protested, Jared was placed in honors biology. Last fall, he entered UC-Davis. The Boyds are proud, but Jared's father, Clarence, doesn't believe Jared got the same education he himself did a generation earlier at a mostly white Catholic school in Detroit.

"Here's the difference: I was one of two blacks, so there was no way you could segregate," said the elder Boyd, an orthopedic surgeon. "I was exposed to the highest level of math, science, English. I had to perform like everybody else."

Unlike the widely discussed academic problems of disadvantaged blacks, the issue of middle-class underperformance has received scant public attention—even though it has been known since the late 1960s.

But with college admissions increasingly a high-stakes lottery only for the best prepared students, the issue demands attention.

A three-month Examiner investigation suggests that explanations for the phenomenon are complex, provocative and disturbing and can be traced to factors inside and outside the schools:

- Historical racism and its impact on school practices.
- Teacher expectations.
- Student attitudes and peer pressures.
- Education levels achieved not only by parents, but by preceding generations.
- Black/white differences in parenting styles.

"People tell me, "You're almost out of school"—I tell them, "No, I'm just starting,"" said 18-year-old Mishea McCoy of El Sobrante, a top-achieving senior at Richmond's De Anza High School who is headed for UCLA as a pre-med major.

"That," she said, "is where a lot of people's minds are at. Not many black kids go on to four-year schools. In fact, people call you names if you excel academically. They look at you like you're different. Like you're, you know, not black anymore."

Disparities in the academic performance of underrepresented minorities—compared to whites and Asians—are prompting a movement to ditch the SAT, one of the most widely used college entrance exams.

Among college-bound students with at least one parent who had a graduate degree, the 1997 mean combined SAT verbal and math score (out of a perfect 1600) was 1165 for Asians, 1130 for whites, 1014 for Mexican Americans and 951 for blacks.

Comparisons by income also showed blacks lagging.

A UC analysis last year of 1995 SAT scores in California found that blacks from the highest-income families scored lower than whites or Asians from the poorest families.

Two years later, well-off black SAT test takers continued to lag behind many lower-income white and Asian families, especially in math.

For example, blacks from California families earning $100,000 or more per year had a mean math score of 498, 1 point less than whites from families earning less than $10,000 and only 7 points more than Asians whose families made less than $10,000.

Similar patterns are found in lower grades.

The 1994 National Assessment of Educational Progress reading test indicates the average score of black high school seniors with a parent who graduated from college was 272—2 points less than for white seniors whose parents did not finish high school.

Granted, the score gaps have narrowed significantly since the 1960s: The gap between blacks and whites in mean SAT scores fell from 258 points in 1976 to 196 points in 1992, a 24 percent reduction. But they have not narrowed enough.

It was the frustratingly tiny numbers of extremely well prepared non-Asian minorities that helped fuel California's affirmative action debate at UC-Berkeley and UCLA—two of UC's most selective campuses.

The backlash resulted in UC regents voting in 1995 to bar the use of race in admissions, starting with the fall 1998 freshman class. A year later, Californians passed Proposition 209, which banned the use of race or gender in state hiring, education and contracting.

Although the real competition at these campuses was between the much more numerous Asians and whites, blacks and Latinos became the focal point in the controversy.

This, in large part, is why:

California SAT scores for 1995 showed that whites accounted for 39 percent of those scoring 750 or more in math (out of a perfect 800), and half of those who scored 600 or more.

Asian American students comprised 46 percent of those scoring 750 or more and 30 percent of those scoring 600 or more.

These represent many of the very best prepared applicants vying for coveted spots at UC-Berkeley and UCLA.

By contrast, blacks, Latinos and Native Americans accounted for just 3 percent of those scoring 750 and 9 percent of those scoring 600.

"With data such as these, it is unsurprising that affirmative action admissions policies in the University of California system have become the subject of debate," said L. Scott Miller of the College Board, which oversees the SAT.

That debate has since spilled over into a controversy about standardized tests themselves.

Upset that already small minority enrollments have dropped without affirmative action, critics want standardized tests eliminated from college admissions.

UC is studying such a proposal.

Not everyone is sure eliminating standardized tests from the admissions process would be a good solution.

"Tests rarely are indicative of everything a youngster can do," said Gloria Ladson-Billings, a professor of education at the University of Wisconsin at Madison. "So we're going to have to make better tests that show us what kids can do. But we can't just blow off the tests and say they're biased. What do they tell us? They tell us kids are exposed to impoverished curriculum, that kids are being undertaught, that kids have skills deficits. And we aren't doing anything about it."

The College Board formed the National Task Force on Minority High Achievement last year to probe the achievement gaps and recommend strategies to increase the ranks of top minority students.

Since such students are disproportionately drawn from the middle class, the underachievement of middle-class youngsters will be a large part of the inquiry.

The task force consists of 34 scholars, including Harvard University's Henry Louis Gates Jr. and National Academy of Sciences president Bruce M. Alberts of UCSF, philanthropists, corporate leaders and minority advocates.

On their plates: a veritable smorgasbord of factors that may interact to result in the achievement gaps.

"There's no one culprit, no single button to push," said Miller of the College Board. "It's a complex, multivariable equation with feedback loops all over the lot."

One major factor might be the long-term impact of slavery and Jim Crow segregation laws that for generations slowed the progress of blacks in society.

National surveys, for example, suggest that as many as 20 percent, or one in five whites, still believes blacks are genetically less intelligent than whites while as many as 35 percent of whites believe blacks are less intelligent for other reasons.

Other factors may involve such school practices as tracking—which critics say segregates blacks and other minorities into lower-ability classes—and low expectations many teachers have of African American youngsters.

Such experiences might make some black students ambivalent about academic success and the value of studying hard. Some might be affected by pressure from peers who reject what they see as white values and equate academic success with "acting white."

Another possible factor might be what experts call the intergenerational accumulation of education, or human capital, that families pass on.

Since blacks until relatively recently were blocked from integrated education, generations—including today's middle-class parents—have less educational achievement than other groups. This might affect what books and magazines are available at home, the content of dinner table discussions, even differences in parent-child relationships.

Still other differences in the black and white middle-class experience might be at work.

Blacks work harder to be middle class. Though their incomes are similar to middle-class whites, they have less accumulated wealth. This, along with segregation patterns, can affect where a family buys a home and result in children having to attend school in less desirable districts, where peers are less likely to aspire to higher education.

Sorting through these complexities is hard enough. But the task force study comes at a time when racial and ethnic group differences remain a volatile subject, thanks to the 1994 publication of "The Bell Curve."

The best-seller by Richard J. Herrnstein and Charles Murray concluded that intelligence is largely inherited and intractable, linking IQ to an array of social problems from poverty to poor schooling. They cited score gaps among whites, blacks and Asians: blacks have an average IQ that is 16 points lower than whites; Asians have an average IQ slightly higher than whites.

Critics blasted the authors for ignoring the continuing controversy over IQ, heredity and environment.

Miller, who is directing the minority achievement task force, believes environmental factors—not genetics—are causing the gaps.

But he said he nevertheless understands why it is difficult to discuss.

"It's a messy area in which stereotypes tend to be reinforced by real performance," he said. "You break the back of a lot of stereotypes with good news, with large numbers of kids who are doing extremely well. We haven't enabled enough minority students to do that yet."

It's just as difficult a topic for African Americans to broach, even as they anguish over the pressing academic issues affecting their children.

Survivors of a rigid racial caste system that for generations was anchored in the belief that blacks were intellectually and culturally inferior, many of them view such discussions with the deepest suspicions.

"You have people who are constantly told they are dumb and ugly, that they're no damned good and their parents are no damned good . . .," said Melvin P. Sikes, professor emeritus of educational psychology at the University of Texas at Austin and one of the celebrated African American fliers of World War II, the Tuskegee Airmen. "They may have stopped the lynching of the body, but they're still lynching the minds of young black people."

But Miller believes the time is right to start talking about what's causing these achievement gaps.

"What's different now is that people's ability to avoid (that discussion) has gotten pretty limited," Miller said. "Heavy immigration from Asia over the past 30 years has led to a large increase in the number of top students, which has helped intensify the competition for admission to selective universities. That's one reason why the affirmative action debate is so hot."

POSTSCRIPT

Should Standard Tests Be Relied Upon to Determine Student Potential?

How does one measure the effectiveness of an education? Typically, the response has been the use of a standardized test. But in a culturally, ethnically, and racially heterogeneous nation such as the United States, how can one rely upon "standardization"? Are we, as a nation, "losing out" by classifying students on the basis of test results that may be biased toward the dominant culture, which is white middle class? Some would argue that the changing demographics no longer reflect the dominance of the white middle class. Quite true in some parts of the country in terms of numbers. But the "dominant culture" is that of established societal values and norms that are slow to change and that have been forged over centuries.

Donna Y. Ford and Deborah A. Harmon argue that as a nation we are "wasting and erasing gifts and talents when we do not recognize the strengths of students." These strengths are not necessarily reflected in standardized test results. Ford and Harmon point out that "culturally diverse students persist in being underrepresented in gifted education," largely as a result of reliance on standardized tests to identify gifted students.

Ford and Harmon review a number of changes schools might undertake. They urge educators to eliminate the barriers that harm students from diverse cultures.

William C. Dowling not only puts a different spin on the issue, he argues for the maintenance of standardized tests. Contrary to those who are "disposed to discount them more as badges of socio-economic status than a measure of verbal aptitude or cognitive ability," Dowling believes that the SATV (verbal portion of the SAT) "measures something real and important." He cites the variety of attackers of the SAT, such as FairTest, the Cambridge, Massachusetts organization adamantly opposed to the SAT as "a direct descendant of the racist anti-immigrant Army Mental Tests of the 1920s," and the *Princeton Review* founder John Katzman, who sees the SAT as "an arbitrary, biased, somewhat pointless exam that doesn't test anything." (*Princeton Review* nonetheless prepares students for the SAT). Dowling provides a useful overview of the origin and intent of the SAT and discusses his own research on the usefulness of the tests as a predictor of future student performance.

Additional readings on this topic include Herman Aguinis, ed., *Test-Score Banding in Human Resource Selection: Legal, Technical and Societal Issues;* Linda M. McNeil, *Contradictions of School Reform: Education Costs of Standardized Testing;* and Rebecca Zwick, *Fair Game? The Use of Standardized Admissions Tests in Higher Education.*

ISSUE 18

Should There Be Federal Education Standards?

YES: Doris Redfield, from "An Educator's Guide to Scientifically Based Research: Documenting Improvements in Student Performance and Supporting the NCLB Act," *District Administration* (January 2004)

NO: Marilyn Gitell, from "National Standards Threaten Local Vitality," *The Clearing House* (January/February 1996)

ISSUE SUMMARY

YES: Doris Redfield delineates the standards set down by NCLB and the research instruments needed to determine the equality of programs across the country.

NO: Marilyn Gitell presents an outright rejection of national standards and argues that local school systems should be financially aided by the federal government rather than having standards dictated to them.

$\mathbf{T}$here would be constitutional, political, and ethical issues surrounding the development of a national curriculum. Yet students across this vast country are not receiving the same education. Should they be, or should localities determine what they want their youngsters to learn? Can these children be treated justly without equality and equity in their education?

Recall, if you will, the precedent set by *Plessy v. Ferguson* (1896), in which the Supreme Court, dealing with the issue of segregated railroad cars, set the precedent for the next 58 years. State laws providing separate by equal facilities, said the court, was constitutional.

But then came *Brown v. Board of Education* in 1954. Aristotle wrote that, "Even when laws have been written down they ought not always to remain unaltered." And so, the Warren Court struck down the doctrine of "separate but equal" as inherently unequal. The states were mandated to desegregate. But what would this mean for the equality of the quality of education?

Many nations around the world have a centralized curriculum. For example, it has been said that the minister of education in France, sitting in his Paris office, can look at his watch at any time of the day and know exactly what every fourth grader is doing." So did the former Soviet Union have such a similar educational system? Do such systems create equity and equality, or do they turn out "Stepford" children? What is the most just manner in which to treat children's futures?

Doris Redfield is a supporter of national education standards—does that translate into a national curriculum? Not necessarily. Nonetheless, Redfield endorses programs that would insure student achievement nationwide. She provides guidelines to educators to implement this equity.

Marilyn Gitell vehemently argues against national standards, be it in the form of milestones to be achieved, or, by logical extension, a national curriculum. Gitell's bottom line is that any attempt at nationalization of education is a threat to local vitality.

Gitell delineates a number of arguments presented by opponents of national standards, including the tradition of local control of education and the greater competence of local governments to determine what is in the interests of their children; the doubt that the national government would provide the necessary follow-though; the notion that national standards or a national curriculum would undermine the states; the importance of diversity in a society; the concern over how the effectiveness of national standards/a curriculum would be evaluated. Gitell summarizes the opponents' arguments by noting that, "the common thread running throughout most of this opposition is this belief: National standards move the federal government from its long-held position of minor partner in American Elementary and secondary education into that of an enforcer, without fundamentally changing its role in finance or governance." Redfield adds her own view that what the federal government should do is provide "equity in funding and Compensatory education."

Gitell argues for equity, not nationalization in education. She concludes by telling us that "American education policy should recognize three goals: equity; expansion of public discourse and participation in school decision making, and excellence. The federal emphasis must be on equality. With our strong tradition of federalism and community-based education, we should be defining standards locally. . . . Although proponents of national standards sometimes claim that standards that apply to all in the same way will produce equity, or that opportunity-to-learn standards encompass equity goals, there is no evidence to support these claims."

Doris Redfield  **YES**

An Educator's Guide to Scientifically Based Research: Documenting Improvements in Student Performance & Supporting the NCLB Act

Dear Readers:

Schools and school districts are under increasing pressure to make sure federal dollars are used to implement programs and practices proven effective by scientifically based research. The No Child Left Behind Act of 2001 (NCLB) mentions scientifically based research 110 times. The phrase has become so common that it has earned its own acronym: SBR.

So . . . what is scientifically based research, or SBR? Who is responsible for doing it? And how can school and district leaders determine the adequacy of SBR claims for a particular program or practice?

To help you answer these questions and address these issues AEL is happy to bring you this Educators Guide to Scientifically Based Research, which:

- provides a definition of SBR
- discusses the importance of SBR to educational practice
- describes who should conduct SBR
- provides a checklist for evaluating research evidence
- lists steps for conducting your own SBR
- offers guidance for identifying high-quality researchers

We'd like to thank the following sponsors for helping to make the distribution of this guide possible: Texas Instruments, American Education Corporation, netTrekker and Inspiration Software.

We trust you will find this guide useful in helping teachers and students in your schools and classrooms benefit from rigorous research.

Sincerely,

Doris Redfield, Director of the Institute for the Advancement of Research in Education at the Appalachia Educational Laboratory (AEL).

(AEL houses one often federally funded educational research and development laboratories. Dr. Redfield's experience as a teacher, administrator, researcher, and contractor to the U.S. Department of Education position her well to speak to the realities of evaluating and implementing SBR in the real world of schools.)

Why Is Scientifically Based Research in Education Such a Hot Topic Today?

It starts with the emphasis placed on the No Child Left Behind Act which mandates that school improvement plans must incorporate strategies based on scientifically based research; corrective action must include professional development based on scientifically based research; and Title III grantees must use English language acquisition approaches based on scientifically based research. This edited Guide provides educators with strategies for evaluating the extent to which products, services, and programs are supported by scientifically based research and conducting scientifically based research, when doing so is desirable.

In addition to SBR's four basic steps—observe, hypothesize, collect data/evidence, and draw conclusions—scientific research in education does six things.

1. Poses significant questions. Scientific educational research seeks to answer meaningful questions—questions that, when answered, will make an important difference that contributes to student learning. An important question relative to educational products, programs, and services is, "will it help teachers teach more effectively or help students learn more or better?"
2. Links to relevant theory. Products, services, and programs that link to theory take findings from prior, relevant research into account. New products should provide logical building blocks for extending what is already known about effective teaching and learning.
3. Uses valid tools. Valid tools are instruments and procedures that are capable of accurately measuring the effects of educational interventions (products, programs, and services).
4. Rules out alternative explanations. Scientific research studies are designed to rule out as many explanations as possible, other than the intervention, that may have contributed to the research findings. The findings of the research study should clearly explain how potential, alternative explanations were counteracted.
   - Experiments. Experimental designs include at least two groups, an experimental group that receives the "treatment" or experimental intervention such as a new program, product, or service and a control or comparison group that does not.
   - Quasi-experiments. Quasi-experiments also include experimental and control/comparison groups. However, the participants in these studies are not randomly selected or randomly assigned to the experimental versus control/comparison group(s).
   - Other approaches. These are not experimental or quasi-experimental; however, other approaches do not, by themselves, demonstrate cause and effect relationships between the "treatment" and the outcome. Such techniques include correlational analyses, case studies, and survey research.

5. Produces findings that can be replicated. Researchers need to describe the methods, instruments, and analyses they used so that another party could replicate the study. This also allows reviewers of the research, such as education practitioners, to evaluate the integrity of the research methods and findings.

6. Survives scrutiny. This may mean that a product developer or publisher contracts with an independent third party to conduct product effectiveness research. When a company's research is not conducted by an independent party, it should, at least, be reviewed by independent and credible third parties.

Quality Controls: How Should Research Evidence Be Evaluated?

In addition to the six tenets of scientifically based research, key phrases from the definition of scientifically based research provided by NCLB provide useful guidance for evaluating the quality of research evidence:

Is it relevant?   Does the evidence provided by the researchers or developers relate to an issue of importance to your needs, particularly student learning needs?

Does the research evidence provided by the developers link to and flow from relevant theory and theory-based research?

Do the research procedures, analyses, and findings support the researchers'/developers' claims?

Is it rigorous?   If the researchers claim a causal relationship between the intervention and an outcome measure such as student achievement, did they include a control or comparison group in the study, in addition to the experimental group?

Were the study participants randomly selected and/or randomly assigned to experimental versus control/comparison groups?

Is sufficient information provided to determine whether the research design, instruments, and procedures are appropriate for answering the research questions posed by the researchers/developers?

Were the research instruments, and procedures applied with consistency, accuracy, and for the purpose intended by the developers of the instruments and procedures? For example, norm-referenced achievement tests were not developed to determine the extent to which students master certain educational objectives. Rather, they are intended to rank order students on their knowledge of the information on the test.

Is it systematic?   Was the research conducted using a carefully planned and logical steps so that "what" questions are clearly and defensibly answered? For example, what interventions or combination of interventions applied to what degrees of intensity contribute to measurable differences in learning?

Is it objective?   Did an independent, third party conduct the research? If not, did an independent third party review it?

Is it reliable?   Could the same researchers repeat the study and obtain time same or highly similar results?

Could other researchers replicate the study's methodology and obtain the same or highly similar results?

Is it valid?   Were the research instruments and procedures accurate in their measurements?

Were the data analyses appropriate for yielding accurate results?

Are the research conclusions clearly linked to the research data?

Seven Steps to Conducting Scientifically Based Research

Briefly, the SBR process includes:

1. Based upon the best available information (e.g., sound theory, prior rigorous research, and/or empirical observation) formulate a hypothesis about the effect of one variable (the independent or "causal" variable) such as a particular instructional strategy on another variable (the dependent or outcome variable) such as student achievement. An example hypothesis might be that when third grade students are exposed to 100 hours of XYZ software for increasing reading comprehension, their scores on a test of reading comprehension will increase.
2. If possible, randomly select participants for the study. Also, if possible, randomly assign individuals to either the experimental or the control/comparison group(s). If random selection and/or assignment are possible, you will have the makings of an experimental study. If not, then you will be conducting a quasi-experiment. Either way, you must have both an experimental group and a control or comparison group.
3. If you are interested in measuring change over time, administer a pretest to both the experimental and control/comparison groups. This is especially important if you are unable to randomly assign participants to groups. Be sure that the pretest is reliable and valid for the purpose at hand. Information about the reliability and validity of commercially available instruments should be available in the accompanying technical manual or in reference books such as Buros Mental Measurements Yearbook or Tests in Print.
4. Apply the treatment intervention to the experimental group, being careful to plan and document the nature, specific elements, length, intensity, and context of the treatment. This will allow for replication.
5. Re-measure (i.e., post-test) both the experimental and control/comparison groups, using the pretest measure or a measure that has been demonstrated statistically to be equivalent to the pretest measure. It is important to document the test-retest reliability of the measure.
6. Analyze the results of the measurements of the experimental and control/comparison groups on the pre and post-test measures. A statistics specialist can help determine the most appropriate types of statistical analyses and tests to conduct. Ultimately, an effect size should be calculated. Effect sizes indicate the practical significance of statistical findings. Large effect sizes tend to be 1.0 or greater, while medium

effect sizes center around .50 and effect sizes of .25 or less are generally considered small.

7. Write a report of the findings that includes a description of the rationale for the study; findings from prior research that contributed to the study's underlying hypothesis; the research procedures and instruments that were used, including information about their reliability and validity; demographic information about the participants in the study, as well as information about how they were selected and how they were assigned to groups; how the results were analyzed; the results of the analyses, including effect sizes; and conclusions that can be supported by the data yielded by the study.

Identifying High Quality Researchers

If instead of conducting your own research, you plan to contract with a research consultant or firm, it is important to get references and establish that they have credentials—for example, advanced degrees with training in research design and methodology as well as active membership and participation in scholarly societies such as the American Educational Research Association (AERA) or the American Evaluation Association (AEA)—that are recognized by professional education researchers. The What Works Clearinghouse (WWC), established by the U.S. Department of Education to review research and evaluate the evidence of effectiveness for specific educational approaches and interventions, plans to establish an evaluator registry of researchers who agree to abide by the WWC standards tot conducting product and program effectiveness research. . . .

NO

Marilyn Gitell

National Standards Threaten Local Vitality

Given the current overwhelming support for national standards, one wonders why it has taken so long to make the creation of standards a national priority. But, in fact, strong opposition to such standards persists and continues to come from both the right and the left. Above all, such opposition points to the weakness of a federal strategy for educational reform that deviates from our national commitment to educational equity. That deviation, and how it can be corrected, is the subject of this article. I will first, however, describe nine positions in opposition to national standards, show what these points of view have in common, and demonstrate how they can contribute to our thinking on educational equity.

Opposition to Standards

Opposition to national standards comes from people with a variety of points of view:

- People who honor and cherish the tradition of local control of education, particularly at the school district level, question why the national government considers itself competent to establish national standards.
- People who give priority to equity and equitable financing of education question the commitment and follow-through of national politicians. They are pessimistic about how a national curriculum can serve these ends.
- People who focus on the role of the states (which provide 50 percent of the funding for education and are legally responsible for providing equal education) and who have spent considerable energy reforming and enhancing state education efforts view the effort to create national standards as undermining the states.
- People who see American federalism as the most effective means of retaining a decentralized and democratic political system question the need for national education standards, which deny the vitality of local responsiveness to local needs.

From *The Clearing House*, vol. 69, no. 3, January/February 1996, pp. 148–150. Copyright © 1996 by Heldref Publications, 1319 Eighteenth St., NW, Washington, DC 20036-1802. Reprinted by permission of the Helen Dwight Reid Educational Foundation. References omitted.

- People who value and encourage diversity in all aspects of American society question how national standards can encompass that diversity.
- People who question the value of the extensive testing in American schools (and challenge the validity of the tests themselves) wonder how the implementation of national standards will be evaluated. What tests, they ask, will be used and how will they affect teaching and learning?
- People who lead school reform efforts-building alternative school models, small-sized schools, and new curricula based on the inquiry method-oppose any national standards that contradict or undermine their efforts.
- People who do not think that foreign school systems are exemplary models of education ask why we would want to emulate systems that use assessments as a means of exclusion.
- People who worked on the national history curriculum or the New York social studies proposal, and have faced the wrath of colleagues who disagree with their suggested standards, predict the difficulty, if not the impossibility, of reaching agreement on the content of national standards across several subject areas.

The common thread running through most of this opposition is this belief: National standards move the federal government from its long-held position of minor partner in American elementary and secondary education into that of an enforcer, without fundamentally changing its role in finance or governance.

I argue that the federal government, rather than focusing on standards and assessment, should concentrate on what it can uniquely contribute to American education-namely, producing greater equity in funding and in compensatory education.

Progressive Federalism

The politics of education in America reflect the competing values that exist in the larger political culture. Americans struggle to balance the need to preserve an inclusive, participatory, and democratic policymaking process with the drive to attain efficiency and economy through professional centralization of decision making. Our federal system allows us to retain local controls and responsiveness through the states and localities while using federal leadership to sustain the values of equity and fairness. Only at the higher levels can we guarantee equity; thus a natural division of roles persists.

The federal government should concentrate on producing greater equity in funding and in compensatory education.

In *Choosing Equality: The Case for Democratic Schooling,* I outlined a theory of progressive federalism based on this division of power. Progressive federalism embraces local governance of local schools, while significantly broadening the participation of stakeholders. It supports public ownership in education that requires "a democratic process guiding the governance process, which goes beyond the election of school boards or public officials." It calls for expanded public discourse. Because states control the largest portion of education funding and institutional resources, progressive federalism views them as the center of political activity and the focal point for reform; they are potential "[agencies] for redistributing school resources and control and for mediating the direction of national and local action." Progressive federalism thus "affirms that government action is the central instrument for achieving egalitarian goals" and holds that it is the duty of the national government to provide leadership to work toward those goals. Plans for national standards reflect many of the key features of progressive federalism; they part with progressive federalism, however, by declining to assert the federal government's legitimate pursuit of egalitarian goals.

American education can only achieve its full potential under a dynamic federal system that encourages all levels to work together to achieve its most important goals. Equality is the essential goal. An emphasis on standards and performance will not necessarily produce equality, as the past fifteen years of education reform have demonstrated. State school reform in the 1980s, so highly acclaimed, did not reduce educational inequities; it improved quality for those who were already advantaged. The results of the educational reforms of the 1960s contrast with the results from the 1980s: those earlier reforms asserted equality as the major priority and achieved quality as a part of that effort.

Sustained support of the democratic process requires greater and continuing public discourse on education goals and standards in an expanded and more inclusive political arena. The federal government's leadership in engaging parents and community in that discourse and in the school decision-making process should be reinforced and enhanced. Only through broad-based participation will the combined goals of equity and excellence be appropriately balanced.

Equity as a Goal

The equity function was initially assumed by the federal courts, first in *Plessy v. Ferguson* when the Supreme Court stated that separate was equal, then dramatically in the 1954 decision *Brown v. Board of Education of Topeka* when it recognized that separate was unequal. Later, in the early 1960s, the national education title acts formulated federal compensatory programs to redress the inequities in school systems. Federal dollars, although never more than 8 percent of education funding nationally, symbolized the commitment to the positive goal of equality. The legislation included financial incentives, but more important, it provided federal leadership and direction to the states. Those programs, and others like them initiated in the decades of the 1960s and 1970s, significantly reduced the gaps in learning opportunities for a broad cross section of the society. Outcomes were certainly essential to program evaluation, although standards and testing were not priorities. Federal support and direction worked well with local programs that were designed specifically to respond to local populations. Some programs, however, such as Head Start, demonstrated the need for other elements, such as compensatory funding and parent participation.

A significant aspect of the educational agenda of that era was the recognition of the political arena in which education decision making takes place.

The Elementary and Secondary Education Act (ESEA) supported mandatory and voluntary parent and community participation in school decisions. The 1975 Education for All Handicapped Children's Act, a landmark in the federal role in education, established detailed requirements that prescribed how schools must make decisions for the future education of children with special needs. The law requires a plan to be prepared jointly by parents, teachers, counselors, and psychologists; parents are integral to the decision-making process, and no decision can be made without their approval. Federal law guarantees that all parents, rich or poor, black or white, will be respected in their judgments of what is educationally sound for their children. This legislation moved the concept of opportunity to learn to another level. Educational standards were henceforth to apply to a population formerly excluded, and the importance of a parental role in the decision-making process was recognized in federal legislation.

Although educational equity is clearly within federal legislative intent, the compensatory priority of federal aid is sometimes undermined by implementation at all levels. Because federal regulations and lack of oversight allow federal dollars to be distributed according to state formulas, federal grants programs can reinforce state inequities. Chapter 1 funding is the most pointed example of a federal policy gone awry. The General Accounting Office (GAO) finds that many wealthy schools benefit from Chapter 1 while schools with considerably higher proportions of poor students are underfunded. Funds appropriated for poor students are routinely distributed to wealthy districts. In Illinois, for example, the formula means that only 64,000 of Chicago's 150,000 officially poor children are served; Chicago has ineligible schools with poverty rates as high as 53 percent. Meanwhile, schools with a 4 percent poverty rate in Schaumburg, a northwest Chicago suburb, receive Chapter I funding. In New York, schools in the Oneonta system, which has a district poverty rate of 6 percent, receive $1,612 per Chapter 1 student, while schools in the Edmeston system, which has a district poverty rate of 34 percent, receive only $761 per Chapter 1 student. Most critics conclude that if Chapter 1 funds were directed to schools instead of to individual children these inequities would be prevented. Better standards for establishing financial equity in those school systems would go a long way toward improving the quality of education, especially in low-income areas.

American education policy should recognize three goals: equity; expansion of public discourse and participation in school decision making; and excellence. The federal emphasis must be on equality. With our strong tradition of federalism and community-based education, we should be defining standards locally. The vitality of our educational goals can best be assured by promoting vigorous public discourse, rather than looking to Washington as the sole source of standards and assessment. Although proponents of national standards sometimes claim that standards that apply to all in the same way will produce equity, or that opportunity-to-learn standards encompass equity goals, there is no evidence to support these claims. Improved governance, broader participation, higher standards, more equitable funding, and encouragement of public debate among a broad cross section of stakeholders should be part of the role of the federal government, which must be straightforward about its priorities. An essential part of the federal role is its assertion of national leadership in confirming social values and priorities. Equitable funding of schools and school districts is basic to our commitment to equality and key to raising systemwide performance. Encouraging these goals through higher state standards would demonstrate the vitality of the federal system.

POSTSCRIPT

Should There Be Federal Education Standards?

Issue 16 explored whether states are providing equal educational opportunity. Issue 17 dealt with potential bias in education as a result of standardized tests. And Issue 19 will deal with the effects of the recent No Child Left Behind (NCLB) Act, which, as shall be seen, set "proficiency" standards. In the midst of all of this controversy, it is only appropriate to discuss whether federal education standards, especially via a universal curriculum might be appropriate.

Imagine that you are 8 years old and in the third grade when your parents move to either a different part of the country or just a different town in your state during the middle of the school year. You are in your new school and told to open your math book to a particular page and work on the problems on that page. You are shocked! You did these math problems three weeks ago. Even worse, you have no idea how to do these math problems because, in your former school, you hadn't yet reached that type of math.

Proponents of a national curriculum would argue that this scenario is all too often the case and that a national curriculum would keep children across the country "on the same page," if not literally at least figuratively. If student performance across the country does indeed "measure, up" then NCLB is working. But can one determine the accuracy of reports of student achievement?

Doris Redfield believes that science-based research (SBR) required under NCLB can achieve this goal. In her succinctly delineated article, which is actually a "letter" to educators that offers an "Educator's Guide to Scientifically Based Research," Redfield defines SBR and provides a checklist of items to ascertain the quality of particular research conducted. This approach takes it as a given that NCLB will work if the correct research methods are in place.

By contrast, Marilyn Gitell argues that national standards—let alone a national curriculum—would threaten "local vitality." She cites a number of reasons to be skeptical of a national curriculum, including: whether the national government is competent to establish national standards; whether there would be the necessary financial follow-through to establish equity; the states' efforts to date would be undermined; local responsiveness to local needs are integral to our system of government; maintaining local control underscores the diversity of this society; how would such a system be implemented and evaluated; efforts to date to build alternative school models and small-sized schools would be undermined; and why should the United States emulate foreign countries who use assessments as a means of exclusion?

The bottom line of opponents, Gitell points out, is that "The common thread running through most of [the] opposition is this belief: National standards move the federal government from its long-held position of minor partner in American elementary and secondary education into that of an enforcer, without fundamentally changing its role in finance and governance."

Gitell argues that a "dynamic federal system" with cooperation among all levels of government can achieve the equity desired in our educational system.

Suggested readings on this subject include two of Diane Ravitch's works, *National Education Standards in American Education: A Citizen's Guide* and *Developing National Standards in Education;* Anne C. Lewis, *An Overview of the Standards Movement;* and Kathy Koch, *National Education Standards: Will They Restrict Local Schools' Flexibility.*

ISSUE 19

Can No Child Left Behind Provide Equitable Education?

YES: Richard L. Simpson, Paul G. LaCava, and Patricia Sampson Graner, from "The No Child Left Behind Act: Challenges and Implications for Educators," *Intervention in School & Clinic* (November 2004)

NO: Lisa Guisbond and Monty Neill, from "Failing Our Children: No Child Left Behind Undermines Quality and Equality in Education," *The Clearing House* (September–October 2004)

ISSUE SUMMARY

YES: Richard L. Simpson, Paul G. LaCava and Patricia Sampson Graner are strong defenders of the No Child Left Behind (NCLB) mandate to the states from the federal government. They believe that the states have already responded with greater educational achievement on the part of children.

NO: Lisa Guisbond and Monty Neill argue that the NCLB demands placed upon the states are strapping the states' already limited resources and that the mandate has only served to exacerbate the problem of educational inequality.

$\mathbf{A}$ major problem with federally initiated programs is that they typically drop the ball in the laps of the states. Politicians at the national pose, posture, and pontificate, and their proposals sound profound. But when push comes to shove, who shoulders the burden? On the one hand, national programs are very appealing, because they typically take a "global" view vis á vis the nation. On the other hand, if there is no federal follow-through, especially financially, what are the states to do?

A current subject of debate on this broader subject is the wisdom, or lack thereof, of the No Child Left Behind (NCLB) Act and program promulgated by the administration of President George W. Bush. Proponents firmly believe this is in the best interest of children nationwide. Opponents vehemently disagree. Which is it?

Richard L. Simpson, Paul G. LaCava, and Patricia Sampson Graner are true believers. They regard NCLB as an extraordinary federal initiative, one of the most far-reaching in decades. The applaud the goal of NCLB of "ensur[ing] that all children have a fair, equal, and significant opportunity to obtain a high-quality education, and reach, at a minimum proficiency on challenging state academic achievement standards and state academic assessments."

Simpson, LaCava, and Graner believe the program can succeed in its mandate to have all children across the nation performing at a comparable level. The method by which to assess this is, of course, the standardized test.

Lisa Guisbond and Monty Neill are diametrically opposed to Simpson, LaCava, and Graner. They argue that the NCLB program, while worthy on its face, only worsens the plight of children across the nation and the states that are left with the burden of meeting the unmandated standards laid out by the federal government.

Guisbond and Neill emphasize that a number of "false assumptions" underlie NCLB, include the national goal that schools should focus on raising the scores on standardized tests and threatening teachers to "perform better" in their profession, lest they face serious consequences.

Guisbond and Neill go so far as to say that NCLB is setting up schools across the nation to fail. They argue that the pace of progress set up by the national government is unrealistic, especially in the face of already inadequate financial resources in many of the schools across the nation. One of the problems, of course, is that the program is forcing teachers to "teach to the test." Is that an accurate reflection of the reality of children's educational achievement? Guisbond and Neill think not.

Guisbond and Neill point to other faults of NCLB. While NCLB loftily speaks about the need for "highly qualified" teachers, the reality is that "a teacher may be deemed 'highly qualified' if she or he has a bachelor's degree and passes a paper-and-pencil standardized exam. This minimal definition can in no way ensure that all children have good teachers. There is no persuasive evidence demonstrating a strong relationship between passing a standardized and being competent in the classroom," argue Guisbond and Neill. They further point out that the federal government is setting standards without being willing to put up the money to help schools across the country—with differential resources and needs—to meet the NCLB guidelines. Is such a program just and equitable?

Richard L. Simpson, Paul G. LaCava, and Patricia Sampson Graner

The No Child Left Behind Act: Challenges and Implications for Educators

The No Child Left Behind (NCLB) Act of 2001, signed into law by President George W. Bush on January 8, 2002, is the most noteworthy of recent congressional attempts to improve student achievement and otherwise reform elementary and secondary educational programs in the United States. Included in the NCLB enactment is the requirement that within a decade, all students, including those with disabilities, will perform at a "proficient" level on state academic assessment tests. Indeed, the assertively stated goal of NCLB "is to ensure that all children have a fair, equal, and significant opportunity to obtain a high-quality education, and reach, at a minimum, proficiency on challenging state academic achievement standards and state academic assessments" (NCLB, 2001).

The standards associated with NCLB represent an unprecedented and Herculean challenge for our nation's schools. By mandating that all students demonstrate annual yearly progress, NCLB serves as the most rigorous and exacting of standards-based strategies yet enacted for reforming schools (Albrecht & Joles, 2003; Center on Educational Policy, 2003). Furthermore, NCLB dramatically extends the contingencies of high-stakes assessments by creating strong rewards and punishments based on students' performance. Under NCLB guidelines, schools that perform well may receive public recognition and financial rewards but those whose students perform poorly could receive sanctions and even be subject to state takeover. As noted by Hardman and Mulder (2003), the NCLB Act expands the involvement of the federal government "from 'assisting States in setting standards and improving local performance,' to fiscal sanctions and corrective action for both States and schools that fail to meet set criteria" (pp. 5–6). So, as Algozzine (2003) pointed out, despite the federal government having no designated power to control education, federal control is exerted through discretionary and other incentives to state and local education agencies, driving the very pulse of each and every U.S. classroom.

The proficiency requirements of NCLB are expected to be a particularly difficult hurdle for the approximately 6.6 million students who are eligible to

From *Intervention in School and Clinic*, vol. 40, issue 2, November 2004, pp. 67–75. Copyright © 2004 by Pro-Ed, Inc. Reprinted by permission.

receive special education services and the educators who are responsible for their learning. That many of these pupils with disabilities have traditionally been excluded from state evaluation and testing programs and other accountability requirements makes NCLB simultaneously a significant opportunity for full participation and a daunting challenge. Thus, in spite of being passed by Congress with overwhelming bipartisan support and in spite of educators recognizing positive features of the enactment, NCLB has been a source of controversy (Robelen, 2002). Relative to students with disabilities, issues of particular concern include

- availability of adequate resources to implement the NCLB mandate;
- allowances for the use of flexible and individualized evaluation accommodations and modifications that address students' unique learning abilities, disabilities, and other needs; and
- support for personnel preparation and professional development needed to successfully implement the mandate.

As of February 2004, approximately a dozen states had rebelled against NCLB on the basis that it imposed costly new requirements without funding to carry them out. State legislators have also passed or introduced legislation or nonbinding resolutions challenging NCLB's standards for licensing teachers and testing students. The Virginia legislature, for example, approved a resolution in January 2004, calling on Congress to exempt Virginia without penalty from "the most sweeping intrusions into state and local control of education in the history of the United States." Despite the controversy surrounding this legislation, NCLB remains the "law of the land," thus one that teachers need to understand and follow. . . .

Major Themes of NCLB

The central and overarching theme of NCLB is accountability, including accountability for positive academic outcomes and related results. To be sure, the idea of accountability is replete in NCLB, and it is this concept that forms the foundation of the Act. NCLB holds individual schools, school districts, and states accountable for improvements in student achievement, with particular emphasis on closing the achievement gap between high- and low-performing students and children and youth from disadvantaged groups and minority populations.

Accountability Through Adequate Yearly Progress

NCLB has established the goal of having every student, including those with special needs, be accountable and meet state-identified standards by the conclusion of the 2013–2014 school year. To meet the aforementioned goals, states have each identified benchmarks by which to measure school and school district progress. States have also identified "adequate yearly progress" (AYP) standards that every student and school is expected to meet. AYP standards, it is thought, will better allow parents, community leaders, and school-district personnel to more objectively identify areas of strength, as well as areas in need of improvement.

Schools and school districts that achieve the AYP goals, as measured by scores on standardized tests, may receive public recognition, and their faculty members and staffs are eligible to receive rewards and acknowledgement. In contrast, schools and school districts that fail to meet their state's AYP criterion for 2 continuous years, either schoolwide or in any major subgroup, are slated to be designated as "in need of improvement." Subsequent to such identification, schools may be given assistance in improving their performance and subjected to various corrective and disciplinary measures.

Accountability Through Highly Qualified Teachers

An important accountability component of NCLB involves states developing plans to ensure that all teachers of core academic subjects are "highly qualified" by the end of the 2005–2006 academic year. The instructional importance of paraeducators is also recognized, and these individuals must also meet minimum qualification standards. There is considerable debate regarding the resources and means of implementing this element of NCLB. Nevertheless, this NCLB accountability caveat is logical in light of reports by researchers and other professionals that have shown a link between the quality of teachers and the outcomes demonstrated by students (Darling-Hammond, 1999; Darling-Hammond & Youngs, 2002; Ehrenberg & Brewer, 1994). Wayne and Youngs (2003) succinctly summarized the importance of qualified personnel: "Both intuition and empirical research tell us that the achievement of school children depends substantially on the teachers they are assigned" (p. 89). Yet, as previously noted, the resources and assessment procedures associated with important elements of NCLB, including the highly qualified teacher component, are clearly controversial.

NCLB and Scientifically Based Research Practices

NCLB promotes the use of effective educational practices based on scientifically based research (SBR), which is defined as methods that have met rigorous standards and that have been shown, when correctly applied, to reliably yield positive results. Typically such practices have been subjected to rigorous peer-review standards.

The U.S. Department of Education (USDOE) has established the What Works Clearinghouse (WWC; see www.w-w-c.org) to promote the use of evidence-based practices. The WWC is designed to provide teachers and others with a reliable and proven source of scientific evidence regarding effective and scientifically supported educational methods. The proposed method for identifying SBR practices is the WWC-developed Design and Implementation Assessment Device instrument and a related protocol to ensure that methods are supported by scientific evidence. The Design and Implementation Assessment Device and its related validation process are controversial because an infrequently used educational research method, randomized experimental group design methodology, is the preferred strategy for showing scientific evidence. Yet, beyond the controversy regarding the precise means of determining scientific evidence, scholars agree that using effective methods bodes well for students, including those with special needs (Algozzine, 2003; Sharelson & Towne, 2002).

Expanded Options for Parents

Another provision of NCLB is that parents are afforded expanded opportunities for decision making and other amplified alternatives associated with their children's education. To be sure, parents are encouraged to become active participants in their child's education under NCLB. Related to the accountability provisions of NCLB, parents are afforded access to information about their child's performance on standardized academic measures, as well as aggregate school and school district performance information. Such data and information are considered to be essential for parents to objectively and conscientiously exercise their NCLB-related rights and options. These options are particularly significant for parents whose children attend schools considered to need improvement. In such instances, parents have the option of transfering their child to a school in their district with a better performance record. Supplemental services, such as free tutoring, are available to some families whose children are enrolled in schools that fail to demonstrate satisfactory AYP.

Interestingly, expanded parental involvement under NCLB is interpreted as the home being a disciplinary model and resource site. That is, parents and families are thought to be an integral educational resource and alternative under NCLB. Moreover, instilling in children the values of home and discipline are thought to be NCLB parental participation components.

Increased School District Control and Flexibility

NCLB supports increased flexibility for states and school districts to exercise discretion in finding solutions to local issues. This decision-making authority includes greater latitude in using federal dollars earmarked for education than previously permitted. The premise behind this allowance for more dynamic decision making and use of resources is that community personnel—educators, parents, and community leaders—can best determine local needs. Of course this plasticity is offered in exchange for school personnel meeting the accountability standards under NCLB. That is, contingent on schools and school districts demonstrating acceptable levels of student achievement, they are allowed increased flexibility under NCLB in making decisions about dealing with local problems and in determining how to best use federal monies to educate pupils.

Technology-based instruction and supporting programs that promote teacher quality and safe and drug-free schools are examples of how money may be used under NCLB.

The highly qualified teacher (HQT) and scientifically based research (SBR) components of NCLB are arguably the most significant and controversial elements of the NCLB Act. Accordingly, these elements are discussed in more detail in the following sections, along with implications and recommendations for educators.

Highly Qualified Teachers

NCLB identifies core content area knowledge and teaching skills as minimum requirements for teachers to be considered "highly qualified." That is, teachers are expected to have expertise in the subject area in which they are teaching, along with the skills to teach what they know (USDOE, Office of the Under Secretary, 2003, p. 11). Even though NCLB gives some leeway to states in developing their "highly qualified" definitions and criteria, they are expected to generally follow the NCLB "highly qualified" provision guidelines. Salient elements of these guidelines are as follows:

- Teachers who are "highly qualified" must . . . have at least a bachelor's degree and demonstrate competencies in each content area as defined by their state.
- All teachers who teach core academic content subjects must be "highly qualified" by the 2005–2006 school years.
- New teachers—Elementary teachers must pass a rigorous state knowledge and skill exam. Middle and high school teachers must either pass a rigorous exam in each subject area they teach or hold an academic major or coursework equivalent, advanced degree, or advanced certification or credentials.
- Experienced teachers must meet the requirements for new teachers or demonstrate competency as determined by each state (USDOE, Office of the Under Secretary, 2003, pp. 12–13).

NCLB supports alternative certification routes as a means of bringing increased numbers of high-quality candidates into the profession. Although the research on this controversial issue is somewhat unclear, many scholars and educators criticize alternative certification programs. For example, Darling-Hammond and Youngs' (2002) analysis of teacher certification and student achievement led them to conclude that traditional teacher education programs were clearly superior to alternative certification options.

Paraeducator Issues

The importance of paraeducators is unmistakably understood by frontline educators. Indeed, paraeducators are of vital importance in implementing Individualized Education Programs and supporting students with special needs in inclusive environments. In recognition of this importance, NCLB contains highly qualified provisions for paraeducators who instruct students. Thus, at least one of the following three requirements must be met by newly hired paraeducators, retroactive to January 2, 2002, and by previously hired para-educators by January 8, 2006:

1. have an associate degree or higher, or
2. have completed at least 2 years of study at an institution of higher learning, or
3. pass a rigorous state or local assessment that demonstrates knowledge and skills needed to assist in teaching reading, writing, and math (USDOE, Office of the Under Secretary, 2003, p. 10).

You could logically argue that requiring schools to hire more qualified paraeducators bodes well for students' progress. Yet, creating higher standards for these often poorly paid and difficult-to-hire personnel without taking other steps to support and compensate them for their work may prove to be of little benefit; indeed, it might do more to increase teachers', parents,' and administrators' stress than to facilitate students' improved learning.

Implications

It is imperative that teachers understand what is expected of them in light of NCLB's higher standards. Teachers who hold licensure from their state within a general area (e.g., elementary education) or a content area (e.g., English, mathematics) will generally be considered highly qualified. Noteworthy for special educators is the Council for Exceptional Children's (CEC) analysis of "highly qualified." According to Egnor (2003), this analysis revealed that in order for special education teachers who teach at least one core content area to be "highly qualified" under NCLB, they must meet both special education and content standards. However, a more recent CEC analysis (Allbritten, Mainzer, & Ziegler, 2004) concluded that the NCLB Act does not comment on special education teachers when addressing core content areas.

Because of severe teacher shortages, many classrooms, including those for students with disabilities, are staffed by uncertified personnel or those personnel who have not vet demonstrated competencies in areas of special education. The CEC (Allbritten et al., 2004) reported a nationwide shortage of 40,000 qualified special education teachers. In the ubiquitous world of teaching short-ages (Darling-Hammond, 2001, 2003) where tens of thousands of teachers are teaching without the minimum required credentials (Allbritten et al., 2004; Ingersoll & Smith, 2003), the "highly qualified teacher" element of NCLB is both a critically important and a troubling component. As of the 2002–2003 school year, 6% of all teachers nationally were not certified. This number increases to 8% for special education teachers and for teachers who teach in high-poverty areas (USDOE, Office of Policy Planning and Innovation, 2004, p. 7). NCLB does include a provision for teachers who have emergency certification or waivers to be considered "highly qualified," contingent upon their working to complete certification that meets NCLB standards (USDOE, Office of Policy Planning and Innovation, 2004, p. 6). Given the reported teacher shortages, it is understandable that government standards would be altered to permit personnel who enter the profession via nontraditional routes to be counted as "highly qualified." Yet, even though teachers who enter the profession via alternative methods are required to demonstrate content knowledge, this caveat nevertheless appears to devalue the benefits of traditional teacher training.

Merely demanding highly qualified teachers, even if the demand is in the form of a federal enactment, will not necessarily increase the availability of such personnel. Indeed, without government support to reach this goal, it will not happen. In this regard, Mathis's (2003) analysis of 10 states' projected costs for implementing NCLB leaves too many questions about where the money to fund the Act will come. One solution may be incentives for teachers to work in areas that are perceived to be less attractive. In this connection, Darling-Hammond (2003) described how the teaching shortage in the United States is a problem of getting teachers to teach in high-poverty areas. That in June of 2003, New York City, Public Schools declared that they had hired more than 3,000 new teachers who were underqualified (Bracey, 2003) is a compelling example of why this matter is so noteworthy.

Despite gloomy statistics regarding teacher shortages, a recent Phi Delta Kappa/Gallup Poll (Rose & Gallup, 2003) concerning the public's attitude about public education highlights several important issues pertaining to highly qualified teachers. Foremost, the public is concerned about hiring and retaining good teachers; and low teacher salaries are perceived to be a significant area of concern. Second, despite reported problems and declining overall trust in U.S. education (e.g., see previous Kappa/Gallup polls, conducted by Rose & Gallup, 2001, 2002), the majority of citizens rated their own community's school as earning the letter grades A, B, or C. In fact, 48% of schools were given a grade of A or B.

Recommendations

We agree that all students deserve competent, caring, and certified teachers. This is sacrosanct to the profession. NCLB's strong stance that those who teach the neediest of students (e.g., Title 1 teachers) be highly qualified is commendable. However, the problems endemic to the educational system's long-term health and vitality (i.e., teacher stress, low pay for teachers and support staff) will not be changed simply by establishing new standards. Although the government has implemented new measures to support existing teachers and encourage potential teachers entering the profession, it fails to go far enough. Accordingly, effective long-term steps for improving teacher quality must involve strategies that address these foundation matters.

The possible requirement that special education teachers, already overburdened with paperwork and stress, be dually certified might prove to be the tipping point that will, at the least, negatively impact the hiring and retaining of an already dwindling supply of personnel. This requirement might also deter individuals from pursuing a career in special education. Moreover, many issues related to this matter require clarification, such as whether or not those who teach in self-contained programs, wherein they instruct students in multiple content areas, will be required to hold multiple certifications in addition to special education certification. It is our recommendation that multiple certifications for special education personnel not be a requirement.

In March 2004, following continual criticism from teachers, professional unions, elected officials, and others, Secretary of Education Ron Paige announced amendments to HQT requirements. These modifications only delayed certification requirements until 2007 for those who teach in rural communities and those who teach science and multiple subjects. It is our recommendation that this same review and consideration be given to other elements of the HQT provision of NCLB.

Scientifically Based Research

As we stated earlier, NCLB promotes the use of effective educational practices based on SBR. Mentioned more than 100 times in NCLB, SBR is defined as "research that involves the application of rigorous, systematic, and objective procedures to obtain reliable and valid knowledge relevant to education activities and programs" (NCLB, 2001), which means products and materials validated by means of research designs that use random samples and control and experimental groups. Relative to NCLB, this model of research qualifies as the gold standard; however, for a variety of sound reasons, randomized control-group designs are more commonly used in medical research than in education.

Explaining the narrow interpretation of SBR, Smith (2003, p. 126) cites the USDOE's "Questions and Answers on No Child Left Behind: Doing What Works," a guidance tool for parents and educators:

> To say that an instructional program or practice is grounded in scientifically based research means there is reliable evidence that the program or practice works. For example, to obtain reliable evidence about a reading strategy or instructional practice, an experimental study may be done that involves using an experimental/control group design to see if the method is effective in teaching children to read.
>
> [NCLB] sets forth rigorous requirements to ensure that research is scientifically based. It moves the testing of education practice toward the medical model used by scientists to assess the effectiveness of medications, therapies and the like. Studies that test random samples of the population and that involve a control group are scientifically controlled. To gain scientifically based research about a particular educational program or practice, it must be the subject of such a study.

This interpretation has broad implications for schools—the understanding that only such wide-scale testing can lead to validated educational practices.

The call for implementation of SBR practices in our schools has been promoted by the Coalition for Evidence-Based Policy. Using the rationale that decades of stagnation in U.S. education be reversed through the promotion of evidence-based practices, the Coalition, in November 2002, proposed that the USDOE

- build a knowledge base of educational interventions that have been proven effective in clinical trials using large-scale replications and
- create incentives for those receiving federal education funds to use such interventions.

Relative to SBR, curriculum materials supported by high-quality research are in demand more than ever before. As a result, educational products are routinely advertised using terms such as "evidence-based," "research-based," and so forth. Indeed, such terms are prominently displayed on the Web sites, catalogs, and pamphlets of companies that sell educational materials. Simply saying that a product is supported by research does not necessarily make it so. Thus, the process by which practitioners and other educators are expected to select SBR-based tools and make related programmatic decisions is an obvious and noteworthy question. To assist with this process, the USDOE awarded $18.5 million in August 2002 to the WWC to assess and report on effective programs (Eisenhart & Towne, 2003). Billed as "a central, independent and trusted source of evidence about what actually works in education," the intent of the WWC is to provide a one-stop shop of reliable, scientifically based research practices and supporting evidence from which educators can make choices. At the time this article was written, the WWC had yet to post the results of their investigation of any products or practices, so it is unclear whether they will be successful in this effort.

Implications

The SBR requirement of NCLB has several significant implications for educators, students, and parents. One obvious implication is that the NCLB interpretation of SBR effectively restricts and even impedes methods of research. This matter is particularly obvious related to students with special needs, especially those with severe and low incidence disabilities. Research involving these students often precludes use of randomized group-design methodology because of limited student samples, heterogeneous educational programs, and so forth. Indeed, such methods are often impossible to use with special needs students. Thus, by narrowly defining the use of federal dollars for research, NCLB has significantly restricted the manner by which educators can be informed of effective practices. Algozzine (2003) recognized that there are important occasions when randomization is not feasible. Yet it is likely that the funding necessary to carry out important lines of inquiry that fall outside the scope of randomized group designs will be negatively affected. We are in agreement with Sailor and Stowe (2003) in concluding, "With passage of No Child Left Behind and accompanying education legislation at the federal level, policy has begun to not only inform inquiry, but also to restrict it." Algozzine (2003) continued this line of logic by advancing the notion that governmental control of "discretionary" and other incentives allows it to wield power over state and local education agencies, institutes of higher education, and any other individual who must "comply" with NCLB, thus effectively tying the hands of all concerned. As evidence of the potential impact of this NCLB requirement, we need only consider that even large-scale research projects, such as READ 180's Great City Schools Validation Study (www.scholastic.org), were unable to apply randomization because parents, teachers, administrators, and students themselves requested—even demanded—that they be included or excluded from the treatment group. Eisenhart and Towne (2003) were pragmatic in their analysis of the NCLB SBR debate, noting that additional dialogue is essential. Their sage words, "Would that there be more of it," make a great deal of sense to us.

The call for reliance on SBR methods is only as good as the stockpile of effective practices and the ability of practitioners to carry them out. When methods for particular groups of students or subjects or needs are unavailable, unpalatable, or when they require complicated and difficult implementation steps, they will not be used and fidelity of implementation cannot be ensured. Cook and Schirmer (2003) pointed out that it is uncertain whether any classroom interventions are used with fidelity, that is, correctly, consistently, and conscientiously implemented using all of the practices, procedures, steps, and techniques required for promised results. Moreover, Allbritten et al. (2004) observed that there is ample evidence that most teachers are not prepared to use research-based interventions, even on those limited occasions when such methods are purportedly known. Hence, the process of complying with the SBR component of NCLB will involve more than simply attempting to identify what works best according to some narrow interpretation of science. Indeed the process will be neither easy nor quickly undertaken. That the NCLB SBR mandate also appears to discount the utility of teacher judgment, that is, their clinical judgment and experience in making educational decisions, only adds to this complexity.

For those who work with students with disabilities, Secretary Paige's February 2003 comments regarding the USDOE foundation principles for the currently proposed reauthorization of the Individuals with Disabilities Education Act (IDEA; 1997) hold significant impact: "IDEA should ensure that schools, local education agencies, state education agencies and the Federal Department of Education quickly adopt research and evidence based practices" (USDOE, Office of Public Affairs, News Branch, 2003). It is highly likely that the SBR theme of NCLB will be a prominent feature in the forthcoming IDEA reauthorization process, and all educators and parents will want to pay close attention and make their voices heard on this significant topic.

Recommendations

With dollars short, and AYP and HQT hanging as double pendulums, educators are frequently left to their own investigation to determine whether a method meets the current SBR standard of NCLB. Thus, as the WWC effort continues to plod toward fruition, the onus for making fiscally and programmatically responsible decisions about the programs and practices that are used in schools continues to fall to local personnel. Accordingly, examining options for SBR interventions for wide-scale or individual implementation requires not only skill in interpreting research but also knowledge of the conditions of implementation necessary to derive expected results. This feature will not change, even as additional information on SBR practices is made available. Thus, decisions regarding that which is most effective for a particular school, classroom, and student must be made at the local level by individuals who possess the most knowledge and information about unique student characteristics and circumstances. For instance, discerning the relative benefits and costs of an intervention that requires 1:1 instruction for two 50-minute periods per day for 30 weeks to derive a promised result versus a method that can be beneficially used within a 1:5 or 1:10 ratio structure for daily 50-minute periods over 18 weeks is only one example of the need for local decision making.

In the final analysis, teachers and other educators must become better consumers in regard to methods available for use with their students. Even if organizations such as the WWC provide listings of efficacious strategies and methods, teachers will still need these consumer skills. In this regard, we offer the following recommendations for assisting classroom teachers in becoming better consumers:

1. Read and analyze professional journals, including those that publish research literature. Being up-to-date on the latest methods takes time, though it is imperative that educators take this important step. Critically consuming such information will require that teachers keep in mind that some groups of students with disabilities, especially those with severe disabilities, will not fit the so-called USDOE "gold standard" of research. Moreover, certain methods that are not based on randomized group-design methodologies will nevertheless yield promising and effective results for both teachers and students.

2. It is essential that authors of research-based journal articles and the editors and publishers who oversee these publications make sure that the information they provide is in a form that classroom personnel can understand and apply in real-world settings. We strongly recommend that teachers make their voices heard: recommend to journal editors that authors clearly inform educators of SBR-related matters, including

   - the research design upon which a method is based,
   - the targeted populations,
   - the outcomes, and
   - the resources needed by classroom personnel to replicate within classrooms the outcomes reported by researchers.

3. Work to develop a critical and discerning eye to determining those methods that are most efficacious and scientifically based. Just as teachers are knowledgeable and savvy at discriminating among non-educational products, they must become better at selecting among the products with which they come into contact, especially those in which

slick packaging and sophisticated advertising outweigh their educational value. Mail and e-mail are rife with products claiming an "evidence" or "research base," hence just as in other sectors of life, being a critical evaluator of educational products is essential. Such a process will require that educators critically review evidence claims, read between the lines of an intervention's claims, call the publisher or developer to ask questions, and so forth.

4. Become familiar with impartial resources that have examined educational products and strategies. For example, SEDL (www.sedl.org) publishes a product guide that evaluates secondary literacy products.

5. Network within professional organizations and with colleagues, local experts, and school district professionals, especially those who have research knowledge and experience. Every teacher must be a product and research evaluator to build advocacy and a knowledge base needed for effective decision making.

6. Network with colleges and universities about conducting and interpreting effective practices and scientifically supported methods. These mutually beneficial and reciprocal relationships are more important now than ever.

7. Collect outcome data in your own classroom. Data are invaluable in decision making, especially regarding SBR matters. Curriculum-based measures, for instance, are an excellent and utilitarian method of understanding what works with both individuals and groups of students.

Conclusion

NCLB Act has established the lofty goal of having every student in the approximately 15,000 public school districts in the United States have an authentic opportunity for educational success. Provisions contained in the Act—

- increased accountability for desired educational outcomes,
- qualified personnel to staff the nation's classrooms,
- reliance on educational programs and practices that are supported by scientific research,
- expanded school district control and flexibility in using federal funding resources, and
- increased parental involvement and authority related to educational decisions

—are having a significant impact on both educators and the general public. Consequently, it is imperative that teachers and other educators be familiar with NCLB and its policy and practice implications.

Equaling the significance of NCLB is its controversy. Some have cast NCLB as an enlightened scientifically based reform effort that will dramatically improve U.S. schools. In contrast, others have described NCLB as a misguided enactment whose foundation is unproven change strategies (McKenzie, 2003). Time will tell which (if either) of these perspectives most accurately describes NCLB. In the meantime, educators must understand and follow this law of the land.

References

Albrecht, S. E, & Joles, C. (2003). Accountability and access to opportunity: Mutually exclusive tenets under a high-stakes testing mandate. *Preventing School Failure,* 47(2), 86–91.

Algozzine, R. (2003). Scientifically based research: Who let the dogs out? *Research & Practice for Persons with Severe Disabilities,* 28(3), 156–160.

Allbritten, D., Mainzer, R., & Ziegler, D. (2004). Will students with disabilities be scapegoats for school failures? *Teaching Exceptional Children,* 36(3), 73–75.

Bracey, G. W. (2003). The 13th Bracey report on the condition of public education. *Phi Delta Kappan,* 85, 148–164.

Center on Educational Policy. (2003). From the capitol to the classroom: State and federal efforts to implement the No Child Left Behind Act. Washington, DC: Author. Retrieved March 29, 2004, from http://www.ctredpol.org/pubs/nclbfullreportjan2003.pdf

Cook, B. G., & Schirmer, B. R. (2003). What is special about special education? *Overview and Analysis,* 37, 200–205.

Darling-Hammond, L. (1999). *Teacher quality and student achievement: A review of state policy evidence.* Seattle: University of Washington, Center for the Study of Teacher Policy.

Darling-Hammond, L. (2001). The challenge of staffing our schools. *Educational Leadership,* 58(8), 12–17.

Darling-Hammond, L. (2003). Keeping good teachers: Why it matters, what leaders can do. *Educational Leadership,* 60(8), 6–13.

Darling-Hammond, L., & Youngs, P. (2002). Defining "highly qualified teacher"; What does "scientifically-based research" actually tell us? *Educational Researcher,* 31(9), 13–25.

Egnor, D. (2003, March). Implications for special education policy and practice. *Principal Leadership,* 3(7), 10–13.

Ehrenberg, R. G., & Brewer, D.J. (1994). Do school and teacher characteristics matter? Evidence from high school and beyond. *Economics of Education Review,* 13, 1–17.

Eisenhart, M., & Towne, L. (2003). Contestation and change in national policy on "scientifically based" education research. *Educational Researcher,* 32(7), 31–38.

Hardman, M., & Mulder, M. (2003, November). Federal education reform: Critical issues in public education and the impact on students with disabilities. Paper presented at the Eagle Summit on Critical Issues on the Future of Personnel Preparation in Emotional/Behavioral Disorders. University of North Texas Institute on Behavioral and Learning Differences, Denton, TX.

Individuals with Disabilities Education Act Amendments of 1997, 20 U.S.C. [section] 1401 (26).

Ingersoll, R. M., & Smith, T. M. (2003). The wrong solution to the teacher shortage. *Educational Leadership,* 77, 30–33.

Leaving some children behind. (2004, January 27). *The New York Times,* p. 22.

Mathis, W. (2003). No child left behind: Costs and benefits. *Phi Delta Kappan,* 84(10), 679.

McKenzie, J. (2003). NCLB: AKA "belter-skelter?" Retrieved from KQWeb, American Library Association Web site: www.ala.org

No Child Left Behind Act of 2001, 20 U.S.C. 70 [section] 6301 et seq.

Robelen, E. W. (2002, January 9). An ESEA Primer. *Education Week,* pp. 28–29.

Rose, L. C., & Gallup, A. M. (2001). The 33rd Annual Phi Delta Kappa/ Gallup poll of the public's attitudes toward the public schools. *Phi Delta Kappan,* 83(1), 41–58.

Rose, L. C., & Gallup, A. M. (2002). The 34th Annual Phi Delta Kappa/ Gallup poll of the public's attitudes toward the public schools. *Phi Delta Kappan,* 84(1), 41–56.

Rose, L. C., & Gallup, A. M. (2003). The 35th Annual Phi Delta Kappa/ Gallup poll of the public's attitudes toward the public schools. *Phi Delta Kappan,* 85, 42–52.

Sailor, W., & Stowe, M. (2003). The relationship of inquiry to public policy. *Research & Practice for Persons with Severe Disabilities,* 28(3), 148–152.

Shavelson, R. J., & Towne, L. (Eds). (2002). *Scientific research in education.* Washington, DC: National Academy Press.

Smith, A. (2003). Scientifically based research and evidence-based education: A federal policy context. *Research & Practice for Persons with Severe Disabilities,* 28(3), 126–132.

Southwest Educational Developmental Laboratory. (2000). Building reading proficiency at the secondary level. A guide to resources. Retrieved February 4, 2004, from http://www.sedl.org/pubs/catalog/items/read 16.html

U.S. Department of Education, Institute of Education Sciences National Center for Education Evaluation and Regional Assistance. (2003). *Identifying and implementing educational practices supported by rigorous evidence: A user friendly guide.* Washington, DC: Author.

U.S. Department of Education, Office of Elementary and Secondary Education. (2002). *No Child Left Behind: A desktop reference.* Washington, DC: Author.

U.S. Department of Education, Office of Policy Planning and Innovation. (2004). *Meeting the highly qualified teachers challenge: The Secretary's second annual report on teacher quality.* Washington, DC: Author.

U.S. Department of Education, Office of Public Affairs, News Branch. (February 25, 2003). *Principles for reauthorizing the Individuals with Disabilities Education Act.* Washington, DC: Author.

U.S. Department of Education, Office of the Under Secretary. (2003). *No Child Left Behind: A toolkit for teachers.* Washington, DC: Author.

Wayne, A.J., & Youngs, P. (2003). Teacher characteristics and student academic achievement: A review. *Review of Educational Research,* 73(1), 89–122.

Lisa Guisbond and
Monty Neill

 **NO**

Failing Our Children: No Child Left Behind Undermines Quality and Equity in Education

The No Child Left Behind Act (NCLB), the title of the federal Elementary and Secondary Education Act, describes a worthy goal for our nation. Tragically, the reality is that NCLB is aggravating, not solving, the problems that cause many children to be left behind. For the federal government to truly contribute to enhancing the quality of education for low-income and minority group students, NCLB must be overhauled.

FairTest, our nonprofit organization that strives to end misuses of standardized testing and promote fair evaluation of both teachers and students, has tracked the first two years of NCLB's implementation and identified fundamental errors in its conception, design, and execution. Rather than accept NCLB's dangerous prescriptions for public education, we propose a new approach to accountability as the basis for a comprehensive revamp of NCLB (Neill and Guisbond 2004).

Many false assumptions undergird NCLB. The most serious of the suppositions are the following:

1. Boosting standardized test scores should be the primary goal of schools. This assumption leads to one-size-fits-all teaching that focuses primarily on test preparation and undermines efforts to give all children a high-quality education. This exclusive focus on test scores ignores the widespread desire for schools that address a broad range of academic and social goals, as reported in public opinion polls. One recent public opinion survey found Americans believe the most important thing schools should do is prepare responsible citizens. The next most important role for public schools was to help students become economically self-sufficient (Rose and Gallup 2000). Another recent survey found that people's key concerns about schools were mostly social issues not addressed by standards, tests, or accountability (Goodwin 2003).

2. Because poor teaching is the primary cause of unsatisfactory student performance, schools can best be improved by threats and sanctions.

From *The Clearing House*, Vol. 78, no. 1, September/October 2004, pp. 12–16. Copyright © 2004 by Heldref Publications. Reprinted by permission.

Such threats encourage teachers to focus narrowly on boosting test scores. However, these punitive actions fail to address underlying problems such as family poverty and inadequate school funding, which are major reasons that many students start off behind and never catch up.

A new accountability system must start from accurate assumptions, including a richer vision of schooling that will lead away from NCLB's test-and-punish methodology. This new approach assumes that educators want to do their jobs but need assistance to do better. We believe that rather than threatening educators with sanctions based on test results, our more effective approach focuses on gathering multiple forms of evidence about many aspects of schooling and using them to support school improvements. Because schools need to build the capacity to ensure that all children receive a high-quality education, all levels of government, therefore, must fulfill their responsibilities to provide adequate and equitable resources. FairTest's proposal also gives parents and the community central roles in the accountability process rather than excluding them through incomprehensible statistical procedures and bureaucratically mandated reports currently required by NCLB.

Set Up to Fail

At NCLB's destructive core is a link between standardized testing and heavy sanctions through the rigid and unrealistic "adequate yearly progress" (AYP) formula. The problem is that NCLB's AYP provision is not grounded in any proven theory of school improvement. As Harvard Graduate School of Education Professor Richard Elmore explains: "The AYP requirement, a completely arbitrary mathematical function grounded in no defensible knowledge or theory of school improvement, could, and probably will, result in penalizing and closing schools that are actually experts in school improvement" (Elmore 2003, 6–10).

Moreover, many other expert analysts also have concluded that the AYP mechanism, the heart of the NCLB accountability provisions, guarantees failure for a substantial majority of the nation's schools. For example, the National Conference of State Legislatures estimated that, according to these standards, some 70 percent of schools nationwide will fail (Prah 2002). More recently, a study conducted for the Connecticut Education Association projected that more than nine out of ten Connecticut elementary and middle schools will fail to meet AYP targets within ten years (Moscovitch 2004).

The reason for the high failure rate is that the pace of progress envisioned in the law—that all students will reach the proficient level within fourteen years of its passage—is implausible. Part of the problem lies in the word "proficiency," which Education Secretary Rod Paige defines as solid, grade-level achievement. In fact, the term comes from the National Assessment of Educational Progress (NAEP), where it has been widely criticized for being an unrealistic and inaccurate standard, as well as a political construct engineered to depict a national academic crisis (Bracey 2003). Only about three in ten

American students now score at the proficient level on NAEP reading and math tests (NCES 2004). Thus, within a little more than a decade, all students are expected to do as well as only a third now do—a goal far more stringent than simply "grade level."

Based on trends on NAEP tests over the past decade, prominent measurement expert Robert Linn calculated that it would take 166 years for all twelfth graders to attain proficiency, as defined by NCLB, in both reading and math (Linn 2003; Linn, Baker, and Herman 2002). In addition, due to requirements that all demographic groups make AYP, several studies have concluded that schools with more integrated student bodies are far more likely to fail than schools that lack diversity (Kane and Staiger 2002; Novak and Fuller 2003). Adding to the confusion, states' definitions of proficiency vary wildly, making it difficult to make meaningful state-to-state comparisons (Kingsbury et al. 2003).

The AYP provisions further reflect the flawed reasoning behind NCLB by assuming that schools already have adequate resources to get all students to a proficient level, if they would only use those resources better. The implication is that administrators and teachers are not working hard enough, not working well, or both. Thus, with willpower and effort, schools and districts can bootstrap their way to unprecedented results. This reasoning ignores real factors that impede improvements in teaching and learning, such as large class sizes, inadequate books, and outmoded technology, as well as nonschool factors like poverty and high student mobility.

The Limits of Test Scores

For NCLB proponents, the law's near-total reliance on test scores to determine the progress of students, teachers, and schools reflects a desire for objective assessments of educational outcomes. For example, President Bush has said, "Without yearly testing, we don't know who is falling behind and who needs help. Without yearly testing, too often we don't find failure until it is too late to fix" (Bush 2001). But standardized test scores offer nothing more than snapshots, often fuzzy ones, of student achievement at a single moment in time. When used to make important decisions about students and schools, they can be misleading and damaging. Moreover, good teachers already know which students are falling behind.

The national obsession with using standardized test scores to drive school improvement and reform is not new. Education researchers have examined this trend only to come up with results that cast serious doubts about the efficacy of test-based reform. Among the findings:

- Test scores do not necessarily indicate real progress when they rise or deterioration when they fall. Annual fluctuations should not be used to reward or sanction schools, teachers or school officials (Haney 2002).
- Many of the tests used to judge our students, teachers, and schools are norm-referenced, meaning they are specifically designed to ensure a certain proportion of "failures" (Haney 2002).

- Errors in question design, scoring and reporting have always been a part of standardized testing and are likely to increase substantially with the increase in testing mandated by NCLB (Rhoades and Madaus 2003).

NCLB's rigid AYP mechanism and the sanctions it triggers exacerbate standardized exams' weaknesses, such as their cultural biases, their failure to measure higher-order thinking, and the problem of measurement error. Exams with such narrow scopes and strong sanctions promote intensive teaching to the test, which undermines efforts to improve educational quality (von Zastrow 2004).

As one seventh-grade Kentucky student explained, "The test is taking away the real meaning of school. Instead of learning new things and getting tools for life, the mission of the schools is becoming to do well on the test" (Mathison 2003).

Even before NCLB became law, there was ample evidence that many of its assumptions and the model on which it was based had fundamental flaws:

- Little evidence supports the idea that the model of standards, testing, and rewards and punishments for achievement is the cure for public schooling's ailments. On the contrary, several studies show a decline in achievement in states with high-stakes testing programs relative to those with low-stakes testing (Stecher, Hamilton, and Gonzalez 2003; Amrein and Berliner 2002).
- Surveys of educators confirm that the model promotes teaching to the test and narrowed curricula, particularly in schools that serve low-income and minority students (Pedulla et al. 2003; Clarke et al. 2002).
- Independent analysts have found that tests often fail to measure the objectives deemed most important by educators who determine academic standards. Thus, students taught to such tests will not be exposed to high-quality curricula, and the public will not be informed about student achievement relative to those standards (Rothman et al. 2002).
- The instructional quality suffers under such a model because it is often assumed that all students who fail need the same type of remediation. On the contrary, researchers have found that students fail for a variety of reasons and need different instructional approaches to get on track (Riddle Buly and Valencia 2002; Moon, Callahan, and Tomlinson 2003; Hinde 2003; Mabry et al. 2003).
- Research refutes the assumption that low-achieving students are motivated to work harder and learn more in a high-stakes context. On the contrary, low-achieving students are most likely to become discouraged and give up in that environment (Harlen and Deakin-Crick 2002; Ryan and La Guardia 1999).
- There is evidence of falling graduation rates in high-stakes states, as well as evidence that schools retain additional students in hopes of reaping higher test scores in key grades. Decades of research support the contention that retained students are more likely to drop out of school (Haney 2003).

Within its more than one thousand pages, NCLB does include some potentially helpful provisions. However, the law's flaws overwhelm them and end up
damaging educational quality and equity, For example:

- NCLB calls for multiple measures that assess higher-order thinking and
  are diagnostically useful. However, these provisions are neither enforced
  nor embedded in most state practices.
- The law mandates school (or district) improvement plans. In practical
  terms, however, improvement means boosting test scores. Disruptive
  sanctions based on unrealistic rates of AYP deny schools the opportunity
  to see if their own improvement efforts work.

Another potentially useful component of NCLB is the call for high-quality
teachers for all students. Unfortunately, the law's requirements fall short of the
attractive label: A teacher may be deemed "highly qualified" if she or he has a
bachelor's degree and passes a paper-and-pencil standardized exam. This minimal definition can in no way ensure that all children have good teachers.

There is no persuasive evidence demonstrating a strong relationship
between passing a standardized test and being competent in the classroom. A
National Academy of Sciences report, Testing teaching candidates: The role of
licensure tests in improving teacher quality, offers the most comprehensive
study of this issue. It found that raising cut-off scores on the exams may reduce
racial diversity in the teaching profession without improving quality (Mitchell
et al. 2001). Furthermore, the study concludes that the tests cannot "predict
who will become effective teachers" (FairTest 2001).

NCLB, however, allows groups such as the American Board for Certification
of Teacher Excellence (ABCTE) to promote quick and inadequate fixes. For
example, the group offers a standardized test as a solution to the serious problem
low-income areas have attracting strong teachers to their schools (Jacobson
2004). ABCTE is a project of the conservative, pro-NCLB Education Leaders
Council, cofounded by Department of Education Deputy Secretary Eugene
Hickok. ABCTE has received roughly $40 million in federal support for this
scheme, although two of the three members of the department's own review
panel rejected it.

A strong definition of "highly qualified" ensures that teachers work
successfully with a variety of students to attain a range of important outcomes, not just test scores. And although NCLB does contain some good ideas
for improving the teaching force, such as mentoring and ongoing professional development, they must be separated from the drive to narrow
schooling to test preparation. These favorable elements easily could become
key parts of revamped accountability and school improvement system that
would replace NCLB.

NCLB also harms rather than helps schools in need in other ways. Sanctions intended to force school improvement eventually divert funds away from
efforts to help all children succeed toward helping a few parents obtain trans-
fers and tutoring for their children. The law's ultimate sanctions—privatizing
school management, firing staff, state takeovers, and similar measures—have
no proven record of success.

As many educators have pointed out, the federal government has failed to adequately fund the law (National Conference of State Legislatures 2004). Just as schools are hit with the demands of the current law, most states' education budgets are shrinking. Worse, neither federal nor state governments address either the dearth of resources required to bring all children to educational proficiency or the deepening poverty that continues to hinder some children's learning.

A Movement for Authentic Accountability

These problems have catalyzed a growing movement seeking to overhaul NCLB. State officials, parents, teachers, and students are mobilizing against the law. Unfortunately, some efforts, such as proposals to modify the AYP formula or spend more money without changing the law, seek only to minimize the damage caused by NCLB and would further perpetuate educational inequality. Others address only peripheral issues rather than the law's faulty premises and assumptions.

Effective opposition to NCLB must embrace genuine accountability, stronger equity, and concrete steps toward school improvement. FairTest has been working with educators, civil rights organizations, parent groups, and researchers across the nation to devise new models of accountability. Based on a set of draft principles, core elements of a better accountability system include:

1. Getting federal, state, and local governments to work together to provide a fair opportunity for all children to learn a rich curriculum. Current governments have failed to meet this fundamental accountability requirement because they have not ensured adequate, equitable funding and have overemphasized test scores.
2. Using multiple forms of evidence to assess student learning. If we want to know how well students are doing, we need to look at a range of real student work. If we want students to learn more or better, we have to provide teachers and students with useful feedback based on high-quality classroom assessments that reflect the various ways children really learn.
3. Focusing on helping teachers and schools ensure educational success for all students. Reaching that goal requires schools to be safe, healthy, supportive, and challenging environments. This means providing schools with data that can help improve academic and social aspects of education and making certain that the schools are equipped to use the data.
4. Localizing the primary accountability mechanisms. These mechanisms must involve educators, parents, students, and the local community. Open, participatory processes, including local school councils, annual reports, and meetings to review school progress, are necessary.
5. Focusing the primary responsibility of state governments to provide tools and support for schools and teachers while maintaining equity and civil rights. Intervention should take place only when localities have been given adequate resources and support but still fail to improve performance or when uncorrected civil rights violations occur.

In the short term, NCLB's rigid AYP provisions and draconian penalties should be amended. States should no longer have to annually test all students in grades 3-8 in reading and math, and the amount of required testing should be reduced. Additional measures of school performance and student learning should be included in progress evaluations. Congress also should appropriate the full amount authorized under NCLB.

FairTest's report, Failing our children, uses work in Nebraska and the Massachusetts Coalition for Authentic Reform in Education's community-based assessment systems as models in the construction of a different approach to accountability.

More fundamentally, policymakers must seriously consider both the damage that NCLB has wrought and the problem of inadequate educational funding around the nation. They should begin by listening to the voices of educators, parents, and community people asking for high-quality education, not test preparation, for children.

Stripped of its bureaucratic language, NCLB is a fundamentally punitive law that uses flawed standardized tests to label many schools as failures and then punishes them with harmful sanctions. NCLB must be transformed into a law that supports lasting educational improvement and makes good on the promise, in the words of the Children's Defense Fund, to "leave no child behind."

Note

FairTest's report on NCLB, *Failing our children: How "No Child Left Behind" undermines quality and equity in education and an account-ability model that supports school improvement,* is available at `http://www.fairtest.org/Failing_Our_Children_Report.html`.

References

Amrein, A., and D. Berliner. 2002. *An analysis of some unintended and negative consequences of high-stakes testing.* Tempe, AZ: Education Policy Studies Laboratory, Arizona State Univ. `http://www.asu.edu/educ/epsl/EPRU/documents/EPSL-0211-125-EPRU.pdf` (accessed June 18, 2004).

Bracey, G. 2003. NCLB—A plan for the destruction of public education: Just say no! `NoChildLeft.com` 1, no. 2 (February). `http://www.nochildleft.com/2003/feb03no.html` (accessed June 29, 2004).

Bush, G. W. 2001. Press conference with President Bush and Education Secretary Rod Paige to introduce the President's education program. `http://www.whitehouse.gov/news/releases/2001/01/20010123-2.html` (accessed June 18, 2004).

Clarke, M., A. Shore, K. Rhoades, L. Abrams, J. Miao, and J. Lie. 2002. *Perceived effects of state-mandated testing programs on teaching and learning: Findings from interviews with educators in low-, medium-, and high-stakes states.* Boston: National Board on Educational Testing and Public Policy, Boston College. `http://www.bc.edu/research/nbetpp` (accessed June 18, 2004).

Elmore, R. F. 2003. A plea for strong practice. *Education Leadership* 61 (3): 6–10.

FairTest. 2001. Reports blast teacher tests. *Examiner.* `http://www.fairtest.org/examarts/Winter%2000-01/Reports%20Blast%20Teacher%20Tests.html` (accessed April 29, 2004).

Goodwin, B. 2003. *Digging deeper: Where does the public stand on standards-based education?* Aurora, CO: Mid-continent Research for Education and Learning.

Haney, W. 2002. Lake Woebeguaranteed: Misuse of test scores in Massachusetts, Part I. *Education Policy Analysis Archives* 10 (24), http://epaa.asu.edu/epaa/v10n24/ (accessed June 14, 2004).

———. 2003. Attrition of students from New York schools. Invited testimony at public hearing. "Regents Learning Standards and High School Graduation Requirements," before the New York Senate Standing Committee on Education, New York. http://www.timeoutfromtesting.org/testimonies/923_Testimony_Haney.pdf (accessed June 16, 2004).

Harlen, W., and R. Deakin-Crick. 2002. A systematic review of the impact of summative assessment and tests on students' motivation for learning. *Evidence for Policy and Practice Information and Coordinating Centre* (EPP1-Centre), Univ. of London.

Hinde, E. R. 2003. The tyranny of the test. *Current Issues in Education* 6, no. 10 (May 27), http://cie.asu.edu/volume6/number10/ (accessed June 16, 2004).

Jacobson, L. 2004. Education Dept. ignored reviewers in issuing grant for teachers' test. *Education Week* 23 (27): 10. http://www.edweek.org/ew/ewstory.cfm?slug=27Amboard.h23&keywords=education%20leaders%20council (accessed June 21, 2004).

Kane, T. J., and D. O. Staiger. 2002. Volatility in school test scores: Implications for test-based accountability systems. Brookings Papers on Education Policy. Washington, DC: Brookings Institution.

Kingsbury, G. G., A. Olson, J. Cronin, C. Hauser, and R. Houser. 2003. *The state of standards.* Portland, OR: Northwest Evaluation Association. http://www.young-roehr.com/nwea/ (accessed June 14, 2004).

Linn, R. L. 2003. *Accountability: Responsibility and reasonable expectations.* Los Angeles: National Center for Research on Evaluation, Standards, and Student Testing, Univ. of California.

Linn, R. L., E. L. Baker, and J. L. Herman. 2002. Minimum group size for measuring adequate yearly progress. *The CRESST Line* 1 (Fall): 4–5. Los Angeles: National Center for Research on Evaluation, Standards, and Student Testing, Univ. of California. http://www.cse.ucla.edu/products/newletters/CL2002fall.pdf.

Mabry, L., J. Poole, L. Redmond, and A. Schultz. 2003. Local impact of state testing in Southwest Washington. *Education Policy Analysis Archives* 11, no. 21 (July 18), http://epaa.asu.edu/epaa/v11n22 (accessed June 16, 2004).

Mathison, S. 2003. The accumulation of disadvantage: The role of educational testing in the school career of minority children. *Workplace* 5, no. 2, http://www.louisville.edu/journal/workplace/issue5p2/mathison.html (accessed April 26, 2004).

Mitchell, K. J., D. Z. Robinson, B. S. Plake, and K. T. Knowles, eds. 2001. *Testing teacher candidates: The role of licensure tests in improving teacher quality.* Committee on Assessment and Teacher Quality, Board on Testing and Assessment, National Research Council. Washington, DC: National Academy Press.

Moon, T. R., C. M. Callahan, and C. A. Tomlinson. 2003. Effects of state testing programs on elementary schools with high concentrations of student poverty: Good news or bad news? *Current Issues in Education* 6, no. 8 (April 28), http://cie.asu.edu/volume6/number8/index.html (accessed July 15, 2004).

Moscovitch, E. 2004. *Projecting AYP in Connecticut Schools.* Prepared for the Connecticut Education Association. Gloucester, MA: Cape Ann Economics.

National Center for Education Statistics. 2004. *The nation's report card.* Washington, DC: National Center for Education Statistics, Institute of Education Sciences, U.S. Department of Education. http://nces.ed.gov/nationsreportcard/ (accessed June 14, 2004).

National Conference of State Legislatures. 2004. *Mandate Monitor* 1, no. 1 (March 31). http://www.ncsl.org/programs/press/2004/pr040310.htm (accessed June 18, 2004).

Neill, M., and Guisbond, L. 2004. *Failing our children: How "No Child Left Behind" undermines quality and equity in education and an account-ability model that supports school improvement.* Cambridge, MA: FairTest. http://www.fairtest.org/Failing_Our_Children_Report.html (accessed June 14, 2004).

Novak, J. R., and B. Fuller. 2003. Penalizing diverse schools? Similar test scores but different students bring federal sanctions. *Policy Analysis for California Education* (PACE), policy brief 03–4. http://pace.berkeley.edu/pace_publications.html (accessed June 18, 2004).

Pedulla, J., L. Abrams, G. Madaus, M. Russell, M. Ramos, and J. Miao. 2003. *Perceived effects of state-mandated testing programs on teaching and learning: Findings from a national survey of teachers.* Boston: National Board on Educational Testing and Public Policy, Boston College. http://www.bc.edu/research/nbetpp/reports.html (accessed June 18, 2004).

Prah, P. M. 2002. New rules may guarantee "F's" for many schools. Stateline.org, December 9. http://stateline.org/stateline/?pa=story&sa=show-StoryInfo&id=275753.

Rhoades, K., and G. Madaus. 2003. *Errors in standardized tests: A systemic problem.* National Board on Educational Testing and Public Policy, Boston College. http://www.bc.edu/nbetpp (accessed June 14, 2004).

Riddle Buly, M., and S. W. Valencia. 2002. Below the bar: Profiles of students who fail state reading assessments. *Educational Evaluation and Policy Analysis* 24 (3): 219-39. http://depts.washington.edu/ctpmail/PDFs/Reading-MRBSV-04-2003.pdf (accessed June 14, 2004).

Rose, L. C., and A. M. Gallup. 2000. The 32nd annual Phi Delta Kappan Gallup poll of the public's attitudes toward the public schools. *Phi Delta Kappan* 82 (1): 41–58.

Rothman, R., J. B. Slattery, J. L. Vranek, and L. B. Resnick. 2002. *Benchmarking and alignment of standards and testing.* Los Angeles: National Center for Research on Evaluation, Standards, and Student Testing. http://www.cse.ucla.edu/CRESST/Reports/TR566.pdf., Univ. of California.

Ryan, R. M., and J. G. La Guardia, 1999. Achievement motivation within a pressured society: Intrinsic and extrinsic motivations to learn and the politics of school reform. In *Advances in motivation and achievement,* ed. T. Urdan, 45–85. Greenwich, CT: JAI Press.

Stecher, B., L. Hamilton, and G. Gonzalez. 2003. *Working smarter to leave no child behind: Practical insights for school leaders.* Santa Monica, CA: RAND Corp.

von Zastrow, C. 2004. Academic atrophy: *The condition of the liberal arts in America's public schools.* Washington, DC: Council for Basic Education. http://www.c-b-e.org/PDF/cbe_principal_Report.pdf.

POSTSCRIPT

Can No Child Left Behind Provide Equitable Education?

$\mathbf{A}$s noted in the Postscript to Issue 16, educational problems in the United States are exacerbated by the fact that the states and localities are "in charge" of providing educational services. The irony is that the political candidates and political leaders at the federal governmental level periodically pontificates about what is wrong with education. To make matters worse, if there is any federal "follow-through," it is often in the form of unfunded mandates. So, for example, when the Reagan administration made much ado about "A Nation At Risk" at the same time federal funding to education was being cut, the states felt the political and financial pinch. Now, the states are beleaguered by Bush's No Child Left Behind (NCLB) Act.

Yet there are those who champion its lofty goals, as do Richard L. Simpson, Paul G. LaCava and Patricia Sampson Graner. These authors actually refer to NCLB as "the most significant initiative to have been enacted in decades."

NCLB has presented a mandate to the states to raise academic achievement levels for all students. NCLB has provided a timetable of one decade during which a particular degree of "proficiency" must be reached. This proficiency will be tested by the states.

NCLB's additional mandate is the state achievement of High Quality Teachers (HQT). There is no doubt that teacher quality is imperative for students to have any modicum of a chance to achieve. But, even supporters of NCLB as Simpson, LaCava, and Graner would admit that "the standards associated with NCLB represent an unprecedented and Herculean challenge for our nation's schools."

These authors applaud NCLB's requirement for accountability. This accountability is being measured already by Adequate Yearly Progress (AYP) reports. The authors also applaud the recognition and sanctions associated with the achievement of or the failure to achieve "proficiency."

By contrast, Lisa Guisbond and Monty Neill argue that NCLB, while a worthy goal, is making things worse. They argue that NCLB rests upon many "false assumptions," including the notion that standardized tests should be schools' primary goal and that threatening teachers will result in quality teaching. The authors argue that the AYP formula has not been proven to effectively tell us anything. They cite studies that argue that based on the required tests, most schools will fail, and that teachers are "teaching to the test." Guisbond and Neill quote one seventh-grade Kentucky student as saying, "The test is taking away the real meaning of school. Instead of learning new things and getting tools for life, the mission of the schools is becoming to do well on the tests."

Guisbond and Neill are also concerned about the assumption that the schools have adequate resources to meet the federal mandate, and just need to better use these resources. They argue that large class sizes, inadequate books and lack of modern technology, coupled with social problems (e.g., poverty) impede any school that may have even the best of intentions. Ultimately, the authors argue that NCLB is undermining quality and equity in education.

Suggested further readings on this subject include Paul E. Peterson and Martin R. West, eds., *No Child Left Behind? The Politics and Practices of School Accountability;* W. James Popham, *America's "Failing" Schools: How Parents and Teachers Can Cope With No Child Left Behind;* and Gail L. Sunderman, et al., *NCLB Meets Realities: Lessons from the Field.*

Contributors to This Volume

EDITOR

MARIE D. NATOLI is a professor of political science at Emmanuel College in Boston, Massachusetts. She holds an M.A. and Ph.D. in political science from Tufts University, a J.D. from Suffolk Law School, and an M.B.A. from the Sawyer School of Management at Suffolk University. She is the author of *American Prince, American Pauper: The Contemporary Vice Presidency in Perspective,* co-author of *Understanding American Government,* numerous articles on the American presidency and vice presidency, and has given numerous television and radio interviews both at home and abroad.

STAFF

Larry Loeppke	Managing Editor
Jill Peter	Senior Developmental Editor
Nichole Altman	Developmental Editor
Beth Kundert	Production Manager
Jane Mohr	Project Manager
Tara McDermott	Design Coordinator
Bonnie Coakley	Editorial Assistant
Lori Church	Permissions

AUTHORS

NORM R. ALLEN, JR. is executive director of African Americans for Humanism.

CARL M. CANNON is a White House correspondent for *National Journal* and the co-author of *Boy Genius,* a biography of White House aide Karl Rove.

CAIT CLARKE is the director of the National Defender Leadership Institute, National Legal Aid and Defender Association (NLADA).

BARBARA CRUIKSHANK is a professor of political theory at the University of Massachusetts, Amherst.

STEWART J. D'ALESSIO holds a Ph.D. from Florida State University and is an associate professor of criminal justice at Florida International University.

TIMOTHY J. DAILEY is a Senior Fellow in Culture Studies at the Family Research Council.

DANIEL ENGELBERG is a law student at Georgetown University Law Center.

DONNA Y. FORD is a professor of special education at The Ohio State University. She specializes in urban and gifted education, where she conducts research on factors that hinder the representation of diverse students in gifted education, and has won numerous awards for her work.

SHIMICA GASKINS is assistant articles selection editor, American Criminal Law Review, Georgetown University School of Law.

ANNA MARIA GILLIS is the features editor of Bioscience, a Washington, D.C.–based publication of the American Institute of Biological Sciences.

MARILYN GITELL is a professor of political science at the Graduate School and University Center of the City University of New York.

PATRICIA SAMPSON GRANER holds an M.S. and is a doctoral student in the department of special education at the University of Kansas.

ELENA GRIGERA holds a J.D. from Duke University School of Law and is an associate at Hogan and Hartson.

LISA GUISBOND is a researcher and advocate for the National Center for Fair and Open Testing (Fair Test).

DEBORAH A. HARMON is an assistant professor of teacher education at Eastern Michigan University. She specializes in urban and multicultural education, specifically developing multicultural curriculum.

EDITH M. HUMPHREY is associate professor at Pittsburgh Theological Seminary.

BARRY L. JOHNSON holds a J.D. from the University of Michigan and is a professor of law at the Oklahoma City University School of Law.

DAVID CAY JOHNSTON is a Pulitzer Prize–winning reporter for the *New York Times* and author of *Perfectly Legal: The Covert Campaign to Benefit the Super Rich—and Cheat from Everybody Else.*

STEPHEN KLEIN is in the criminal justice program, RAND Corporation, Santa Monica, California.

PAUL G. LaCAVA holds an M.S. and has worked as a teacher and consultant for students with disabilities.

PRESTON LERNER is a writer for *Washington Monthly.*

HEATHER MAC DONALD holds a Ph.D. from Stanford University Law School and is a John M. Olin Fellow at the Manhattan Institute and a contributing editor to *City Journal.*

SUSAN E. MAYER is associate professor at the Harris School of Public Policy Studies at the University of Chicago.

MIKE McCONVILLE is a professor of waw at University of Warwick in Coventry, England.

CHESTER MIRSKY is a professor of saw at the New York University School of Law.

MICHELE MOSER is an assistant professor of public administration at George Washington University.

CHARLES MURRAY holds a Ph.D. in political science from the Massachusetts Institute of Technology and is the Bradley Fellow at the American Enterprise Institute. Murray has been affiliated with the American Enterprise Institute since 1990. In addition to his books and articles in technical journals, Murray has published extensively in *The New Republic, Commentary, The Public Interest,* the *New York Times,* the *Wall Street Journal, National Review,* and the *Washington Post.*

ILENE H. NAGEL received and Ph.D. from New York University and received her masters of legal studies from Stanford University School of Law.

ANNIE NAKAO is a staff writer for the *San Francisco Chronicle.*

MONTY NEILL holds an Ed.D. and is the executive director of the National Center for Fair and Open Testing (Fair Test).

JIM NINTZEL is a writer for the *Tucson Weekly.*

ELLEN C. PERRIN is a professor of developmental-behavioral pediatrics at the Floating Hospital for Children of Tufts-New England Medical Center in Boston.

JOAN PETERSILIA is a professor of criminology, law and society in the School of Social Ecology, University of California, Irvine.

FRED L. PINCUS is an associate professor in the department of sociology and anthropology at the University of Maryland Baltimore County.

DORIS REDFIELD is director of the Institute for the Advancement of Research in Education at the Appalachia Education Laboratory (AEL).

DAVID RISLEY is assistant U.S. attorney for the state of Illinois and is the lead organized crime drug task force attorney. Risley also serves as legal advisor to Drug Watch International.

ROSS RUBENSTEIN is an associate professor at the Center for Policy Research at the Maxwell School of Citizenship and Public Affairs of Syracuse University.

TIMOTHY SANDEFUR is the lead attorney of the Economic Liberties Project at the Pacific Legal Foundation, and a contributing editor of *Liberty Magazine.*

RICHARD G. SCHOTT is a special agent and a legal instructor at the FBI Academy.

LARA SCHWARTZ is the Human Rights Campaign's senior staff counsel.

EKATERINA SHIRLEY is a graduate student at the John F. Kennedy School of Government, Harvard University.

RICHARD L. SIMPSON holds an Ed.D. and is a professor of special education at the University of Kansas.

VIRGINIA E. SLOAN is the president and founder of the Constitution Project.

PETER SPIEGLER is a graduate student at the John F. Kennedy School of Government, Harvard University.

RON STEWART holds a Ph.D. in sociology from Harvard University. He is an associate professor of sociology at SUNY-Buffalo State, Buffalo, New York.

LISA STOLZENBERG holds a Ph.D. in criminology from Florida State University and is an associate professor of criminal justice at Florida International University.

ANDREW SULLIVAN holds a masters degree from the Kennedy School of Government at Harvard University and a Ph.D. in government from Harvard University. Sullivan served as editor of *The New Republic* for a number of years, and works as a contributing writer and columnist for *The New York Times Magazine* and the *New York Times Book Review*. He also writes a weekly column for the *Sunday Times of London*.

SUSAN TURNER is in the criminal justice program, RAND Corporation, Santa Monica, California.

CATHY YOUNG writes a column for *The Boston Globe*. She is the author of *Cease-fire! Why Women and Men Must Join Forces to Achieve True Equality* (Free Press).